Also by Susan Jane Gilman

Kiss My Tiara
Hypocrite in a Pouffy White Dress

UNDRESS ME
IN THE
TEMPLE OF HEAVEN

SUSAN JANE GILMAN

GRAND CENTRAL
PUBLISHING

LARGE PRINT

Grand Central Publishing
Hachette Book Group
237 Park Avenue
New York, NY 10017

Visit our Web site at www.HachetteBookGroup.com.

Printed in the United States of America

First Edition: March 2009
10 9 8 7 6 5 4 3 2 1

Grand Central Publishing is a division of Hachette Book Group, Inc.
The Grand Central Publishing name and logo is a trademark of Hachette Book
Group, Inc.

Library of Congress Cataloging-in-Publication Data
Gilman, Susan Jane.
    Undress me in the Temple of Heaven / Susan Jane Gilman.— 1st ed.
      p. cm.
    Summary: "In her hardcover debut, bestselling author Susan Jane Gilman
describes a very different kind of backpacking trip to China in which she and her
college friend set out to conquer the world only to be conquered by it"—Provided
by publisher.
    ISBN: 978-0-446-57892-9 (regular ed.)
    ISBN: 978-0-446-54125-1 (large print ed.)
    1. China—Description and travel.   2. China—Social life and customs—20th
century.   3. Gilman, Susan Jane—Travel—China.   4. Gilman, Susan Jane—
Friends and associates.   5. Backpacking—China.   6. College students—
Travel—China. 7. Authors, American—Biography.   I. Title.
DS712.G544 2009
915.104'58092—dc22
                                                        2008019490

This Large Print edition published in accord with the standards of the N.A.V.H.

for
Bob Stefanski
my Beloved, my fellow traveler, my North Star

Author's Note

THIS IS A TRUE STORY, recounted as accurately as possible and corroborated by notes I took at the time and by others who were present. However, given the sensitive nature of what unfolded and the conditions under which many of the people in this story continue to live, I have changed the names of almost everyone unless given their permission. I have also altered distinguishing characteristics of several people—most notably of my friend "Claire Van Houten" and her family—to the extent of rendering them unrecognizable. It is my intention to protect their identity and privacy.

I've also spelled some Mandarin words the way they sounded to me at the time rather than as they're actually written.

Except for these alterations, this remains a work of nonfiction. All these events happened, and the people are real. God knows, I couldn't make this up.

—*Susan Jane Gilman*

To become wise, one must *wish* to have certain experiences and run, as it were, into their gaping jaws. This is, of course, very dangerous; many a "wise man" has been swallowed.

— Friedrich Nietzsche

Two Air Signs are fun to watch, like trapeze artists at the circus... Since Librans can never make up their minds, and Geminis are continually changing theirs, it's hard to know what to predict will happen in an association between them.

— *Linda Goodman's Love Signs*

—

Chapter 1

Kowloon

NO ONE ELSE seemed concerned when our plane took a nosedive. We banked sharply to the left, then plunged toward what looked like a tongue depressor, a tiny spit of land jutting into a titanium sea.

Our tray tables in their upright positions, our carry-ons stashed in the overhead bins, the plastic seat frames rattled violently. Below us, the earth went haywire. And yet the flight attendants remained placid at their stations. One of them was even leafing through—was that a golf magazine? The other picked at her cuticles. The plane continued plummeting. I gripped the armrests. *Dear God, we are all about to die with a splat!* Across the aisle from me, a businessman tossed his newspaper aside and yawned.

The cabin rang with the high-pitched whistle of deceleration. "Wow, check it out." Claire leaned across me. Beyond the little oblong window, gargantuan mountains rose up wildly in the twilight; a phalanx of apartment buildings suddenly appeared. High-rises seemed to be lining the runway, providing some sort of sadistic buffer between our 747 and the peaks. They were so close, I thought I could see light fixtures silhouetted in their windows, clotheslines jiggling on their balconies. On the other side of the plane was the bay. If we didn't land precisely, we'd careen into either the mountains or the sea.

"It's like Scylla and Charybdis down there," Claire laughed, spooling the cord from her headphones around her Walkman. She had majored in philosophy, so she tended to view the world through a prism of Greek mythology and nineteenth-century German depressives. The cabin began filling with the smell of sewage, jet fuel, rotting fish. Seeing my distress, she squeezed my arm. "Oh, sweetie. Relax. It's all part of the adventure."

There was a screaming roar; my heart went staccato in my chest. I flashed miserably on my teary-eyed parents, on my little brother back in Manhattan listening to all the record albums I'd left behind. A ribbon of asphalt swelled beneath the plane. I shut my eyes and braced myself for impact. The fuselage seemed to tear through a membrane. Everything convulsed, then shuddered, then released with an ear-splitting squeal.

We stopped. For an instant, there was silence.

"Ladies and gentlemen," the pilot said cheerily over the loudspeaker, "welcome to Kai Tak Airport." The passengers applauded politely. I'd never heard people applaud a landing before—though to be fair, this was only the third time in my life I'd ever been on an airplane. As we taxied toward the gate, I exhaled and imagined that they were really clapping for Claire and me. Our arrival was momentous. It was unbelievable to me that we'd actually pulled it off. We were now truly here, on the other side of the earth. All that remained was for us to step out onto the glistening tarmac and into the gloriousness of our lives.

───────────

In 1986, my classmate Claire Van Houten and I decided to backpack around the world for a year. Neither of us had ever traveled independently before or been to a country where we couldn't speak the language. The farthest west I'd ever been, in fact, was Cleveland. Nonetheless, the two of us became convinced that we should not only embark on an epic journey, but begin someplace incredibly daunting and remote where none of our friends had ever set foot before. And so we decided to kick off our adventure in the People's Republic of China. At that point, Communist China had been open to independent backpackers for about all of ten minutes.

The summer after our graduation from college,

we'd purchased around-the-world airline tickets, which began with a flight from New York to Hong Kong that September. By slowly plane-hopping around the waistline of the planet, we'd figured we'd circumnavigate the globe in exactly a year, returning just in time for my student loans to come due.

We had no idea, of course, of how complicated the world could be, or of our place in it, or of just how much trouble we were in for. We didn't even comprehend what it would feel like to lug water purifiers, sleeping bags, and leaden pairs of hiking boots around the globe. All we'd thought was: Hey, let's be Odysseus. Let's be Byron. Let's be Don Quixote, Huck Finn, and Jack Kerouac all rolled into one—except with lip gloss. Let's conquer the fucking world.

As we alighted from the gangway, Claire pirouetted. "Oh my God! We're in Hong Kong! Can you be-lieve it?"

We each gave a trilling, girlish squeal—no doubt exactly as Odysseus would've done—and sashayed through passport control. We hadn't even reached the baggage claim, however, before I got a massive nosebleed.

Blood pooled in my left nostril, dripping down my face. A sweet, meaty taste filled the back of my throat. Although I'd been sure to stuff a half-pound bag of M&M's, my diaphragm, and my 913-page astrology guide, *Linda Goodman's Love Signs,* into my carry-on, it hadn't dawned on me to pack Kleenex. I found a

crumpled, lint-ridden United Airlines cocktail napkin and stuck it up my nose.

"Ow." Claire winced as she drew closer. "That
looks nasty. Here."

She guided me like a blind person across the con-
course to the ladies' room. Thousands of women had
passed through it during the day; streamers of wet
toilet paper lay matted across the floor. Claire eased
me down onto a dry spot near the sinks. Leaning my
head back, I almost choked on my own blood.

She rummaged through her purse, pulling out the
split of champagne we'd bought at the duty-free shop
back in San Francisco, her Mason Pearson hairbrush,
a paperback copy of *The Genealogy of Morals*. Claire
was perhaps the first person to insist on bringing the
complete works of Friedrich Nietzsche on a backpacking trip. But she hadn't thought to pack tissues,
either—which was ironic because we'd otherwise
prepared for this voyage as if it were the invasion of
Normandy. The bags we'd checked were laden with
no less than fourteen Berlitz phrase books, two different types of malaria pills, earplugs, first aid kits,
inflatable pillows, sarongs, flip-flops, bug spray, Kwell,
anti-diarrhea medicine, canteens, condoms, six Pen-
guin literary paperback classics by authors ranging
from Cervantes to Virginia Woolf, and enough tampons to last us a year.

"Stay here," she instructed, pivoting around. Even
when she was exhausted, Claire moved with the disci-

pline of the ballerina she'd once been, her feet turned out, her carriage erect, her chin elevated. With her long neck and aristocratic features, she looked like a Dutch Renaissance Madonna—albeit one in a polo shirt and pleated khakis from L.L. Bean. She had an air of certainty about her, a regal loveliness. Me, I was all breasts and flyaway brown hair and enormous, mismatched rhinestone earrings; half the time, I flounced around in black ripped-neck sweatshirts with my bra strap showing. I'd cleaned up my act for traveling, but just barely.

The ladies' room door *fwooshed* open and shut. An announcement crackled over the PA in English, then Cantonese. Women came in to pee and stepped around me with annoyance. I felt foolish, wildly disoriented. We'd left New York over a day ago; we'd crossed the international dateline. It was eight a.m. back home, nine p.m. here. Time had collapsed in on itself like a soufflé.

Claire returned, dragging both our backpacks. "Fuck, we overpacked," she said.

Gingerly I stood up. My reflection in the mirror was a catastrophe. The lower half of my face was caked with dried blood. It looked like a Ming vase that had been smashed, then glued back together. Claire handed me a fistful of napkins from the airport snack bar, and I cleaned myself up as best I could.

Now, if you've never really traveled before, and you've just flown over thirty-one hours in economy class—two rows up from the smoking section—to a foreign city in an upside-down, day-is-night hallucinatory time zone—and you're filthy: your mouth feels encrusted with airplane pretzels and you haven't showered in over a day—and you both have splitting headaches from dehydration and from watching endless loops of *The Goonies* and *Ferris Bueller's Day Off* on the minuscule screens throughout the airplane—and at least one of you has just had a massive nosebleed—and as soon as you step outside the airport, a wall of tropical humidity hits you that makes you feel as if you're standing behind the exhaust pipe of a city bus—then as a general rule of thumb, it's a good idea to take a room at a Holiday Inn for a couple of days to get acclimated.

But Claire and I would have none of this. We were determined to check ourselves directly into a shit-hole.

"I want us to be *travelers,* not pampered little tourists," she'd declared during our many phone calls that summer. "No air-conditioned buses, no idiotic tour guides, no Hilton hotels."

"Absolutely," I'd agreed, twirling the phone cord around my knuckles. "The whole point of this trip is to experience the *real* world. Stay off the beaten path entirely. Stay only in local places, eat local food. Be totally hard core and authentic."

All our lives, Claire and I had been ambitious, straight-A students who built dioramas of Aztec vil-

lages for extra credit in social studies; who recited
Robert Frost poems for our parents' unsuspecting
dinner guests; who took AP French in high school
and edited the yearbooks and wrote honors theses in
college. It wasn't enough for us to merely navigate the
world on our own. Oh no. We had to prove to everyone, in the process, just how expertly and imagina-
tively we could do it too. Like everything else in our
lives, we seemed to believe our trip was something
we'd be getting graded on.

In 1986, there were no regular commercial flights
between the United States and Beijing. Independent
travelers had to enter China through Hong Kong.
We'd purchased an obscure budget guidebook, *Southeast Asia on a Shoestring,* published by a bunch of
hippies calling themselves Lonely Planet. They recommended staying in Hong Kong's Kowloon section at a place called Chungking Mansions. This was
not only a great base for backpackers, they said, but a
good source for information about obtaining Chinese
visas and arranging transport across the border.

So that's where we decided to go. Chungking
Mansions. Just the name alone appealed to our sense
of adventure and romance.

"It sounds sort of gothic, doesn't it?" Claire said
as we slid into the taxi with our backpacks. "Like
some sort of abandoned plantation with vines growing over it?"

"Wild peacocks roaming the verandah," I suggested.

She laughed, nodding. "Shutters banging in the wind."

Until our precipitous landing at Kai Tak Airport, Hong Kong had been an abstraction to me. Despite my education, my conception of the world at that point was about as sophisticated as a kiddie ride at a theme park. Other nations were a blur to me of strange alphabets, kitschy costumes, tiresome folk songs, and snow globes. Mostly I assumed that what made a country foreign was the degree of its deviation from the standard of America. If a country had skyscrapers, refrigerators, and televisions, I figured it was pretty much the same as the United States. If it had houses, diets, or skirts made entirely of foliage, it wasn't.

My concepts of places were nothing less than bad poems: clichés lazily cobbled together. Hong Kong, to me, was simply an abstraction—the home of cheap novelty key rings, yo-yos, see-through pencil cases. I somehow imagined we'd be sleeping in a rice paddy.

Yet when I showed our driver the address, he gunned the cab onto a wide concrete access ramp looping down into a tunnel, a serpentine of white tiles and sodium lights sucking us back and forth beneath the bay. We emerged onto a chaotic intersection that looked like a compression of Times Square,

the streets claustrophobic jumbles of high-rise buildings with enormous electric billboards for Toshiba,
Aiwa, Kent cigarettes. Neon signs flashed "Pearls,"
"Watches," "Lucky Peking Duck." Whole roast pigs
dangled by their ankles like lanterns in the restaurants. Buses, old cars, and motor scooters ground
out bluish-black plumes of exhaust; crowds elbowed
each other at crosswalks. Honking trucks, mirrored
bunting: The streets had a whorish, carnival quality
that defied nighttime or any semblance of order.

The driver lurched onto a huge main road with
three lanes of traffic running in each direction, then
came to an abrupt stop in front of an arcade full
of lurid discount stores. "Okay." He pointed to the
meter. "Two hundred twenty dollar."

Claire and I looked out the window. "What?"
I leaned forward and pointed to our guidebook.
"Chungking Mansions *on Nathan Road.*"

The driver looked at me furiously. Jabbing the page
with his finger, he pointed outside. "This Chungking
Mansions!" he shouted. "This Nathan Road."

Claire rolled down the window and poked her head
out. "Shit," she said after a moment. "He's right."

We paid him with our strange-looking Hong
Kong dollars, and his cab screeched away, leaving us
with our backpacks on the edge of the gutter. A sign
above the arcade read: "Chungking Mansions, 36-44
Nathan Road, Kowloon." It looked nothing like a
tropical villa and everything like the Port Authority

Bus Terminal back in New York City. Inside was a warren of convenience stores selling cheap electronics and knock-off designer handbags. Music blared, a drum machine punching out a bass line. Young Asian and African men in grease-stained T-shirts slithered out of a newsstand drinking beer out of brown paper bags. In an instant, they descended upon us. "You want wristwatch? For you, special price. You want guest house, come on. I show you." The stench of sweat, urine, and frying pork was dizzying. Already, we were drenched in perspiration. The tropical air was broth. My traveler's checks and passport were strapped beneath my clothes in a money belt. It felt like a damp tourniquet, but I kept checking to make sure it was still there.

"Okay, clearly, this is not the Chungking Mansions in the guidebook," I panted.

We were the only Westerners on the entire block, as well as the only women. With our bulging backpacks and our deer-in-the-headlights faces, we might as well have had giant bull's-eyes painted on our chests.

A Western couple emerged from the arcade.

"Excuse me." I flagged them down. "Do you know where Chungking Mansions is?"

They looked at me as if I were mentally retarded. "Right here," the girl sniffed, pointing to the elevators.

Reluctantly Claire and I hoisted up our packs

and trundled inside. Above a bank of decrepit steel
elevators were plastic slats listing restaurants, massage parlors, and guesthouses in no particular order.
Chungking Mansions wasn't a hotel at all, but a ware-
house for transients.

"I don't know," I said warily. I'd grown up in a
rough inner-city neighborhood in New York. I'd
gotten harassed often enough to know when something looked like a bad idea. It didn't take much
imagination to see the entire filthy corridor cordoned
off with yellow crime-scene tape.

Claire sighed and raked her hands through
her hair. Of the two of us, she was by far the more
optimistic. "Well, we won't know until we see."
She jammed the button for the elevator. "Let's start
with the Lucky Guesthouse at the top. If we don't
like it, we'll just work our way down till we find
something."

I tried to keep my pulse in check. Claire had been
raised in New Canaan, Connecticut, in a colonnaded
house with a circular driveway flanked by topiaries
and a swimming pool that looked like a giant turquoise paramecium. When the Van Houtens had
invited me and my family up for a little post-graduation
party, their maid had greeted us at the door with a
tray full of champagne and lemonade.

The door to the Lucky Guesthouse had a frosted
window like an old detective agency. The proprietor
sat behind a dented metal desk smoking a cigarette

and staring at a television mounted high on a shelf in the corner. Two men onscreen appeared to be beating each other with sticks.

"Hello," Claire said. I had to admit, I admired her fearlessness. She just walked right in on her long, caliper legs.

The proprietor continued staring at the TV. An electric fan whirred on his desk, making the papers flutter. The tiny room smelled like an ashtray. Somewhere a toilet flushed gaseously. "Room or dormitory?" he said gruffly.

"A room," Claire said crisply. "With a private bathroom and two beds, please."

The man yanked open a drawer and tossed a key at her, never once removing his gaze from the screen. "Number six," he said. "Down hall, on right. Eighty dollars. Cash only. You pay first thing in morning." Eighty Hong Kong dollars was roughly eleven bucks.

Claire strode down the corridor. I bumbled along behind her. Room 6 was a concrete cell with two denuded mattresses. A bare plastic lamp molded in the shape of a candlestick sputtered on the floor between them. When we tried the light switch, the overhead bulb blew out with a spark and a pop and a huge cockroach scuttled out from a crack in the ceiling.

Without a word, Claire spun around and walked back down the hall. When she dropped the key back on the desk, the manager never even took his eyes off the television.

Riding and stopping at each floor in Chungking Mansion's elevator for the next twenty minutes was like reading one of those pop-up books I'd had as a child in which you pulled open little paper flaps to reveal tiny domestic scenes behind each one. Except in this case, each time the elevator door slid open, it unveiled a tiny tableau of squalor and depravity.

On one floor, we saw an obese Chinese man sitting on the landing in a giant diaper. His hair was matted; he was masturbating, weeping, and growling like a rabid dog. On the floor below that was an empty hallway heaped with garbage, a sole lightbulb swinging overhead like a noose, the walls gouged with graffiti. On the next was a red and gold sign for a massage parlor and the sound of people fighting. Puffs of greasy, garlic-scented smoke filled the hallway in front of the Happy Family Hostel.

With each stop, our trepidation increased. But when I finally suggested we take out the credit card we had for emergencies and check into the Kowloon Holiday Inn, Claire cried, "No!"

"Please," she said more gently, "if we check into a fancy place for one night, soon we'll be, like, 'Oh, let's just stay here.' It would be too easy. We've got to stay strong, okay? I promise we'll find something, okay?"

Eventually we arrived at the Boston Guesthouse,

whose name, at least, sounded promising. "Hello. Welcome. I am Mr. Chung," said a studious-looking young man behind the counter. "Come." He smiled extravagantly. "I have nice rooms. You want with air-conditioning or fan?"

"Air-conditioning," we chorused wearily, our foreheads glistening. So much for roughing it.

In its previous incarnation, the Boston Guesthouse had clearly been a bathhouse; the rooms were windowless, aquamarine tiled stalls with an asterisk of a drain embedded in their floors. Each was blindingly lit by a fluorescent tube running the length of the ceiling. Tiny bathrooms were sectioned off from the beds by a shiny plastic shower curtain. A few ants scurried across the tiles, but otherwise, the rooms seemed clean enough. In fact they reeked of chlorine. Air conditioners were bolted unevenly to the walls just below the ceiling. It was now almost eleven p.m. We were running out of options.

"They're fine. We'll take them," Claire sighed, tucking her hair back behind her ears. She had an opalescent complexion, like milk glass; you could see the fine blue veins at her temples. In the queasy fluorescence of the guesthouse, her hair looked almost green.

We paid Chung seventy Hong Kong dollars apiece, and he handed us keys to two small, adjoining rooms. And there we were: officially ensconced in Asia.

I closed my door and dropped my backpack on the

floor, the *thunk* reverberating off the tiles. I sat down on the bed. In a few minutes, Claire would come over to uncork the champagne we'd brought to toast our arrival. Yet somehow I couldn't bring myself to move. Although the air-conditioning was on high, I couldn't stop sweating. Perspiration bloomed in the armpits of my T-shirt, damp flowers of exhaustion.

From overhead came the sizzle of mosquitoes frying against the fluorescent bulb. I looked around. Without any windows, it was impossible to get oriented. I sat on the edge of the metal-framed bed, trying to catch my own breath.

It was the first time I'd ever been alone in a foreign country.

It didn't feel triumphant or glorious at all.

Like most grandiose ideas, ours had begun stupidly. Claire and I had first conceived of our little adventure at four a.m. at the International House of Pancakes fifteen days before our graduation from Brown. We were both drunk and bemoaning the fact that we had no idea what the hell to do with ourselves once we tossed off our mortarboards. We were, I suppose, typical twenty-one-year-olds: We believed we were exceptional.

Both of us had had big plans for ourselves after college. Mine had been to write the Great American Novel by the end of senior year and publish it to international acclaim. Claire's had been to win a Rhodes scholarship. Yet somehow neither of these had panned out. All that awaited Claire was a gelatinous summer at her family's beach house in Hilton Head, where her stepmother (whom she called "the Lady Macbeth of the dog show circuit") would dote on her six pedigree bichons-frises while yelling at Claire not to spill Tab on the slipcovers. All that awaited me was moving back home with my parents and pretending that a job at Lady Footlocker was some sort of feminist activism.

At the IHOP, a beleaguered waitress had set a couple of paper place mats in front of us with the menu printed on them. "Pancakes of Many Nations!" they'd read. Beneath this were little pictures that reduced the world's great cultural differences to a matter of hotcakes and waffles: *Vive La France:* crepes. *Polynesia Paradise:* pineapple and ham. *O, Canada:* flapjacks, maple syrup. The pictures had a faded, nostalgic quality: they appeared to have been taken in the fifties. Presented this way, the vast world we were about to enter suddenly appeared cheery and infinitely manageable; there was not a single nation on earth, the IHOP menu implied, that couldn't be mastered with a fork.

Staring at it, we'd had a jolt of inspiration. Why not eat pancakes of many nations *in* many nations? Why not travel the world? Oddly, barreling headlong into developing countries with a backpack somehow seemed far easier to us than simply getting a job.

"Oh my God, let's do it!" we cried. "Let's literally circle the globe."

Neither of us knew the other terribly well. Our freshman year at Brown, we'd lived on the same hallway and taken comparative literature together. Although Claire had gone on to join a sorority and to frequent football games while I'd installed myself at the Womyn's Center with other leftie malcontents, once a semester or so, we went out for coffee. We'd end up laughing so hard that the proprietors of the café invariably asked us to leave. Parting, we always blew each other silly, exaggerated air kisses, said "Au revoir, darling," and left flushed with goodwill and kinship.

Deciding to travel the world together on impulse didn't strike either of us as unreasonable. We were at that age when we still believed that genius arrived in bolts of lightning and shrieks of "Eureka!" We still believed in love at first sight, not just with people, but with ideas—that in a single instant, you could *just know.*

What's more, we'd been raised to assume that one day we would in fact conquer the world. Claire and I had come of age during that rare moment in human history when little girls were pumped full of the steroids of feminism, told en masse that we could do anything, be anything, go anywhere. During our freshman orientation week at Brown, the university president had addressed us as "the best and brightest, the future leaders of America."

Whenever we'd read books about bold, romantic, heroes who'd sailed the oceans, climbed the mountains, and ventured into uncharted territories, we'd been supremely irritated that almost none of them had had a vagina. Why couldn't women be heroes in great epics too?

That night at the IHOP, Claire had reached into her purse, pulled out a ballpoint pen, and clicked it expertly, as if preparing to administer an injection. "Let's star in our own epic. Let's write down every place in the world we've ever wanted to go." Flipping over her place mat, she'd scribbled down the words *Katmandu, Thailand, Greece,* then passed it to me.

Marrakech, I'd jotted down. *Paris. Bali.* I could barely identify these places on a map, but they sounded cool. I couldn't quite believe we were actually going to go through with this, but so what? *Italy,* I wrote. *Sri Lanka.*

In the scheme of human history, 1986 is not long ago. And yet as we made our lists, the foreign countries we were naming seemed a lot farther away than they do now. With the Cold War raging, the entire Eastern Bloc was sequestered behind the iron curtain, and mass tourism beyond Europe was only nascent. This was years before the Internet; before routine transpacific flights; before American jobs were outsourced to Mumbai and Manila; before overseas direct dialing and cell phones; and before CNN, Sky TV, and the 24-hour news cycle regularly transmitted images around the globe into everybody's living rooms. And this was, of course, before September 11.

Oblivious to the ickiness of our presumption that we would discover cultures that were actually far older and far more evolved than we were, we believed that there was still a great frontier left to explore — a frontier, in fact, that eagerly awaited us. *The People's Republic of China.* It seemed so vast, so unknown, so pregnant with promise! "Look out, world," we giggled. "Here we come!"

As we scribbled, the sun started to rise, inflaming the windows of the IHOP, blinding us with hot slats of gold reflected off the Formica tabletop. Claire glanced up at me, brushed her white-blond hair back with her wrist, and smiled a dazzling, exuberant smile. "We're really going to do this, you know," she said rapturously. "We're going to have an adventure worthy of great literature."

Across from us, four truckers stood up, hiked up their pants, adjusted their belts, inserted toothpicks between their lips. The waitress wiped down their table and reset it. Then she untied her apron and sauntered off.

The restaurant was empty. The stillness felt like relief. We could hear the clanking of pans in the kitchen, a griddle being hosed down, a time clock chomping a punch card. From the parking lot came the first tentative peeps of sparrows. As we wrote, scribbling down budgets, listing the supplies we might need, we became more and more giddy. Our laughter rang out like a carillon in the morning. We grew increasingly delirious with our newfound sense of possibility, our widescreen visions, our raw, voracious ambition. We were young, brilliant, and drunk. We were the future leaders of America. We were off and running. We now had a plan.

———

When Claire's mother had died, she'd left Claire a trust fund. I, however, had grown up in a government-subsidized housing project and attended Brown on financial aid. To pay for our trip, I'd had to defer repaying my student loans and work multiple jobs. That summer I'd answered telephones during the day at a real estate office, then waitressed at a grungy Upper West Side bar at night. The bar was notorious for serving alcohol to minors. The fact that I could get arrested for this didn't bother me nearly so much as the fact that teenagers never tipped.

By the time the jukebox was switched off at the end of my shift each night, it was close to three a.m. To save money, I walked home. The dark, cracked pavement glittered in the heat. Back at my parents' apartment, I'd tiptoe into the kitchen and make myself a Kahlúa and milk, then carry the clinking glass to my bedroom and sip it as I counted out my tips. I'd smooth each dollar bill lovingly, fanning them out on my bedspread. On a good night, I earned over seventy-five bucks; on a bad night, less than forty.

My parents' apartment overlooked rows of dilapidated brownstones, their backyards strewn with rusted baby carriages, disemboweled sofas, plastic pink flamingos bleached to the color of an infection. Beyond these towered ugly, Braque-like buildings like our own. As the sun came up each morning, I'd stare out the window and listen to the sound of jackhammers, to the police sirens ripping by and our neighbors yelling from fire escapes, "I kill you, you dumb fuck," and I'd think with relief: *In just a few months, I'll get out of here and bestride the world like a goddess.*

Now, sitting on a metal bed ten thousand miles from home in a cell the pale blue-green color of chewing gum, listening to two people yelling in Cantonese through a grimy ventilation duct, I realized what a mother lode of stupidity this had been. Claire and I didn't speak a word of Chinese. What if we got sick? Our guidebooks were full of warnings about parasites, worms, fungi, fevers. What if we were molested or robbed? What if we got lost?

We didn't know one soul in the entire hemisphere. We'd landed in Asia without a single name scribbled on a napkin. No friend of a friend's cousin teaching English. No army buddy of her father's. No Brown alumnus to call in case of an emergency. When we'd finally made it into the arrivals hall at Kai Tak, there'd been absolutely nobody waiting for us. For all my talk about wanting to be a bold, independent traveler, I'd never considered what it would actually feel like to journey halfway around the world with no one to greet me on the other end.

The reality of how utterly alone we were was starting to hit me; the loneliness of it was sonic. We could disappear or die here—who would even care?

It was, I realize, a Copernican moment. For perhaps the first time in my life, it became viscerally clear to me just how little I mattered, just how much I was not in fact the center of the universe. It was like a swift kick to the gut.

I had just spent two thousand dollars on a nonrefundable around-the-world airplane ticket, received a battery of vaccinations against everything from tetanus to yellow fever, and traveled halfway across the globe for what was clearly a hideous mistake.

My teeth began chattering so hard I thought they would crack. Shutting off the air-conditioning, I curled up in a fetal position in my sleeping bag and tried to think of how to break it to Claire that I was sorry, that I just wasn't *that type of girl* after all—that this was all wrong—and I had to go home immediately.

As if on cue, there was a knock on my door. "Susie?"

Leaping up, I switched the AC back on and tried

to recompose myself. Claire hurried in. Her hair was wet from showering. She was clad in light-blue-and-white-pinstripe pajamas that smelled of fabric softener.

"The champagne. I'm sorry. I think I left it in the bathroom at the airport. Oh, Susie!" She sat down on my bed and buried her face in her hands.

"Claire, what is it?"

"This place! My mattress is crawling with ants. The AC is broken. My room's like an oven. And it's so strange. There are all these weird noises. And I suddenly feel so *completely* alone. What are we doing here?"

I dropped down beside her. "I don't know." I hiccuped. "I was just thinking the same thing."

"I'm so sorry," Claire choked. "First I go, 'Hey, let's travel the world. Let's go totally off the beaten path.' And then I'm, like, 'We're going to rough it. No Hilton hotels for us. I'm not some pampered little princess.' But you know what, Suze? I *am* a pampered little princess. I didn't think I was, but I am. Tonight has totally creeped me out. My father is right."

When he'd seen us off at JFK, Claire's father had paced around the departure gate, chain-smoking and cracking his knuckles, his sport coat tugging across his shoulder blades. "They're making a terrible mistake," he told my parents, shaking his head gravely.

"Don't say I didn't warn you, princess," he said to

Claire. The muscle in his jaw spasmed. He had a long patrician face and pewter-colored hair clipped close to his skull. He looked like a pained greyhound.

Asia was a cesspool, he said loudly. Didn't we know that? It was Third World, rice fields and shanties, filthy children, beggars in the streets. Of course, he'd only been to Tokyo, back in the seventies. But trust him. Oriental culture was perverse. Those men had schoolgirl fetishes. They read pornography openly on the subways, and nobody ever went jogging. Worse yet, they considered us white people to be monkeys. "And this after we rebuilt their country. They bombed Pearl Harbor, and we gave them Toyota," he said. No, sir, he was 100 percent opposed to us setting foot in Japan.

"We're not going to Japan, Daddy," Claire had said irritably. "We're starting in China."

"The People's Republic. A Communist empire." He'd snorted. "When you come crying home to us, princess, don't say I didn't warn you."

"Your father's wrong," I told Claire now. "There's a difference between being a princess and not wanting to spend the night in an ant-infested shit-hole with guys in diapers jerking off by the elevator.

"Look," I said, "if it's any consolation, I'm completely freaked out, too. In fact I've been freaked out since the minute we got off the plane."

"Really?" Claire sniffled.

"Uh-huh, totally. The heat, the noise, the craziness. And the idea of going to China, this Communist country where no one speaks English —"

"We don't have to, you know," she said quickly. "I mean, I was thinking. At least maybe we shouldn't start there, you know? Maybe we should get our bearings somewhere else a little easier first. Like Bali."

"Bali?"

"Sure. It's supposed to have tropical beaches. Palm trees. We could go there, acclimate, and then if we feel like it, go to China."

"True," I said after a moment. "I guess I was thinking of someplace even easier."

"Like?"

"Chicago. Or Philadelphia. Philadelphia's probably my speed."

Claire stared at me.

"But they're not even in Asia," she said after a moment.

"I know." Then, unable to contain myself, I wailed, "Oh, Claire. I'm not like you. I've never traveled the way you have. You at least spent a semester studying in Paris.

"No one ever tells you this," I said despairingly, waving at the turquoise tiled walls, the bare, hissing light fixture. "All those travel magazines. People with their vacation photos. They just make it look so easy."

Claire looked at me sympathetically. Suddenly she clamped her hands over her mouth.

"What?" I said.

She shook her head back and forth like a horse breaking free of its bridle. Then she started laughing. "Oh, my God. 'Let's go to Bali. Let's go to Philadelphia. There are ants in my bed.' Suze, would you listen to us? What kind of wusses are we?"

"You know what this is?" Claire said. "Jet lag. And culture shock. The two of us are so exhausted and disoriented, we're practically psychotic. So we're getting freaked out. Over nothing."

Hugging myself, I wiped my nose on the back of my wrist.

"I'm serious, Suze. You know my stepbrother? Dominic?"

I nodded feebly. Claire had three stepbrothers, Alexander, Edward, and Dominic. They were all gorgeous, strapping, and redheaded, and I couldn't tell one from the other. They treated Claire like their mascot. "Every time Dominic goes anywhere — England or just back to Wharton — the first night he arrives? He always has a meltdown. He gets obsessed with the bed pillows, the noises in the street.

"So what we're feeling here? It's totally normal. We've just got to get through this first night, is all, and we'll be fine." She tilted her head at me, her hair falling across her forehead, her lips pursed. "Sweetie, you think you can sleep?"

I shrugged.

"Nah. Me neither, I guess." She sighed and threw

up her hands. "This place is a dump. But we just have to stick it out. Here. Move over. This way at least we won't have to go it alone."

I rolled against the tiled wall and made room for Claire on the flimsy narrow bed. She was extremely thin and much taller than me — five-nine — a former dancer, a horseback rider, all legs and ribs and elbows and knees. As she wedged in next to me, we kept knocking up against each other, apologizing as we shifted about trying to get comfortable. The bed squeaked insanely. The air conditioner grunted and belched. Claire started giggling. "Oh my god! This is absurd!" she hooted at the ceiling. "Look at us!"

Rolling onto her stomach, she propped herself up on her elbows. "Okay, right now, at this very moment, this feels like hell, right? But in the morning, I promise, Hong Kong will seem so much better."

She snuggled up against me and sighed.

After a moment, she said, "Want me to burp 'The Battle Hymn of the Republic'?"

"Nuh-uh," I said miserably.

This was a talent she'd picked up from her stepbrothers. Normally it cracked me up. Now I worried it would only make me more homesick.

"You sure? Okay. Well, you just let me know if you change your mind."

With a little flounce, she turned over on her side. From the way she went about adjusting her pillow, plumping and re-plumping it, I could sense her acceptance of our situation, her growing contentment with it, and this only made me feel more wretched.

Amazingly, while I was growing up, my hippie mother had gone through an Eastern religion phase, during which she'd compelled us all to practice Transcendental Meditation and listen to a guru named Baba Ram Dass. "Be here now," he'd instructed. "Live completely in the moment." But the moment was all I ever lived in, and it made me fucking miserable. I could never see beyond whatever emotion had me directly in its grip.

As she lay beside me, I knew that Claire was already seeing in her mind's eye the Yangtze River, shining like mercury. She was standing in chartreuse rice paddies and talc-like sand. She was climbing the Great Wall and twirling ecstatically in the Temple of Heaven. Despite her trepidation, she was off—off and soaring above all expectation and constraint. Me, all I could see were filthy hotel rooms swarming with ants, yawning toilets, and demented men in diapers wailing amid the remnants of vegetables. All I could see were the other passengers from our flight, leaving Kai Tak Airport with their families in a great yarn ball of love, leaving me to bleed alone, scared and incompetent on the floor of a public bathroom. All I could see were street signs like hieroglyphics that I would never be able to understand, convoluted neighborhoods I would never be able to navigate, and the endless, interminable trek I would have to make beneath the weight of my backpack in an idiotic Bataan Death March of Tourism of my own making—to be endured across one alien land, then another, in order to finally make it home a year later deranged with exhaustion. All I could smell and taste was fear, hot as curry at the back of my throat.

"You'll see, sweetie," Claire murmured as she finally began to drift off to sleep. "A few months from now, this will all just seem really, really funny."

Even then, when she said this, I had the terrible feeling that it wouldn't.

Chapter 2

Hong Kong

I DON'T KNOW how many of the world's great explorers called home in tears immediately after they arrived someplace strange. I suspected I might have been the first.

When we finally awoke — hours, days later — unable to discern if it was morning or night, Claire hopped out of bed positively mentholated with energy. "Wow, I feel so much better. Don't you?" She pirouetted, grabbed her room key. "Let's wash up, then go explore."

The moment I heard the arrhythmia of the shower in her bathroom, I yanked on my clothes, dashed out into the reception area, and begged Mr. Chung to help me.

As the overseas operator tried the connection, I wiped my nose on the back of my wrist and bit down on my knuckle. Finally there came a click.

"MOM?" I shouted. My voice echoed over a crackle of static.

"SUSIE?" my mother shouted back. "WHERE ARE YOU?"

"Hong Kong—"

"Are you all right? The Van Houtens are worried. They haven't heard from Claire." Our voices overlapped, then cut each other off abruptly like fingers blocking and releasing an air valve.

"We've both been sleeping. We're really jet-lagged."

"Good. I'll let them know you arrived."

"Oh, Mom, I'm really homesick. I'm kinda freaked out."

"Oh, honey, I'm sure you'll be fine."

"I'm thinking of cashing in my plane ticket and just coming home."

There was a pause, a lunacy of high-pitched whistles. I heard my mother exhale. I imagined her standing over our kitchen sink in her purple leotard, filling a steamer with organic brown rice. She'd been uneasy about my trip from the beginning. At JFK, when I'd finally turned and headed down the gangway, her face was so wet and palsied with emotion, she could barely say goodbye.

But now she shouted across the hemispheres, "What? You can't just fly back home. You just got there. What are you going to do for money?"

The week before my departure, I'd had a false

pregnancy scare, followed by an unfortunate night of drunkenness, and a big fight over doing the laundry. We had our issues, my mother and I. Now, as I clutched the telephone receiver in Hong Kong, it suddenly occurred to me that her sobs at the airport hadn't been those of a distraught parent at all. Rather, they'd been like those of a death-row inmate receiving a last-minute reprieve from the governor. I'd be departing the country for an entire year and inflicting myself on the Communists instead; she couldn't believe her good luck.

"No, if you come back, you have to have a plan," she announced now. "I think you should stick it out in Asia awhile. You'll see. In a few days, you'll feel better."

"But, Mom—"

"Listen. This call is costing us a fortune, and we're about to sit down to dinner. I'm thrilled you called. Really I am. Tell Claire I'll call her folks for her, and let me know when you get to China. Hang in there, girl. Your mama loves you."

With that, she hung up.

I stood there incredulous, the gunmetal receiver heavy in my hand. Mr. Chung waited respectfully off to the side, pretending to sort a pile of tourist brochures.

Of all my family members, my grandmother had always been my staunchest ally. For years, she'd fancied herself a Communist. When she wasn't berating her housekeeper—whom she degradingly called "the domestic"—she'd sit back in a crushed velvet armchair with an enormous gin and tonic and speak glowingly of Trotsky.

"You're not a Communist, Ma," my father would say with irritation. "You're an alcoholic. There's a difference."

Real Communists didn't have country houses and tennis club memberships, he pointed out. Real Communists didn't play the stock market.

Luckily for me, though, my grandmother did. For a Bolshevik, she was somehow the only person in our family with any disposable income. When she heard I was planning to backpack around the world, she said ecstatically, "The only thing that could make me any happier, *bubeleh,* would be if you married a Negro."

Grasping both my hands, she whispered, "Years ago, I bought some bonds. Today, they're worth three thousand dollars. I'm going to cash them. As long as you go to China, the money's yours. Otherwise, you pay me back with interest."

Now, standing amid the file cabinets at the Boston Guesthouse, I considered calling her collect, too. But then, I knew exactly what she would say.

———

Claire emerged from the bathroom smelling of peppermint castile soap. We'd each brought quart-size bottles for the trip; according to the label, it was 100 percent biodegradable and could be used interchange-ably as shampoo, toothpaste, and laundry detergent.

"So how's this for a plan?" She flounced onto my bed, her towel draped around her neck like a stole. Whipping out a comb, she pulled it briskly through her hair. "We go get some breakfast, then head to the Chinese consulate to get visas. After lunch, we take the cable car to Victoria Peak."

I studied the mattress ticking as if I were actually considering this. Reaching behind her head, Claire gathered the damp skeins into a ponytail and secured it expertly with an elastic band. "Well?"

Her gas-blue eyes fixed on me expectantly. On the floor, ants congregated around the drain.

When Claire had urged me to travel with her that night at the IHOP, I hadn't quite believed it. Claire Van Houten and me?

Most of my time at Brown, I'd felt like geometry: a collection of unlovely, isolated parts that needed to be proven over and over. I'd sauntered around campus in miniskirts and fishnet stockings and gold leather ankle boots, trying desperately to convince people that I was this sophisticated and outré New Yorker. But I didn't think I fooled anyone.

As part of my financial aid package, I'd served tur-key tetrazzini to my classmates at the dining hall for four years while dressed in a paper hat. Otherwise, all I'd managed to do at college was gain weight, have my heart broken, and write term papers with titles such as "A Post-Lacanian Analysis of Valorizations of Gender" that even my professors found tedious. Junior year, when my father secretly telephoned to tell me that he was thinking of leaving my mother, I'd checked into health services for a week.

My friends had been equally neurotic—arch, hyper-articulate young women with asymmetrical haircuts and black eyeliner who sat around quoting obscure French feminists and rolling their own cigarettes. And yet, for women obsessed with liberation, they were as rigid and sensitive as tuning forks: Everything set them off. Freud offended them. Non-vegetarian lasagna offended them. The words *fascinating*, *natural*, and *objective* offended them. Money offended them, too—I suppose because, unlike me, they'd always had more than enough of it.

Any time I made a smart-ass remark—say, if I suggested that we call our feminist coffeehouse Girls, Girls, Girls!—they glared at me with thinly veiled contempt.

Claire, by contrast, had a laugh like a waterfall. You could hear its cadences building and spilling clear across the dining hall. Her great-uncle had donated a rare books collection to the John Hay Library. Her stepbrother Alexander had been roommates one semester with JFK Jr. Yet she was a standout in her own right. With her height, her cascade of pale hair, and her milky skin, she was hard to miss. Plus, she was smart. Whiplash, magna cum laude smart. Everything that I didn't know, she did. Latin. Supply-side economics. How to play tennis. How to drive a car, change a tire, ride a horse. How to follow the stock market. How to read Plato and Aristotle in the original Greek. How to make chicken tarragon in our Soviet-style dormitory using only a saucepan and a fork. She was self-assured and utterly at home in the world in every way that I was not.

Perhaps most importantly, she was kind. Rich, beautiful girls weren't expected to take a special ed student to his prom. But on Claire's bulletin board freshman year, I'd seen a snapshot of her in a fuchsia taffeta dress, smiling over a tuxedoed boy in a wheelchair. "Him? Oh, that's Jimmy," she'd simply shrugged. "A kid I used to tutor."

Okay, so she voted Republican. And she could listen to the Gary Numan song "Cars" fifteen times in a row. And she'd decorated her freshman dorm with puppy calendars. But in the end, I found her an enormous relief to be around. Striding purposefully across campus in her puffy white ski jacket, oblivious to her own dreamy-faced beauty—her hair dancing in the wind, catching in the corners of her mouth—she looked to me like normalcy. She looked to me like happiness. I secretly hoped that by traveling with her, some of her gold dust might rub off on me.

Yet now, at the guesthouse, my gutlessness was palpable, ungainly. It filled the room like a hideous air

bag. I'd been unmasked as the weak link, the albatross, the sissy.

"Look, Claire," I said after a minute. "I just. I don't
know. I still feel really, really...*unsure*."

She set down her tortoiseshell comb. "What's to be
unsure about?"

I shrugged miserably.

"Okay, look," she said after a moment. "You're
still acclimating. And China isn't exactly a luxury
destination. But Suze, what's the worst that can possibly happen to us? We hate the food? The hotels
are uncomfortable? The scenery sucks? So what?
We move on. But shouldn't we at least try? We have
the chance of a lifetime here. We'll hate ourselves
if we don't seize it. It's like Joseph Campbell says,
'Follow your bliss.' "

I gnawed at my thumbnail. "Usually whenever
I follow my bliss," I said quietly, "I end up with a
rash."

Claire narrowed her eyes. "C'mon, Suze. I'm serious. We've been planning this for ages. We've come
all this way—you can't just back out now." Her voice
rose. I could sense her struggling to contain her frustration: the wild pony of it thrashing against the
reins.

"I mean, I'm sorry," she declared, "But this is our
big chance. We do this, and for the rest of our lives,
we're going to have this extraordinary experience
under our belts. We're going to know certain things

that almost nobody else does. I mean, do you really think the world needs just a couple more Ivy League assholes—two more people like us who go on to become corporate weenies or lawyers, sleepwalking through life?"

"I know, but—"

"You want to be a great writer? Great writers always go abroad. Twain. Hemingway. Steinbeck. You think they just sat on their beds moaning, 'Oh, I'm afraid. Oh, I'll get a rash'?"

She leapt up, exhaled, and paced around the bed, vibrating with exasperation. "Okay, I'm sorry." She pivoted around. "But I will *not* let you give into fear here. We're *going,* Suze, whether I have to—I don't know—throw you over my shoulders and *carry* you there myself. You are not leaving me to go it alone, and I'm not letting you back out, either. We are young and brilliant and capable. If we can't do this, nobody can. We are going to fucking China."

Her words resonated in the air like a gunshot.

For a moment I just stared at her.

I leaned my head back and blinked desperately at the ceiling. "Claire," I whispered. "I'm sorry. But I'm *just not you,* okay? I'm not."

I couldn't help it. I started to cry. I felt so foolish. Whatever made me think I could do this?

My pathos seemed to drain all the fight out of Claire. She sat down heavily beside me and sighed. After a moment, she got up, walked into the bathroom, and came back with a handful of toilet paper. She took a wad of it, dabbed her eyes, and handed the rest to me. Her own unhappiness was peculiarly reassuring. I blew my nose a couple of times, and so did she.

"I'm sorry, I was too harsh," she said finally. "I guess with all this newness…and the jet lag…I just really, really want us to go to China, is all."

She scanned my face with heartfelt concern, her eyes red-rimmed and puffy. "Oh, Susie. We could have such an amazing time together. Just think of the adventures we'll have. You may not have much con-fidence in yourself," she said gently, "but, sweetie, I do. You are so smart and funny and sexy. And a great writer. You're an amazing woman. Trust me. I have faith in you. You can do this."

She glanced down at her hands. "But I can't force you to go someplace you really don't want to go."

I nodded, swollen with gratitude. "Thank you," I mouthed.

"At the same time," she continued, her voice nearly a whisper, "I can't *not* go someplace just because you're too weirded out, either.

"I'm sorry, Susie," she added, "but I just can't."

———

The Star Ferry wobbled in the stewy bay. People scrambled across the swaying cabin, vying for seats on slatted wooden benches. The steaminess of the day weighed on us like netting. All the windows were open, yet even when the horn sounded and the engines began grinding, there was no breeze. Passengers waved folded newspapers and paper plates in front of their faces, trying to generate their own weather.

Across the harbor, the Hong Kong side of the city was barely visible. Enormous neon billboards for Carlsberg beer, Longines watches, and Coca-Cola lined the waterfront, creating a relentless seawall of advertisements, a barricade of corporate graffiti. From behind them, the skyline and mountains of Hong Kong rose up in a blur, decapitated by a veil of lavender haze.

Claire and I stood at the bow, squinting at the greenish water, the glaring, primordial ooze of it. It stank of algae, gasoline. Pearls of sweat ran down my neck.

"Well, you can't say it's not atmospheric," Claire teased. Holding on to the ferry rail as if it were a ballet barre, she did a little plié. "Look!"

An old-fashioned Chinese junk bobbed across the water, its webbed sails fanned out against the sky like the plumage of a magnificent bird. A group of sailors bent over the hull, hoisting emerald nets out of the sea. Water runneled out of them, catching the light.

"Photo op," Claire sang. Reaching into her leather bag, she pulled out her Instamatic. When she was done, she lowered her camera. "Okay, now you can't tell me that *that* isn't totally amazing."

The Star Ferry docked at the opposite pier. Slowly we trudged through the Sheung Wan quarter toward the consulate. A hot breeze came down from the mountains, whipping up dust until it felt like we were inhaling chalk. Neither of us said anything. Already I'd decided I hated Hong Kong. It seemed like the worst of the city and the worst of the tropics combined: skyscrapers; ugly fast-food chains; hot, cramped alleyways stinking of incense, wet bamboo, rotting melons; pushcart hawkers; sizzling concrete; viscous, malarial air. It took all my concentration to put one foot in front of the other. All those famous adventurers like Captain Cook and Ernest Hemingway: How the hell had they traveled around the world so blithely? Then it dawned on me: Most of them had been completely drunk all the time.

By the time we reached the consulate, our clothes were lacquered to our skin. "Well, this is good practice for Indonesia and India," Claire panted. "They'll be at least this hot, too."

I couldn't believe that she was actually thinking that far ahead. *Indonesia? India?* Her optimism was daunting. For a moment I nearly hated her: her pearly beauty, her bake-sale enthusiasm. That morning after our argument, she'd suggested, "Why don't we adopt special travel names for ourselves—something with a whiff of espionage, say, like Zsa Zsa and Genevieve." She'd taken out her camera and made me pose in front of Chungking Mansions, saying, "Oh, that's it. Work it, Zsa Zsa. The camera loves you, baby!" She'd photographed me in front of the seagulls, a motorized rickshaw, a sign for McDonald's in Cantonese. She'd pirouetted. She'd said that we should have a champagne breakfast to celebrate our arrival. She'd quoted Rilke. At the ferry terminal, she'd purchased a small bag of M&M's, even though she was eternally on a diet. "Here, you want the green ones?" she'd said magnanimously. "They're supposed to make you horny. Ha-ha."

She was determined to gloss over my blubbering cowardice, to put it behind us and pretend, in fact, that it had never happened. She was insisting that we were still a team. She was generous and patient with me to a fault; her kindness made me feel so callow, I almost couldn't bear it.

At the visa office, we took our seats on metal folding chairs and began filling out applications. An official behind the counter gave us a list of rules we had to agree to beforehand.

As tourists, all our travel inside China would have to be authorized by the government's China International Travel Service (CITS). All train and airplane reservations, sightseeing tours, and theater tickets would have to be booked through them. That September, CITS had designated approximately fourteen cities as open, meaning we could visit them freely without prior approval or alien travel permits. But we'd also be issued a separate currency: FEC, or foreign exchange certificates. These would insure that we paid "foreigner" prices for everything.

Prior to entering China, we'd also have to fill out customs forms documenting each item we were bringing into the country. Upon leaving, our luggage would be searched. If any item on our list—say, a Walkman or a camera—was unaccounted for, we'd have to explain its whereabouts to the authorities.

All in all, it didn't seem like we were being given visas so much as being put on a retractable leash.

As I shifted in my chair, the door buzzed. Another Westerner lumbered in. He slung down his rucksack, then stood there scratching his belly. He was tall and bulky, with massive tree-trunk legs. A ribbon of gut peeked out above the elasticized waistband of his shorts; I could see curls of brown, pubic-like hair ringing the puncture of his navel. On his feet were ribbed socks and Birkenstocks. With his shaggy hair and beard, he looked vaguely like Jesus—or rather, like Jesus's older, dumber brother. His eyes were deep-set and slightly too close together. There was a thickness to his face, a suggestion of vague, affable dementia.

"Is tsis tsee place for tsee wee-zah?" he said, pointing to the counter. Claire and I nodded. His German accent was so heavy, it was almost a parody: You could hear the beer and mustard in it, the bratwurst and pretzel salt. The smallness of the office highlighted his size, making him seem gargantuan by contrast. As he tramped past us to take a clipboard, Claire made a goofy face and mimed a Nazi salute. I clamped my hands over my mouth to keep from giggling.

Once I'd confessed to Claire that as a Jew, I felt a gut-level distrust and hostility toward Germans, even the younger ones. I couldn't help it, I said. I assumed they all wanted to kill me. To my great irritation, Claire had scolded me. "That's so prejudiced. Isn't that making the same generalizations about them that they once made about you?" She hadn't been the first person to say this, either; several classmates at Brown had sighed aloud that they wished "the Jews would just get over the Holocaust already." One of these was a Southerner whose grandmother was still complaining about General Sherman stealing the family silver. Another had been in Jungian psychoanalysis since she was six. If you asked me, it seemed that nobody anywhere ever got over anything.

But now, in the name of solidarity, I suppose, Claire whispered in my ear, "I know nut-tink!" mimicking Colonel Klink from the TV show *Hogan's Heroes*. "Is tsis tsee place for tsee wee-zah?"

"Stop," I giggled as my clipboard slid to the floor with a clatter. "I'll pee."

As the German stumbled back with his papers, he reached down, picked up the clipboard, and handed it to me.

Lowering himself carefully into the narrow chair,

he motioned to my visa forms. "Do you speak Mandarin?" he asked.

I shook my head. "Do you?"

Claire and I were both surprised when he nodded. "For some reason, it is very funny. I am speaking better than I am reading."

"You're fluent?"

The man tilted his head from side to side. I noticed he wore a stone arrowhead around his neck on a leather cord. "Not so much, not so little. I can ask for pork. I can ask for water. I can ask for the hotel. But I cannot be making the jokes. I cannot be talking of the philosophy."

We looked at him, impressed. "Whoa, that's more than we can say," Claire admitted.

"Hey," I asked as a thought suddenly occurred to me. "Can you show us the Chinese character for *ladies' room*?"

The German leaned over and dutifully scribbled a single character on the corner of Claire's visa application: a crosshatched stick figure.

"How do you say it out loud?" Claire asked.

He said something completely incomprehensible, a garbled, throat-clearing grunt.

"Oh, well, we'll just stick to pointing to the character," I said.

"How are you going to China?" he asked.

Claire shrugged. "Train, I guess. Or maybe a hydrofoil to Guangzhou. What about you?"

The German untied the drawstring of his rucksack and began rooting through it. "First, I am thinking I am taking the train, too. But then I am learning there is the sailboat." He pulled out a mimeographed flyer and handed it to Claire. It read:

SAIL TO CHINA!!!
JORNEY TO THE MAINLAND ON THE
HIGH SEAS!!!
Weeky sailings on the Jin Jiang.
Depart Kowloon Thursday, Arrive Shanghai
Sunday.
HK$630
Port tax inclus.
Must Have Valid Visa for PRC
RESERVE NOW!!!
An EXCLUSIVE Jade Buddha Travel Agency
Exclusive.

"This, she is from the budget travel agent near the Star Ferry," said the German. "I am thinking it is looking very interesting, no?"

I glanced at Claire. Everything about the flyer smacked of fraud — from the lousy photocopying job to the misspellings to the suggestion that a tourist pay $630 Hong Kong dollars for the "exclusive" privilege of sleeping on a hammock in a Chinese fishing boat for three days. It might as well have read: COME TO THE JADE BUDDHA TRAVEL AGENCY AND WE WILL

TURN YOU UPSIDE DOWN BY YOUR ANKLES AND SHAKE
ALL OF THE MONEY OUT OF YOUR POCKETS.

Claire studied the flyer.

"Wow, it sails tomorrow?" she said.

The German nodded. "Jah. That is why I am bringing the extra money to be getting the instant visa."

"Have you booked your ticket yet?"

The German shook his head. "You need to be showing them first the visa. Just like with the train."

"Do you think there are any more places left?"

I could hear the gears in her head clicking. "Claire," I said anxiously, nudging her. "This doesn't exactly look legit."

The German shrugged. "I ask the lady, and she is telling me there is still room but that the reservations for the boat, they have to be made by three o'clock today."

Claire's eyes glittered as she did the calculations. "So, if we get our visas now, here, today, we could be on a boat to China by tomorrow?"

The German nodded. "If you want, we can be going together to the travel agent."

"Oh my God, that is *beyond* awesome," Claire exclaimed. She turned to me. "Can you imagine? Sailing to China on one of those boats we just saw? How cool would that be?"

"Claire, look," I said. I began to feel queasy, a wave cresting in my gut. The Van Houtens were avid sailors. Claire had her own Sunfish. At the graduation party in Connecticut, Claire's father had given us a tour of his den. Decorated in a nautical motif, it was designed to resemble a captain's cabin, though mostly it reminded me of a New England seafood restaurant. Photographs of his boats hung on paneled walls, and a model of a Spanish galleon was displayed atop a sea chest. Mr. Van Houten explained the history of each one to us in great detail. My family and I had stood there with our half-finished flutes of champagne, feigning comprehension. Finally my mother could no longer restrain herself. Leaning over to my brother, she whispered, "John, darling. Our own family's boat. You did take it out of the bathtub this morning, didn't you?"

Now Claire was imagining Odysseus, Magellan, Columbus and being on the open seas doing something bold that no one we knew had ever done before. All I could envision was fending off water rats with a shovel, peeing in a bucket, and projectile vomiting into the Straits of Taiwan.

"Six hundred and thirty Hong Kong dollars? That's only ninety U.S.," she exclaimed. Leaning across me, she offered her hand to the German. "I'm Claire," she said enthusiastically. "This is my friend and co-conspirator, the Divine Ms. Susie G."

"Hello. I am Gunter." The German shook her hand, then mine. "In Chinese, to say hello, you say *nee how*."

"Nee how!" said Claire.

"Yah," said Gunter. He turned to me. "Now you," he prompted. *"Nee how."*

"Nee how," I said dispiritedly.

"And to say 'Thank you,' you say *Shay shay nee.*"

"Shay shay nee," I said.

"See." He smiled. "You are learning the Chinese already."

三

Chapter 3

The Straits of Taiwan

THE PIER WAS deserted. Garbage in the water bumped listlessly against the pylons. Just as I'd anticipated, the excursion to Shanghai aboard the *Jin Jiang* had been a scam, a version of three-card monte for Western suckers like us eager to plunk down HK$630 for the dubious thrill of sleeping on a fishing junk.

"This can't be right," Claire said anxiously. "Where's the boat?"

Across the bay, there wasn't so much as a dinghy in sight. Yet over by the ferry terminal, hundreds of Chinese lined up along the waterfront. Many stood beside refrigerator boxes. Others were surrounded by pieces of furniture wrapped so snugly in brown paper, it looked as if they'd simply moved entire living rooms of their apartments out onto the sidewalk. Others sat fanning themselves atop piles of enormous shopping bags made of candy-striped plastic. The bags looked toxic and indestructible, taxidermied with clothing and bedding. Odder still, everyone carried grocery sacks bulging with oranges, pineapples, and cabbages. They didn't look like passengers so much as refugees.

"Maybe I ask?" said Gunter.

Claire and I watched uneasily as he lumbered across the street. As he approached a Chinese couple, they looked at him with alarm. A moment later, Gunter waved us over.

Claire frowned. "He can't be serious. *All* these people are going with us? On a fishing junk?"

In 1986, China was a country with one billion people. And yet until that moment, it had never occurred to us that we might actually be sailing with any of them—or that the chances of doing anything exclusively was in fact pretty much nil. Now it was starting to appear that the *Jin Jiang* might not be a fishing boat so much as a great floating gulag crammed full of China's great unwashed proletarian masses. Judging from these masses, all of us were expected to supply our own food, bedding, and linens for the trip, too. The People's Republic of China was the no-frills concept applied to an entire nation.

While Gunter held our place in the line, Claire and I hurried into the terminal to see if we could stock up on provisions and make a couple of last, desperate calls home. Once we docked in China, we had no idea if or when we'd have access to telephones again.

While I bought snacks, Claire hunched over a pay phone. "Daddy, I told you —" she whispered fiercely, her hand cupped around the mouthpiece, a lock of hair falling over one eye.

"Daddy, what don't . . . Shanghai. It's right there in the folder . . . No, look again — I'm not —"

She shot me a furious look and mimed shooting the receiver. Turning back around, her hair drawn over her face like a curtain, she hissed, "Daddy, please don't cry. Nothing bad is going to —"

A little boy ran by holding a finger puppet, his pregnant mother waddling after him. A garbled announcement came over the loudspeaker.

Claire slammed down the receiver so hard it rang back at her, reverberating in its cradle. "Augh!" she cried. People seated in the waiting room looked over at us.

"You know, if it was Alexander or Edward or Dominic, he would not be doing this. He goes to me, 'Oh, princess, when are you coming home to Daddy?'"

With a great sweep of her hand, she motioned toward the red aluminum can I was holding. "I mean, for chrissake, you're standing here drinking a *Coca-Cola*. I *told* him that. What on earth does he possibly think is going to happen to us?"

She whirled around and struck the pay phone with

the side of her fist. Families glanced over at us again. I had no idea what to say, how to react. It was hard to imagine Claire's truculent father, his feet propped up on his mahogany desk, blubbering into the telephone like a twelve-year-old girl.

"Fuck." Claire pressed her forehead against the receiver. "It is so. Not. Fair."

Gently I moved beside her and put my arm around her shoulder. She reached up and squeezed my hand. For a moment we just stood together, breathing. It was odd. Back at college, my other friends and I had been touchy-feely to the brink of lesbianism. But Claire's greetings consisted of a stiff nod that seemed to say *Yes, I'm here and so are you, so let's not make a big deal about it*, followed by a perfunctory pair of air kisses. Once when I'd gone to hug her goodbye on campus, she'd flinched. "I'm sorry," she said, stepping back awkwardly, "but in my family, we've just never done that."

Now we stood intertwined in front of the pay phone while strangers circled us, angling to make a call.

"I'm fine," she said after a moment. Disengaging, she ran a finger under each eye and shook her hair out as if that would free her of all unpleasantness.

"He just—he thinks I can't possibly do anything without his supervision, without...Aw, fuck it," she announced. "I'm going to get a Coke. Phone's all yours, Zsa Zsa." She pressed a handful of coins into my palm and strode off to the snack bar.

I watched her get in line beneath an arrow reading "Order Here," then slotted my coins into the phone. In 1986, there were no phone cards or credit card calls. If you wanted to call overseas, your only option was to feed fistfuls of unfamiliar change into a public phone, contact the operator, and pray that she could get a connection and reverse the charges while the line crackled and hissed like a campfire.

This time I dialed my grandmother. After a minute of excruciating static, I heard her raspy, brittle voice fizzing across the Pacific.

"Susie?"

"Grandma!" Her saying my name made me melt with homesickness and love. My heart throbbed anxiously in my rib cage. *Oh, please, Grandma, don't let me get on this crazy Chinese fishing boat! Tell me to come home!* Back in New York, it would be twilight. I imagined my grandmother sitting at her dining table, the sky beyond her window blushing pink over Central Park.

"Oh, Grandma! It's so good to hear your voice. I miss you!"

I expected her to say my name repeatedly. Whenever I telephoned, she always sighed, "Oh, Susie love," luxuriantly, each intonation making me feel that she was stroking my hair, touching my cheek with fingertips as translucent and powdery as moth's wings, pressing me to her bosom.

Instead she bellowed, "What the hell's all this nonsense about you coming home? You just got there. What's wrong with you?"

"Oh, Grandma, I'm so homesick—"

"Don't give me that bullshit, *bubeleh*. You stick it out. Enough with the melodrama."

"I am sticking it out," I said, wounded. "Claire and I are sailing to Shanghai in a few minutes. It's just, oh, Grandma—" I gulped, trying not to cry. Somebody had gouged a heart into the metal plating of the pay phone. I traced it with my finger. "It's just so much harder—"

"So who ever said travel was easy? You think it was easy when my whole family came over from Poland, not speaking a word of English? Where on earth did you ever get that *fakaktah* idea? Even on a package tour. They schlep you here, they schlep you there. You don't know the language, where to look for the toilet. Now, at least, you have airplanes. Now, at least, when the stewardess isn't looking, you can take a little Delta silverware and slip it into your purse—"

"Oh, Grandma!"

"Don't 'oh Grandma' me. I don't want to hear it. And I don't want to hear about any more weepy phone calls home to your parents, either. They're having a rough enough time of it. You're not to add to their burdens, you understand? You're twenty-one years old. You've got three thousand dollars, an Ivy League education, and an enormous pair of bazooms. The world should have your problems, *bubeleh*. Now you get your *toches* on that goddamn boat and sail to China."

With that, she hung up.

For a moment I stood there, staring at the receiver.

Claire sidled back over, sipping a Coke. "Uh-oh," she said. "You don't look so good, either. What happened? Your folks start crying and begging you to come home, too?"

"Mm," I said. "Something like that."

——————

In our absence, the line for embarkation had only grown longer, but Gunter was impossible to miss. He towered above everyone else, a shaggy, walleyed giant with his meaty hands open by his sides, his belly like a presentation, an offering. Strapped to his back was the same small rucksack he'd been carrying the day before; on his massive frame, it looked ridiculous, like a child's.

"*Nee how*," Gunter said, waving. He pointed toward the bay. "This *Jin Jiang*. I am thinking: she is not the kind of boat we are thinking she is."

As if on cue, a thunderous foghorn sounded, and a huge white cruise ship appeared, plowing straight for the pier.

We watched, stunned, as it cut its main engines and maneuvered effortlessly into the slip like a massive wall sliding between us and the sky, obliterating the cityscape of Hong Kong behind it. There was a deep, reverberant rumbling, a tremble of the dock. Sailors leaned over the bow, shouting out orders and tossing coils of ropes down to men on the pier.

"I don't believe it," Claire said. "We're sailing to Shanghai on the fucking Love Boat."

When a boat sailing to Communist China in 1986 was dubbed exclusive, this is what it turned out to mean: We round-eyed, big-nosed Westerners were summoned to the front of the line and ushered up the gangway while the Chinese—hundreds of hoi polloi with their mountains of possessions—were left waiting behind the ropes on the pier below, roasting in the sun, looking on sloe-eyed while cargo trucks pulled up and unloaded their freight onto the melty asphalt, and the air filled with the oversweet stench of motor oil. Stranger still, no one seemed to question it. The crowd just stood there, docile and enduring.

Meanwhile, a uniformed Chinese porter led Claire, Gunter, and me across a grand carpeted reception area with a voluptuous staircase, then down a hallway illuminated by brass wall sconces shaped like paper fans. Faint Muzak played over the PA system—a xylophonic rendition of the Pointer Sisters' "Jump (For My Love)."

Although our cabin was barely big enough for all three of us to stand in at once—it wasn't so much a cabin as a *cabinet*—compared to the Boston Guesthouse, it was a palace. Three modular bunks gleamed with serenity and corporeal order. Invisible hands had fastidiously arranged jasmine-scented guest soaps like party favors by the sink. They had even placed one of those paper belts around the toilet bowl announcing in both English and Chinese that it had been "freshly sanitized for your cleanliness pleasure." A printed card in the ashtray explained—also in English—what times breakfast, lunch, and dinner were served in the dining room. Apparently we were not expected to prepare our own food after all.

Claire frowned, tossed her sunglasses on the night table, and massaged the bridge of her nose. "Christ," she groaned. "There's even a swimming pool. What do you think we should do?"

I flopped down on the bottom bunk. The mattress was cool and unyielding. I felt myself relax instantly. "Ooh, aah," I said. "Comfy pillow."

"Yah," said Gunter, hoisting himself onto the uppermost bunk. "I think I am liking the cool air."

A crease of vexation formed on Claire's brow. "C'mon, you guys, this is not budget traveling. This isn't what we signed up for."

"Look. This isn't exactly a tragedy." I laughed.

"So we paid ninety bucks and wound up comfortable anyway. Why not enjoy it?"

"Yah," said Gunter, closing his eyes, his face positioned directly beneath the air conditioner so that the steady breeze tickled his beard. "Three meals a day for free? That is being quite a bargain!"

"No, I will not enjoy it," Claire said sourly, yanking open the door. "I'm going to see the head purser."

"And do *what* exactly?" I laughed. "Have him flag down a rowboat for us?"

Claire slammed the door behind her with such vehemence, it was almost comical. I'd never seen her so incensed before.

Gunter looked at me, perplexed. "Your friend," he said, glancing at Claire's backpack on the floor. "I am thinking. She is maybe a little crazy in the head, no?"

"Nah." I yawned. "Just moody. Just your typical Gemini."

After a minute I sat up. "I should probably go after her, though."

I found Claire above deck near the bow, her eyes shut, her face tilted like a mirror toward the sun, her hair blowing wildly around her in a corona of platinum.

The *Jin Jiang* was already sailing toward the open sea. Somehow I'd missed the sonorous fart of the air horn, the lurch of the ship sliding away from the dock. Now the only vestige of Hong Kong was a purple-blue nipple on the horizon between the ocean and the air.

A lone steward stood by a lifeboat. Otherwise, Claire was completely alone.

"Where are all the other passengers?" I said.

She shrugged.

"Any luck with the purser?"

She shrugged again. "No one on board seems to speak any English."

"You okay?"

She turned to me desperately, her eyes welling with tears. "I mean, we tried, right?"

"Absolutely."

"And maybe Daddy won't even find out that the *Jin Jiang* is not actually a fishing boat—"

"Well, of course not. How would he?" The very idea struck me as bizarre; I didn't follow her logic. "How on earth would he find out if you never tell him?"

Claire looked at me oddly then, her face furrowing. "You don't understand," she said in a low voice. "My father can do things."

"Excuse me?"

She squinted out at the horizon, then down into the sea churning below us. "Ah, forget it," she said with a forced little laugh, pushing away from the railing. "C'mon, Zsa Zsa. If we're going to sail to Shanghai on the Love Boat, we might as well put on our bathing suits."

Evidently the masses gathered back on the Tai Kok Tsui pier had been waiting for an entirely different ship. The *Jin Jiang* was nearly deserted; the stewards stationed around the deck fidgeted like hosts at a party where the guests had failed to show up. At a loss for something to do, they continually mopped and remopped the floors and rearranged the lounge chairs as if, by expending enough effort, they might magically compel a ship full of people to materialize.

Oddly, they all wore English name tags: JONNIE, TED, GEORGE. (Later we would discover that this was common practice in Chinese tourism.) Claire, Gunter, and I seemed to have our very own steward, TED, a man with a goiter who stood vigil in the corridor directly outside our door at all times.

"Hello, I am Ted. I am your steward," he recited whenever we walked past. Then he'd smile uneasily, revealing a mouth of graying, ramshackle teeth. "Where are you going?"

Otherwise, the ship felt abandoned. In the "casino," a lone bank of slot machines sat unplugged beside gaming tables shrouded in drop cloths. In the dining hall, only a few tables had been set up at the far end; the rest remained folded and stacked along the walls like ghosts of weddings and bar mitzvahs past. Floor-to-ceiling mirrors on one side of the room reflected blankly in the mirrors on the other.

"Is this a cruise or a crypt?" I whispered. All Claire and I could hear as we moved through the ship was the deep, pulsing groan of engines.

We had an unnerving sense, though, that activity was percolating *somewhere*. Occasionally, in my peripheral vision, I'd glimpse a lone waiter, scurrying across the far end of a darkened room with an enormous soup tureen. From somewhere beneath us came the rumbling of a cart rattling with glassware or cutlery. We sensed doors being hastily opened and bolted; people breathing in unison behind a porous wall; a heart, perhaps, embedded in the floorboards, thudding ominously. Walking through the corridors, pockets of cold air would suddenly pass over us like high-voltage shocks. We'd hear momentary voices: the high, shrill jabber of Chinese. But when we whirled around, we saw nothing. Nothing except a lone steward standing sentry in the hallway.

"Hello, I am Ted," he announced. "I am your steward. Where are you going?"

"This place is creeping me out," Claire said "It's like a cruise ship after a hydrogen bomb." She stopped abruptly, listening. After a moment, she said sotto voce, "You hear them?"

"What?"

"The voices."

I nodded.

"Something's going on here," she whispered. "Something not good."

Only the pool area seemed to be functioning normally: striped lounge chairs, fluffy towels. The glitter and the thrash of the sea all around us, merging with the sky, felt symphonic. Seawater sprayed across the deck like diamonds.

It was there that we met the few other passengers onboard. Martin was a jaunty, unshaven Australian who sauntered around in fraying shorts and flip-flops, a can of Tsingtao beer in his hand. In the span of an hour, he'd somehow managed to familiarize himself with the entire crew and given them all nicknames.

"*Nee how,* sea horse," he called out jocularly to a waiter, giving a little salute. "How's about a round of Tsingtaos, *ching,* for my new friends here?"

Martin was a linguistic anthropologist heading to China on a research fellowship. He was fluent in half a dozen languages. Or so he told us. It was hard for me to believe him, given his diamond stud earring and the glossy centerfold of *Juggs* magazine spread open on his lap.

"Ay, I'm a scholar, luv," he said, raising his beer, "not a corpse."

The other passenger we befriended was a leggy blond divorcee from Southern California. Cynthia Lukens strode onto the *Jin Jiang* in high heels with ankle straps and big white movie-star sunglasses, moving across the parquet as if jazz cymbals were tapping out a rhythm with her hips. As soon as she arrived at the reception desk, a bevy of cabin stewards flocked around her like eager-to-please chorus boys.

Behind her, two little tow-heads barreled across the lobby, shrieking, "*Cowabunga!*"

With a flying leap, the older, slightly knobby-kneed boy lunged at the smaller, rounder one and tackled him onto the carpet. The younger one, however, managed to roll over and straddle his opponent's face, hollering, "*Noogie patrol!*" The older boy giggled, his squeals muffled by the other's buttocks.

The crew looked on, alarmed.

"Boys," the blonde said mildly. Instantly both children got up, brushed themselves off, and raced over to her. "If you two want to run around, do it outside."

"Aw, Mom," they groaned in unison before dashing out.

"Remember," the blonde called after them cheerfully, "don't push each other overboard."

Cynthia and her two sons, Anthony and Warren, ages seven and eleven, were backpacking through Southeast Asia for six months using the same Lonely Planet shoestring guide, water purification tablets, and youth hostel discount cards as the rest of us. In Hong Kong, in fact, they'd stayed at the Happy Family Guesthouse on the sixteenth floor of Chungking Mansions.

"You've gotta be kidding," Claire and I said almost in unison. "That shit-hole?"

"Oh, it wasn't bad at all," Cynthia said breezily,

reclining in her deck chair and kicking off her sandals. Her feet were pedicured, her toenails glazed a candy-apple red. "The boys really liked the ants," she said. "They even made a game out of smushing them for math practice."

"Math practice?" I said.

"Every morning, before breakfast, we do our math." Reaching into her coral-colored handbag, Cynthia fished out a small tube of zinc oxide, dabbed a bit onto each of her fingertips, then massaged it neatly over her face and throat. She was classically California beautiful: blond, tanned, pert. Her disposition itself was sunshine. I suddenly wanted her to be *my* mother, too.

"I made sure their teachers gave me all their homework assignments before we left so they won't need to repeat a grade. Math is easy when you're traveling. Time zone changes. Currency rates." She smoothed the residual cream into the backs of her hands. "After we finish our lessons, we spend the day sightseeing. We've seen Hong Kong, Macau already. Now, of course, China. Then Indonesia, Thailand. Maybe India, if we have the time."

Claire and I stared at her, flabbergasted: an American housewife traveling with two little boys off the beaten path in Southeast Asia? It was beyond the range of anything we ever could have imagined. We were hugely impressed.

"The way I see it, they'll learn more this way than by sitting in a classroom." Cynthia shrugged.

Just then Warren raced across the deck and cannonballed into the pool, detonating a great explosion of chlorinated water. "Hey, Mom," he shouted when he resurfaced, "did you see?"

"Mom, look!" Anthony cried, bobbling after him, his chubby arms sheathed in inflatable plastic water wings the color of maraschino cherries.

"They're such great kids." Cynthia gazed at them beatifically. "And they're up for anything." Almost as an afterthought, she looked at us. "Of course there's one thing that does worry me a little, taking them through Asia like this."

"What's that?" I asked.

"Neither of them likes rice."

———

Later that morning, Gunter appeared on deck. "I am meeting someone new who is also traveling," he announced. "This is Jonnie."

He presented a young Chinese man dressed in business slacks, a cheap, pressed shirt, a loosely knotted nylon tie.

"Hello, I am Jonnie," the man said melodically. "Your friend, Mr. Gunter, he has told me that you would all be interested to meet someone from Mainland China. Well, that is me."

With his boyish, wide-open gaze and his slim build, it was hard to tell Jonnie's age. He could've been twenty-four or a full two decades older. His hair had been cut in a bowl shape, making him look vaguely like an Asian Paul McCartney. Certainly he had the same gentle sweetness about him, the same puppy-doggish wonderment, the same newly poured pancake look.

Like a young politician, Jonnie began moving among us, earnestly shaking each of our hands, including those of Anthony and Warren.

"Hello. Hello," Jonnie kept saying agreeably and nodding. He spoke with precision and tenderness, like someone carefully measuring out tablespoons of sugar, wanting to ensure that everyone received an equal amount. "I would say 'Welcome to China,' but we are not yet there. Also, you should know, I do not live in China. I live in Ghana. I run Chinese restaurant in Ghana, but my home is in China. So maybe I am what you look for, maybe I am not." He laughed, and we all laughed with him, tickled and enchanted.

"Well, *nee how* there, Jonnie," Martin saluted.

"*Nee how*," I parroted.

"You speak Chinese, too?" Jonnie asked, surprised.

I shook my head.

"Oh. Yes. But not to worry. Then I teach you to speak Chinese," Jonnie said enthusiastically, sitting down on the edge of a deck chair across from me and Claire. "I teach you everything you need to know about China. You tell me, please. Where are you from?"

"America," said Claire. She set down her copy of *The Fountainhead* and studied him outright.

"Oh, America!" Jonnie exclaimed, his face illuminating like a flashbulb. "I love America!"

"You've been there?"

"No, no." He looked crestfallen. "But one day"—he brightened—"I will go. I love America. *Wizard of Oz*. Hamburgers. Stevie Wonder—"

"You like Stevie Wonder?" Cynthia laughed.

"Oh, yes," he exclaimed. Leaping to his feet, he began singing:

I just called, to say, I love you—

Although Jonnie's English was excellent, he was unable to reproduce certain sounds. Instead of *love*, he said *ruv*, and instead of *Susie* and *Claire*, he said *Sushi* and *Crair*. His accent laid bare all his hopes and vulnerabilities. I suddenly understood why people struggled to get rid of their accents and teased others for theirs. An accent is a form of public nudity. Listening to Jonnie, I felt a strange mixture of bemusement and protectiveness. Soon enough in China, others would feel this for me.

———

At lunchtime, we all sat together in the nearly empty dining room. The fact that we were all literally in the same boat created an instant sense of intimacy.

Ironically, the fact that we would likely never see each other again only accelerated this. In this way, I suppose, travel is a bit like the Internet—there's a protective anonymity to it. Cast into a situation with people you never have to see again and shielded from repercussions, you turn brazenly candid.

As waiters set before us steaming bowls of egg-drop soup and pork dumplings, Martin told us about a tribe in Indonesia that demanded he dress up as a woman in order to meet with their village elder. "It was only after I was completely kitted out in lipstick, a bra, and an enormous flowered housedress that I realized my colleagues were playing a joke on me," he chuckled.

Everyone laughed—except Claire.

She sat with uncharacteristic sullenness, pushing her food around with her chopsticks, bringing slices of beef and chicken to her mouth, then changing her mind and setting them down.

"Mom," Anthony begged, tugging at Cynthia's forearm as she spooned prawns with chili sauce onto his plate. "Tell them the story of me and Warren. How we were born."

Cynthia found herself confessing to us that her pregnancies had been so risky, her doctor had required her to spend the last three months of each one in bed, completely immobilized.

"Three months!" Anthony repeated with awe, unable to fathom such a thing. "Warren and me are the two most wanted children *ever*." Impaling a prawn on a chopstick, he sucked into his mouth.

"That's 'Warren and *I*,' not 'Warren and *me*,'" Cynthia corrected. "And that's not how we eat. Use your chopsticks correctly, please." She glanced sheepishly around the table. "I did want them fiercely," she said softly.

Claire stood up abruptly. "I'm sorry. You'll have to excuse me." She dropped her napkin onto her chair. As she wobbled off clutching her stomach, I pushed my chair back to follow.

"Susie. I'm fine," she insisted. "Finish your lunch."

When I persisted, she said in a low voice: "Please. Let me be alone. Don't make this a big deal."

Reluctantly I sat back down. "Don't worry. She sails a lot," I reassured everyone at the table, even as I glanced after her.

Jonnie told us about his family then, his mother and father, an aunt and cousin, who all lived in a small village a day's journey south from Shanghai. He hadn't seen them in more than seven years.

"Travel to and from Africa, it is very difficult," he said. As he spoke, an uneasy silence came over the table. Even *I* knew enough then to know that there was far more to Jonnie's story than he was saying—than perhaps he was permitted to say. After all, he spoke fluent English. He also had a Chinese passport, travel privileges, residency overseas; in 1986, these were almost unheard of for Chinese citizens.

Most lived in a state of lockdown. They needed the government's permission simply to change apartments. Clearly Jonnie was exceptional. But how? And why? We somehow sensed that it was rude, perhaps even forbidden or dangerous to ask.

"Now, I am going home. I am bringing my family a refrigerator. I am bringing them tape deck," Jonnie informed us happily.

"Oh, so you're one of the people with the refrigerator boxes," I leaned across the table with my chopsticks to pluck two garlicky stalks of broccoli from a platter. "Claire and I were wondering what happened to all those people on the pier."

Jonnie looked pained. A hush fell over the table. I saw Cynthia shoot Martin a look. Martin shrugged. I looked at Gunter, but he was focused on picking the rice out of his bowl grain by grain with his chopsticks. It was impossible to tell if he was deliberately avoiding the conversation or just being Gunter. Clearly I had missed something crucial.

A waiter hastily gathered up the remains of our lunch with a clatter, then set a plate of cut-up oranges on the table. For a moment, we regarded it uncomfortably.

"Yes, I bring refrigerator to Dinghai," Jonnie said finally. "Dinghai such a nice place. I wish all of you to come, meet my mother. Meet my father. Show them you are my new friends." Then he turned to me. "Tell me," he said. "What is it like in America?"

When I returned to the cabin, I found Claire propped up in her bunk, writing fervently in her journal.

"Is your stomach better?" I asked.

"Uh-huh," she said, not looking up.

"Cynthia and everyone were really worried about you."

Claire set down her pen. She seemed to consider this a moment. "They're worried about me?" she said with an incredulous little snort, her pale brows arching. "Well, they should be, I guess. I'm onto them, you know."

"Huh?"

She leaned in toward me. "Gunter?" she said. "Susie, do you think he's really *that* oblivious?"

I made a face. "Actually, I think he's pretty perceptive."

"Exactly. He's got a whole other hidden side to him."

"Well, he is German," I said, pulling the last of my M&M's out of my backpack. "Just play 'Flight of the Valkyries' and see what happens."

"No, seriously. How does a German just happen to be fluent in Mandarin? And Martin? With that earring? Do you really think he's a professor? I mean, 'studying languages in Borneo'?"

"It's probably a line he uses to pick up women," I suggested. "You know 'Hello, I'm a cunning linguist.'"

I expected Claire to laugh, but she didn't. She shut her journal sternly and set it on the night table. "And tell me. Why would a woman take her kids out of school for an entire semester, especially when summer vacation just ended? Why wouldn't she have left with them in June instead?"

"I dunno," I shrugged. Growing up in New York, I'd known numerous parents who'd pulled their kids out of school on a whim. Granted, they'd mostly been hippies—fathers in ponchos and clogs, braless mothers with harpsichords—and they'd taken their kids to join communes in the Ozarks or attend rainbow gatherings on Indian reservations. But the only thing that struck me as unusual about Melinda was that she was backpacking with a pedicure and a Hermès scarf.

"Suze," Claire whispered, leaning in close, "Cynthia is a kidnapper."

I stopped eating M&M's and let out a whoop. "What? Oh my God. That's brilliant, Claire. She's actually a Romanian gypsy who moved to California to open a hair salon as a front for a white slavery—"

"Please. I'm not kidding. Think about it. She's divorced, right? I'll bet she's embroiled in a vicious custody battle. Her ex-husband hired some big-gun lawyer, so Cynthia yanked her boys out of school, put them on a plane to Hong Kong, and voilà! This sort of thing happens all the time, you know. But traveling the way she is, staying in places like Chungking Mansions, that's the really ingenius part, you see. Because the feds aren't going to be looking in the Happy Buddha Guesthouse. No. They're going to be checking the Hyatts. The Hiltons. She could go undetected for months.

"For all we know," she added, gazing at the evacuation instructions mounted on the door, "Martin's in on it, too."

"Martin?"

"Yes," Claire said with gravity. "Martin. How do we know he's not her lover? Sure, he and Cynthia *seemed* to meet onboard, but maybe they just planned it this way so her kids don't suspect. How much do you want to bet that once our ship docks, they'll just happen to end up traveling together?"

I looked at her, awaiting some sort of punch line. But there was none. An uneasy feeling came over me.

"What?" Claire said after a moment. "Why are you looking at me like that?"

"Are you sure you're okay?" I said. "You seem, I don't know. Different. I guess I'm just not following you."

"I'm perfectly fine," she sniffed, sweeping back her hair with a flick of her hand. But then she slumped forward and buried her face in her palms. "Oh, Susie. There *is* something else. It's big and it's secret. Promise you won't freak out?"

She glanced around the cabin dramatically as if

she was afraid someone was eavesdropping. "This summer," she whispered, "I had this *thing*. With this *guy*."

She sat back and gave me a fierce, freighted, prompting look.

"Oh my God," I said as the possibility unspooled before me. Cynthia's confession during lunch—that was when Claire had stood up abruptly. "Claire. Are you pregnant?"

"Oh no!" she cried. "But it's complicated. In June, my father hired this new boat hand. An Israeli named Adom. Fresh out of the army. And oh, Susie. He was so gorgeous. I mean, when I saw him, I nearly died. He looked just like JFK Junior, except, you know, one of *your* people."

One of *my* people. Once certain Christians learned you were Jewish, that was the foremost way they defined you thereafter. Even if you had a zillion other outstanding characteristics, even if you didn't keep kosher or go to temple, even if you were like me and had been educated by Presbyterians, Quakers, and a bunch of crackpot maharishis, you were regarded as almost a separate species. Jewishness marked you forever, like a radioactive isotope.

This time I let it slide. "So you slept with him?"

"Well," Claire said slyly, letting her voice trail off. When it came to sex, Claire was surprisingly prudish. She spoke mostly in ellipses, bashful glances, allusive *you know*s.

To be fair, there had never been much for her to tell. She'd had the same boyfriend since sophomore year at Brown. Parker had the number III after his last name and his hair parted so stringently to the side it looked like a toupee. He wore lemon-colored cardigans and webbed belts with little whales on them. He was so wholesome, he was basically neutered.

Once when I'd asked her, "Where's the wildest place you've ever had sex?" she'd replied earnestly, "On my stepmother's Louis the Fourteenth reproduction couch."

When this failed to impress, she'd added quickly, "*without* the slipcovers."

"The thing is, Adom had to go back to Israel at the end of the summer," Claire told me now. "And of course Parker kept coming down to visit…but from day one with Adom. Oh, Suze."

In a feverish whisper, she described how an attraction had roiled between them, how they'd watched each other across the deck, tension and longing carbonating the air around them as the yacht thrashed through the sea. Finally one evening after they'd docked back at the marina and Claire's father had headed back to the house for a conference call, she'd been standing at the sink in the galley rinsing out a glass when Adom had come up behind her, wrapped his arms around her waist, and kissed her hotly on the neck.

"And it was like…Oh. My. God." Claire rolled her eyes back in her head and let out a moan of ecstasy.

"After that, any time my father and I took the boat out...I mean, Suze, it was un-be-lievable."

"So? Are you still in touch with him?"

"That's the thing. It's complicated. You see, Adom is...Suze, he told me *stuff*."

"Stuff?"

"Well, I can't be 100 percent certain, but, Suze," she whispered, "I think he's with the Mossad."

"You're kidding." I sat back and cackled. "He's an Israeli spy? He *told* you that?"

My skepticism and amusement seemed to wound her. "Well, obviously they can't come right out with it," she said defensively. "Like no one in the U.S. goes 'Hi. I work for the CIA.' But first of all, okay, what's an Israeli guy doing at a yacht club in Hilton Head anyway? And second of all, I could tell from things he said. Little asides, details, observations. So now, with Gunter and Martin showing up like this—and they're clearly not who they seem to be and they know all these languages—I can't help but think that, you know, maybe they're in intelligence, too, and somehow connected to Adom."

When she said this, I wasn't sure what to do with it. For a moment I just sat there.

Someone else, someone older, perhaps, might have been alarmed by such a confession. But my reaction, as it formed, was simply one of relief: So Claire Van Houten was as neurotic as the rest of us after all.

Until now Parker had been the first and only guy

she'd ever slept with. Yet some hot Israeli had just swept her off her feet and made her writhe. Now, she didn't know what the hell to do with this. She hungered for him; she was clearly obsessing. But she couldn't reconcile the fact that this monumental lay had been just some deckhand—a Jew, no less, with a thick, guttural Israeli accent—employed by her father for $6.50 an hour. And so she'd built him up, transformed him in her mind into something far more palatable and dashing. He wasn't really a boat hand: why, he was actually a spy for the Mossad! Of course! We girls did stuff like that all the time: slept with underachieving, half-formed guys, then made them over in our minds, polishing them, nudging them up to the next level. We told ourselves that the guitar-strumming pothead we were fucking was really a future rock star, the waiter at the juice bar was really a poet.

Sex was perhaps the one area where I felt I had far more expertise than Claire. And when it came to obsessing, I myself was a pro. The guy who'd broken my heart in college had been a bass player; I don't know how many hours I'd spent imagining elaborate scenarios in which I became a famous blues singer who won him back, or how often I'd interpreted certain songs on the radio as signals that he still loved me and wanted me to call him.

I looked at Claire tenderly. Then I couldn't help it. I started to laugh. "Oh, Jesus, Claire," I said. "You think Gunter and Martin are secret agents because you fooled around with some Israeli guy in Hilton Head?"

"An Israeli guy from the Mossad," she corrected. "How else do you explain what I've just told you?"

I sat down beside her and touched her shoulder lightly. "Claire," I said gently, "what I think is that you're fantasizing a little too much about your hot yacht stud. You're overheating. That's all. It's okay. Great sex will do that to you. Think of it" — I laughed — "as a sort of emotional culture shock."

She struggled to smile. "So I'm not crazy?" she said with uncertainty.

I shook my head. "Nah, just horny. Welcome to my world."

She gave me a look of grateful relief, and we laughed. And that was that. She went back to writing, and I headed up to the pool.

In retrospect, I often wonder what would have happened if I hadn't dismissed her suspicions so quickly.

———

That afternoon an announcement came warbling over the PA system: *Ladies and gentlemen, today, for your entertainment pleasure, the* Jin Jiang *will show in the lounge the Hollywood movie* Gone With the Wind.

"*Gone With the Wind*?" Cynthia said. "Did I just hear that right?"

"Oh my God," Claire groaned, looking up from

The Basic Writings of Friedrich Nietzsche. "They have *got* to be kidding."

"Maybe it's a revised Communist version," I suggested. "Mammy and Miss Prissy overthrow Scarlett and Rhett as capitalist oppressors and seize the means of production."

Claire laughed. "Oh, that's brilliant. They'll re-title it 'Gone with the Window Shopping.' "

"Let's all go," Cynthia said, gathering up her guidebooks. "The boys love anything with horses and soldiers."

En route to the lounge, however, we took the wrong stairwell. We found ourselves in a low-ceilinged corridor in the bowels of the ship before a pair of dented metal doors that seemed to flap back and forth of their own accord. Each time they opened, they brought forth a great gust of noise: plates clattering, the sizzle of fat, piles of silverware raining metallically against each other, the occasional shattering of a dish, a baby crying, the violent *pppzzzzztt!* of water being tossed on a grill.

Warren ran up and peered in. "Mom, it's another restaurant."

Inside we saw a steaming hall crammed full of tables with hundreds of Chinese diners squeezed in around them. They were intently bowed over large tin bowls of muddy liquid from which they shoveled limp bits of grayish cabbage into their mouths with chopsticks. An oppressive cloud of cigarette smoke hung over the room, along with a sharp, sour smell of body odor, scallions, and wet cardboard. It was unventilated, and the wheeze and grind of the engines reverberated through it relentlessly. The din and the humidity were almost unbearable.

"Mom," Anthony asked tremulously, "who are all those people?"

Soberly the five of us climbed back up to the second floor. There, we were greeted by a tsunami of refrigerated air, by the mellow, easy listening sound of Lionel Richie's "Say You, Say Me" as interpreted by a Moog synthesizer, and by a steward in a polite white jacket who just happened to be waiting for us outside the stairwell.

"Hello," he said, revealing a mouth full of small, pointed teeth, "my name is Victor. I am your steward. Where are you going?"

A VCR had been rolled into the lounge, and a dozen chairs arranged in an intimate crescent. But none of us was in the mood to go in anymore.

For the duration of the voyage, *Gone With the Wind* played over and over, in one continual unedited loop. The crew never seemed inclined to shut it off; perhaps it had been pre-programmed. Heading to the dining room for breakfast each morning, we would hear Butterfly McQueen crying out, "Miss Scarlett, I don't know nuthin' 'bout birthin' no babies!" Coming in from swimming in the afternoon, we'd be treated to the sight of Scarlett declaring "As God is my witness, I'll never be hungry again!"

Scarlett flounced, Atlanta burned, and Rhett scoffed, "Frankly, my dear, I don't give a damn," over and over, their ghostly blue images flickering out through the porthole across the vast dark Straits of Taiwan, heard and seen by no one.

———

To entertain ourselves, Claire and I debated. We debated whether Tess of the d'Urbervilles had been raped or seduced. We debated whether sci-fi novels qualified as art. We debated: Whose life would make a better musical, Socrates' or Dolly Parton's? We debated about which was more user-friendly, astrology or *The Basic Writings of Friedrich Nietzsche*.

Okay, I argued for astrology. In my defense, I'd brought along *Linda Goodman's Love Signs* simply because I didn't own a guitar or a harmonica. Ideally, I believed, travelers abroad should carry something with them to endear themselves to the natives. Since I couldn't play a musical instrument, I figured I could always read people their horoscopes. No matter how skeptical they were, people everywhere always seemed to love hearing about themselves.

Plus, truth be told, astrology was my own secret little self-esteem program. Whenever I felt riddled with anxiety, I flipped to my horoscope at the back of a magazine for guidance. If I felt particularly bad about myself, all I had to do was open up *Love Signs* and read about how fabulous I was for simply being born in October. According to Linda Goodman, Libras were endowed with an innate "intelligence, charm, gentleness, and emotional balance."

"Oh, please." Claire rolled her eyes. "I'm sorry, where I come from, we believe in free will and self-determination. You want real wisdom?" Opening her paperback at random, she read: "'One has to test oneself to see that one is destined for independence and command—and to do it at the right time.' C'mon. There's far more truth in that than insisting that everything is predetermined and that the whole world is divided into twelve personality types."

To annoy me, she referred to astrology as "hope for lazy people." To annoy her, I began calling her book her Nietzsche Board.

It was silly and good-natured, and it was like we were back at Brown, bantering at a café. But every once in a while, a look would pass over Claire's face like a shadow across a prairie. "Excuse me," she'd say abruptly. "I need to go do something." She'd hurry across the deck and disappear for a while. Sometimes she'd reemerge sullen, other times with a pirouette and a wave. I assumed she was thinking about Adom.

Cynthia leaned over to me. "I don't mean to pry,"

she said softly, removing her sunglasses, "but your friend. Are you sure she's all right?"

"Oh sure. She's fine."

Cynthia frowned. "The other day?" she said hesitantly. "She told me she kept hearing voices."

"Oh, *those*." I nodded. "Yeah. I was hearing them, too. They were from that kitchen down below, though we didn't realize it at the time." I laughed. "We really freaked out. We're a Libra and a Gemini, you know. So we're like two total drama queens."

———

Yet even then it began to dawn on me just how little I actually knew about Claire. The witticisms; the bitching about food, roommates, term papers; the romantic confessions that passed for intimacy at college somehow fell short here. One afternoon as we were sunbathing, I rolled over on my side. "Tell me about your mom," I said. "What was she like?"

Claire propped herself up on her elbows and stared out at the sea. "There's not much to tell, really," she said, rubbing her midriff. "I barely remember. She died when I was three. Car accident. We lived in Arlington at the time. Virginia. I don't remember if Daddy was there or not. I think he was away. All I remember was our chocolate lab, Ruffles, who was blind in one eye, barking a lot. He seemed to bark for days. And our housekeeper, Sonja, kept giving me bowls of strawberry ice cream, even for breakfast."

Claire made a little lopsided face. "I guess I cried. My grandmother thought I was too little to attend the funeral. Mostly what I remember about my mother was a pair of these pearl-drop earrings she used to wear. Clip-ons. And me playing with them, snapping them open and closed. And a sweater she had with this thick yellow, white, and navy blue stripe across it. I have an image in my head of her pushing me on the swing in our backyard, saying 'Up, up, up' with her hair tucked under this chiffon scarf to keep it from blowing. But I'm not sure if that's a memory or something I got from a photograph."

The afternoon sun was lowering. Claire's profile appeared stark against the sky.

I said dumbly, "I'm sorry."

She shrugged without taking her eyes off the horizon. "People always act like it was this great tragedy. But the truth is, it's hard to miss something you never really knew, you know? The year after she died, Daddy married Lady Macbeth—ugh—but then I also got Dominic, Alexander, and Edward, these three amazing new brothers who played with me all the time. We had this fort in this tree. And Sonja was still there. So in a weird way, it was like there was this *party* after—I don't know—all this quiet."

Around us, the ocean heaved. We were too far from land for any seagulls to appear. There was nothing beyond the railing but a great plain of blueness.

"I suppose I could get all bent out of shape about it."

She sighed. "Sometimes I used to get really sad, thinking about how great it would be to have my mother. And I'd imagine her talking to me from on high, you know. But her voice was never her voice. It was always the voice of Florence Henderson. And I'd imagine her looking like Florence Henderson, too, instead of like she did in the photos. How pathetic is that?"

"It's not pathetic at all," I said. It seemed that virtually everyone who'd grown up watching *The Brady Bunch* had dreamed at one time or another of trading their own parents in for Florence Henderson and Robert Reed. I know I certainly did.

Claire sniffed. "Sometimes I feel like people want me to dwell on it. But I just can't. It's just too vague. Besides, like Nietzsche says, 'That which does not kill me makes me stronger,' right?"

She swung her pinkened legs over the side of her deck chair and stretched. "Which reminds me" — she reached for her leather bag — "I probably should do some more reading."

Suddenly she nudged me. Across the deck, Martin and Cynthia were standing by the railing. He was leaning in close to her, murmuring something; she was tossing her head back into the wind and laughing. "See?" Claire whispered. "What did I tell you?"

———————

On the third afternoon, Jonnie shouted from the bow of the ship. "Look!"

We ran over to the railing and saw the People's Republic of China looming off the starboard side. Against the sky in the distance, the granite-colored mountains looked like the jagged line of a heart monitor, an EKG reading reflecting my own sudden panic.

China.

For three days, the salt air had lulled me. For three days, despite Claire's protests ("Why can't we eat the real Chinese food that everybody downstairs is eating?" she'd asked the headwaiter. "Oh, no," he said, shaking his head vigorously. "You no like that. This food much better."), I'd managed to eat without my stomach seizing up. For three nights, I'd been rocked to sleep in the amniotic sac of my bunk bed, soothed by the sea. For three days, all of us had been a kind of family.

But Martin had colleagues awaiting him in Beijing. God only knew what Gunter had in mind. Cynthia had reserved a room for herself and her boys at a big foreigners' hotel that had to be booked months in advance through CITS. Once we docked the following morning, Claire and I would be on our own again.

I squinted across the water as if it might be possible to actually see the Chinese. I imagined them pulling rickshaws and performing tai chi in the parks, cooking stir-fry and working in factories—all one billion of them, indifferent to our arrival.

I had no idea how we'd get from the pier to downtown Shanghai. The port wasn't even on the map in our guidebook. Would there be taxis available? Was there even a bus?

"Wow," Claire gasped, standing on tiptoes by the rail. "We're here."

"China," Jonnie said, gazing at the coastline. I tugged lightly at his sleeve.

"Jonnie," I said softly. "How do you say in Mandarin, 'I'm scared'?"

"Sushi, why you scared?" Turning away from the coastline, he regarded me with a mix of compassion and sadness. Perhaps more than any of us, Jonnie knew what it was like to be a stranger in a strange land.

I tried to shrug it off. "Just a little nervous, that's all. We don't even have a hotel—"

"No need to be scared," he said emphatically. "Please do not worry. When we get to China, you and Crair are my guest. I have many friends in Shanghai. We know good hotels, good restaurant. We take you there. We give you tour. You not have any problem. Shanghai is beautiful city and we take good care of you. Then you come home with me. You come meet my family in Dinghai. You see the real China."

"Really?" Claire clapped. "You'd do that? Show us your hometown?"

"Yes," said Jonnie. "Special honor."

"Oh. That. Is. Awesome," she cried. "Jonnie. You're

amazing!" She gave a little twirl against the railing. "Of course," she added quickly, "you know we're totally fine on our own, if it's too much trouble."

Jonnie beamed. "No trouble at all. I show you very special places. You meet my friends."

I exhaled. The prospect was almost too fabulous and too much of a relief to contemplate. "Are you sure?"

Jonnie nodded. "We make a big feast, big special meal for you. You do not worry. You be my guest."

"Thank you *so* much," said Claire. And I could tell what she was thinking: that we were going to get to see the real China far beyond anything in any guidebooks. That we were on the brink of something spectacular. That already we were earning gold stars, extra credit, an A+. "How can we ever thank you?"

Jonnie continued smiling his same boyish, exuberant smile. "Maybe I go with you to Beijing later," he said almost casually. "I show you around Beijing. And then maybe you take me to American embassy. Maybe I be your guest then."

四

Chapter 4

Shanghai

IT WAS BARELY daybreak when we were ushered down the gangway with our backpacks. In case we'd had any doubt that we were now in a Communist country, at four o'clock that morning, rapid-fire Chinese anthems began playing at full volume over the PA system.

Jerking awake, we scrambled out of our bunks. In distinct contrast to our days at sea, the mood aboard the ship was one of anxiety. Now that the *Jin Jiang* had docked in Shanghai, no one was allowed out on deck. The stewards stopped smiling and nodding agreeably; instead, they tromped through the boat, pounding on cabin doors and ordering people out into the corridor. "You take bags now," they barked. "You go to dining room." It didn't feel like we were disembarking so much as being evacuated—or perhaps arrested. Through the portholes, we couldn't see any trace of Shanghai or even daylight, only inky black circles like giant, unblinking pupils staring back in at us.

Within half an hour, we were all fed tea and a greasy fried egg slapped on a piece of white bread, then herded into the reception hall with our baggage, at which point, we waited and waited, eyeing each other with trepidation. Clearly we were in a different sort of territory now. We sat fondling our cameras, wondering just what awaited us on the other side of the hull. Only Anthony and Warren lay motionless, pressed against Cynthia in heavy-lidded, liquidy half sleep. Gunter sat in a corner, *ppffuuuhhffing* as he studied his guidebook.

Although Claire and I assumed he'd be heading off on his own, he'd said to us that morning, "So Jonnie, he will be showing you around, yah? I think that I will be coming with you."

This had irritated us to no end. Gunter, with his Luftwaffe accent and incessant chewing—Gunter, with his marshmallow temperament: Gunter had been getting on our nerves. Just the way he audibly exhaled, the way he galumphed into a room, then stood there expectantly, smack in the middle of everything, filling up the space like a La-Z-Boy recliner without ever really being present. His mind was inverted somehow. He seemed more captivated by a scrap of Chinese newspaper or the rivets on his backpack than by any conversation taking place directly in front of him. Getting his attention was like trying to operate a shortwave radio. Although this might have been due, in part, to the language barrier, in retrospect, I suspect he may have had Asperger's syndrome. At the time, though, Claire and I only experienced him as frustrating.

Claire herself was in high spirits. "Finally!" she sang. She paced the reception hall, pantomiming tennis serves and ballet positions, then sat back down again and jiggled her leg. She looked around expectantly. She chewed a piece of gum. She spit it out. She leafed through our guidebook. She brushed her hair absentmindedly, then sighed *C'mon already* at the ceiling. She took out her Instamatic, insisting we photograph each other for "before" pictures. Then she accidentally sat on it and broke it.

"Piece-of-shit camera," she laughed, trying to piece the chassis together. "Ah well. Maybe it's for the best."

"You can use mine."

"Oh, you are too sweet. Nah, it's probably better this way. If you have a camera, you sometimes get so busy taking pictures you forget to actually see stuff. Hey" — she glanced mischievously at my Instamatic — "want me to sit on yours too? Watch out!" she giggled and did a little butt wiggle. "Here comes the ass of mass destruction!"

Cynthia glanced over at us, frown lines on either

side of her mouth like inverted parentheses. "Hey you two," she said, clearing her throat. "Are you going to be okay once we disembark?"

Claire did a little plié. "Sure. Why wouldn't we be?" She stopped and crouched down to examine something at the baseboard. "Oh my God. Look. It's a Chinese ladybug. *Nee how!*" She hooked the Walkman headphones over her ears. "Time for one last shot of Oingo Boingo before we hit the mainland."

Cynthia watched us uneasily.

"We're okay," I said, not entirely convincingly. I held up our Lonely Planet guidebook. "See. Bible."

"Cynthia, please. Don't worry," said Claire, pulling the headphones away from her ears. "Jonnie is getting us a hotel." She pressed a button on her Walkman and began tapping out a tattoo in the air in time to the music only she could hear.

Cynthia and I watched her. I envied Claire's confidence. Maybe that's what it was like to be rich: If you grew up with housekeepers and deckhands, you took it for granted that other people would take care of your problems. I scanned the reception hall. Jonnie was actually nowhere in sight. His absence filled me with a mixture of dread and relief. *Maybe you take me to American embassy. Maybe I be your guest then.* I was pretty sure I'd heard him correctly. His words made me leery. It was unclear exactly what kind of quid pro quo we were tacitly agreeing to by accepting his hospitality. Did he merely want to *visit* the embassy and get his picture taken beside the American flag? Somehow I doubted it.

But now Jonnie hadn't even shown up for breakfast. Maybe we were better off going it alone: We could just swan-dive into Shanghai and hope to God we didn't go *splat!* on the asphalt.

The ship's air-conditioning had been turned off. The reception hall grew yeasty with body odor and listlessness.

At five a.m., there was still no sign of Jonnie. Chinese officials in military regalia boarded the ship and moved from passenger to passenger, checking our passports, visas, paperwork. Quickly we gathered up our tourism paraphernalia and stashed it, then stood rigidly at attention, shining examples of purity and rectitude. We Americans, I noticed, smiled winningly, as if this might not be merely a border control, but a dental inspection.

An official grabbed Claire's passport, then mine. After a disconcertingly long time, he stamped them and handed them back without once making eye contact. There came a great metallic drumroll and a voluminous rattle; suddenly the hatch opened. All the stewards began shouting at once and motioning toward the doorway. "Okay, you go out now," they barked.

We stumbled outside, tripped down an aluminum plank, and found ourselves discharged onto a rotting pier in the predawn chill of the People's Republic of China.

We were greeted by the briny smell of seawater and the mournful caw of gulls. The sun had only just risen, bronzing the world with light. We were nowhere near a city. We were standing on a small rural fishing wharf.

The water beside the pier teemed with rudimentary bamboo boats bobbing and knocking against each other like buoys, old tires lashed to their sides. Beyond them was a muddy quay lined with crumbling concrete stalls whose thatched roofs were collapsing in places; piles of sodden, tangled netting and decaying cabbages lay abandoned in the grime. A handful of men in flip-flops and coolie hats crouched in the dirt, waving away flies, chewing something fibrous. Farther down, a few in Mao jackets straddled rusty bicycles.

Besides the gulls, the only sounds were that of a lone dog barking and the rhythmic slap of water against the pier. Occasionally one of the men would summon up a great mouthful of phlegm from the depths of his throat, making a *haaaccchhh* sound like a windup before a pitch. Then he spit into the dirt by his feet, leaving a jewel of saliva glistening in the dust. As we would soon learn, China rained phlegm.

It felt not just foreign, but other-dimensional, as if we'd stepped off the *Jin Jiang* into a nineteenth-century sepia-toned photograph. It was as if we'd gone to sleep, then woken up a hundred years earlier— Rip Van Winkle in reverse.

Bicycles and battered carts began pulling into the dirt lot at the end of the pier. Beside it was a squat, arcaded building that looked like an abandoned aviary. Inside, I could see two officials at a desk and a large blackboard covered with Chinese characters. Some of the Chinese passengers from the *Jin Jiang* began forming a line in front of it. Others crammed their bundles hurriedly into the backs of arriving wagons, trucks, and dented, corroding cars. There were great gales of shouting, engines chugging, axles squeaking. I searched frenetically for Cynthia and her boys, but they had disappeared. Through the sea of heads, I glimpsed a tall white man in a leather hat folding himself into the back of a small, mud-splattered sedan. Behind the windshield, I thought I saw a blonde with a scarf tied over her hair twisting around to assist him, but I couldn't be sure. "Martin?" I shouted across the quay. "Cynthia?" The car door slammed shut. The sedan backed up with a squeal, then gunned forward and vanished in a plume of dust.

"See?" Claire whispered.

I stood watching the cloud disintegrate. It was hard to tell what I'd just witnessed. Before we'd disembarked, Cynthia had pulled us aside and handed us a sheet of paper with the name and address of her hotel in Shanghai: not exactly the behavior of a kidnapper, a woman on the lam with her lover. "If you two need anything at all, promise you'll contact me?" she'd said. "You can even travel with us, if you want."

Now the dock was deserted.

Claire, Gunter, and I stood alone on the tamped plot of earth. We had no idea how far the wharf was from the actual city of Shanghai. The three of us walked to the end of the pier to assess our position. All we could see lining the muddy harbor were a couple of low-slung petroleum tanks, an outcropping of smokestacks, cargo cranes like monstrous high chairs.

The morning was now almost eerily still, bathed in dust and the washed-out light of overexposed film.

I looked at Claire. She was surveying the scene grimly, a cleft deepening in her brow. "Christ," she said softly, slinging her pack down into the dirt. From somewhere a lone dog continued barking.

"What do you think we should do?" I asked.

Her eyes narrowed as if she was trying to thread a needle. It was a look she got whenever she was concentrating hard on something. "Okay," she said after a moment. "We're fine. We're good. We're excellent. Everything's under control. Gunter." She turned to him. "What's going on?"

To our great annoyance, Gunter just shrugged.

"C'mon, Gunter," Claire said, pointing to the makeshift terminal. "You speak Chinese. Can't you go inside and maybe see if there's some way to book a hotel or a taxi?"

Gunter stood there like an office building whose lights were only just being turned on by the cleaning crew. "Yah, okay," he said.

We slung our packs over our shoulders again and lumbered back toward the quay.

Just as we reached the terminal building, we heard a voice: "Sushi, Crair, Gunter, wait for me! It is Jonnie."

In a moment Jonnie caught up to us, breathless, an enormous camera bag slung across his chest. He smiled anxiously. "Where are you going? Why you not wait for me?"

"Jonnie," I cried happily. "We thought we had lost you!" And then I actually threw my arms around him and hugged him, a gesture that embarrassed just about everyone.

"We are thinking we are booking the hotel, yah?" Gunter said.

"No, no need to book a hotel," Jonnie insisted, struggling to maintain his smile. "I told you. I have friends. They come. We take care of everything." He glanced nervously back at the *Jin Jiang*. "I get my luggage. You wait here. Please. One moment."

"One moment" quickly turned into half an hour, but none of us seemed inclined to invent a Plan B.

We stood watching a few people come and go on

bicycles. One man pushed a rusty wheelbarrow with a slaughtered pig hanging out of it; another pedaled a cart piled with corrugated sheeting and onions. The air stank of fish oil, fermenting garbage.

"Watch out," Claire shouted. She pulled me out of the way of an oncoming van. The driver stopped abruptly and leaned on the horn. With the engine still running, he bounded out of the driver's seat. I thought he was coming to yell at me, but instead he ran to Jonnie, who'd suddenly reappeared, and greeted him exuberantly.

"This is my friend Harry," Jonnie announced happily.

Harry was a compact man with a receding hairline. Dressed in polyester pants and a tweed slouch cap, he looked older than Jonnie, more weather-beaten. His teeth were crooked. Sweat stains bled through the armpits of his plaid shirt. A small scar ran from his left ear neatly along his jaw, a shiny threadlike seam. "*Nee how.* Hello," he said warmly, shaking our hands. "Hello" turned out to be one of the few words Harry knew in English. The others were "yes," "thank you," "have a nice day," and "Ronald Reagan."

For a few minutes Harry and Jonnie walked over to the other side of the van and conferred. Claire, Gunter, and I stood there dumbly like babies waiting to be diapered, fed, burped. Being a tourist, I was beginning to see, meant being infantilized much of the time. All power is contextual. Take a brain surgeon in Uzbekistan and stick him in Manhattan; take the toughest homeboy from Compton and leave him in Tuscany. Drop any of us, anywhere, in an alien environment, and you'll see our IQ plummet. "IS THIS THE BUS STOP?" we'll holler at strangers, while dementedly pointing to the bus stop. To buy a sandwich, we'll pantomime chewing. This is why, I suspect, so many otherwise decent people back home behave like assholes abroad: There's nothing quite like feeling helpless to turn you into a world-class control freak, to make you forget your manners and throw a tantrum if your room isn't ready and there's no ice in your drink. In a strange environment you feel like a baby, and you're often treated like a baby, and so you act like one. Claire, Gunter, and I were no exception. We stood there stupefied, fretting.

Finally, Harry waved us over to his van. Ignoring two decades of warnings to *never get into cars with strange men*, Claire and I squeezed in. The van didn't actually belong to Harry, but to the company he worked for. In China, Jonnie explained, almost no one owned a car. If you needed a vehicle, you had to lease one from your employer ahead of time. "It is not like in America," Jonnie said. "In America, people sing songs about their cars. Everyone, they have a Cadillac, yes?"

"Not really," Claire said vaguely, staring out the window. "The best cars now are all foreign." Harry eased the van out of the quay down into the street.

Soot-darkened tenements appeared on either side of us garlanded with laundry.

"It's true, though," I laughed. "About the songs. Let's see, there's 'Pink Cadillac.' 'Little Red Corvette' —"

"Except Stevie Wonder," Jonnie said happily. "I never hear Stevie Wonder sing about cars."

"That's because he's blind," Claire said. "Blind people don't drive cars."

"Stevie Wonder is blind?" said Jonnie.

Our van turned right, then left, then left again for a few hundred yards, then stopped.

"Here we are," Jonnie announced. For an instant I thought he was kidding. We were no more than eight minutes from the pier. "This is a very good, very nice hotel."

He pointed to a hulking sheet cake of a building that looked like a Victorian sanitarium.

Gunter leafed through his guidebook, trying to figure out where we were. "Puijang Hotel," Jonnie said, motioning us out of the car. "Harry know the manager. Please, come."

He ushered us over to a bench and instructed us to wait while he and Harry approached the woman behind a reception desk. The lobby was high-ceilinged and pillared. Back in the 1920s, it had probably had Persian carpets and elaborate chandeliers. Now it had the drafty, utilitarian feel of a high school gymnasium.

A moment later, Jonnie returned. "Okay, Harry

book you three beds. Now you give us passports and change your money. Okay?"

Claire and I exchanged uneasy glances: hand over our passports and traveler's checks? It occurred to us that we didn't really know Jonnie or Harry at all—we didn't even know their real Chinese names. For all we knew, they could be in cahoots with the hotel staff, getting kickbacks for every Westerner they brought in off the boat. For all we knew, they would cut and run with our stuff. All the smiling, all that *you be my guest* could be a con. Certainly it would be back in New York.

"Wait a sec. I'm sorry," I said. "But how do we know this is legit?"

Claire cleared her throat and ran a hand through her hair. "Jonnie, is it possible for us to see the rooms first, before we book them?"

Jonnie continued smiling at us. "Yes, okay. Harry book you three beds. Now you give your passports and pay."

Claire looked at Gunter. He had pulled a granola bar out of his tiny rucksack and was struggling to rip open the wrapper with his teeth.

"Gunter!" she shouted. "Can you help us here, *please*? How do you say 'We want to we see the rooms first'?"

Gunter looked confused. Suddenly neither Claire nor I had the energy to deal with him. It was clear: Either we trusted Jonnie and Harry or we didn't. We were in a Communist country halfway around the globe, amputated from everything we knew and understood. Before I'd left home, a boyfriend of mine, Jake, who'd backpacked through India, had told me, "Remember, when you're traveling, you're in *their* sandbox. Either play by their rules or go home."

Reluctantly we surrendered our passports. We wrote our names on a form where Jonnie told us to. We cashed our traveler's checks at one counter, then counted out several hundred yuan in special foreigners' FEC money and handed them over to Harry. He returned to the receptionist. We watched her take out an abacus and slide several beads around on it. A moment later, Harry handed us each a key, as well as our passports and three receipts written in longhand on slips of rice paper. The total cost of our lodging was $3.50 per person per night.

"Dormitory is on fifth floor," Jonnie said. "Very nice beds. Okay?" Exhaling, he wiped his hands on the thighs of his pants. "Okay. Now Harry and I, we must return to the pier for the refrigerator for my family, yes? We come back for you later. We take you to lunch. We have friends who have a very good restaurant. We give you special tour of Shanghai. We take care of everything for you. You understand? You stay right here, okay?"

As soon as Claire and I were stuffed into the tiny elevator with our backpacks, she said, "Wow. Was that ever weird or what?"

"What should we do?" I said. "He's going to bend over backwards for us."

She frowned. "I know. I mean, I really want to go around China with him, but there's just no way we can waltz him into the American embassy."

"Should we even have lunch with him?"

"I'm not sure." After a moment she said cryptically, "It's actually not Jonnie I'm worried about. It's Gunter."

"Him? Why?" I forced a little laugh. "What'd he do now?"

Claire gave me a peculiar, guarded look. "I can't say. It might upset you too much. But, Suze. You might be right about those Germans."

The elevator stopped abruptly. "I actually don't think we can trust them," she said.

Before I could press her to elaborate, she strode out onto the landing.

The women's dormitory was in a big, drafty hall with narrow iron beds arrayed in rows beneath a ceiling fan. At the far end, a pair of French doors opened onto a small wrought-iron balcony. We could smell the exhaust and hear the traffic from the street below.

It was only 6:45 a.m. The other travelers were still asleep, tangles of russet, blond, and chocolaty hair splayed across the pillows—maps, guidebooks, bags of cough drops, flashlights piled on the floor near their beds.

Down the hallway was a communal bathroom with a row of sinks and four poorly concealed toilets. A small sign taped to the mirror informed guests that the showers were on the second floor next to the hotel kitchen. Clutching our towels, flip-flops, and peppermint soap, Claire and I made our way downstairs to what turned out to be one large concrete cell with a bent pipe jutting out of the wall.

"Wow. Plumbing—as brought to you by Charles Dickens," I said.

Claire didn't laugh. She glanced around worriedly. "There's no curtain?"

Cowering in the corner, she removed her bra from underneath her shirt and waited until the last possible minute to take off her chinos. "Don't look," she begged. "Please. My thighs are a nightmare."

Her embarrassment was painful to me; I wondered how she'd survived as a school athlete all those years. From what I could glimpse, she didn't have an ounce of fat on her. The keys of her spine pressed through her back. Her legs were so narrow, the space between them was concave. Why were the girls with the best bodies always the most self-hating?

As we rode upstairs in the elevator afterward, she looked despondent. "It's bad enough the showers are freezing," she said bitterly. "But just how am I supposed to function here with everybody watching me?"

"Well, we wanted to go hard core," I said. "I guess this is budget traveling."

Claire looked at me darkly. "I'm sorry. This has nothing to do with budgeting."

———

Although it had been our plan to ignore Jonnie's instructions and go outside, it hadn't been our plan to go outside with Gunter. But Gunter, being Gunter, was waiting for us in the lobby. What's more, he'd thoughtfully procured a set of maps for us from CITS printed in pinyin, the Chinese system of writing out characters phonetically using the Roman alphabet. These proved to be a godsend. It hadn't occurred to Claire and me that most Chinese maps would be labeled only in Chinese characters. When Gunter handed us the map, my heart broke a little. *Poor big dumb Kraut*, I thought guiltily, *he's doing the best he can.*

In the morning light, Shanghai looked like a city that had belonged to somebody's grandparents: a formerly splendid metropolis now moldering in dust and neglect. The hazy streets were a riot of telegraph wires, old enameled bicycles, and outmoded buses shaped like breadboxes. Along the riverfront stood a row of majestic European buildings left over from colonial times. Fanning out behind these was a maze of walled alleyways, dirt lanes, ancient tile-roofed tenements. Nothing appeared to have been constructed after 1932. The colors were muted: slate, dun, sage.

All the signs, of course, were in Chinese. Although I'd anticipated this, I'd underestimated the impact. It was as if a computer glitch had converted everything into dingbats, squiggles, and glyphs. No matter where I looked, I couldn't read anything. It made me feel brain damaged.

The only English appeared atop an abandoned hotel at the north end of the river. A giant white neon aspirin tablet—an advertising billboard left over from World War Two—flickered above the city reading

B
A
B A Y E R
E
R

like a crucifix, a strange set of crosshairs.

Our hotel was located not far from this Bayer sign, across an industrial canal called Suzhou Creek. To reach the heart of downtown, we had to walk over a small iron footbridge. A great cascade of bicycles flooded past us toward the main riverfront road known as the Bund. As we stood watching, a crowd of Chinese surrounded us. While we stared at the traffic, they stared at us.

In 1986, the People's Republic was still a closed society. Most mainland Chinese had never seen us white-skinned, big-nosed Westerners before. Two girls pointed at Gunter, at the sheer enormity of him, then covered their mouths and giggled. Several old women baldly sized up Claire and me. Our round eyes, mine behind big owlish 1980s glasses. Claire's size 9½ feet in their Timberland boots. My 36-DD breasts pushing like fists through my lavender sweatshirt. We must have looked like Amazons to them, albino gorillas, freaks of nature. Back at college, I'd decried the ways in which guys had sexually objectified me. Now I saw that I hadn't experienced the half of it.

"*Nee how,*" Gunter said, giving a little half wave at the crowd.

Taking our cue from him, Claire and I chorused, "*Nee how.*"

People burst out laughing. "*Nee how,*" they replied. A father in a Mao uniform urged his daughter forward. She couldn't have been older than seven. Her long hair was tied with red strings into two pigtails.

"Hello. How. Are. You?" she said shyly, tentatively, shaping each syllable with practiced care as her father looked on proudly.

I kneeled down. "Hello, I am fine." I overenunciated. "How are you?"

The girl dashed back to her father and buried her face in his leg. The crowd roared with approval.

The circus had come to town, and we were it. We walked to Huangpu Park. The crowd walked with us. Gunter stooped down to tie his shoe. The crowd stooped with him. We strolled to the waterfront and gazed across the river at the barren mudflats of Pudong. The crowd strolled with us and gazed at us gazing. I have to say, as much as I'd always fantasized about having an entourage, it was wildly unnerving.

"I'm not liking this," Claire murmured under her breath even as we smiled at the crowds and tried to wave affably. "It's weirding me out. Can we try to keep moving?"

As we made our way across the street to the famous Peace Hotel, the crowd finally dispersed.

Two types of currency existed in China back then, the FEC money we tourists were issued, and local renminbi money issued to Chinese citizens. Only FEC was accepted at Friendship Stores — government-run emporiums that sold the best Chinese and imported goods. And so a black market had sprung up. Local renminbi was being traded for FEC at rates of up to 1.4 to one.

The Peace Hotel was the center for this. No sooner did we approach the steps than Chinese men with hats tilted over their faces sidled up, whispering, "Change money? Good rate."

Without a word, Gunter nodded to one of them,

who pointed down the street, then hurried off. Before we could say anything, Gunter followed, disappearing into an alley, leaving us alone on the steps.

"See? What did I tell you," Claire fumed. Back in Hong Kong, we'd overheard backpackers bragging about how they'd made a fortune off the locals on the black market in China. We'd thought this was despicable. "It's like charging people admission to a lifeboat," Claire had said disdainfully. Although trading on the black market was apparently a necessity—you couldn't travel independently without renminbi—we ourselves vowed never to do this.

"C'mon," Claire said now. "Run." Rounding the corner, we made a mad dash down the street, then turned into an alley, then ran down another street, then collapsed in a doorway breathless and giggling as if we'd just orchestrated a prison break.

"Oh, thank God we're free of him," Claire panted. "Okay. Now where the hell are we?" Amazingly, we hadn't brought our guidebook with us because *we didn't want to stand out like tourists.*

She yanked open the map. The names of the streets—Nanjing, Jiangxi, Guangxi—all ran together. "Oh, let's just wander," she said. "Worse comes to worst, we'll just head back toward the water and look for the big, white aspirin."

Shanghai. Pearl of the Orient.

Nanjing Road was lined with low ice-cream-colored storefronts with Chinese characters painted on their walls in red. Most opened directly onto the street like garages, revealing cheap, modest goods. Crates of tangerines. A grease-spattered hot plate, a wok surrounded by flies. Polyester blouses. Underfoot, the sidewalks were fractured and chalky. It was as if every structure had been ground down into filaments over the years. More overpowering than anything else were the smells. Wave after wave of pungencies and perfumes came over us. Urine. Jasmine. Roasting pork. Mildew. Sandalwood. Gasoline. Decomposing vegetables.

We walked slowly, quietly, waving away the dust.

In the lanes, bamboo scaffolding had been erected in front of tenements to create makeshift balconies. So many wires, tubes, cords, and laundry lines were connected to them, they looked like giant electrical outlets. Chickens hopped in the dirt.

"I'm thirsty," Claire said. "Let's try our communication skills." At a small grocery, plastic crates filled with glass bottles of orange soda were stacked on the sidewalk. A teenage boy stood behind the counter, watching us with fascination.

"*Bonjour,*" I said to the boy. "*Comment allez-vous?*"

French. Why had that come out of my mouth? I supposed because it was the only foreign language I even remotely knew. Having taken it in high school, I could possibly, if pressed, order a croque-monsieur and a café au lait in Paris. Now it seemed my brain had clicked into it as a default mode.

Claire laughed. "Want to try that again in Chinese, Zsa Zsa?"

She turned to the boy behind the counter. "*Nee how.*" She pulled two bottles of orange drink from the crate and set them on the counter. Handing me our Berlitz phrase book, she said, "Find out how to say 'please.'"

I riffled through the pages in a panic. "*Ching*," I said finally, pointing to the sodas and gesturing.

The boy nodded. I beamed.

We had one moment of perfect, shining, cross-cultural communication. Then he said something completely incomprehensible.

"He's probably telling us how much it costs." Claire pulled out her leather Gucci wallet. She insisted on keeping her money in her purse instead of strapped beneath her clothes in a money belt like I did. This drove me crazy. As I saw it, she might as well just tape a sign to her ass reading, "I'm wealthy and careless. Come pickpocket me." No one from New York City ever flashed money around like she did.

While she dug around for her FEC, the boy held up two fingers and said, "*Bah.*"

"*Bah?*" Claire chuckled. "What do you suppose *bah* is?"

"I think it's 'two,'" I said. "He's holding up two fingers."

Claire slid two FEC notes toward him. The boy shook his head. He held up his his thumb and index finger again. "*Bah.*"

"Yes. I know. *Bah*," said Claire, pointing to first one FEC note, then the other.

The boy shook his head. "*Bah*," he repeated, pointing to his fingers.

"Christ, is he retarded?" Claire whispered.

I flipped hurriedly through the phrasebook to the section "Counting and Numbers." "It looks like *bah* is eight."

"He's saying eight but holding up only two fingers?"

"Maybe he thinks he's a Magritte painting," I said.

Claire snorted and slapped six more FEC notes down on the counter. "Jesus," she said soberly. "You'd think at least that counting on your fingers would be the same. I mean, since when are two fingers not two?"

We stood there for a moment considering this. When we looked up, mothers, fathers, grandparents, and small children had gathered around us, gawking. Word seemed to have gotten out around the neighborhood.

"Yep, that's right, everybody. Drop everything and get over here." Claire groaned, raking her fingers through her hair. "Two Americans are standing around drinking orange soda. Will the excitement never cease?"

"Boy." I laughed. "I wish I found us nearly as fascinating as they do."

While I'd been unnerved by our anonymity in Hong Kong, the relentless attention we received now in China was at least as unsettling. As we hurried from the grocery store, people everywhere pointed and hollered any little bit of English they'd ever learned. "Hello!" A man dogged us across a pedestrian footbridge. "Miss America! Nuclear missile! Hamburger!" We felt besieged.

Our only respite came in Renmin Square, a thickly wooded park in the middle of the city with a duck pond and gazebo. Yet even here, a young Chinese man approached us. "Excuse me, but are you busy?" he asked furtively. "I would like to talk with you a few minutes, if that is possible."

Unlike other strangers we'd encountered, his English was impeccable. He was also dressed in Western blue jeans and a plaid button-down shirt, his hair cut in modern punkish spikes. He was our age, possibly younger—a contemporary, someone we might really be able to talk to.

"Please. Sure. Absolutely," we said.

He glanced nervously around the park. "Do you mind if we go here?" He motioned to a small thicket of azalea bushes off the side of the path.

With the Cultural Revolution so fresh in everyone's memory, some Chinese were reluctant to be seen with foreigners. Once we were seated on a bench, the young man exhaled, though he continued to look around.

"Thank you so much," he said, leaning in close. "It is so rare that I get to practice my English. If I do not practice it, I am afraid I will lose it."

His name, he told us, was Tom. His father had been a diplomat. When Tom was twelve, his family had lived in England for two years. He was pleased to learn that we were from America. Back in London, he had seen several American movies, including *Star Wars* and *Grease*. "Please," he said. "It is not too rude that I ask about your country?"

"Fire away," we said.

His questions came so quickly, it was hard to keep up: Why has America's influence been so great when it is such a young nation? Children in America, you are so independent — is there any sense of family? There is a lot of divorce, no? Why are people in America ever discontent when you are so wealthy?

While Claire and I could've responded with aplomb to any questions, say, about Plato's concept of eudaemonia, Maslow's hierarchy of needs, or the Treaty of Versailles, Tom's questions completely stumped us. We'd never been pressed to explain our country in quite this way before.

When we finally managed to deliver what were largely defensive and inchoate answers, Tom considered them politely. Then he asked haltingly, "In America, do you get arrested for reading magazines?"

I laughed. "Are you kidding? Why would a —"

Shamefully, he looked away.

"Oh my God." Claire covered her mouth. Gently, she shifted toward him on the bench. "Was it something political?"

Tom shook his head. "*Playboy.* A classmate in England gave it to me when I was fourteen. When they found it, I was sent to reeducation camp for two years."

I flashed on Martin, casually thumbing through *Juggs* magazine, then of myself at college. I'd spoken out vociferously against pornography, declaring that it was violence against women and ought to be illegal.

I suddenly felt despicably naïve.

Tom stood up. "Yes, well, okay. I think I should be going now. Thank you."

Before we could respond, the azalea bushes rustled and he was gone.

Numbly we made our way out of the park. As soon as we stepped back onto Nanjing Road, an old man with a thatch of white hair grabbed me by the forearm.

"Hello! Welcome to China!" he bellowed, thumping his chest. "I learn English during World War Two." He had on Mao pants, a brown-and-white-checked shirt. "I work with Americans. Americans very nice. Have good friend in America. He live in Cincinnati. You from Cincinnati?"

"No, New York City," I nodded.

"Oh, New York! Big Apple. Yankee baseball.

Brooklyn Bridge!" As he spoke, another crowd began forming.

"You've been to New York?" I asked.

"Oh no. My friend from Cincinnati, he send me postcards. Postcard of Statue of Liberty. Postcard of World Trade Center."

He drew closer to Claire and me, clutching our wrists to steady himself, his hands as small and bony as starfish. "New York, big city. One day, Shanghai be number one city like New York! How many people live in New York?"

"I dunno. Seven million?"

"Seven million!" The man took a step back in disbelief. "But that not so big! Shanghai bigger! Shanghai twelve million! You say Shanghai bigger than New York?"

"I guess so." While Shanghai certainly didn't feel bigger, it seemed to have at least as many people in it—most of whom now seemed to be standing around gaping at us.

The man turned to our Chinese audience and said something that generated a lot of excitement. "I am telling them that you are from America. That you say Shanghai bigger than New York City. That New York City have only seven million people."

Another man in the crowd pushed forward and shook my hand. "Shanghai bigger!" he said exuberantly. "Shanghai have fourteen million people!"

"Shanghai have fifteen million people!" A woman leaned over, poking Claire.

"Shanghai very big city. Twenty million people!" announced a young man straddling a bicycle.

Standing there surrounded by traffic and exuberant loudmouths, I felt curiously at home. I was used to being the only white girl in a subway car, on a city street, in an entire neighborhood, in fact. I was used to being jostled by crowds. And the Chinese? All of them talking at once, arguing over whose version was right, insisting you pay attention to them — why, they were pretty much like Jews.

Claire clutched me. "Susie," she whispered, "can we get out of here? I'm hot. I'm dizzy. And I really need to go to the bathroom."

Her face was flushed. For all her self-assuredness, I realized, she was still a child of the suburbs. Her world was one of oak trees and horse farms, country clubs, golf greens, and quaint New England towns dotted with colonial banks. When she looked out her dormer windows in Connecticut, she saw only people like herself reflected in the swimming pool. For once, my upbringing put me at an advantage.

"Okay," I said. "Let's head back to the Pujiang."

"No," she cried desperately. "I mean, I really need to go. *Now*."

She appeared to be in pain. *Help me*, she mouthed. I had no idea what to do. We were somewhere on the map in a tangle of streets, all named Donglu. I looked around. "Maybe back down that street with the store. I think there was a restaurant."

Urgently we tried to retrace our steps, hurrying down one alley, then another. Dust, scaffolding, walls, chickens. Dead end. We doubled back, crossed a street. A lattice of overhead wires, laundry. More tenements. A shirtless old man on a folding chair, fanning himself. An abandoned bicycle. An outdoor sink. A woman with a baby in one arm, washing clothes in a plastic bucket with the other. Everything smelling like a musty throw pillow. Go left. Scallions frying. A man crouched on the curb before a broken louver door. Another alley.

I hurried through the lanes, searching. Claire stumbled behind me, clutching her stomach as if she were holding her internal organs together. Finally we came upon a tiny restaurant. A few people seated around a crude wooden table looked up, set down their chopsticks, and stared.

"Quick," Claire cried, leafing through her phrase book. "How do you say 'toilet'?"

"Claire." I pointed. The cover read *Cantonese for Travelers.* In her distress, she'd pulled out the wrong one; we needed Mandarin. She gave a little cry. "I have to go!"

I ran up to the woman behind the counter. "*Bonjour.* I mean, *Nee how. Ching?*" I pointed to Claire and pantomimed squatting.

"Ah!" The woman smiled. She was plump, dressed in a Mao uniform and an incongruously frilly apron. Motioning us back through the kitchen, she led us out down a narrow alley full of weeds and tiny houses.

"Where is she taking us?" Claire cried, hugging herself. "Did you explain?"

The woman led us around the corner to a low concrete barrack with two cutaway doors. She steered us into one, urging us inside, pointing and nodding.

"*Merci beaucoup. Shay shay nee.*" I bowed idiotically. Claire hesitated. The woman took her by the elbow and guided her in.

The low concrete room was bare except for a trough running down the middle of the floor. Two women were both squatting over it with their Mao pants and underwear pushed to their ankles. They glanced up impassively as they defecated. At the far end of the room, water ran out of a rusted spigot and trickled down the trough toward a drain. The place stank of feces and urine—though it was not any worse, I supposed, than the New York City subway system or of any gas station bathroom off Interstate 95.

Claire let out a cry, then backed out. It was odd. China was supposed to be a closed society, yet almost every basic aspect of life seemed to be lived out in the open—cooking, eating, washing, and shitting were all carried out in full view of others. Standing there, I grasped a fundamental irony. If you wanted to live freely, in an open democratic society, you had to be able to shut your door. You had to have the privacy to pee or think or speak away from the relentless gaze of your neighbors, the public, and your government. While I supposed that going to the bathroom publicly en masse was in a certain way a great leveler—perhaps even perversely democratizing—to Claire and me, it just seemed degrading.

"I can't go in there! That's disgusting." She was now in tears, half doubled over, leaning against a wall.

"I know, sweetie. But I don't think we can make it back to the hotel, do you? Better to pee in there than in your pants."

She looked at me in horror.

"Look." I took a deep breath. "We are two young, brilliant Ivy League graduates. If we can't use a public bathroom in the People's Republic of China, who the hell can? I'll even pee with you." I dug into my pocket and pulled out two tissues. "We can have a contest. Who can finish first. Or who can pee on their shoes the least."

Bracing herself, Claire turned reluctantly and walked with me back to the doors.

"Good thing I got that nosebleed in the airport, huh?" I said. "Otherwise, we might not be carrying around Kleenex."

Stepping back inside, we tried hard not to breathe through our noses. Mercifully, the two other women had left.

Claire walked to the far end of the trough next to a little window and stood with her back to me. I stood at the other end, facing the door. It was as if we were preparing to duel.

"Okay. Ready?" I giggled, straddling the trough, pulling down my pants. "On the count of three, drop and pee."

I heard her inhale miserably, then her khakis unzipping and the stereophonic *fwish* of our pee simultaneously hitting the floor.

Suddenly Claire screamed, "*Stop looking at me!*"

I glanced over my shoulder and saw her bent over, struggling to pull up her pants while waving furiously at the window. "*Get the hell away from there!*"

"Oh, God, Susie," she cried, pointing. "Those women were watching us."

Back at the Pujiang, the dormitory was empty. We both went to our narrow iron beds and lay down on them, listening to the sounds of the traffic below without saying anything. A moment later, I heard a sniffle.

"Sweetie," I said gently, "you okay?"

"I'm fine, I'm fine," she said bitterly, blowing her nose. "I just don't understand how I'm supposed to function with everybody looking at me all the time."

As she said this, dozens of Western women tromped into our dormitory, talking and laughing, dropping their day packs heavily on the floorboards, kicking off their shoes, unbolting their lockers, flouncing on their creaky beds. It was lunchtime. They had returned to the hotel to eat.

We were the only Americans in the entire dorm. Everyone else was Canadian, Australian, Kiwi, European. Virtually all of them had been on the road for months, if not years. Their skin had been burnished to the color of burnt sugar. Their faces had the flinty-eyed look of war veterans. Dressed in patchwork drawstring pants and batik tunics purchased from street markets across Asia, they'd dispensed with all Western frivolities a long time ago. They were expert navigators now, muscular with experience. Sitting among them with our brand-new backpacks, my snow-white virginal Reeboks, our crisp pastel-colored L.L. Bean sportswear, Claire and I weren't impressing anybody.

"Siberia is Siberia," a Danish woman shrugged. She yanked off her grimy T-shirt and used it to blot her armpits. "But Outer Mongolia...now *that* was worth going to."

"Well, it took a while, but eventually the Brazilians realized they'd made a mistake and released me," someone else said. "The good thing was, I met another gal from Brisbane who was jailed by mistake too, and we hitchhiked down to Patagonia."

A Swiss woman in the bed next to Claire's had just returned from Lhasa. Embarrassingly, until that moment, I'd thought Lhasa was a yogurt drink, a sort of irritatingly nutritious Indian milk shake. But no, it turned out to be the capital of Tibet.

As the woman recounted her journey, others congregated around her bed. Not only was traveling to Lhasa technically prohibited at the time, but nearly impossible, requiring two grueling weeks of travel. During her trip, the woman had contracted dysentery. She became so weak, she'd had to be hauled to the monasteries on a yak.

"But oh." She sighed rapturously. "Tibet is the most extraordinary place on earth. Even if you are hallucinating."

When an angelic-looking Canadian mentioned that she'd participated in a smuggling ring that paid Western women to fly to South Korea with Rolexes stitched into their coats, Claire and I were just about ready to kill ourselves. We had been in Shanghai exactly five hours. All we had managed to do was walk a few miles and buy a bottle of orange soda, and the most risqué thing either one of us had done so far was pee. And already we felt overwhelmed.

———

When Jonnie arrived, we climbed gratefully into the back of Harry's van without protest, and gazed out the windows, happy to be borne aloft through the streets. Jonnie held up a small tape recorder. "Look what I brought." As the soundtrack from *The Woman in Red* began playing scratchily, he sang along. Soon all of us—even Harry—joined in.

I just called to say I love you.

Gunter sat between us, his hands on his knees, leaning forward to peer out the windshield. He hadn't bothered to ask where Claire and I had gone while he traded on the black market—either our absence hadn't registered or he took it in stride. Seeing him, I felt strangely melancholy. As he sang, his voice was surprisingly high and tender. Around us, soft gold autumn light filtered through the sycamore trees along the boulevards.

At the restaurant, Jonnie's friend "Mike" insisted we sit at the best table. He brought out hot and sour soup. Dumplings in hot sesame oil. Chicken with chilies and curlicues of onion. Barbecue pork. Piles of freshly sautéed greens. Prawns the size of tangerines, still in their shells, coated in salt. Crispy glazed duck. Bottles of Tsingtao beer. Even Claire ate without hesitation. The platters kept coming. So did the beer. Through the ginger-scented steam, we grinned at each other dopily and tilted our glasses: *To arriving in Shanghai*, we chorused. *To our new friends Jonnie and Harry! To Victor and his restaurant!*

The meal grew increasingly raucous. More friends of Jonnie's and Mike's arrived, pulling up chairs and picking up chopsticks. By the end we could only sit back with glassy looks on our faces, watching a social interaction that looked increasingly like water ballet, until there was nothing left to drink or eat at all, and a bill suddenly appeared, brought to the table on a little porcelain dish that somehow wound up before me, Claire, and Gunter, the three of us digging into our money belts and wallets. I had the vague impression we'd insisted on paying.

After that, back in the van. Jonnie had another friend. "Please come meet Tony. Tony speaks English."

Harry steered us into a narrow cobbled back alley where a man was waiting for us dressed in a cheap button-down shirt, Mao pants, and rubber flip-flops.

"Hello, welcome to China," Tony cried. "Please, come to my house." He led us through a back door up a narrow flight of cement stairs. From everything we'd heard, it was highly unusual to be invited into a Chinese home; the government apparently forbade it. But if what Tony was doing was risky or illegal, he didn't seem the least bit concerned.

Tony and his wife lived in what Americans call a "studio" or an "efficiency" that was probably all of 350 square feet. Although Claire and Gunter seemed appalled by its compactness, by New York City standards, it looked pretty fabulous to me. "Wow," I said as I walked into the rectangular living area. "You know, this would rent for, like, seven hundred dollars a month back in Manhattan?"

Off the main room were a separate dining and kitchenette alcove and a bathroom. The modern furnishings were unlovely, but functional. A tweed couch. An oak veneer sideboard draped with a cheap doily on top of which sat a small boom box, a vase of plastic roses, and a porcelain kitten. I'd expected Chinese apartments to double as shrines to Mao Zedong, but in Tony's home, at least, there were family photographs everywhere and not a trace of the chairman.

"Wow, this place is really, really great," I said. I must have said this several times, because Claire finally had to tell me to cool it.

Tony made us all tea and insisted that Claire, Gunter, and I take seats on the couch; he then gave Jonnie and Harry the two folding chairs. He himself stood in the archway between the living and dining alcoves. We all sipped our tea, made polite remarks about the tea— *Yes, it's very nice. No, it's not too hot at all*—then hit the inevitable wall of silence that rises uncomfortably between any group of six strangers with absolutely nothing in common.

Finally Claire cleared her throat. "Tony, do you mind if I ask what kind of work you do?"

"I am teacher at technical university," he said. "I teach mechanical engineering."

"Oh, wow. And your wife?"

"My wife, she a teacher, too. She teach biology. And my daughter, she go to university."

"Oh, you have a daughter?" I said. "How old is she?"

"She is seventeen. She be eighteen next month."

"Oh, so she's a Scorpio?" I exclaimed. "Uh-oh, watch out. Scorpios are tough. Incisive. Analytical. Passionate. Suspicious. And highly sexual, of course. In fact, you know, they say Scorpios are the real nymphomaniacs of the—"

Claire shot me a vicious look and I shut up. I realized I was much drunker than I'd thought.

Tony, however, was intrigued. "Scorpio?" he smiled, not comprehending. "Please. What is this word?"

"It's a zodiac sign," Claire said, rolling her eyes. "Susie here doesn't believe in self-determination. She thinks our fate is entirely written in the stars."

"Not *entirely*," I corrected.

"Self-determination?" Jonnie smiled. "Please. What is this word?"

"Oh, astrology. Chinese love astrology," Tony exclaimed. "I am born the Year of the Horse. What year you born?"

"Self-determination?" Claire turned to Jonnie. "It means that you exercise free will and shape your own destiny. That you, yourself are responsible for your choices in life. Nobody else."

"Both Claire and I were born in 1964," I told Tony. "The Year of the Dragon."

"I see," Jonnie said to Claire. "You think this is possible?" He smiled at her so strangely, I almost felt embarrassed for her.

"Oh, Year of the Dragon very good!" Tony said to

me. "Most auspicious sign in whole zodiac. Very pow-
erful." He turned to Gunter. "What year you born?"

"The Year of the Yeti," I murmured to Claire.

"Nineteen sixty-one," Gunter said.

"Oh. That Year of the Ox. Quiet, steady, but very
smart."

Claire wriggled around on the couch as if by doing
so she might be able to redirect the conversation. "So,
Tony, please, back to your daughter. Where does she
live?"

A look of confusion passed over his face. "Why,
here, of course."

Claire paused and blushed. "Oh, of course. How
silly of me. Do all Chinese have apartments as nice as
this one?" She smiled prettily.

Tony beamed. "Not every apartment as special as
this. This very good apartment."

After that, we stared down into our cups and
glanced around the room. It seemed unimaginably
rude and intrusive to ask all the questions that I was
really dying to ask. Are you happy? Do you have any
idea what the world is like outside of China? Do you
long for freedom? Do you feel hopelessly oppressed,
a mere cog in the wheel of a totalitarian Communist
regime? Are you allowed to read books? What's with
the public squat toilets?

Instead, I sat on the couch alongside Claire and
Gunter, my hands knitted respectfully in my lap like
a guest in a museum.

Tony, however, seemed to feel no such compunction. "May I ask, please, some questions to you?" He set down his teacup and kneeled before us by the couch. "Is it true that in United States you have to pay for health care? The doctors, they are not free?"

He asked not antagonistically, but with genuine curiosity.

"Well, yeah. Sure." Claire shrugged. "We're not Communists, you know."

"Yah, but West Germans are not Communists either," Gunter interjected. "And we are not paying for the medical care."

"If I may ask, please," Tony continued. "Are the doctors expensive?"

"That depends," said Claire.

"Absolutely," I said. "They're a fortune."

Claire turned to me. "C'mon, you get what you pay for."

"How can that be?" said Tony. "Is that not like paying for air?"

"Well, for starters," Claire took a deep breath and twisted her watch around on her wrist, "doctors have to put themselves through medical school, and that's very expensive."

Tony looked stunned. "You have to pay for university? Doctors have to pay to train themselves?"

"Yeah, but they make the money back once they graduate," Claire said. "It's an investment."

"You can take out loans," I interrupted. "Borrow

money from the banks and the government to go to school."

Tony seemed floored by this. Jonnie, too. "Borrow money?"

I shrugged. "I did it. To go to my university."

Tony looked from me to Claire. "You go to university too?"

"Uh-huh, both of us did," she replied. "That's where we met."

"Oh," said Tony, pressing his hands together and bringing them to his lips. "So both of you are very rich, yes?"

As the afternoon wound down, we all said goodbye. Jonnie had business to take care of, and Harry had possession of the van for only another hour. "Do not worry. I come see you soon," Jonnie insisted. "I will make arrangements. In a few days, we will all leave for Dinghai together, yes?"

Claire and I nodded hesitantly, guiltily, noncommittally. We set off with Gunter through the old Shanghai Concession neighborhood, working our way back toward the riverfront.

It was twilight. The sky had ripened to dark violet. The Bund was cordoned off, each palatial European building illuminated with ribbons of fairy lights. It was the night before China's National Day—the anniversary of the foundation of the People's Republic, Communist China's very own version of the Fourth of July. All of Shanghai seemed to take to the streets carrying sparklers and sticks of candied fruit. The crowds kept accumulating, tributaries feeding into each other, people gathering and pressing in around us as the three of us walked arm in arm along the Bund, swept up in the tide of celebration. As soon as night fell, there was an explosion, followed by a collective chorus of oohs and aahs, which appear to be the same in any language. Fireworks rocketed up and bloomed over the Huangpu River in great sunflowers and starbursts, brilliant geysers of red, silver, and gold reflecting off the faces of people like firelight.

Amid this jubilant crowd, I experienced a rush of pleasure, something close to ecstasy. Standing in the middle of the Bund, feeling the breeze from the river tangling in my hair, seeing the faces of the children as they waved their sparklers giddily, spraying white hot glitter into the dark, I felt my fear dissolve. For the first time I felt suddenly capable—as if everything might, in fact, be all right. My life, this trip: It could be a torrent of wonder.

"Claire!" I shouted, pirouetting in the middle of the street the way she so often did. "Claire! We did it!" As fireworks exploded above us, I grabbed her hands and spun her around deliriously, tossing my head back and laughing. "Claire, we've made it to fucking China!"

五

Chapter 5

The East China Sea

THE FERRY TO Dinghai reeked of bilgewater and gasoline. On the pier, everyone was pushing, loaded down with bedding, cabbages, melons, rags, nets of silvery, stinking, dead-eyed fish. In the midst of the melee, some people lit cigarettes and started spitting even as they jockeyed toward the gangway. Military officers blew whistles attempting to corral the crowds. It was amazing no one fell in the water.

Nighttime in Shanghai, we'd discovered, was almost a blackout. Except for a few pale lamps along the Bund, all the street lights went off at once, plunging the boulevards into darkness. It was as if someone had pulled a plug on the entire city each night.

"Please, you follow me." Jonnie shouted.

It was hard to see the gangway. We burrowed headlong into the crush. Claire, Gunter, and I gripped each other's hands. People were packed so tightly, I could've lifted my feet off the planking and been carried along. But then our Western faces caught the beams from the officers' flashlights. A murmur rippled through the crowd, and people began stepping back, giving us a wide berth and staring.

"See, being a freak has its privileges," I whispered to Claire. Then I began coughing so violently, I doubled over.

"You okay?" she said. "Take a moment."

I stood panting with my hands on my knees while she whacked me on the back. Like the Chinese around me, I spit a huge gob of congestion down into the bay.

———

Days earlier, on our first morning in Shanghai after the riotous night of fireworks, I'd awoken at the Pujiang Hotel to a symphony of bronchial infections.

It began innocuously enough, with the squeak of a bedspring and a lone sandpapery little cough. But within minutes women across the room were keeled over in their beds clearing their throats, sniffling, wheezing, expectorating into their fists. It sounded like a tuberculosis ward.

"It's the 'Shanghai hack,'" the British woman in the bed next to me rasped. "Give yourself two days, luv, and you'll be spitting your lungs up like the rest of us. It's from the bloody pollution. The Chinese burn coal for everything."

Claire was gone. Her bed was already made, the top sheet pinioned to the frame with military tautness, *The Basic Writings of Friedrich Nietzsche* propped against the pillow like a Gideon Bible. As I got up she reappeared, fully dressed, her face scrubbed to a waxy sheen, her wet hair wrapped in a towel. She'd taken great pains to rinse her extra polo shirt out in the sink; the white knit fabric clung to her skin damply, as did the gold bracelets on her wrist and her horseshoe charm necklace.

"Even at six a.m., the water's still freezing," she said. "I swear. The plumbing alone in this country is a human rights violation."

We had assumed, of course, that traveling would elevate us to a higher level of consciousness, that by backpacking through China, we'd absorb great wisdom the way a chunk of bread might soak up a plate full of sauce—that our minds would dilate with insight—and wherever we went, we'd spout razor-sharp cultural observations worthy of great philosophers. Instead, as we trudged around Shanghai the next few days, our thoughts became nearly pre-verbal: *Can I eat that? This is itchy. I need to pee.*

We took a boat tour of the muddy Huangpu River. We visited the Yuyuan Gardens and the decrepit

Shanghai museum full of forgotten treasures. But the grime from the streets clung to us, and our clothes became saturated with a chemical stench of car exhaust and shellac. We had trouble finding drinking water. Claire got blisters. We found ourselves preoccupied not with Ming dynasty porcelain or Maoist ideology at all, but with figuring out how to read the goddamned bus map, hunting down extra Band-Aids, and finding time to wash our socks out in the bathroom sink at the hotel.

Most of all, we became preoccupied with food.

In 1986, there were few Chinese restaurants outside the tourist establishments. Unless you could read Mandarin or didn't mind risking hepatitis from street carts, you were pretty much the culinary hostage of your hotel.

And in a poor nation of one billion, the Chinese ate things we average Americans found repulsive. At the Pujiang Restaurant, "chicken" consisted of feet, necks, and chopped-up spinal columns; "pork" meant bone shards with strings of fat clinging to them; "beef" was tendons, joints, and gristle. Any vegetables that had not been cooked to a sodden mess were to be avoided as health risks.

Plus, every meal at the Pujiang quickly became a standoff between hungry tourists and the apathetic waitstaff. The dining room would fill to capacity with desperate diners, who'd then wait and wait.

When a single waitress finally emerged from the kitchen, the place was like an auction house, everyone waving napkins, hands, and menus, bidding for her attention while she glided around the tables as if it were her job not to serve us but to model. She seemed to have decided *I'm not getting tipped and I'm never getting fired, so why the hell should I bother?* Having waited tables myself, I couldn't say I blamed her.

The only places where Claire and I could eat outside the hotels were in the ancient back-alley neighborhoods called *hutongs*. They had dumpling houses—storefronts, really, consisting of little more than a hot plate and a wok. All we had to do was buy a ticket and stand on line as a woman sautéed dumplings in hot oil and her daughter wrapped them in squares of brown paper. As soon as we got our order, we'd rip the steaming bag open and devour the contents right there in the street. For the very first time in our lives, we were chronically hungry.

Each day that we ran around sightseeing, we grew more acutely aware of just how coddled we'd been all our lives and just how foolish we were.

Without knowing Mandarin, we were, in the end, just voyeurs. All that set us apart from any other slack-jawed, gum-chomping tourists was the fact that neither of us had a camera. Our second morning at the Pujiang, I'd pulled my Instamatic out of my backpack to find its shutter button had jammed.

Inside the Dinghai Ferry, it was bedlam. People elbowed their way through the corridors with enormous bundles wrapped in cheap, sulfurous green plastic. Relentless broadcasts blared over the ship's PA system. Inexplicably, members of the crew had decided that this was a good time to wash the decks. They stood amid the mayhem with soapy buckets, swishing mops over people's feet as they passed. Through the din, I also heard — was I making this up? — chickens squawking.

Jonnie pointed proudly to an enameled door on the left. "We get number one cabin. I tell them you very special guests."

He unlocked it, but the door wouldn't open all the way; it banged against a rusty iron bunk bed. All told, there were three such bunks in the tiny cabin — one against each wall. The four of us squeezed inside. An elderly Chinese couple arrived, loaded down with a twin-size mattress stuffed into a garbage bag and three wicker baskets secured with packing tape. They elbowed their way in, dropped their belongings on one of the beds, then disappeared back into the corridor with what looked a like a bag full of dried ears.

"Well, at least there won't be any crowds in here staring at us," I said as Claire and I surveyed our medieval bunks with their bare chain-mail mattresses.

Claire sighed, pushed up the sleeves of her smoky

gray cardigan, and slung her backpack onto the top bed.

Jonnie sensed her dismay. "You want I find blanket for you?" he said anxiously. "You want I show you to ladies' toilet?"

Claire shook her head. Jonnie was like all the nice guys you always dated once but could never bring yourself to go out with again; his very goodness, obsequiousness, and eagerness to please somehow made him slightly repellent. He hovered. He smiled too much: *The food, it is okay, yes? Do you like the hotel, it number one hotel, yes? You do not like the tea?*

While both Claire and I knew we should be prostrate with gratitude, we found ourselves bristling, experiencing his fussing over us as bossy and meddlesome even as we grew increasingly dependent upon him. We were still at that age when we regarded kindness as some sort of character flaw — the gambit of the weak, the elderly, the perennially uncool.

Plus, in fairness, we sensed Jonnie's desperation. *Please take me to the American embassy:* We heard this subliminally in every gracious thing he said to us. We tasted it in every cup of tea he insisted on pouring, in every extra bowlful of soup he urged us to eat. He naively believed that by virtue of simply being American, Claire and I could open the golden door for him — and we just couldn't bring ourselves to tell him otherwise. Although we told each other we didn't want to break his heart, that it was cruel to extinguish his hope, the truth was, we were simply too callow to level with him. We were afraid that if Jonnie stopped seeing us as his ticket to freedom, he would refuse to take us to Dinghai or help us navigate China. As long as he believed we were his salvation, he would be ours.

Each time Jonnie smiled at me, though, with his pure, almost elated smile laden with admiration and trust — each time he began to sing in his sweet, earnest tenor, "I just called, to say, 'I love you'" — I felt increasingly guilty.

On our third morning in Shanghai, as we were walking across the bridge spanning Suzhou Creek, I said to him quietly, "Jonnie, do you understand that Claire and I — just because we're Americans — it doesn't mean we're special, okay? Back home, we're just students. Nobodies. We don't have any influence with the American embassy here. Do you understand?"

For a moment he paused. He blinked into the sunshine and smiled abstractly. Then he pressed his hands together, brought them to his lips, and nodded. "Yes, yes," he said agreeably. "We go to American embassy in Beijing together. We are friends, yes?"

Although both Claire and I were reluctant to tell Jonnie the truth, when I look back at the situation now, I wonder if on some level Jonnie wasn't equally reluctant to hear it. All three of us, I suspect, tacitly agreed to pretend.

————

The cabin was claustrophobic. Gunter and I opted to head out and explore while Jonnie lay back on his bunk listening to his tape recorder and Claire sat propped on her sleeping bag, writing intently in her journal.

On our fourth afternoon in Shanghai, she'd turned to me with great solemnity. "Listen. I think it's only fair that I tell you. I've got to do something that's going to require me to go off on my own during the days."

We were sitting on a bench in Renmin Square. "Excuse me?" I said. Something in her tone made my heart lurch.

"I'm working on a world curriculum," she said distantly, twisting her watch around on her wrist. "A compendium of insights on all the nations we're visiting. I have to profile their cultures, their histories, their outlooks. Eventually it will be adapted for grade schools, high schools, universities, and think tanks in Washington. It'll be a prototype—you know, a sort of Proustian examination of the world today? But it'll be practical, too. Kids like Cynthia's boys, whose parents can't take them to China and India, they'll be able to access it like a database."

She squinted across the park, a steely look on her face, and fingered the gold horseshoe charm at her throat. In the shadowy light, her skin looked almost lavender. "It's something I've just got to do," she said. "It's crucial. One day it might become a component of our national security."

Create a world curriculum? A Proustian examination? National security?

To someone else, this undoubtedly would have sounded bizarre, disturbingly grandiose. But Claire and I had gone to Brown. Our classmates had talked this way all the time. The university practiced a sort of free-range intellectualism; students were routinely encouraged to design our own majors, create our own courses. I had friends who crafted independent study programs with names like "Ethno-Music-Semiology" in which they traveled to the Australian outback to play the didgeridoo for a year, then wrote a thesis about the meta-language of aboriginal music as deconstructed through psychoanalysis. If you were brilliant enough, creative enough, and inquisitive enough, the thinking at Brown went, then you should boldly forge your own academic path — no matter how crackpot or pompous it sounded.

Which is exactly what I assumed Claire was doing now. China was making her feel stupid and irrelevant, so she was going to embark on a research project that would elevate her beyond mere tourist status and restore her sense of dominion. When she announced her "world curriculum," all I'd felt was a niggling prick of envy. Why hadn't I been so clever?

"Cool. Can I help with the research?" I said. "We could do it together."

She frowned, her pale brow furrowing. "I'm sorry, but with the contacts I have to make—" Her voice trailed off. "Listen, please don't ask me to explain. This is just something I have to do by myself, okay?"

She patted the cover of her notebook into the side pocket of her leather saddlebag and stood up. "I'll meet you back at the hotel."

"What? You're going now?"

"I promise if I find out any really useful information, I'll share it with you."

"But wait? Where—"

Claire fixed her gaze on me. Her blue eyes appeared glacial. "Susie, please. I just need a little space to operate on my own, okay? Don't make this difficult."

I sat back down on the bench heavily. "Oh. I'm sorry. I get it." I tried not to betray my hurt. Before we'd left the States, we'd agreed that if we ever needed a little space apart, we should never be afraid to ask for it. It was unrealistic to expect we could spend every single moment of every day together for an entire year.

Still, as I watched Claire saunter off through Renmin Square with her assured, athletic gait, her leather bag slung across her back like weaponry, her gold head bobbing with purpose, I felt a sting of rejection. We'd been in Shanghai barely four full days, yet already she needed to distance herself from me. With all my bleeding, cowering, and melodrama back in Hong Kong, I suspected I'd already exhausted her.

Only after she was gone did I realize that she hadn't told me where she was going, whom she was meeting, or even when she'd be back.

———

Trevor Fisk was a sailor from a small town near Perth. He had the wispy goatee of a young pirate and slate-blue eyes that pillaged everything they looked at. His shoulders were pinioned with muscle. He was so swaggering and lascivious, he was practically feral. So of course, I was instantly attracted to him.

I slammed into him before I even saw him. After Claire abandoned me in the park, I'd headed back to the Pujiang. Rounding the corner in the lobby, I'd collided with him by the elevators.

"Oi, watch it, girlie. Those are some of my best body parts you're charging over," he laughed, grabbing my elbow.

Girlie. Only the Aussies could get away with that one.

Meeting like this could've been a groaning cliché — except that as soon as he introduced himself, Trevor began showing off his tattoos to me as if they were art installations in a gallery. This was still a good decade before tattoos became the trendy accessory for every high school kid in Dayton and Scarsdale; in 1986 they were still, for the most part, the markings of an outlaw.

"This here's Leila," he said, rolling up his right sleeve to show me a teal-colored, topless Polynesian woman with a bowl of fruit on her head. "Got her in Fiji. And this one here" — he turned and flexed his left triceps — "is Sofia. Got her in Bangkok." Sofia the mermaid (also big-breasted, topless) gracefully swam up along his arm toward his shoulder.

"How very unsexist of you," I said drily.

"Oi." He grinned, rubbing his biceps with mock defensiveness. "It gets lonely out at sea. This way I always got me girls to talk to. But wait," he said exuberantly. "You haven't seen the pièce de résistance yet."

Undoing his pants with lightning speed, he pulled down his underwear and mooned me right there in the lobby. "Check it out." Following the curvature of his right buttock was the name *Trevor* in elaborate curlicue script that looped off after the last *r*, culminating in a little smiling black-and-yellow bumblebee.

It happened so quickly, I didn't have time to register anything close to shock. All I could think to say was "You got your own name tattooed on your ass?"

"Oi. Could've been worse," he laughed, yanking up his pants. "Could've had someone else's name put there. Or could've had my own name misspelled."

"I'm sorry, but can I ask you something?" I rubbed my temples, trying to understand the turn the afternoon had taken. "Why on earth would you do that?"

Trevor laughed again, a deep, happy, lecherous laugh. "Ah, who the fuck knows? I was drunker than shit. Somewhere in the Philippines, one of me mates said to me, 'Trevor, you are so drunk right now, I bet you wouldn't remember your own fuckin' name if it was tattooed on your ass.' And so I thought *Why not?* Bet him five bucks. And from what he tells me, I won, too! Of course," he suddenly turned pensive, "I suppose if I'd been really smart, I would've had them tattoo it on backwards, so that way, when I looked in the mirror —"

"Okay," I held up my hand. "Getting the picture."

Sidling up to me, he snaked his arm protectively around my shoulder. His skin was warm and smelled of cloves. I could feel his biceps pressing against me, the tautness of his abdomen. "So how 'bout it, girlie?" he gave me a squeeze. "You've seen me good, me bad, and me ugly. Think you can handle me taking you out to dinner?"

———

Trevor had been in Shanghai long enough to learn to say, "Another Tsingtao, please," expertly in Mandarin. He took me to the Peace Hotel for dinner, then to a nightclub at the International Seamen's Club on the Bund that "officially" did not exist.

Stepping inside was nothing short of hallucinatory. In the center of an abandoned rococo ballroom was a huge table full of Sudanese men playing bongo drums accompanied by a lone Belgian accordionist. Backpackers, black marketeers, aid workers, entrepreneurs undulated to the beat, clinked bottles, and bellowed out rounds of increasingly incoherent toasts. The din was phenomenal.

Trevor knew everyone. He was like the mayor of the nightclub. Leading me through the crowd, he introduced me to an Austrian woman dancing sinuously with a Senegalese man; to a half-Canadian, half-Indian man who called himself Tai and shouted over the music that he worked in computers; to a stunning Icelandic blonde who eyed me coolly and blew smoke rings over Trevor's head; to a robotic-looking, square-headed German who said, "I am German. I am psychotic," over and over while gulping beer; and to two highly amused Swedes, who, upon hearing I was American, felt compelled to launch into their own imitation of the Swedish chef from *The Muppet Show*.

In the midst of all this, an elderly, rotund Chinese man went around hugging everyone and dancing in an artful, angular manner that reminded me of Kabuki. I had spent my teenage years in New York drinking illegally at Studio 54 and Danceteria, yet nothing came remotely close to this. It was *Star Wars* meets the UN.

Trevor and I danced and drank; danced and flirted; flirted and drank, shouting to each other at close range over the music. It turned out he was a Libra, too! *Oh my God! No wonder we're so instantly compatible! We're starmates! Let's celebrate our birthdays together on the Great Wall,* we cheered, collapsing into each other's arms. *Let's have another toast! To Libra, the scales!* until suddenly we looked around the International Seaman's Club and realized it was empty except for a lone busboy stacking the chairs, and that we'd been dancing together for at least twenty minutes without any actual music.

And then we were waltzing out on the landing and sitting on the cold stone steps of the Peace Hotel. It was after midnight.

Swashbucklers, explorers, those mythological Greeks: Our legends are misleading. Most people who travel overseas — ostensibly on a quest — are fleeing something, too. Captain Cook set out not only to chart the Pacific but also to escape provincial England. Huck Finn was sprinting from the Widow Douglas. And although back in 1986 it never occurred to me that Claire Van Houten could be on the run from anything, I knew on some level that I certainly was.

As we sat with our hands knitted, I found myself telling Trevor about the fault lines in my parents' marriage. About my mother's fierce mood swings. I told him how I'd watched my beloved little brother suffer and diminish from the tension—and about my father's secret phone call to me at college to say he was thinking about moving out.

"I mean, just how was I supposed to respond to that?" Without meaning to, I started to cry.

Trevor reached over and pressed the back of his hand to my cheek. Staring somberly out at the river, he told me haltingly about how stultifying his hometown had been—the drunken marinade of it, full of posturing and gossip and petty Saturday-night brutality—and how his father had cut out when he was six. "Bastard even took my model train collection. Pawned it for beer money.

"You and me, girlie." He smiled sadly. "We're not so different, are we?"

It was one o'clock in the morning. We stood up stiffly, brushed ourselves off, and slowly made our way back through the shadowed pathways of Huangpu Park toward the hotel. The city was so quiet, we could hear the tide licking the seawalls. Although the night had turned bittersweet, once we found ourselves on the Suzhou Creek Bridge, we started kissing.

And then suddenly we were kissing some more, and then we were sneaking into the women's dormitory back at the Pujiang, tiptoeing past the sprawled and sleeping women and stumbling giddily out onto the wrought-iron balcony overlooking the streets of Shanghai, and we were kissing and shushing each other drunkenly and covering our mouths with each other's hands to keep from making noise and then kissing some more, and then Trevor was kneeling down and lifting up the hem of my thin purple jersey tank dress, whispering "Just close your eyes now, girlie. Don't look." And as I felt the first wet flicker of his lips, I started to giggle again.

When I told Claire about it the next morning at breakfast, however, she failed to find it funny.

"Ew. You fooled around with that sleazy sailor guy from the men's dorm? The one with his name tattooed on his butt?"

I sat back. "How did you know about that?"

"When I came off the elevator yesterday morning, he was showing it to two German girls. In fact he was showing it to everybody. Watch out, Suze, okay? That guy is a nut job."

She looked at me with displeasure and drew in a breath. She scratched her neck. A patch below her left ear had grown raw and irritated. "Look, there's something else. Early this morning, Jonnie stopped by. You were still asleep. Anyway, he's already gone ahead and bought tickets for us to sail with him on the ferry to Dinghai. Tonight."

"What? Tonight?" I said. "But we never—"

"I know. But he already paid for the tickets. And he's even arranged for somebody with a car to bring us to the pier."

"Whoa," I said. "I don't know about this."

She sat up stiffly, her nostrils flared, her arms crossed. "What's not to know?"

Her sharpness took me aback. "I just thought we didn't want to be indebted to him," I said.

"And pass up a once-in-a-lifetime opportunity? I mean, I'm sorry, but how many of the other people here have gotten invited to someone's Chinese hometown?"

"I know. But, Claire, he thinks we're going to help him defect."

She looked at me with annoyance. "What's the problem? You don't want to leave your sailor now?"

"What? He's not my—"

"I thought you wanted to have great adventures, not just the usual—"

"I do, it's just—"

"But, I mean, if you'd rather stay here with some little fling instead of boldly venturing off the map, far be it from me to—"

"Claire, c'mon. Don't be ridiculous."

"Okay, then," she said in a tone that implied it wasn't okay at all. "We're going to Dinghai with Jonnie." She grabbed her shoulder bag and started to get up, then thought better of it and plunked back down.

"I'm sorry," she groaned. She stretched her arms out over the tabletop and dropped her head down on them, her hair falling over her face, her bracelets sliding down her wrists. "I'm being an asshole."

"Well, you're certainly not being fair."

"Oh, Suze." She turned her face toward me helplessly. "I'm just so tired. I feel all filthy and gross. I'm not sleeping well. Everyone's always watching us. There's never any quiet."

"Yeah. I know."

"And it *is* a once-in-a-lifetime opportunity, going home with Jonnie. I mean, we can't pass it up, can we? I promise we'll let him down gently. When the time is right, I'll think of something. I mean, we're young, we're bright—"

"And you can burp 'The Battle Hymn of the Republic,'" I conceded.

Claire gave me her most dazzling smile, her upper lip stretching above her teeth like a ribbon. "Think of the stories we'll be able to tell. It certainly beats smuggling wristwatches, no?"

I said that I supposed it did.

"I owe you." She stood up, flung her hair over her shoulders, and smiled at me indulgently. "Go. Take a few hours to say goodbye to your crazy tattooed love boy. I'll pack up our stuff and deal with the hotel."

Trevor, dressed in nothing but cutoff shorts, was sorting through a mountain of dirty laundry on top of his bed. "You're leaving me already?" he cried when I told him the news. "But you're my dream girl. And we've only just...Okay. Quick." He pulled me across the hall to the women's dormitory, which, unlike his, was empty.

Afterward he said, "Where will I find you again? Where are you going after this village?"

"Beijing." I traced the outline of his Leila tattoo with my finger. It was odd to be in the arms of a man whose arms were literally covered with other naked women; it felt like competition. I flashed on Tom, punished by the Chinese authorities for owning an old *Playboy*.

Trevor reached for my guidebook and pointed to a map of downtown Beijing. "October nineteenth, it's me birthday. We'll meet here, just outside the Forbidden City. Fourteen hundred hours. That's the time I was born."

I smirked. "Will you have a password, too?"

"I'm serious, girlie." He tossed aside the book and tucked a lock of my hair behind my ear. "We've got a date. We said we'd celebrate our birthdays together on the Great Wall of China. So? Let's do it. One of my mates says we can even sleep out there—"

"Oh, yeah. Right. Sleep out on the Great Wall."

Trevor gave a low, wicked laugh. "Oi. The Communists don't give a shit what we do. They're too busy policing their own."

"It's not the Chinese government I'm worried about." I wiggled my eyebrows.

"Aha! Just you wait, then." He laughed, nuzzling

my neck. "I'm going to take you all over Beijing. Do forbidden things to you in the Forbidden City, undress you in the Temple of Heaven . . ."

At the time it had all seemed so promising and possible. Of course we would meet up weeks later and find each other. Of course we would live out some epically tawdry romance. We were two Libras, charmed, seductive, and daring. We were up for anything. We were not so different after all.

———————

Yet now, standing alone by the railing on the outer deck of the ferry, I knew better. It had been a sweet, ephemeral moment, nothing more. Already it seemed very far away.

Around me, families huddled on straw matting they'd brought, their belongings piled against the bulwarks like barricades. Crates of live poultry. Bags of clicking crabs. Bundles of bok choy, newspaper, and clothing. As the ship chugged through darkness, I could hear the swishing against the hull, the leviathan throb of the engines. In the moonlight, the silhouette of the mountains on the shore looked like ripped black paper against the sky. I had no idea where we were heading. None of the maps had Dinghai on them.

I felt a shiver of ecstatic terror. Except for Trevor, not a single person in the entire world knew that I was on board a night ferry right now, plowing through the darkness in the East China Sea. Since our arrival in Shanghai, Claire and I hadn't been able to contact our families. I stared at the black water forlornly. In the end, I realized, *this* was all there ever really was: dark mountains, a turbulent sea. A boat hurtling through a vacuum toward an unknown port. The true condition of anyone once you stripped them of their loved ones, their culture, and their passions was just this: Loneliness. An incurable longing. Insecurity. And grief.

Suddenly I started to cry. I felt foolish, but then, who would hear me? Who would even care? I leaned against the railing, feeling pitiful and forsaken. I pulled out a Kleenex and blew my nose unglamorously.

In the distance, a man began singing. It took a moment for it to register. At first I was certain I was imagining it.

But from across the deck came the thin, fragile, unmistakable words:

Country roads, take me home,
To the place, I belong
West Virginia, Mountain Mama

John Denver? Who the hell was singing John Denver? A few yards to my left, a slim young Chinese man in a white button-down shirt and Mao pants was pressed against the railing. His head was thrown

back, his eyes closed, his small, tapered hands pressed
to his heart.

Take me home, country roads

"Country Roads" had been one of the preeminent
songs of my childhood. My whole family sang it in
the car when we drove up to Silver- Lake — a bunga-
low colony north of Manhattan where we went to flee
the heat every summer. It was a song of gilded late-
afternoon light shimmering on the lake, of walking
barefoot on dirt roads after a rainstorm, delighting in
the mud and the thrum of crickets from the marshes
near the handball court. It was the song of uncompli-
cated happiness, of a time when my family was at its
best — before my parents' marriage began shredding,
before my father began disappearing and my mother
began storming through our apartment slamming
drawers and screaming with frustration. It was the
song from when I was six years old and felt loved and
serene, when I never felt a yearning to be anywhere
else. Now, halfway around the world, a young Chinese man just happened to be singing it beside me in
the darkness aboard a ferry bound for a hidden recess
of the People's Republic of China.

I hear her voice,
in the morning hour she calls me
The radio reminds me of my home far away

He seemed strangely unfazed when I drew up beside him and began singing along. We sang as if it were the most natural duet in the world, as if it had been preordained, the two of us harmonizing without once glancing at each other, just gazing straight ahead at the sea in tandem.

When we finished the last verse, however, we turned and shook each other's hand. *"Nee how,"* I gushed. "Oh my God. Do you know what that song means to me? I spent my whole childhood singing it."

The young man smiled at me glassily. I realized he had no idea what I was saying. He didn't speak a word of English.

How the hell had he learned an American folk song? This was 1986. People were still listening to record albums on turntables. The Internet and MP3 files were more than a decade away. MTV was an American novelty. There was no independent television in China, no pop radio, no Western movies, and in some places, no electricity. And yet—John Denver?

Gesturing, I managed to persuade the young man to come with me to find Gunter.

"Gunter, this man was singing a song from my childhood. Please," I begged when we'd found him. "Ask him how he learned it."

Gunter translated. The young man's name was

Wen. "Wen is saying that he has learned this song a long time ago from his English instructor. But he is saying that his instructor only teaches him the song phonetically. He says he does not know the meaning of the words. He is asking to you to explain them, please."

I had Gunter tell Wen that "Country Roads" is about a man who is far from his mountain home in West Virginia. Everywhere he goes, he misses it and hears its beauty calling to him. He yearns for the country roads to carry him back there.

When Gunter finished, Wen looked at both of us sadly. He spoke at length to Gunter.

"He is saying he is understanding the song very well," Gunter relayed. "He is saying in China, many people are being made to work very far away from their homes. He is saying that many people in the world are missing this West Virginia."

The three of us were quiet for a moment. Some things needed no translation at all.

———

After Wen departed, Gunter said, "I have also met a singer on the ship. I invite him to sing for us, yah?"

A small, smiling, middle-aged man in a blue Mao uniform arrived at our cabin. When Jonnie saw him, he leapt up from his bunk, flabbergasted. It turned out Gunter had befriended a famous Chinese opera star. Yet the star shook our hands as if we were the celebrities.

"He says you are very special guests. That he never meet foreigners on boat like this before, only overseas, when he give concert in Europe," Jonnie translated. "He will now give special concert for you."

Gripping the side of one of the metal bunks, the man drew himself up and positioned himself with balletic precision, placing one foot perpendicular to the other, puffing out his chest and tucking his right hand theatrically into his jacket, as if emulating Napoléon. Then, he began to sing.

In Shanghai, Claire and I had gotten tickets for the opera through CITS one night. Chinese opera, we'd discovered, was a very big deal. Troupes performed in towns and villages across the provinces, so that the Chinese grew up knowing classic librettos the way we Americans grew up conversant in movies, cartoons, and sitcoms. In China, a nation with hundreds of regional dialects, opera was a lingua franca.

The opera that Claire and I had seen was about a concubine in love with the emperor. Since there was no English translation, all we could glean from the histrionics on stage was that the emperor forsook the concubine and she committed suicide.

As an overall cultural experience, it was illuminating (the Chinese ate and talked throughout the performance). But the music itself was excruciating. It was simply beyond the range of Western aural comprehension — atonal, shrill, nerve splitting.

As the opera singer in our cabin arranged himself before us, I steeled myself. But when he opened his mouth, the elegiac notes of "Ave Maria" rose over the bunks and hung in the air like nebulae. Above the chickens squawking, the unremitting prattle of the PA, and the guttural *haaatchhh*ing of people spitting in the corridor, his exquisite tenor sounded even more incongruous than John Denver.

Ave Maria.

Jonnie, Gunter, Claire, and I stood mesmerized, almost unwilling to breathe for fear of interrupting him. When he finished, we applauded wildly, Claire and I woo-hooing in that barnyard way Americans do. The man beamed. Inhaling, he launched into a weepingly beautiful rendition of Puccini's "Nessun Dorma."

He must have sung at least three other arias, each one more unearthly than the next, until sheer fatigue forced him to stop for a sip of tea from Jonnie's thermos. Claire and I exchanged looks of gleeful disbelief: Not only were we sailing to a town no Westerner had ever visited before, but we'd just had a private concert performed for us by the Communist equivalent of Luciano Pavarotti.

"Please," we begged Jonnie, "ask him what we can do to thank him."

The opera singer removed his cap, thought for a minute, then whispered bashfully.

Jonnie grinned. "He says that when he was in Europe, he saw an American performer on an American TV show. He says that he would like you to teach him to dance like this person you call Michael Jackson."

"Michael Jackson?" I laughed. "Are you kidding?"

Claire riffled through the cassette tapes in her backpack, held one up triumphantly, and slipped it into Jonnie's little tape recorder. "Oh, this is going to be good," she said. "Okay, Zsa Zsa." She turned to me. "This one's all yours. Teach Pavarotti here to shake his booty."

What can I say? I can dance like Michael Jackson about as well as I can sing like Aretha Franklin. But spending my adolescence running around Studio 54 in my underwear had its benefits. Shamelessly I took the Chinese opera singer by the hand. In the narrow confines between the bunks, I got him shimmying with me to the Jackson Five's "I Want You Back," gyrating to Prince's "1999," and bumping and grinding our way through "Rock Me Amadeus." We waved our hands in the air to "The Roof Is On Fire" and did the bump to "Superfreak." Disturbingly, the opera singer had more energy than I did. By the end, he was practically improvising a moon walk to the A-Ha song "Take on Me."

Finally the tape was over and we were both breathless. The opera singer bowed.

"*Shay shay nee*," I replied, attempting a curtsy.

"He says he will always remember this night," Jonnie translated. "He is saying for once he has danced like an American."

After the singer departed, the steady commentary over the PA system was replaced with a low, crackly patter of Chinese music. Despite the lights being left on mercilessly and our bunkmates' incessant cigarette smoking, Jonnie and Gunter fell asleep folded into their bunks like origami. The cabin took on a strangely subterranean feel. Claire propped herself up on her elbows and whispered from the adjacent bunk, "Okay now, you see? *This* is what I had in mind. *This* is what we came here for. Am I right?"

"Uh-huh," I whispered, inhaling the cold air through the porthole, the salty chowder of the sea. "Tonight was absolutely amazing. Thank you, my friend. Thank you for getting my sorry ass over here."

"Look at us," Claire said with amazement. "Can you believe where we are? I mean, seriously, Suze. You and me. We're really doing it. We're conquering the fucking world."

The next morning we disembarked groggily onto a clumsy wooden pier in Dinghai. We found ourselves miles from anywhere, in a muddy, hut-lined alley-

Susan Jane Gilman

way. There was no sign of the young man who'd sung "Country Roads" with me. Nor was there any sign of the opera star. But at Dinghai's one Overseas Chinese Hotel, where we checked in ten minutes later, the military police were already waiting for us.

六

Chapter 6

Dinghai

WHEN JONNIE HAD described his hometown to us, he'd used the word *village*. He might have used this word because his English was limited. He might have used it because his family's home itself was on a remote hillside shrouded in fog. But as we quickly discovered, the "village" of Dinghai actually had a population of 830,000 people. What's more, it was home to a large, high-security Chinese military installation and an even larger, higher-security hydro-electric facility. It had not appeared on any published Western map for a reason. And for this reason it was not on the PRC's official list of approved backpacking destinations. No American apparently had ever been allowed to set foot in Dinghai before.

Which is why, I suppose, the Chinese military police were extremely curious to know what Claire and I were doing there that morning in our wine-dark lip gloss, arriving merrily at the region's one Overseas Chinese Hotel without an alien travel permit, official Communist Party invitation, or approved CITS government escort, yet loaded down with backpacks that, when searched, revealed a great cache of phrase books, maps, cameras, film, batteries, cassette tapes, water purifiers, binoculars, Swiss Army knives, flashlights, and notebooks.

No sooner had we checked into our room than an official from the Bureau of Foreign Affairs appeared on our doorstep. How he'd located us so quickly was a mystery. In 1986, both electricity and telephone service were in short supply around China. Whole cities appeared to be lit by a single forty-watt lightbulb, and the only telephones available to most people were public pay phones housed in corner stores or post offices. Our own hotel room, ostensibly the fanciest in all of Dinghai, had a bulbous plastic telephone with fraying wires; the only illumination came from an anemic fluorescent doughnut bolted to the ceiling. But somehow—without benefit of cameras, computers, telecommunications, or searchlights—the Chinese government had tracked us down within ten minutes of our arrival.

The foreign affairs officer stood in our doorway dressed in full military regalia, epaulets bracketing his shoulders, his officer's cap emblazoned with the red-and-gold insignia of the Chinese army and tilted downward over his brow so that it eclipsed the upper half of his face.

"Hello," he said in Chinese as Jonnie translated. "Welcome to Dinghai. I need to ask you some questions, please." Then, as if to quash any imminent panic, he added awkwardly: "Do not be alarmed. I am your friend." This "friend" then marched into the center of our room and gestured commandingly at the twin beds. "Please," he instructed, "have a seat." Claire and I collected ourselves and sat down rigidly on the edge of one of the mattresses while Jonnie hovered nervously beside us. Not coincidentally, the military officer also seemed interested in him. Only Gunter, it turned out, had been excused from any questioning and was allowed to wander off through Dinghai unmolested; only Gunter, it turned out, had been canny enough to obtain an "all entry" alien travel permit back in Hong Kong using a letter from his Chinese language school in Bavaria.

The officer asked us to surrender our passports. He flipped through them almost casually. With his face half shadowed by his cap, it was impossible to gauge his reactions. "How long are you planning on staying in Dinghai?" he asked. As we answered, he wandered over to the low wooden banquette near the door, nonchalantly yanked open the zippers of our backpacks, and began sifting through their contents almost absentmindedly. He was standing behind us now, just beyond the range of our peripheral vision.

The *ttzzzzzppp* of pockets being opened, the pluck of snaps unsnapping, the crackle of Velcro being unpeeled, sounded discordantly musical. Overhead, the fluorescent light flickered berserkly. It made the room appear as if it were having convulsions. "What are your professions?" the officer asked.

Growing up, the only interaction I'd ever had with the police had been in kindergarten, when a local traffic cop came to teach us how to cross the street. But the NYPD in my neighborhood were generally viewed with suspicion and hostility: "pigs" who shoved black teenagers up against squad cars for no good reason, took kickbacks from drug dealers, and beat antiwar protestors with nightsticks. Now, confronted by a bona fide officer, I froze. It seemed like a trick question: What exactly were our professions? The only thing that came to mind was "unemployed backpackers," which I suspected was not any kind of answer you should ever give law enforcement.

Claire, however, straightened her posture, crossed one leg over the other, and gave a small toss of her head as if gearing up for a job interview. "We're scholars, Officer. From Brown University. Thank you for asking."

Her voice had the creamy, artificially sweet cadence of a beauty contestant. Back at school, she'd once mentioned she'd never gotten a speeding ticket even though she'd been pulled over three times in

Pawtucket. "It's no biggie," she'd said airily. "You just *talk*."

Like many of my classmates who'd been educated at exclusive prep schools, Claire seemed perfectly at ease with authority and had a reflexive talent for winning over her superiors with cleverness and charm. She seemed to approach people in positions of power not as entities to be thwarted, feared, or defied, but as equals to be reasoned with.

As we sat there in the anemic light of the Dinghai guest room, I watched her slip on her good breeding and pedigree like a camel hair coat. Twisting around to face the officer directly, she smiled at him winningly— her white teeth winking—then spoke to him as if he were an old, familiar friend. I had to admit, she had nerve. It was really something to see.

"Please understand. We've meant no disrespect or offense by coming here," she said, touching her hand to the milky hollow of her throat, her tone carameliz-ing. "As two scholars from one of America's top universities, we're just so eager to see as much of your beautiful country as we possibly can. And it is such an honor to be here, Officer. Really, it is. And we are so grateful to be welcomed here by you like this, to be shown such hospitality and concern."

As Jonnie translated, she unsnapped her wallet, pulled out her old Brown University ID card, and presented it to the officer like a diplomatic creden-tial. Taking my cue from her, I poked through my money belt to do the same. However, I'd left my old college ID back in New York, so I handed him my International Youth Hostel Association and Student Discount Travel cards instead, hoping he wouldn't be able to discern the difference. "You see, we come from a very elite academic institution in the United States of America," Claire pressed. "And it's our hope that our presence here will only bolster more goodwill and understanding between our two countries."

The officer nodded and looked at our ID cards. For a moment, he seemed prepared to acquiesce.

But then he gave a little grunt and took a step backward. He'd arrayed on the desktop many of our possessions: our fourteen different Berlitz phrase books for languages ranging from Cantonese to Urdu; our Michelin maps of various Southeast Asian countries; our cameras, film, and batteries; our hastily marked homemade cassette tapes; our Swiss Army knives; our electrical adapters; our flashlights and notebooks; our water purifier; Claire's miniature binoculars.

Something among them had caught his eye anew. He turned around and picked up Claire's canteen. It had belonged to her stepbrother Dominic, who'd purchased it years ago from a camping and military surplus store. It was still snapped in its original, khaki-colored canvas case with "Property of the U.S. Army" stenciled on it in fading black letters.

Until that moment, I'd assumed the officer's visit was mostly a formality, a bureaucratic ritual designed to impress and intimidate visitors. As he'd questioned us, I'd even started imagining how I was going to embellish this story later telling it to loved ones back home. It seemed obvious to me that Claire and I were innocents; what's more, we were U.S. citizens with valid American passports—golden tickets, I'd presumed. What could the Chinese really, possibly do to a couple of red-white-and-blue girls armed with nothing but backpacks and good intentions?

Yet seeing all of our travel gear displayed atop a cold metal desktop in the eerie half-light of Dinghai, it suddenly didn't look like innocuous crap to me anymore so much as it looked like incriminating evidence. *Property of the U.S. Army?* All those wires and documents? A twisty unease came over me as I began to see Claire and me not as the bright, lovable Americans we believed ourselves to be, but as Chinese eyes might view us instead. From their vantage point, we were two aliens half a world away from anyplace where we were supposed to be, who'd arrived in Dinghai with unconvincing student ID cards and what appeared to be a cache of rudimentary surveillance equipment. If this Chinese military officer thought we were guilty of espionage—well, I couldn't say I blamed him.

I glanced anxiously at Claire. "That's not a real U.S Army canteen, Officer," she said, straining to sound mollifying.

"It's just a decorative trademark they put on," I

interjected. "You know, a brand name, like Coca-Cola or McDonald's?"

Claire made a quick, decisive slicing gesture with the side of her hand as if to say either "shut up" or "decapitation."

The officer turned to us, set down the canteen, then presented us with another object he'd unearthed. "What is this?" he asked.

He held up Claire's waterproof Sony Sport Walkman encased in bright yellow plastic.

"That's for listening to music. See?"

Claire stood up hurriedly. Unfolding the headphones, she placed them gently around his chin and over his ears, then directed him to press the turquoise play button. I guess the volume had been set on 10 because a second later, the synthesized drum-machine riff from Dead or Alive's "You Spin Me Right Round, Baby" could be heard blaring through the headphones, and the officer winced and pulled them off.

He then picked up our two cameras, shook them, and opened the film compartments. "Did you know that foreigners taking photographs in Dinghai was strictly forbidden?" he asked.

The fact that Claire and I had somehow managed to break both cameras within a day of arriving suddenly seemed like a phenomenal stroke of luck.

While Jonnie translated, we proudly showed off the jammed shutter button on my Instamatic and the cracked plastic chassis of Claire's. "See? See?" we nattered. "They're broken! They don't work! We couldn't take any pictures even if we wanted to—which we don't!"

Then, in case we hadn't driven the point home clearly enough, Claire pantomimed sitting down on the cameras by accident. In her nervousness and desperation, she delivered quite a performance; it was practically an *opera*. She leapt up from the bed, rubbing her backside in distress, then faked crying, rubbing her eyes with her fists and pointing melodramatically at the broken equipment.

This must have convinced the officer that he was not dealing with two international military spies at all, but with a pair of world-class dimwits, because after that, he stood up, sighed, massaged the bridge of his nose, and wearily announced that we were free to stay—providing that Jonnie accepted responsibility for us as our officially sanctioned host.

"But if Chinese officials give you orders, remember, you must obey," he warned us. "You must follow all instructions, rules, and laws. You must respect all representatives of the People's Republic of China. And again, no pictures."

Claire and I nodded puppyishly. "Tell the officer that of course we will obey everything and cooperate fully," I said to Jonnie.

"Tell him that not only do we thank him," Claire added with a regal flick of her hair, "but that my father does as well. Tell them that my father is a very rich and very important businessman in America."

When she said this, I made a face.

"What?" she said defensively, touching her hand to the base of her throat again and fingering her gold chain. "It's true. I think they should know exactly who they're really dealing with."

Ignoring us, the officer walked over to our nightstand, picked up the clunky plastic telephone, and called someone. Then, inexplicably, he remained in our room, lingering wordlessly by the window with his hands clasped behind his back. Unsure of how to proceed, Jonnie and Claire and I remained frozen in our places, glancing furtively at him, then at each other.

The stark hotel room felt like a morgue. Its two twin beds were bandaged in white sheets and swaddled in thick, gauzy mosquito netting. Except for the metal desk, the metal chair, and a lone dented metal nightstand, the room was empty and bathed in jaundiced light. There was absolutely no sound in the hotel at all, either, except for the occasional *haatcch* of someone spitting in the street below and the rattle of the elevator shaft.

Finally there was a knock on the door. A second military officer arrived with two alien travel permits filled out for Claire and me, which were presented to us as if they were some sort of civic award.

After wishing us a pleasant visit, the two officers smiled, nodded, and left.

As soon as we heard their footsteps fading down the corridor, the three of us exhaled in unison like criminals who'd just barely pulled off a heist.

"Wow." I laughed nervously. "Talk about a welcome wagon."

"And they didn't even bring a Bundt cake," Claire said drily.

Jonnie stood up and wiped his hands on the thighs of his pants.

"Everything, it is okay now, yes?" He smiled anxiously, his eyes darting between Claire and me. "Everything is now official?"

Claire and I nodded. "I suppose," she said abstractly.

"Now I must go home to see my family. You stay here, yes?" said Jonnie. "You have very nice lunch here. Overseas Hotel have number one restaurant in Dinghai."

Claire frowned and crossed her arms. "Well, wait a minute. I thought we were going home with you," she said. "I mean, isn't that why we just went through all of this questioning? I'd much rather meet your family than hang around here all day."

"Jesus, Claire," I murmured. "The guy hasn't been home in seven years. Let him have some alone time."

"You want come home with me now?" Jonnie said.

Although he was smiling, I could see the distress bloom-
ing in his face, the calculations scrolling in his head.
"My mother, I tell her you coming *tomorrow*. Tomorrow
we make special feast. My brother, he take car back to
his company already. Now I walk home. Over one hour.
Special friends should not walk home over one hour."

"Jonnie, please, don't worry about it." I glared at
Claire. "We're actually *very* tired and would prefer to
stay here. Right, Claire?"

Claire shrugged noncommittally. When I shot
her a prompting look, she managed to fake a yawn.
"Sure," she said.

"Yes?" said Jonnie uneasily. "You do not mind?
You are comfortable?"

"Go see your mom, Jonnie," I said. "We're happy
to meet her tomorrow."

"Yes, yes, okay," Jonnie nodded, clasping his hands
together. "But if you want, maybe I still come back
for you later today, yes? This afternoon, I see if my
brother, if he can reserve car again, okay?"

"Whatever," Claire said with a little flutter of her
hand.

"Okay," he said, but he sounded unconvinced. Even
as I began to close the door behind him, he insisted
on poking his head back in and waving. "Okay, Miss
Crair?"

When he was finally gone, I scowled, but all Claire
did was smile at me fakely and curtsy. "There. He's
gone, and we're not. Better?"

She pushed back the mosquito netting around her bed, flopped down on it, and exhaled toward the ceiling. "I can't believe you'd rather stay here all day. We're in the middle of nowhere." She stretched, feline and indolent. "So. Who did you think was more annoying just now?" She settled a pillow beneath her head. "Jonnie or the cop?"

"You weren't nervous?" I said. "When he emptied our backpacks—"

"Please. We're Americans, for Chrissake. One call to my father or the U.S. embassy—" Suddenly she sat bolt upright. "Wait, let's not lay down," she said. "Let's go out."

"Out?" I motioned to the window. All there appeared to be outside were a few dilapidated yards and a jade-green mountain with a radio tower impaled on it. We had no map, no guidebook, nothing even scribbled in our journals to indicate where we were.

Claire picked up her silver Windbreaker and knotted the sleeves around her waist. Then she hoisted the strap of her shoulder bag over her head. "Let's just explore," she said. "Maybe I can do some research here. Make some contacts for the world curriculum. Grab the phrase books. I'm sorry, but there's just no way we're sticking around here all day, even if we're not going to Jonnie's. Let's face it." She smiled. "This place is about as interesting as a cryogenic freezer."

Back home, when Claire and I had first dreamed of venturing into uncharted territory, we'd somehow assumed that *uncharted* meant *exotic*—lush jungles dripping with vines; toucans; natives in feathers; and some sort of untouched Eden at the end of a dirt trail.

Certainly neither of us had imagined that uncharted territory might instead mean being stranded in a dusty industrial park on the outskirts of a Chinese military installation without any street signs or a road map.

Downstairs, the lobby of the Overseas Chinese Hotel was deserted and as spartan as our room. Certainly there were no little information racks by reception full of pamphlets for petting zoos, coal mining museums, miniature golf. Nor was there so much as a "You Are Here" sign tacked to a wall. From the rows of keys hanging behind the reception desk, it appeared that Claire, Gunter, and I were the only guests in the entire hotel.

Neither Claire nor I had the faintest idea where we were. When we'd left Shanghai the night before, the shoreline had been on our right, so we knew we'd sailed south—but just how far? That morning the boat had seemed to dock in some sort of estuary. Was Dinghai an island or on a delta close to the sea? We'd been too frazzled to take much notice of our surroundings. At the pier, we'd simply squeezed into the van Jonnie's brother had borrowed, then headed away from the dockland in a whirl of dust into what seemed like the countryside. At the time I'd been captivated by the surrounding mountains, majestic blue-green peaks, soaring and angular like those a child might draw, and by a grizzled man walking barefoot along the road, a crude wooden yoke across his shoulders with an enormous basket of cabbages suspended from each end.

Now when Claire and I walked outside the hotel, we saw that it was a desolate concrete high-rise built on a small hillock of asphalt flanked by a shuttered gas station and two cinder-block shells of half-constructed buildings. A driveway leading down from the hotel fed into a road lined with weeds and piles of gravel. Behind it were dilapidated stone houses and one ugly modern apartment complex. Small yards were crisscrossed with laundry lines. A rusted cement mixer sat abandoned in an empty field. In the distance were mountains. But there you had it. That was pretty much it.

The sky was overcast, so it was impossible to tell east from west, north from south. There was no way of telling where the road in front of the hotel led to, or where we were in relation to the rest of Dinghai. Jonnie had said that it took an hour to walk to his family's house, which meant that the town center was probably between three and four miles away. Our only option was to randomly pick a direction, just start walking, and hope to God we didn't get lost.

Claire looked at me. I looked at her. We stared out at the gritty, unappealing pavement. Despite traces of domestic life, there was absolutely no one around. The eerie silence was punctuated only by a strange intermittent crackle of static and high-pitched whistling that seemed to be coming from the transmission tower atop the mountain.

On the ferry from Shanghai, the lights and the loudspeakers had remained on all night. The elderly couple in our cabin had stayed up talking and chain-smoking. When Claire had hissed, "Could you please be quiet?" they'd only smiled and encouragingly offered us cigarettes. We'd ended up pushing open the rusty porthole as far as it would go, filling the minuscule cabin with frigid, pickle-scented air and the grinding sound of the engine. When Gunter began snoring, we gave up trying to sleep entirely. For the duration of the trip, we sat up shivering in our sleeping bags and listening to our Walkmans, ticking off the hours by watching the sky outside the porthole dissolve from black to indigo to amethyst.

Now my cough had sunk deeper into my chest, and Claire's hair hung lankly against her cheekbones. The prospect of blindly hiking along an asphalt road for an hour in the middle of nowhere seemed thoroughly unenticing.

"You know something," said Claire, pressing her

slender wrist to her forehead, "suddenly I'm feeling hungry and maybe a little tired."

"How about instead of exploring, we check out the number one restaurant in Dinghai, then go take a nap?" I suggested. "I promise I won't tell anyone if you won't."

If our brush with the Chinese military police was jarring, lunch at the Dinghai Overseas Chinese Hotel was simply bizarre. After we waited in an empty, curtained antechamber on the top floor for ten minutes, a silent young woman materialized and led Claire and me into an antiseptic dining room overlooking the mountains. Everything in the room was a glaring, retina-searing white: walls, floors, tables, chairs, linens, upholstery. It was as if someone had run a gargantuan roller of white reflective paint over the entire room. The effect was that of dining in a decontamination center. We were seated alone at a round white banquet table big enough to accommodate eight people. The place was utterly silent. Claire and I sat on our white chairs and waited.

And waited.

Both of us grew increasingly antsy, hungry, and quietly distressed, but what were we supposed to do? We had no idea where else we could possibly eat. Certainly we had no language skills.

After a while, Claire said sullenly, "Wow. This must be what purgatory's like."

I nodded glumly. "It's like *Waiting for Godot: The Restaurant.*"

Finally the waitress reappeared from behind a large, greenish white scrim. Without a word, she placed on the table a whole cooked silvery-brown fish on a bare white plate — then vanished. Claire and I looked down at the fish. Its head was still on and its eyes were still open, so it appeared to be looking back at us. When I studied it more closely, it seemed to have some kind of whiskers, a fringy fish mustache. We wondered if perhaps there wasn't something more to go with this fish: sauce, perhaps, or a bowl of rice? Surely, a utensil to help us cut it up? But the wait-ress never reappeared. We were left alone with only our white chopsticks and our white plates and a fish that looked so alive, we expected it to jerk and writhe when we poked at it.

Today I would've seen this fish for the gourmet extravagance that it undoubtedly was; what's more, I would've dug in happily and gratefully. But for four years at college, I had honed my juvenile palate almost exclusively on potato skins bathed in bacon bits, chocolate milk shakes, Jell-O shots, Kraft mac-aroni and cheese, Egg McMuffins, Domino's Pizza, Diet Pepsi, and low-fat frozen yogurt. My idea of exotic and adventurous eating was falafel. The fish, glimmering in a puddle of mottled brownish oil, was repulsive to me.

It was to Claire, too. Despite all her summers

spent sailing, she absolutely hated all seafood except shrimp cocktail and lobster Newburg. "Ew," she cried when she saw the fish. "I'm sorry, but I just cannot eat that."

When the waitress finally returned, Claire had the phrase book open and ready. "Please. *Ching*. Fried rice?" she said, tapping the appropriate translation page. "Or noodles? Fried noodles?"

The waitress looked at her uncomprehendingly, picked up the plate of untouched fish, and left. A moment later, she returned with a different broiled, whole fish, this one metallic blue and shaped like a flattened enema bag. "No," Claire cried. But the woman simply set it before us and left. When she returned twenty minutes later, Claire said, "Please. We're so hungry, and we hate fish. Please?" She rubbed her stomach with exaggeration, then mimed eating from a bowl with chopsticks. "Rice? Noodles? Even, *ching*, chicken?"

What followed next can perhaps only be described as a fish beauty pageant. Our waitress determinedly brought out and set before us one fish dish after another. A long plate of small fried bronze-colored fishes stacked up like cordwood. A silver, trout-like fish in a pool of scalliony sauce. A pile of enormous prawns curled up like fetuses in their shells with their eyes and antennas still intact. Bowls of fish soup with what appeared to be fish eyes floating in oily broth. Eventually, seized by hunger and the grim realization that all there was to eat was fish—period—Claire and I tried to make the most of it. I skinned and ate some of the trout, gulped down the fried fishes with tea, and devoured most of the prawns. Claire ate a prawn or two and a few spoonfuls of soup before choking and setting down her utensils in tears. "Oh, God. I'm sorry, but I just can't eat this," she said, gagging.

Only then did the waitress arrive with two bowls full of steamed white rice. We accepted them gratefully, intoning *Shay shay nee* over and over again. (No one had explained to us yet that in China, steamed white rice was considered not only a luxury, but dessert.) We sat in the blindingly white room and shoveled rice into our mouths with sloppy, lupine fervor in total silence.

Back in our room, Claire locked herself in the bathroom with the water running, then staggered out looking sweaty and flushed. She announced. "I really need to sleep now." Sprawling out on her bed, she fell instantly into a deep, drooly slumber with her hiking boots still on, her nautical watch ticking away loudly on her wrist. While she slept, I puttered about the room. I felt too unmoored to nap. The loneliness and isolation I felt were like being in free fall. Just where on earth were we?

I stared out the window at the few meager back-yards and the one ugly high-rise fronting the mountains. I considered taking a shower to relax, but only an icy dribble sputtered out of the faucet. I sat back down on my bed and stared out the window again. I guess I hoped that if I stared at the mountains and overcast sky long enough, I'd suddenly have some sort of epiphany and know where I was.

It occurred to me that I'd never really seen mountains before—only the Adirondacks in upstate New York, which looked much more like foothills. In fact the whole morning in Dinghai had been full of firsts. My first time truly not knowing where I was. My first brush with the police. My first time eating fish that had not been battered, deep-fried, and premolded into little fingers. I had always assumed that firsts would feel triumphant—didn't parents spend hours documenting the firsts of their newborns?—but somehow here it felt like I was inching farther and farther toward a precipice, away from everything normal and familiar. I didn't feel accomplished or enriched at all, only profoundly anxious. There seemed to be only the thinnest veneer of common reference points here, of recognizably modern civilization—a small dented car, an old telephone, a squeaky elevator—beneath which nothing functioned as we knew it, beneath which was total, seething chaos, an abyss of the unknown.

Eventually I climbed underneath the mosquito netting of my bed and tried to read.

Back in college, I'd spent an inordinate amount of time participating in multicultural awareness dialogues. The goal of these seemed to be to impress upon all of us a terrific contradiction, namely, that every ethnic group had its own distinct culture—that needed to be celebrated and respected—but that in no way should ever be used to stereotype them.

As a Jew, I'd understood this paradox innately. At college, my sensibilities had often seemed strangely out-of-synch with those of my blue-blooded classmates; our differences lay dormant beneath the surface until something caused them to flare up like a muscle spasm. Often I sensed it when they exclaimed, "You're so *funny*" with a mixture of admiration, surprise, and discomfort on their faces, as if humor was a strange food that they almost never ate but enjoyed—provided it was served in small, elegant doses. My way of talking, my unvarnished passion, my offense at the "Campus Crusade for Christ" banner draped across the green—all of this was like a pair of hands clapping off-beat in a room full of applause.

But ironically, while I longed for my classmates to understand my perspective, I was also loath for them to view me as "a Jew"—or to assume that everyone I came from kept kosher and walked around in a yarmulke. I didn't want to be reduced to any sort of caricature. "Stereotypes are not only wrong and racist, but intellectually lazy," I once declared.

Yet lying beneath a mosquito net in a deserted hotel in an uncharted backwater in the People's Republic of China, in a place that I literally could not locate on a map in a culture that I could not even begin to comprehend — I realized that everything I'd known up to that point about China was, basically, a gross cultural stereotype. What's more, I realized that I would welcome still more of these gross cultural stereotypes — or pre-masticated facts, or massive generalizations — or anything, really, that would at least give me a clue about where I was and whom I was dealing with.

Embarrassingly, until that moment, everything that I knew about China could be boiled down to a single list: Confucius, gunpowder, printing press, noodles, dynasties, concubines, foot-binding, opium, Communists, tai chi, acupuncture, and pandas. And oh yes, the Gang of Four, which I knew first not as the instigators of the Cultural Revolution, but as my freshman roommate's favorite punk rock band. A few dates, names, and facts also floated around in my head from high school history class. I knew, for example, that the Empress Dowager had once been a concubine with fingernails like curly fries. There was the Boxer Rebellion, Chiang Kai-shek, the Great Leap forward. But there you had it. That was pretty much it.

Now that Claire and I were actually in Asia, I was determined to spackle these holes in my education. Mostly, I did this by reading the background chapters in our guidebook.

Lying on my bed in Dinghai, I skimmed a few

paragraphs about Chinese culture, then promptly fell asleep.

I awoke suddenly to a tightening around my left forearm. Someone was shaking me. Claire loomed above me tearfully, dressed only in her sports bra and the pair of Parker's boxer shorts she slept in. Her face was flushed; her brow sparkled with sweat.

"Susie, you've got to help me. I'm burning up."

I disentangled myself from the mosquito netting, and felt for my glasses. Claire's normally pale skin was now an angry reddish pink; it made her blond hair, her delicate eyebrows, and her lashes appear blanched by comparison. She looked like an albino aflame. I pressed the back of my hand to her forehead. It was scalding.

"Oh God. I'm so sick," Claire gasped, keening over on my mattress. "I had to crawl across the floor just to get to your bed. I think it's from the fish." Her hair was damp with sweat; her boxer shorts were matted to her lower back. Her chest heaved in what were either breaths or sobs.

Scrambling up, I rummaged through my backpack for the first aid kit. "Did you take any medicine?" I tried to sound as calm as possible.

"Uuuh-huuhh," came a groan. "I took two Tylenol. They've just made me more nauseous. The whole room. It's spinning."

I looked around the hotel room as if the walls and the few bits of furniture might suddenly, magically present some solution. Then I remembered that

I had one small bottle of club soda left in my day pack. Claire and I had purchased three apiece from a vendor in Shanghai before boarding the ferry. It had been an ordeal to get him to part with the glass deposit bottles.

Pulling out my Swiss Army knife, I uncapped the soda and handed it to Claire. At first she refused it with a "Nnuuugghh," but then took one sip, then another, then downed the whole bottle in a swallow. "Oh, God," she cried, falling back on the bed.

Despite all we'd packed, neither of us had brought a thermometer, our thinking being that we might break it by accident and get mercury all over our backpacks.

"Water," Claire said. "Can you please find me some more? Or some soda? Anything cold?"

Of course we'd packed a water purifier and charcoal tablets, but we hadn't bothered reading the instructions or testing it out yet; in my panic, I knew that this was not the time to start. If I screwed up, I'd only make Claire sicker. In the bathroom, I pressed a towel beneath the frigid dribble of water and made a compress.

Claire screamed when I draped it across her forehead. "Oh, God, no! I'm freezing!" Grabbing her sleeping bag off her bed, she wrapped it tightly around herself. "Oohh," she moaned, shivering so hard she seemed to be seizing. "So cold. Oh, Susie, I think—I think I need a doctor."

Grabbing the phrase book, I hurried across the hallway and pounded on Gunter's door. But there was no
answer; I imagined him lurching through the center of
Dinghai with his backpack and a dopey grin, clutching a bagful of hot dumplings. "Big dumb Kraut," I
swore under my breath. On the way downstairs in the
elevator, I felt my heart thump in my rib cage. *Please,*
I thought, *let somebody be manning the reception desk.
And please let them speak a modicum of English.*

A woman was in fact sitting behind the front
counter, yet when I tried to communicate with her,
she stared at me with the cool impassivity of a toll-
booth clerk. Not only didn't she understand English,
but any attempt I made to pronounce the Mandarin words in my phrase book appeared to irritate her.
Apparently, "Call a doctor" was *Ching jyao ee-sherng
gwor-lai.* In my panic, I had absolutely no idea how to
pronounce this; even the phonetics seemed like gibberish. *Ching, ching!* I cried, pointing dementedly at
the printed phrase. The woman glanced at the page
and shrugged.

I tried another one: "My friend is sick." *Wor-der
perng-yo sherng-bing*...oh, fuck me. "Orange juice?"
I attempted. *Cherng-jir?* This the woman seemed
to vaguely understand. Sighing, she said something
back—a question of some sort. Of course I couldn't
understand. As I stammered, she turned away and
resumed doing her paperwork.

Cherng-jir, I cried again. *Ching! Shay shay!* I

mimicked someone drinking. *Parlez-vous français?* I pleaded. I pantomimed coughing, sneezing, vomiting. Surely there had to be some cross-cultural frame of reference, some international language for *illness* and *doctor.* When the woman glanced over at me indifferently, I burst into tears.

I guess this must have been the international language I'd been looking for, because finally, wearily, she set down her abacus and gestured for me to wait. She disappeared into the back room and returned with another woman, this one wearing an ill-fitting white polyester blouse that I assumed was meant to distinguish her as the manager.

No sooner had I wiped my eyes on my sleeve, reopened the phrase book, and attempted to pronounce "Please call a doctor," than the manager's eyes glazed over, too. Whatever I was saying clearly wasn't getting through to her either. I thought of Claire upstairs, going into convulsions. From there, it wasn't hard to imagine her slipping into a coma or dying of dehydration. I had no transportation and no way of contacting Jonnie (his family, like most Chinese families, did not have a telephone). And then, of course, I didn't even know where I was. *"Please,"* I cried.

Just then, someone said *"Nee how"* with a distinctive German accent.

Gunter!

He had lumbered into the lobby carrying what looked like a fistful of twigs.

"Look, tsis man I meet on zee road, he give me something from which you can be making tsee tea," he said, holding up the cluster of leaves proudly.

"Gunter," I cried. "Oh, thank God you're here. Gunter, Claire's very sick. Can you ask the hotel staff in Mandarin to please to call her a doctor and bring her some orange juice or some soda water or something?"

Gunter looked at me, then at the receptionist and hotel manager, who were eyeing him with horrified fascination. In the modest scale of the lobby, he looked like the King Kong of China.

With his free hand, Gunter stroked his beard contemplatively. "Yah, I can try, but they do not understand Mandarin."

"They don't speak Mandarin?"

Gunter shook his head. "The people of Dinghai, they are speaking the special dialect. All over China, most people are speaking only the dialect. They are not understanding the Mandarin, only maybe reading it."

"So you're telling me my phrase book is useless? That not even you or Jonnie can communicate with them?"

"Jonnie, he is speaking the dialect here in Dinghai, but me?" Gunter shrugged and held open his broad palm. "I try, but I am not thinking anyone will be understanding."

I pressed my hands together. "Please, Gunter," I begged.

Gunter cleared his throat and said something to the two women. They said something back. Gunter tried again. This time the women giggled. Everyone seemed to be shaking their heads helplessly in a volley of incomprehension. Finally the manager disappeared and returned with another hotel worker. He apparently was able to grasp what Gunter was saying just enough to understand that we needed orange juice. Somehow a bicycle was procured and a young man in an oversize Mao uniform was prevailed upon to pedal into Dinghai to buy several bottles. The gist that there might be a medical emergency was starting to sink in.

Finally the hotel worker who spoke a little Mandarin managed to locate a former teacher in the area who spoke a little English. The woman was elderly and slightly stooped, with a proud, dust-streaked face and wild gray hair coming lose from its chignon. In her soil-stained Mao uniform, she appeared to have been brought in directly from the fields. When she saw me, she smiled and said, "Hello. How do you do?" with a triumphant finality that suggested that these five words were her entire repertoire of English.

Still, I made an attempt. "My friend is very sick."

The woman smiled at me with almost grandmotherly concern. "Yes. How do you do?" she said again.

"My friend," I said. "Sick." I pantomimed coughing and vomiting again.

The woman smiled. "Yes. How do you do?"

"We need a doctor," I said despairingly.

"Doctor?" the woman repeated.

I nodded. "Doctor," I said, then coughed for real.

"Doctor," the woman said again. Suddenly she pressed her fingertips gently to my forehead, then reached for my wrist and acted as if she were taking my pulse. "Doctor, yes?" she said encouragingly.

"Yes!" I cried. "Doctor!"

The woman turned to the receptionist and hotel manager and said something to them. Reaching under the counter, the manager pulled out a rice paper notebook and consulted it for a few minutes. She lifted the telephone receiver and dialed.

When I arrived back upstairs, Claire was sleeping, curled tightly under her puffy down sleeping bag. The curtains had been drawn, and the room felt overheated and bacterial, as if it had absorbed her fever and was beginning to sweat itself. The hotel manager's brother had returned from Dinghai clutching five dusty bottles of warm orange soda and a paper envelope full of small green tangerines. I tiptoed around in semi-darkness looking for Claire's collapsible travel cup and my Swiss Army knife. Since the military officer had rummaged through our belongings, nothing was where it was supposed to be, and everything stank of my peppermint castile soap, which had leaked all over my toiletry bag. As I stumbled around, I heard a wan "ahem" followed by a small croak. "I'm not asleep."

I carried the cup and orange soda over to the nightstand, then sat down on the bed beside her. "How are you feeling?" I asked. Claire rolled over and pressed her forearm to her forehead. Her face was still damp, her eyes glassy.

"Uhh," she swallowed, then closed her eyes again. "Not great," she whispered hoarsely.

I reached over and touched her brow, which was now clammy and cadaverously cool, then stroked her sweat-drenched hair. "A doctor should be coming," I said. "I got you some orange soda. It's all they had. You want to sit up and drink a little?"

Claire just lay there breathing, letting me stroke her hair. She whispered almost inaudibly, "Oh, that feels so nice."

"My mother always used to do this to me when I was sick," I said gently, my voice lulled to the rhythm of my hand. "You know . . . just sit beside me . . . stroke my hair . . . holding my hand if I got the chills."

After a moment Claire said softly, "I wish I'd had my mother. I wish I had her back." She looked away toward the wall. "I wish I had her here now." Slowly her face crumpled, and she started to cry. "Oh, Susie," she sobbed.

Her sobs were heartbreaking; hearing them made me feel like crying myself. What were we doing here?

Oh, God. Look at us. I blinked up at the ceiling and swallowed.

"Hey, it's okay, it's okay," I lied, still stroking her hair.

At that moment, there was a knocking. An officious iron-haired woman with spectacles and a canvas jacket strode into our room, accompanied by the elderly former English teacher. "Hello," the teacher said again. "How do you do?" She pointed to the woman in the canvas jacket, who was carrying a cumbersome leather satchel. "Doctor."

Claire visibly relaxed. She sniffled, rubbed her eyes, and struggled to sit up in the bed. *"Nee how,"* she said weakly.

The doctor acknowledged her stiffly. Picking up Claire's damp wrist, she took her pulse. She felt the glands on either side of Claire's neck. She pressed the back of her palm to Claire's forehead. She shook her head and said something to the teacher.

"Hot," said the teacher.

Claire nodded, rubbed her stomach with exaggerated motions, then mimed throwing up and shivering. The doctor pointed to the bottle of Tylenol on the nightstand questioningly. "Yes, yes," we both said.

"Two," I said, holding up my fingers in what I hoped was the Chinese counting style. It occurred to me that if dialects were regional, maybe hand gestures were, too. What if here in Dinghai the gesture for two really meant seven?

Reaching into her satchel, the doctor pulled out a thermometer. She tucked it under Claire's armpit and stood there timing it with her watch. From outside came another spitting sound, then someone yelling sharply across the yard. I looked at Claire and smiled weakly; she nodded at me with relief. We were in the hands of a professional now.

The doctor plucked out the thermometer and showed it to us.

It read 40.1.

"What's 40.1?" I asked.

Claire groaned. "It's Celsius. What's that in terms of Fahrenheit?"

Goddamned President Nixon. Back when I was in kindergarten, his presidential commission had promised us that America would go metric by the time we were in high school. Now I tilted the thermometer and held it up to the light to see if maybe it had the Fahrenheit gradations on the other side—which, of course, it didn't.

Throughout my schooling, I'd been a stellar math student. I loved the puzzle, the symmetry, the intrinsic justice of mathematics: the fact that what you did to the numerator you had to do to the denominator. I loved its certainties. Right answers were concrete, immune to opinions. Best still, I loved that I was great at it. The quadratic equation. Sine, cosine, tangent. The Pythagorean theorem.

And, yes converting Fahrenheit into centigrade. I couldn't tell you how many times in class I'd been required to memorize this formula, and how adept I'd become at computing it in my head.

$F - 32 \times 5/9 = C$. For years, I'd carried this around in my brain, where it took up mental space along with television jingles, the preamble to the U.S. Constitution, and the calorie count of assorted fruits. Yet of course, now that I finally needed it—now that I had to unpack it from its cerebral mothballs and put it to use—I had no fucking idea how the inverse was supposed to go. If $F - 32 \times 5/9 = C$, than what was F? Wasn't it $C + 32 \times 9/5 \ldots$ or was it $32 \times 5/9 + C$? In my panic, I forgot. Frantically I scribbled calculations on the cover of our guidebook. "Goddamn it," I said. According to what I came up with, Claire's fever was either 129.7 or 57.8 degrees Fahrenheit, both of which were obviously beyond wrong.

But the doctor, who didn't need to remember any convoluted formula she'd learned back in high school, took one look at the thermometer and said simply, "Hospital."

"Hospital?" Claire said.

The doctor and the teacher both nodded.

I looked at Claire uneasily. "I'm not sure that's such a good idea," I said. "We have no idea what the hospitals are like here."

Claire swallowed and tugged the sleeping bag more tightly around her shoulders. Her teeth had started chattering. With her chin, she gestured around the stark hotel room with its lone metal chair, its one nightstand, its ice-cold plumbing. "It's got to be better than this." She trembled. "At least there someone will look after me."

"Hospital," said the doctor again insistently. She and the schoolteacher reached over, yanked the sleeping bag off Claire, and pulled her abruptly to her feet. "Ow," Claire said, rubbing her elbow.

"Doctor say you very sick," said the schoolteacher. "Must go hospital now."

The doctor picked up the pair of Timberlands Claire had kicked off beside the bed and thrust them at her.

"You come now," the teacher commanded. "You go to hospital."

Suddenly my hackles were up. I was back in the playground in Central Park, watching a little girl getting bullied. "Hey, don't you be telling her what to do," I snapped, sounding oddly like every New York City cabdriver and Puerto Rican homegirl I'd ever grown up around. "You get your hands off her."

The teacher simply ignored me. "You very, very sick," she cried shrilly, tugging at Claire's arm. "You can no stay here. You go hospital."

"She doesn't have to do anything she doesn't want to," I yelled. The two women continued to prod and pull. Claire stood between them limply like a rag doll they were fighting over. "Uuughh, I don't feel so good," she groaned.

"Wait here," I commanded. The word *hospital* suddenly sounded ominous. "Don't agree to anything, Claire," I instructed. "Don't even put your shoes on. I'll be back in a sec."

I dashed out into the hallway and pounded on Gunter's door. "Gunter," I hollered. "Gunter, we need you."

Gunter opened his door abruptly. He was wearing his Windbreaker zipped all the way up to his chin. He had his rucksack on with the fistful of tea twigs poking out of the top, his passport holder dangling around his neck, and his little canvas carrying bag in one hand. He stepped out into the corridor, set down his bag, and methodically locked the door behind him. "Jah," he said. "I was just coming to say goodbye."

"Goodbye?" I said. "What? Where are you going?"

Gunter reached down and picked up his bag again. "Today I am seeing Dinghai, and I am thinking that it is not being a very interesting place. So I have bought a new ticket for the ferry back to Shanghai."

"What? You're leaving?" I said. "Now?"

"I am feeling very lonely," said Gunter.

"You've got to be kidding me," I said. "Gunter, we need you."

"The ferry, she is leaving in half an hour. The hotel manager, she is driving me."

"Gunter," I pleaded. "Please. Don't leave. Claire is really sick, and the Chinese are insisting on taking her to the hospital, and the whole thing—"

Gunter shrugged. "Tomorrow, there is maybe not being a ferry. It is very hard to get tickets here. They do not have tickets for foreigners. They are not used to us. So if I give up my ticket, maybe I cannot go back."

"But, Gunter, we're really in trouble," I pleaded. "I don't know what to do. I can't communicate with anyone."

Gunter shrugged again. "I am sorry, but the manager, she is waiting for me. She can only use the car one hour."

And with that, he turned and galumphed down the hall. At the elevator, seemingly as an afterthought, he turned and called back, "Please be telling Claire and Jonnie auf Wiedersehen for me." Then he stepped inside the elevator. The jaws of it closed shut across him, and he was gone. Watching him disappear, standing alone in the narrow hallway, I suddenly flashed upon the *Gone With the Wind* video playing over and over onboard the *Jin Jiang,* upon Scarlett O'Hara at the end of part one, falling to her knees on the war-scorched earth utterly alone.

———

"No, this is good. This is better," Claire murmured as we sat in the back of the doctor's tiny, rusted car. She closed her eyes and pressed her forehead against the spotted glass of the window. "I'll be more comfortable this way. I'll get more attention."

The prospect of comfort seemed increasingly dubious to me. As the car bounced along the rutted road, the outskirts of Dinghai became visible. The countryside was stunning. The clouds had dissipated and the majestically lush emerald mountains were now ribboned with undulant light, as if reflected in a swimming pool. But once we entered the city, the streets themselves became a parched conglomerate of squat gray-stone houses and filthy cinder-block buildings. Women with faces like dried apples wore coolie hats and rough-sewn kerchiefs over their heads. They squatted in the dirt along the highway selling greasy machine parts, a few small green oranges, and woefully blackened bananas. Skeletal men and women trotted barefoot in the dust carrying enormous baskets of produce and charcoal dangling from yokes on their desiccated shoulders, or pulling carts laden with live geese, chickens, nets full of dried eel skin and shrimp. A few people pedaled rusty bicycles. The road was inexplicably littered with crab claws. All along it, piles of gravel, tile, and brick lay untouched before half-constructed buildings. A hot wind blew.

The car lurched on, past lean-tos; past squat houses with scalloped roofs; past an entire family—father, mother, sister, brother—in identical Mao uniforms, trudging solemnly up a hill, farm implements slung over their shoulders. Dinghai was one of those rural farming communities that flouted the government's "one child" policy; I could see six- and seven-year-old children helping to till the fields in the sun, their tiny backs bent forward like plowshares jutting into the furrowed land.

Soon we were past the city, and the road gave way to the idyllic countryside again: gold and chartreuse fields, mountains framing the distance. The doctor maneuvered the car onto a rutted path. The frenzied wobble of the chassis seemed to stir Claire out of her sleep. The car continued down the road for about a hundred yards beneath a canopy of trees, then pushed into a clearing through an iron gate, scattering a bevy of chickens and whipping up a swirl of dust as it did. Abruptly, it stopped. The doctor and the former school-teacher scrambled out, opened the passengers doors, and ushered Claire and me onto a wide dirt path.

"Come," commanded the teacher. She and the doctor led us up a stony incline. Claire and I followed reluctantly, but what else could we do? *If Chinese officials give you orders, remember, you must obey. You must follow all instructions, rules, and laws. You must respect all representatives of the People's Republic of China.*

Before us stood what looked like a wooden stable and concrete barracks with a shaded porch. At a short remove, nestled among tall grasses and silvery weeds, was another concrete structure and a crude wooden building on stilts that looked like a chicken coop.

"Here," the teacher commanded again. She and the doctor each placed a hand on the small of our backs and steered us toward the buildings.

"I thought you said we were going to the hospital," Claire said.

"This hospital," said the teacher.

With that, both Claire and I stopped violently. "This is it?"

"This hospital. You very sick. You go hospital now. You no stay in hotel. Hotel no good."

Only then did it become apparent that the hotel manager, the teacher, and even the doctor were not nearly so concerned about Claire's illness as they were about the prospect of being held responsible for it. None of them wanted the shame of having word get back to the authorities that Dinghai's first American guest had fallen ill on their watch.

As we drew closer to the buildings, we saw that the structures were filthy: moldy walls streaked with mud and dirt. I'd grown up around poverty and slums, but this was of a different league—a different century, really. There wasn't even a front entrance to speak of, only a rudimentary doorway cut out of the concrete. The interior felt like a cave: cool, clayey, dim. At the front desk a woman stood arguing with two farm-hands. The floor was powdery cement. Directly to the right of the doorway, in full view of anyone who entered, an old, half-toothed woman lay uncovered on a wooden pallet with an oxygen tube taped beneath her nose. As she rasped and moaned, people walked past her as if she were a piece of furniture, all of them smoking, spitting, arguing, carrying baskets of food. Chickens hopped around the entryway, scratching and pecking at the dirt. From somewhere, another woman was screaming, and there was the smell of frying onions mingled with the sharp scent of ammonia.

My impulse should have been to turn around then and simply run, but by that time, a peculiar sort of fatalism had set in. Claire and I were both so helpless and so clearly no longer in charge of ourselves; the surrealism of it all had overpowered us. We had surrendered now, and I was aware that my consciousness seemed to have bifurcated. I was both experiencing the situation of the hospital and passively observing it from a distance, as if I were watching myself on footage from a security camera.

The doctor steered Claire out to the other concrete building across the pathway. I followed her, I suppose still hoping that maybe, just maybe, it would get better. Maybe, as with so many other Chinese facilities, there was a separate, superior facility for foreigners. But while the second building proved larger and brighter, there were still intensive care patients crowded onto beds in the reception area, chickens clucking, and hordes of people standing around coughing and spitting. At the sight of it, Claire buckled over. "Oh, God," she groaned, clutching her stomach. "I need the bathroom. *Now.*"

Taking her by the elbow, the doctor hustled her outside and around the back of the building. Hurrying after her, I descended with them into a rancid basement. The doctor kicked open a rough plywood door, then pointed Claire to a steaming trough gouged into the earth. Claire let out a cry and I ran back upstairs. "Someone," I shouted, "is there even someone else here who speaks English?"

How did you say it in Mandarin? Both Jonnie and Trevor had told me.

"Ni shou ying wen ma?" I cried.

The schoolteacher and the receptionist fell upon me then, each grabbing an arm. While the schoolteacher barked repeatedly, "You must sign papers," the receptionist thrust a sheaf of printed forms at me covered with official-looking seals. The schoolteacher literally jammed a pen into my hand, motioning. "You sign, yes?"

"I don't know what they say," I cried. "I can't read Chinese." There seemed to be pages and pages, line after line of characters blurring together into gibberish, a rain of cross-hatchings and pen strokes. For all I knew, signing them would authorize the Chinese to give Claire a frontal lobotomy. "I'm not signing anything," I shouted.

When the schoolteacher refused to let go of me, I yanked my arm away, slapped the papers down onto the desk, and threw down the pen. I might as well have detonated a stink bomb. As soon as the pen hit the floor, everyone began yelling at me: one nurse, another, the schoolteacher. Forms were being waved, pushed back into my face, papers creasing and flying. Chickens were hopping around clucking in an uproar. A male doctor appeared holding a syringe and pointing. Suddenly Claire had rematerialized; he and the female doctor were hustling her down a long hallway. All I could see was the back of her yellow-gold hair shaking like a mop and her voice crying "Ow! Ow!"

"Claire," I yelled.

"You sign papers," cried the schoolteacher, literally twisting my arm now in a panic, her fingers hot on my wrist.

"Get away from me," I bellowed, yanking my arm back. As I pushed past the nurses and paper-wavers, I knocked into a pallet of empty wooden stretchers, sending them clattering. Elbowing through the gawking spitters, smokers, and farmhands, I ran down the dank hallway after Claire, shouting, "Someone, please. *Ni shou ying wen ma?*" My voice broke then; tears dripped down my cheeks. I couldn't find Claire; she'd been taken from me. This was far too much, way out of my league. "STOP" I yelled hoarsely down the empty corridor to no one, my voice dissolving into the damp vegetable air. "STOP!"

"I'm sorry, milady. But may I be of some assistance to you?" a voice behind me said in breathless plummy English.

An elegant middle-aged Chinese man in a three-piece pin-striped suit with a polka-dot necktie and a bowler hat appeared before me.

"Excuse me?" I said, wild-eyed.

Bowing every so slightly, he said in impeccable British-accented English, "Allow me to introduce myself. My name is Victor. I am a friend with the Foreign Affairs Department. I wondered if I couldn't perhaps be of service to you."

In my panic, I never stopped to ask Victor how he just "happened" to be nearby so fortuitously, where he'd learn to speak English so perfectly, or even how he'd known exactly where to find us. In fact I never stopped to question him at all; I accepted him as I accepted the rest of the situation, in all of its improbable, hallucinatory strangeness.

"Yes, help me," I cried. Trying to contain my hysteria, I explained the situation as best as I could. Victor appeared unfazed. Immediately he led me down the fetid hallway to an examination room. He seemed to know precisely where to go.

In the dark concrete room, Claire appeared to have revived considerably. She was standing defiantly away from the doctors, flailing her arms anytime they tried to get near her. "NO HOSPITAL!" she hollered. "NO VACCINATION! HOTEL, NOW! DO YOU UNDERSTAND? HOTEL!"

When Victor appeared, all the Chinese began pointing at her and pleading their case to him at once. The male doctor was still holding his syringe and waving it for emphasis. I wish I could say I was making this up, but I'm not: I could actually see beads of rust along the injection needle.

"The doctor would like to give you a vaccination," Victor explained gently to Claire. "He says that it will make you feel infinitely better."

Claire, like me, did not even pause to consider Victor, to ask who he was or why he was there. She cried only, "Tell him to keep his hands off me. I'm not getting any shots. I just want to go back to the hotel."

This seemed to distress the hospital staff greatly. As Victor escorted us out onto the crude breezeway, they hurried after her, swiping at her arm in persistent attempts to vaccinate her while she flailed at them shouting "Off! Get off me!" Finally Victor turned to them and said something that seemed to put an end to it once and for all. In an instant, the staff scurried back inside the hospital.

"Please," said Victor with a graceful sweep of his arm, "allow me now, if you will, to escort you back to your hotel."

Parked at the end of the dusty driveway by the gate, surrounded by the ubiquitous chickens, sat a voluptuous white 1940s limousine with a running board and toile de Jouy curtains in the windows. It appeared to have been modeled on a Rolls-Royce. Gallantly, Victor opened the back door and ushered us inside.

As soon as we slid into its cool, generous interior, Claire gave a moan of relief, then fell asleep almost immediately. An austere-looking man sat behind the wheel dressed in full military regalia. Oddly, I assumed he was a chauffeur.

"I fear that you may have found the standards of this hospital are not what Westerners are used to," Victor said apologetically as the driver eased the car over the ruts in the road. "I am sorry if the best intentions of our medical staff have in any way caused you and your friend distress."

There was something about his voice, the Shakespearean tenor and delicacy of it, that made me inexplicably sad and ashamed. We had so much, we Americans, yet we demanded and expected so much, too. The Chinese had done the best they could with what they had. They were so fearful of making a mistake. They were determined to the point of mania to give us the best of the meager medical care that they had. The bullying at the hospital: Even then I understood that it had stemmed from a code of hospitality, a peculiar generosity. It was flawed and likely dangerous. But when had we in the United States ever been so obstinate about caring for strangers?

"No, it's our fault," I said diplomatically—and suddenly I meant it, too. Surely we should have known better. Surely we had to learn to be more patient and understanding.

"We're just not used to Chinese medicine," I said. "We shouldn't have put everybody to so much trouble."

I exhaled and sat back. The sun filtering through the ruched curtains, the leathery smell of the upholstery, the sense of being in someone's care—all of it came as a balm, an enormous wash of relief.

———

Back at the hotel, Victor saw us to our room while the driver stood out front like a sentry. Claire hobbled across the lobby, then propped herself up against the corner of the elevator. "Oh, I feel so tired," she said, pressing her cheek to the elevator paneling. Back in our room, she sank down into the lone metal chair by the window and let her head loll against her chest for a moment. She appeared to be breathing heavily. When I touched her forehead, however, it was smooth and cool.

"Please," Victor said. "Does your friend require anything else? Is there anything in particular that I can arrange for you?"

I thought for a moment. "I think she's pretty dehydrated. And she hasn't had much to eat, either. She's not really big into fish. Is there any way you can maybe get her some bottled water and some plain white rice? And crackers or bread, if you have any?"

Victor smiled faintly with a tinge of what was either amusement or pity. "Certainly," he said with a slight bow. "I will see that it is arranged and brought to your room."

"Wow," I said. "Thank you so much. *Shay shay nee.* Really."

At that moment, it seemed to me that living in a Communist country was not actually half bad. If you had a problem: *poof!* Officials were at the ready to arrive like the cavalry to rescue you, to disentangle you, to provide you with the appropriate paperwork, and even, it seemed, to arrange for hotel room service. Was that really so horrible?

I thought of my grandmother back in New York.

She had been born with a deformed leg in Bialystok, Poland, during a wave of pogroms in which lynch mobs thundered through the streets with torches, shrieking, "Kill the Jews!" She was less than a year old when her family fled to America. They had arrived with nothing, of course: a few suitcases bound together with rags. As an immigrant, she had not exactly begun life auspiciously.

Given all the meanness around her, I could never for the life of me understand why she flirted with communism the way she did.

For a while I'd wondered if maybe, perversely and unconsciously and steeped in self-hatred, she secretly craved its cruelty and conformity, the punishment and absolution of a totalitarian regime. Perhaps she longed to be absorbed into the great proletarian masses until there was nothing left of her individuality at all, until every trace of anything that set her apart from other people had been bled away—a twisted wish for assimilation and camouflage. Communists always liked to purport that their societies were thoroughly egalitarian. Well, what could be more appealing to someone so outcast?

But standing there in Eastern China, I realized that this was not it at all. Although she was only four-foot-eleven, my grandmother was a force of nature: cultured, opinionated, bellicose with intelligence and passion. If she longed for a totalitarian regime, it was because on some level, she assumed she'd be running it. In her Communist utopia, legions of Hispanic cleaning women, Yiddish waiters from Barney Greengrass ("The Sturgeon King!"), Asian dry cleaners, Irish parking garage attendants, black store clerks, teenage cashiers, and everyone else in the service industry whom she routinely bossed around and abused would now legally be required to abide by her wishes. Her Marxist utopia was not economic or even political. It was simply the dream of an entire nation functioning as her own personalized maid service. *Here's your medical care, Mrs. Gilman. Here's a lovely dacha for you to live in. Here's your laundry. You don't have to lift a finger anymore. Workers of the world have united: for you.*

Now, a dapper and attentive man named Victor from the Foreign Affairs Department had just intervened on my behalf at a rural Chinese hospital. My grandmother, I knew, would've loved this. In the end, I suppose, she just wanted someone to take care of her.

"Very good, then," Victor said, gesturing around

our hotel room. "If everything is in order, then shall I leave you to rest?"

"Sure," I said. "Again. I can't thank you enough. Really, Victor, you've saved our lives." I stepped forward to hug him. Victor looked at my outstretched arms with horror. The best I could do then was to try and pretend that I was merely demonstrating the size and volume of my appreciation. I took a step back, my hands frozen awkwardly in midair. None of the multicultural workshops back at Brown had prepared me for this. I'd never understood before how communication went so far beyond language.

"You've done so much for us," I said inanely.

"No, please." Victor smiled, but I could sense his displeasure and embarrassment. "It is no trouble at all. I am merely a friend."

He touched the brim of his bowler hat and stepped into the hallway. As I watched him hurry to the elevator, something else occurred to me.

"Victor," I called from the doorway.

He stopped.

"There is one other thing you could do, actually, that would really help Claire and me. Do you think you could find us a map of some sort—it doesn't have to be anything fancy—just a little tourist map or a diagram or something to give us a sense of where we are?"

Victor glanced back at me, his face arranged in an insistent smile. He jammed the elevator button. "The countryside here in Dinghai," he said, "is considered one of the most beautiful landscapes in all of China. I find it is particularly beautiful at this time of year. I do hope that when your friend improves, you might be able to admire it."

The elevator doors slid open, consumed him, and he was gone.

———

A porter arrived carrying a tray with two bowls of white rice, four dusty glass bottles of orange soda, and a cellophane package of bright yellow sponge cakes. The waitress from the restaurant stood behind him bearing a thermos of tea and two small, scuffed cups. They set everything down wordlessly, then fled.

Claire stirred, moaned. She sat up and ate a bit of the rice and the tasteless, oversweet cakes. I ate, too. Both of us were drained. Slowly the color returned to Claire's face. She stood up gingerly and unpeeled the blankets we'd draped around her. Her hair was still sodden and her clothes smelled stale and oniony, but there was a feeling in the room of a storm having passed. I looked at her with affection. It was good to have her back.

"Well," she smiled wanly, glancing out the window, "that's one for the history books, I guess. Let's hope my father never hears about this one."

Walking around the room stiffly, she gathered up her toiletry bag. "Okay." She exhaled. "Time for a shower."

A moment later, I heard the squeak of the faucet followed by "Fuck, that's cold! Fuckity fuck fuck!" When she emerged, dressed in her same dusty khakis and polo shirt, towel-drying her hair, she looked miserable. She sank back into the chair, uncapped one of the bottles of orange soda, and downed it in one prolonged swallow.

"The water is freezing and the soda is hot," she panted. "Go figure."

There was a pounding on the door.

"You know, for a place that's deserted, it feels an awful lot like Grand Central Station in here," I said.

Jonnie rushed in, accompanied by his brother, who stood warily on the threshold in his worn blue Mao uniform.

"Sushi? Crair? Are you all right? They tell me you are sick," Jonnie said with distress. "They say you have gone to hospital. They say you have very bad fever."

Claire glanced at Jonnie wearily, then set her empty soda bottle down on the windowsill and shrugged. "Nah," she said. "I'm okay now."

"You are okay? You are not sick? They tell me you very sick." Jonnie bent over her chair, his face mapped with worry and concern. I could tell already he was irritating her. "You need medicine? You want me to find doctor?"

"She had a fever and some stomach problems," I said. "But they seem to have passed. Right now she just needs to eat."

"So you are okay now?" Jonnie pressed.

Claire nodded.

"Oh, that is wonderful," Jonnie clasped his hands together rapturously. "Because I have very big surprise for you. My mother, she has prepared the big feast for you today. And my brother, he has gotten the car again from his company. So we can go to my house after all."

Claire blinked at him. "Today?" she said. "Right now?"

Jonnie nodded proudly. "You say this morning, you do not like to wait to meet my family. And I am thinking, you are right. You come all this way. You come far. Making you wait is not hospitable. So my family and I, we go to the market. We prepare big feast in your honor. We prepare many special dishes, best food in Dinghai. My brother, everyone comes. So you come now, yes?"

I have no recollection of how we managed to rally. All I remember is the oppressive sense that the visit to Jonnie's house was mandatory and inescapable, that declining his invitation was not an option. Both Claire and I felt bloated with dread and exhaustion, but somehow we combed our hair and put on lip gloss and squeezed ourselves back into Jonnie's brother's company van, because I vaguely remember it pulling us back through the tumbleweed city, then up into the luscious hillside.

I have a memory of stopping somewhere along the way, of Claire, Jonnie, and me standing on a ridge in the golden late-afternoon sun overlooking a valley stitched with fields, of seeing a pool of platinum water shining on a plateau in the distance and thinking, *Oh, that must be part of the hydroelectric facility.* I remember rippling foothills giving way to mountains on the horizon, mountains as final and declarative as punctuation. And I remember that a rainbow appeared, transforming the whole vista into a postcard. For one moment I felt elation, all the previous crises of the day evaporating. Then we were somehow back in the humid, spluttering van, on a dirt road snaking up the mountainside, and the farmland gave way to forest and Jonnie's family's little house, nestled in a remote wooded glen at the very end of a pockmarked road, smoke chugging out of its chimney in puffs.

There was a little boy, a couple of young girls. In all, I recorded later in my journal, a dozen people lived in Jonnie's family's little stone house—though I have no memory of them and no further notes. The magnitude of the day, the weirdness and adrenaline of it all, left me in a fog. No one truly registered with me beyond Jonnie's mother, who seemed to be flanked by an entourage of relatives. When Jonnie introduced me and Claire, she smiled toothlessly, touched a leaf-trembling hand to our cheeks. No one except Jonnie, of course, spoke even a word of English, yet somehow people were parroting "America, America" over and over, and I had a sense that we were all talking at once.

Children pulled us inside. Someone gave us a tour. The small stone house was bisected into four rooms. Only the front two had electricity. In the brightly lit sitting room, there was a concrete floor, a modern couch, and a state-of-the-art boom box that sat by the window like a shrine. In the adjacent dining room, the uneven whitewashed walls were grimy with age. The enormous white refrigerator that Jonnie had brought back from Hong Kong stood in the center. The family seemed to be using it as a storage chest. It stood in the middle of the room, unplugged, its doors gaping open. Dozens of stiff, dried whole fish were stacked up in the freezer, one on top of the other like firewood, their heads and tails jutting out.

Stepping into the two rooms behind these was to step back in time several centuries. The filthy cave-like kitchen was medieval—a lean-to, really, with dirt floors and chickens hopping around inside beside piles of blackened pots, pans, wooden crates, a rusted oil drum. Through a curtain was a darkened bedroom with a mud floor and a chamber pot between its two beds.

To straddle the threshold between any two rooms in this house was to stand between the past and the future, tradition and modernity, poverty and promise. Looking back on it now, I realize the house was emblematic of the entire condition of the People's

Republic of China at that precise moment in time, though of course I didn't know this and I didn't have wisdom yet to even sense the metaphor. At the time, I was simply shocked and captivated by the fact that there were actually live chickens in the kitchen.

"Wow," I whispered to Claire. "This place is wild. Twelve people live here?"

Claire shook her head in amazement. "Okay, not to be an asshole or anything," she whispered slyly, "but this house is smaller than my parents' Jacuzzi."

It has long been a tradition in the West to mythologize peasants as being happier and purer than those of us corrupted by materialism and ambition. Having grown up in a rough neighborhood in New York City, where my brother and I were routinely mugged and harassed by kids from the surrounding housing projects — and where our parents themselves were often strapped for cash — I never for a moment harbored any illusions about the nobility or innocence of the lower classes. The poor kids I knew were tough. They would kick your ass, break your nose, wreck your bicycle, and steal your lunch money without another thought. What's more, they were far savvier, tougher, and more cynical than any of my milquetoast, middle-class friends.

I hate the idea of the poignant peasants, with all its implicit judgment, condescension, paternalism. And so I hesitate to write that Jonnie's family was unlike any other I had ever encountered. But they were. They seemed otherwordly—physically radiant, as if Titian had painted light emanating from their bodies. The children, the parents, the aunts and the uncles: They positively beamed at one another, addressing each other with such tenderness and adoration that, even without understanding their language, we could see the profound respect and joy among them.

Spend fifteen minutes with my own extended family over dinner and you were inevitably treated to a parade of pathology: whining, hyperactive children; furious, beleaguered-looking mothers; drunken uncles; husbands making inappropriate jokes about their wives in front of their wives; sullen, seething teenagers (okay: me); and a dictatorial grandmother badgering her dithering husband with a soup ladle. You heard doors slamming and caught vicious, fleeting looks. At Claire's, it really wasn't that different. Despite the maid and the swimming pool and the marble entranceway and the hushed tones floating over the garden parties, it didn't take long to sense a cat's cradle of tension and resentment strung between her and her stepmother, her stepmother and her father, her father and his three stepsons. To me, any group of people who shared a household, DNA, or both was by definition a hotbed of misery and conflict.

But Jonnie's family? They were all truly and utterly in love with each other.

To this very day, I don't know what to attribute it to. Perhaps it *was* the agrarian simplicity of their lives. Perhaps it was cultural. Or perhaps it was just endemic to Jonnie's family itself. But whatever the reason, when I saw Jonnie among them, patting his niece on the back of her head, lovingly assisting his mother as she maneuvered the steps, laughing with his brother, I understood: He was not a supplicant at all. He had not brought us to Dinghai as bribery so that we would feel indebted to him or sorry enough for him that as quid pro quo we'd take him to the American embassy afterward. Nor had he brought us to Dinghai to show us off to his family like two trophies: Look at my two shiny new American friends. On the contrary, Jonnie had brought us to Dinghai to show his family off to *us*. Though he looked young, he was a *man*. He had traveled and experienced far more than Claire or I ever had, and he had provided for twelve people by working halfway around the world from them. Furthermore, he was wise enough to know how truly extraordinary they were.

We were not the prizes on display in Dinghai at all, I realized. What hubris! What presumption! No, Jonnie had wanted Claire and me to see what *he* had.

"Please," he said generously, "come and eat." He ushered Claire and me to the only two chairs at the table. Only after we were seated did the others take places around us on rough-hewn stools and benches.

From the kitchen, the women brought out one

plate after another and set them on the table: enormous prawns cooked in salt, sautéed greens, steamed crabs, a whole fish buried in scallions, a huge tureen of soup, platters of root vegetables and noodles, a cortege of delicacies. The children danced around, almost insane with anticipation and glee. This was clearly a momentous occasion.

"Please," Jonnie said. Claire and I alone were handed bowls and chopsticks. The family pressed in, staring at us expectantly. It became clear that no one else would touch the food until we did. I looked at all of the plates spread before us. There must have been at least fourteen. The abundance was embarrassing. Where were we supposed to start? I reached for the only dish that looked vaguely recognizable—the huge prawns encrusted in rock salt, glistening like crystal.

"Ah," Jonnie's mother exclaimed, nodding appreciatively. A murmur of approval went around the table. I supposed I'd demonstrated good taste. They continued watching me. Picking the prawn up with the chopsticks was a challenge, and their stares made me infinitely more self-conscious and inept.

"Sorry." I grinned apologetically. "I'm not very good at this."

I glanced over at Claire. She was clutching her stomach and leaning forward in her chair, her chopsticks untouched on the empty bowl before her. I motioned for her to eat something.

She glared at me desperately and shook her head. "It's all seafood," she whispered.

Seeing her empty bowl, Jonnie's mother reached over and held out a dish to her, a jellied mass of what looked like fish eyes and pea pods. Staring at it, Claire gave a little cry and jumped up, knocking over her chair.

"Crair," said Jonnie, alarmed, making his way around the table toward her. "Are you okay?"

Claire looked at him, flustered. "I have to go to the bathroom," she stammered. Jonnie said something to the little girl across the table. Dutifully she got up and led Claire behind the curtain into the bedroom.

I got a terrible feeling just then: During the tour of the house, I'd noticed the chamber pot. I sensed what was coming. As quickly as I could, I began reaching for the various dishes, shoveling delicacies onto my plate and offering them around, urging the others to please begin feasting with me. I began eating everything as fast as I could—something eggy, something with fish, the prawns still in their shells, bitter greens that I could barely swallow, something slimy and something with crunch. "Oh, my God," I said in my exaggerated, imbecile tourist's voice, "is this ever delicious. Jonnie, please tell your family that this is delicious."

A moment later, just as I'd anticipated, Claire hurried out from behind the curtain. She grabbed her silver Windbreaker off the back of her chair and yanked it over her shoulders. "I'm sorry," she announced, lifting the strap of her leather saddlebag over her head, "but we have to go back to the hotel. *Now.*"

Jonnie looked stricken.

"I'm not feeling well," she declared. "I'm sorry, but we have to leave."

I couldn't help it: I glared at her. I suppose I was a terrible friend. But though her face was flushed, I simply didn't believe her. It was too patently convenient. I'd seen Claire when she was sick, and I'd seen her when she was being extravagantly theatrical. I was still confident that I could tell the difference.

"Can't you wait just a little?" I pleaded under my breath.

She looked at me, furious. "Susie, I'm not feeling well. Goddamn it, what don't you understand about that?" There was a prick of hysteria in her voice.

"Please, look at this," I whispered, gesturing to the feast. Clearly the family had been working for hours to prepare it; clearly, they'd spent everything they had on it, perhaps a month's savings. From what I'd read in our guidebook, the Chinese lived in mortal fear of losing face—of appearing in any way unworthy, inhospitable, flustered, deficient. Preventing loss of face required tacit cooperation among all concerned; causing someone else to lose face was just as bad as losing it yourself. Rejecting Jonnie's family's hospitality would be humiliating for them and a terrible affront on our part.

His family looked bewildered from Claire to me to Claire again as if watching a Ping-Pong match. "They've gone to all this trouble," I begged. "Can't you just hold out for fifteen minutes?"

"Jonnie." Claire turned to him abruptly. "Jonnie, I feel horrible. I think my fever is coming back. Please give your family my apologies, but you and your brother are going to have to take me back to the hotel." She bowed, then hurried out of the house.

The family looked after her, then at me, then down at the abandoned feast.

"No," I announced, "Claire isn't going anywhere until we're finished, Jonnie. What she means is that she'll wait outside until you can go. So sit down. We're all going to eat for a few minutes."

He looked at me uneasily. "Sit," I said.

For the next five minutes we all ate mechanically, in quiet misery. Outside, the sun was low in the sky, and I knew Claire would be pacing by the van. But suddenly I didn't really care. Let her wait, I thought. All day long people had been doing their best to take care of her. It was time she gave a little and let this poor family enjoy the biggest meal they'd probably had all year. But it was ruined and we all knew it. Finally Jonnie set down his chopsticks.

"I think we go now, Sushi," he said quietly, standing. "Crair has been sick all day. I do not want her to have to go back to the hospital."

On the ride back, Claire stared out the window

at the sherbet-colored sunset and hummed. When we reinstalled her in the hotel room, she poured herself three cups of now-tepid tea and swallowed them in rapid succession. As Jonnie and I looked on, she ripped open a second package of the yellow cake and devoured it.

"Oh, God," she sighed, rubbing her stomach in exaggerated circles, "that feels so much better." She waved aside the mosquito netting and jounced down on the bed. "My insides are just a mess," she said almost happily. "Jonnie, I don't suppose there's any place I can get some soup around here? Just something very simple like broth with maybe some dumplings or noodles?"

At that moment, I remember thinking that if Jonnie turned on his heels and slammed the door on us both, I'd applaud him. And then I remember feeling guilty for thinking this. For weeks, Claire had indulged my anxieties and pulled me along when I was too homesick and freaked out to function properly. Now, when our roles were reversed, I was hard-nosed and resentful. But I somehow just couldn't believe that she was still sick; something rang false. But why should it? Just a few hours before, she'd been taken to the hospital, yet I was second-guessing her. I was not only a coward, but a bitch.

"I'll go with you, Jonnie," I said guiltily.

It was dark when we set out on foot through the narrow cobblestone streets. The low stone houses lining the alleys had barred windows and no electricity. I would've thought they were deserted except for the occasional fragments of voices and cooking sounds wafting from them as we passed. Without a flashlight, it became increasingly hard to see, but Jonnie seemed to know exactly where to go. We turned a corner and reached a small clearing strung with bare lightbulbs. A generator growled behind a lean-to of corrugated tin, in which a man and his family had set up a little restaurant. Jonnie bought us each a pink ticket at a side window, then handed it to the proprietor. He and his family began cooking soup and dumplings for us on a hot plate. We helped ourselves to bowls, spoons, and chopsticks from a pile on top of the counter. All of them were filthy, with stuck-on food left over from the previous diner, but I'd given up caring. I figured if it hadn't killed Jonnie, it wouldn't kill me.

When the food was ready, Jonnie and I served ourselves, then carried our bowls to a rickety wooden table covered with a plastic cloth that felt like contact paper. Both of us were ravenous. We slurped in silence.

"It is good, yes? You like the food?"

I nodded vigorously. It really did seem to be some of the best soup and dumplings I'd ever eaten. The proprietors waved over at me proudly. When Jonnie got up to buy us a second round of tickets, they refused our money. On the shelves behind them were displayed a few paltry bottles of Chinese wine, beer, "fruit tonic," and dusty canned goods, and in the glass counter were bags of hard candies, nuts, and packages of biscuits. To show my gratitude, I shopped extravagantly, buying as many packages of nuts and biscuits and bottles of fruit tonic as I could carry. Meanwhile, Jonnie arranged for the restaurant to lend him an enamel pot full of soup and dumplings for Claire.

Yet by the time we returned with our bounty, she was already asleep.

———————

The next morning, when Jonnie bicycled back to the hotel to check up on us, Claire was still sleeping. I longed to buy him breakfast but realized I'd used up all my Chinese money the night before. I didn't even have enough for our ferry tickets back to Shanghai.

Jonnie appeared unfazed.

"No problem," he said cheerily. "I take you to the bank."

There was a little metal pallet on the back of his bicycle. I perched on it backward, straddling the fender with my knees bent, while Jonnie pedaled. I was amazed how fast we went, bouncing over asphalt, gliding down dusty roads. Jonnie insisted on bringing his tape recorder with him, and as we tore along the streets of downtown Dinghai, I held it on my lap, the volume dialed up to 10, and we both sang along to

Stevie Wonder with gleeful abandon. As we passed, people pointed at us smiling and waving.

"*Nee how!*" I shouted, grinning and waving back. I felt ridiculous and exultant. "*Nee how!*"

We rode alongside bicycle carts, tractors, army buses. We rode past fields, construction sites, and open fruit stands on the roadside. We became one with a sea of other cyclists, everyone pumping away in unison, waving and nodding in a community of labor and recognition. By the time we'd gone to the bank and returned to the hotel, I was completely disheveled, breathless, and covered with dust. "Oh, Jonnie," I cried, reluctant to get off and return to the privileged sterility of our room. "That was amazing."

Jonnie laughed with genuine pleasure. "Last night you eat in a local restaurant, and today you ride a bicycle many miles," he beamed. "You are a real Chinese now."

七

Chapter 7

Beijing

WE ARE HIS friends now, truly his friends. We have traveled the high seas with him. We have warbled songs in harmony and peppered him with fantastical stories about America. We have kissed his mother's papery cheek. When Claire insisted on cutting short our stay in Dinghai, he took leave of his own family in order to return to Shanghai with us on the ferry. For three weeks he has been our guide, our guardian, our companion.

So when we abandon Jonnie on the platform of the Shanghai Terminus, when we leave him to his fate by dashing abruptly onto the last night train for Beijing while shouting at him, "Jonnie, the train is leaving! Hurry up! Where's your ticket?" knowing full well he doesn't have a ticket—he's been under the impression that we'd bought one for him—he looks stricken. His eternal smile collapses. He can't help it. His face becomes a landslide of confusion and panic. "Sushi, Crair!" he cries, running after us. The train grinds and chugs forward, accumulating velocity. He cannot keep up with it. We are standing in the vestibule, breathless and shaking. Our faces slide past him. Does he know that we've betrayed him? Or does he believe what we hope he'll believe — that it was simply a terrible misunderstanding, that we hadn't actually intended to leave him behind?

From the doorway of the train, I watch his little cardboard suitcase tumble onto the concrete. I watch his hands go up to his face. I watch his bereft figure grow smaller and smaller on the edge of the platform, until it is just a pinpoint absorbed into the violent glare of the station, and then the train rounds a corner, and there is just blackness, and he is gone.

It's over. We have amputated him from ourselves entirely. Just like that. And for the first time in my life, I feel like I've committed murder. He has been nothing but generous and kind to us. And look what we've done. We've not only rejected but humiliated him. We've caused him to lose face. Hundreds of his countrymen have witnessed his desperation and unraveling in public.

Grimly we stumble through the corridor with our backpacks, moving in counterpoint to the *slong*ing of the train. It has taken us five days to obtain tickets for the hard sleeper, an open compartment in second class with six bunks. The train ride to Beijing is fourteen hours. Even Lonely Planet advises not to attempt this journey in third class, ominously called *hard seat.*

People lean out of their compartments to stare at us. Their faces emerge in sequence, like a silk fan, opening.

"Look, we did him a favor," Claire says unconvincingly, slinging down her backpack. Our reserved bunks are on the bottom and in the middle in the last compartment, by the acrid toilet.

"Even if by some miracle we helped him defect, do you think we'd be allowed to just waltz back out onto the streets afterward and continue traveling?" She unrolls her sleeping bag and shakes it out over her sleeper. "Our own lives might have been put at risk."

I glance at her bitterly. Claire had told Jonnie "Meet us at the train station. We'll have the tickets," but had then deliberately given him the wrong departure time.

I tell myself that betraying Jonnie had been her idea, her problem, her responsibility, not mine; after all, wasn't she the one who'd insisted we go with him to Dinghai in the first place? Hadn't she promised me that she'd be the one to deal with him? But I know better. I feel dirty and monstrous, and rightfully so. I have been complicit. I am the Vampirella of the backpacking circuit. Claire and I should've been willing to forfeit our own adventures to help a friend break free of an oppressive regime. *That's* what the heroes in great books did, after all.

"Look," Claire said flatly, "Jonnie had an agenda. Okay, he smiled, and he introduced us to his family and blah blah blah. But c'mon, Suze. How do we know he wasn't a spy?" She pulled a Wash'n'Dry out of her purse, tore it open, and ran the towelette briskly over her hands.

"A spy? What kind of a spy sings Stevie Wonder songs and takes you home to meet his mother?"

"Please. Don't be so naive," she said tightly. "That's exactly how those people operate, you know. Befriend you, then exploit you." She dropped the used Wash'n'Dry into the bag she used for garbage, then tossed it on top of her purse.

"You think everyone's a spy, Claire," I said meanly.

"So okay, then. How did he know English so well, huh? And how did he get to live in Ghana? You saw where he grew up. How does someone from Dinghai get to travel halfway around the world when most Chinese can't leave their village without permission?"

Dropping to her haunches, she riffled agitatedly through her purse, pulling out books and slapping them down on the padded bunk.

"Besides, spy or no spy, *you* know he wouldn't take no for an answer. He just would not stop pushing."

Stiffly, miserably, I hoisted myself up onto my

sleeper. Even with my sleeping bag spread across it, the bunk felt like an ironing board against my spine. I shifted about, struggling to get comfortable as an old woman in the berth directly across from mine stared at me unremittingly. Above her, another woman chewed sunflower seeds and spit their shells on the floor. She, too, stared at me. Their gaze felt like an indictment.

I rolled over onto my stomach. Beneath me, Claire sat in her berth with her journal spread open across her knees.

"Oh, Claire," I said over the ledge, "it was just so heartbreaking, seeing him standing alone like that—"

Slowly she set down her pen. "Yeah. I know." She sighed. "He just—he just didn't know what he was playing with, Suze, you know? And I don't want to spend the next, like, seven years in a Chinese prison. Do you?"

Beneath us, the muddy, felt-covered floor of our compartment was littered with sunflower shells. Already the air was growing milky and bluish from cigarette smoke. A sharp chemical smell emanated from the toilet, and the emergency bulbs overhead bathed everything in a nicotine-tinted light. The train jiggled. Slowly I shook my head.

"Here. Take some." She held up a cellophane package of peanuts. "It's all we've got. We'll toast. To Jonnie."

She strained upward toward me, proffering the bag, and I stretched down to meet her and scoop up a handful of nuts. "To Jonnie," we said solemnly, knocking our fists together. The Chinese looked on, perplexed.

After that, Claire and I sat somberly in our berths, quietly eating our peanuts.

And that was it.

For the first time since our arrival in China, we were truly on our own.

———

Throughout the night, the dim lights remained burning while our bunkmates bantered, spit, smoked, peeled oranges, offered around bags of boiled sweets, laughed uproariously, and coughed deep, labored coughs. Intermittently, broadcasts blared over the loudspeakers in long-winded monologues. Public announcements were so ubiquitous and relentless in China that they'd become white noise to us. The train squealed and stalled, jerking along from station to station in the darkness. Occasionally a man came down the corridor with a rattling metal trolley, and our Chinese bunkmates clamored out of their bunks with tin cups and enamel thermoses, which he filled with boiling water before rattling on. The air smelled of axle grease and a pungent, mushroomy soup. By now both Claire and I knew better than to try to sleep. Using our flashlights, we sat up reading—me *Tess of the d'Urbervilles*, she *The Fountainhead*—and listening to our Walkmans while the train slowly chewed up the miles beneath us.

The relentless rocking of the car became numbing, then peculiarly erotic. I found myself returning to licentious thoughts of Trevor. My precarious time in Dinghai had revived my desire to see him. Travel, I realized, made me lonely, and loneliness made me horny. Hot, crazy Trevor. I began reminiscing about our fling, investing it with far more emotion and significance than I'd ever originally accorded it: perhaps traveling does this to all people, but at age twenty-one, this was pretty much my standard operating procedure anyway.

The delay in getting our train tickets had set Claire and me back several days. Now we'd be arriving in Beijing exactly *on* Trevor's birthday. When Trevor first proposed meeting at the Meridian Gate to celebrate, I'd half figured he was kidding. But now, each rotation of the train's wheels brought me closer to him, stoking my anticipation, the rhythm synchronizing with the throb of my desire to see him. I imagined him pressed into the dingy berth beside me, his smooth hip bones grinding against my thighs, the minty taste on his tongue. On my Walkman, I replayed "Espresso Love" and "Little Red Corvette" as a soundtrack, then I invented insipid dialogues, then envisioned Trevor sliding his cool hands up the back of my shirt and kissing me fiercely in Tiananmen Square. Trevor undressing me slowly. Trevor nuzzling me from behind.

When Claire leaned out from her bunk and said suddenly, "I can't sleep. What are you doing?" I got flustered and snapped off my cassette player.

"Oh, just taking notes," I lied. "You?"

She stammered, "Just working on my world curriculum."

She studied me for a moment, fingering the thin gold chain around her neck.

"Actually, I can't stop thinking about Adom," she confessed shyly. "Imagining, you know, that he was here with me. And *stuff.*" She giggled and blushed. "Is that terrible?"

I shook my head. "Not at all. I want Trevor so badly, I *ache.* I know you think he's a lunatic. But oh, my God, Claire, he is so fucking hot."

"Ooh, so is Adom," she whispered. "I can't get him out of my head. Everywhere we go, I keep thinking I see him. I keep imagining he's sending me little messages, little signs—"

"I keep thinking about having sex on the Great Wall of China."

Claire laughed and clamped her hands over her mouth.

"Oh, sweetie," she scolded, "we are *so* bad."

Beijing was oppressively gray. The vast boulevards, inhuman in scale, were gray rivers of concrete teeming with black and gray bicycles. The massive, oppressive-looking stone buildings were gray. And the sky was gray, too. Even though the sun was out, it hung like a small dull pearl behind a gauze of smoke, glowing weakly without emitting any light. The air, heavy with dust from the Gobi Desert and decades of burning coal, existed in a permanent state between mist and particle, powdering the trees in the city with whitish ash, coating the rooftops, buses, and shop windows with fallout.

And Beijing was cold. As soon as we emerged from the train station, wind iced through our clothing. At the guesthouse in the south of the city, we were not upset when the proprietor informed us that he only had a twin room with a private bath available. All we cared about was a shower. We had not had a full, decent shower since Hong Kong. For three weeks now, washing had consisted of tentative forays beneath frigid spigots and searingly cold, masochistic sponge baths. My cough had crept across my chest and taken deep root. My lungs now felt knitted together with congestion. I craved eucalyptus, menthol rub, fresh orange juice. If I could just sit in a hot, steam-filled bathroom for a few hours, I thought, maybe I could breathe again.

"Yes, yes." The proprietor nodded when we asked him if there was hot water. "Number one room."

When we switched on the light to the room, we saw a private bathroom to the left with turquoise fixtures, including a turquoise Western toilet with a black plastic bagel of a toilet seat. We couldn't believe our good luck. The room itself had chunky, lacquered twin beds, a black bureau with ornate drawer pulls, and gold-flocked wallpaper that looked like it had a moiré pattern superimposed on it. Little brown polka dots streamed over it, moving in great reflective arcs across the walls.

Claire screamed.

What is it about cockroaches? People live with houseplants that grow spiky and grotesque as they creep over bookshelves, strangling things with their overgrown tendrils, their genitals exploding every spring, littering the gardens and tabletops with rotting petals. People live with cats who claw their furniture, coating it with dander and millions of adhesive hairs, filling the bathroom with ammonia-scented feces and tracking urinous kitty grit all over the floor. And dogs? Those slobbering, defecating, crotch-sniffing, face-licking shit-eaters? I've seen people literally clench bits of breakfast sausage between their lips and let their schnauzer eat it out of their mouth in an act of low-grade bestiality. And yet it's cockroaches that propel us into a frenzy of primeval disgust.

"Oh no." Claire announced, doing an about-face with her backpack. "I can't stay here."

But back downstairs, the proprietor pointed to the empty row of key hooks behind him. "No more room. You have number one room," he insisted.

Before we could protest, two blond boys came careening into the lobby shrieking, *"Cowabunga! Die!"*

Strolling behind them coolly was none other than Cynthia, dressed now in slacks and a beige cashmere sweater, a plum-colored backpack slung over one shoulder. The moment she and I saw each other, we shrieked with delight. *Oh, my God! Are you a sight for sore eyes! What are the chances? Let me get a look at you! How are you? When did you get here?* There were hugs all around.

"Anthony! Warren!" she called across the lobby. "Look who's here. It's Claire and Susie from the boat!"

Warren raced over. "Guess what? Mom lost money on the black market this morning."

"This man was going to give her a hundred and ten Chinese yuan, but he ran away," Anthony interjected, bouncing up and down, delirious with excitement.

"So I chased after him on my bicycle—"

"And Warren caught him! Warren caught him!"

"Anthony!" Warren slugged him on the shoulder. "You're not supposed to tell. This is *my* story—"

"This is *everybody's* story," Cynthia corrected. "No

hitting." She smiled at us helplessly as if to say *What can you do?* "We've been having quite a time of it here," she said, not unhappily.

"Beijing is awesome," Warren declared. "We saw a dead body."

"That would be Chairman Mao," said Cynthia. "Honestly, Warren. You *know* that—"

"We saw Tiananmen Square! And the Great Wall of China! And a lake full of ducks! And we fed all the ducks!" cried Anthony, leaping up and down. "Quack! Quack! Quack! And we saw a man peeing in the street! And we saw the Temple of Heaven! It's round, and if you spin around in it, you get all dizzy like—" He started spinning and making a shrill, regurgitative *Waaahhhhoooo* sound.

"There hasn't been a dull moment yet." Cynthia laughed. She took my hand and squeezed it. "So how have you two *been*?"

"Uh, good, I guess. We've had some adventures," I said.

Claire looked at her wearily. "We have to find someplace else to stay. Our room is crawling with roaches."

Cynthia pursed her lips. "Oh, dear. I hate to tell you, but this is *it*, I'm afraid." She gestured at the sparse lobby with its cheap silk banners dangling from bamboo dowels, its brown pilling sofas. "The boys and I were at two other hotels before this one. It's the best of the bunch. It's where everyone stays."

"There's nothing else at all?" Claire said. "But this is a capital city."

"There's the Holiday Inn Lido. But it's miles outside of town, and apparently it's in some sort of compound. And there's the Grand Hotel Beijing downtown, but it's very expensive, and I'm not even sure it's open to Westerners."

Claire looked deflated.

"If it's any consolation, we've got roaches, too. The boys just killed three in the bathtub this morning. They're keeping score, actually."

"Yeah and so far," said Warren, puffing out his bony rib cage and pounding on it, "we're winning."

"When you put the lights on, they run. But if you put toothpaste on your shoe, you can get them to stick to it," Anthony reported. "And then you can smear them along the edge of the bathtub and—"

"Okay, Anthony," said Cynthia. "That's enough."

"Mom," Warren whined, tugging on Cynthia's arm. "You said we could rent bicycles."

He and Anthony pulled at Cynthia, prodding her toward the door. She looked back at us in delighted surrender. "Get settled in, you two," she called out. "You can rent bicycles at the stand next door. We're going to spend the day at the Forbidden City, if you want to meet up with us. Otherwise, we're in room 214."

As the glass door swung shut behind them, Claire sank down on the bench near the reception desk.

"Well?" I said.

She sat staring at the crude brass key in her palm, turning it over and over as if doing this long enough would transform the key into something leading to a better room in a different hotel.

Finally she said, "How do we know Cynthia's right? I'm sorry, but you can't tell me there isn't another decent guesthouse in all of Beijing." She whipped out the Lonely Planet guide and pawed through it furiously.

I stood over her, shifting my weight. I was disgusted by cockroaches too, but Claire's squeamishness somehow brought out my bravado. We were seesawing, Yinning-and-Yanging, the two of us adhering to the laws of physics: *For every action there is an equal and opposite reaction.* I found myself thinking impatiently: *So what if there are a few cockroaches in our room? Big deal. They're everywhere in New York, too. What planet do you live on?* I didn't want to waste time hotel-hopping. I didn't want to go on a quest for the holy grail of guesthouses. I just wanted to take a hot shower and cough up as much phlegm as possible, then meet up with Trevor at the Meridian Gate.

Yet just as Claire and I were about to face off in the lobby, I heard a distinctive Australian voice saying, "Of course, if I'd been really smart, I would've had him put the tattoo on backward, so when I looked in the mirror—"

Cynthia was right: This *was* where all the backpackers stayed. Rounding the corner, with a girl tucked under each of his sculpted, tattooed biceps, was Trevor. As soon as he spotted me, he shouted "Oi!" unhooked his arms, rushed over, grabbed my chin in his hands, and kissed me full on the mouth. His goatee was prickly and rough. "Girlie, you made it!" he cried, throwing his arms around me sloppily. There was something performative about his gestures; his breath was hot and oversweet. He seemed to have already been drinking. He pulled me tightly against him, his belt buckle digging into me. "Oi. Where've you been? Adele, Luxana." He called over to the two girls. One was skinny and blond, pocked with acne. The other was chubby and sullen, with dyed black hair and red lipstick. They both wore peasant blouses and ill-fitting canvas hiking pants. They looked completely uninterested. "This is Susie." Drawing close to me, he stage-whispered, "They're from fuck-knows-where in Eastern Europe. Hardly understand a word of English. Oi, you're just in time for me birthday!" He threw his arms around me again.

I asked uncertainly. "Do we still have a date today at the Forbidden City?"

Trevor wobbled and took a step backwards. "Whoops. Sorry. Change of plans. We're going to the Great Wall tomorrow instead. We'll celebrate me birthday up there. Me and Adele and Luxana here...an' about six other people. We're just on our way to get some beers and rum from the Friendship

Store. It's going to be brilliant. This guy I met on the train up here, Wolfgang. Oi, you've got to meet him—a total fucking madman, he's this little Austrian guy who's been running around Borneo and Tibet for, like, years, with nothing but a banjo and a toothbrush. He's got this Mekong whiskey that's like fucking turpentine. He's going to come, bring his banjo. We got a couple of Kiwis that we met, plus maybe this British girl and her friend, and we're all going to sleep out—sleep out on the Great Wall of China for me twenty-second fucking birthday! How's that? So grab your sleeping bag and get ready, girlie. This is going to be the party to end all parties." He pulled my face into his and kissed me hard on the mouth again, making a smacking sound like *Mmmahh!* "Fucking brilliant," he said, more to the lobby in general than to me. "Okay, off to the Friendship Store. See you later?"

———

And then he was gone. Though the taste of him was fresh on my mouth, the image of him with his arms around those two girls was seared into my mind like a photographic negative, their faces in light and dark, echoing.

The rental bikes were old and rusted, thick-fendered, flaking black paint. They had only one gear, and they squeaked and clanked as we pedaled.

But they liberated us. Not only was the scale of Beijing massive — each city block was at least a quarter of a mile long — but once we were in motion, people no longer surrounded us, gawking. Instead they waved as they pedaled past, as if to say, *Welcome to the club!* Cycling down the boulevards with the millions of other bicycles sifting through the streets of Beijing, I felt part of something bigger.

I glanced over at Claire. She was pedaling with grim determination. We'd mapped out a route from the hotel, heading east along a canal lined with market stalls called Hucheng City Moat, then turning left up a big street past the Temple of Heaven. The streets were lined with dumpling houses, minuscule groceries selling bottles of fruit liquor and canned goods, tool and die shops, all of them opening directly onto the sidewalk: no storefronts, no doors. Men were drilling, repairing cracked roof tiles amid great clouds of dust, whacking noisily away with ball-peen hammers. The streets were laced with sycamore trees and an elaborate corseting of electrical wires.

Down the side streets, the roads turned to dirt: more *hutongs,* those ancient, labyrinthine neighborhoods built around courtyards and communal plumbing. We veered into one to explore, but the narrow road was muddy and pockmarked, and my bicycle chain snapped.

"Oh, fuck," I said. Claire and I kneeled in the

dust beside my bike, fingering the dry, broken chain. We'd left our Swiss Army knives back in the room, and our phrase book contained nothing regarding bicycle repairs. Around us, a crowd began to gather, and as they pressed in more closely, I could sense Claire's uneasiness. A man in an oil-stained Mao cap pushed through. Smiling, he pointed to the bike and motioned for us to follow.

He led us back through an alley, past a stack of crates and debris. If this had been America, we'd never have followed, but what were our options? He brought us to a dilapidated shed in a courtyard and pulled out a pair of pliers and a small can. After expertly repairing the chain, he nimbly rethreaded it around the gear and gave it a salutary glug of oil. When we attempted to pay him, he refused adamantly, smiling and waving us on.

We cycled north, past the ominous stone Qian-men Gate, past Mao's tomb, into Tiananmen Square. At the far end, on the massive crimson wall guarding the Forbidden City, the enormous framed portrait of Mao stared down beneficently. Our guidebook said Tiananmen was the largest public square in the world, but it didn't look like a public square so much as a giant parking lot.

Wind whipped across the pavement. Except for a lone man sweeping around a flagpole and the soldiers standing sentry at the entrance to the Forbidden City, it was eerily empty. There were no people in this "people's square," no hint of passion or lifeblood: no sense at all of what would occur just twenty-seven months later. At this particular moment in time, Tiananmen Square was still simply just the world's largest rectangle of poured concrete.

And so we continued on, coaxing our rusty bicycles through the vast gray streets, breathing in the sooty mauve-colored air. We located the Main Post Office, where we could wait for hours in a Plexiglas booth to place a collect call to the United States. We passed the Grand Hotel Beijing. The Friendship Store.

Although we were cycling through one of the most populous cities on the planet, the boulevards had a peculiarly empty, post-apocalyptic feel. Pedaling along the main east-west thoroughfare, Chang'an Avenue, we came across one of the only signs of life. Bizarrely, on a corner near the train station was a lone low-slung gray building with a bold red awning. Maxim's, it read in puckish gold letters. The plate glass windows were tinted black, like a limousine's. Yet inside we could make out the hallmarks of the famous French eatery: white-clothed tables, crystal glasses, fully intact but utterly empty.

"What the hell is Maxim's doing in Beijing?" Claire said. Across the enormous avenue, we spied a tiny French bakery selling a few trays of fresh croissants and crème-filled coronets. Other than that, the neighborhood was cracked and dusty, with the feel of a war zone salvaged by bureaucrats. Who shopped at the little lemon-yellow bakery? Who frequented Maxim's?

"Let's get out of here," Claire said. "This place is weirding me out."

———

It was on this first day in Beijing that I began to notice the change in Claire's mood. She seemed unusually petulant, contrary, disengaged. The expression on her face grew fretful. It was like an abrupt shift in the weather, a surprise cold front, a bank of clouds rolling in, eclipsing the sun. Stranger still, she barely spoke.

When I asked her where she wanted to bicycle to next, she crossed her arms and scowled. "I don't *know*. Christ. Where do *you* want to go?" For the rest of the afternoon, she refused to make eye contact with me.

It seemed I must have done something to offend her, though I couldn't imagine what. As we cycled through the city, I replayed the day's events. The only variable, the only anomaly that I could think of, was Trevor.

Ah. I had a guy. Never mind that Claire thought he was creepy and crazy and more than a little vulgar. Trevor had kissed me right in front of her that morning, while she was relegated to pining away for a boat hand who was growing more and more illusory each day. In spite of herself, she was jealous. That had to be it.

As we pedaled furiously to get back to the hotel before sunset, Claire's bike got a flat tire twice. Each time we found ourselves stranded in different neighborhoods, and each time, local people rushed to our rescue with pumps and duct tape. There was much merriment in helping us, lots of pantomiming and laughter. One grandmother insisted we hold her infant grandson; another came running out to us with a bowl of soup and two spoons. There was such an outpouring of kindness shown to us that by the time we returned to the hotel, Claire and I were fairly in love with the Chinese. Certainly their generosity was unlike anything we Americans had ever showed to foreigners back home. In fact, it was more than either of us had experienced back home ourselves.

The goodwill seemed restorative. Claire was now buoyant, pirouetting. "Can you get over that?" she said as we entered the lobby. "They have nothing, nothing at all. But look at them. *Those* are good people, Suze. Those are people we can be safe with. Hey," she said. "Let's go have a drink and toast to our rescuers."

At the hotel bar, travelers sat around in loose groups smoking and trading stories. Most were dressed in rough Tibetan sweaters and batik drawstring pants, and no one was much older than we were. It was like a scruffier version of college. I recognized a few faces from back at the Pujiang Hotel in Shanghai. The backpacking community was proving to be a small, recycled pool.

Back in Shanghai, however, our fellow travelers had been positively magnanimous, routinely lending out shampoo, trading guidebooks, and giving away their leftover foreign currencies. *You're going to Katmandu? Here. Take this card for this guesthouse. Tell the owner that Molly and Angela sent you. And do you want these two sweaters? No, please, take them. We're off to Bali, so we don't need them anymore. Save your money.*

But in Beijing, the mood had turned noticeably frostier. Perhaps it was the cold. Perhaps it was the pollution exfoliating our lungs. But people leaned back in their chairs with their arms crossed, sizing each other up shrewdly. *Who exactly are you?* And conversations quickly turned competitive: Who was the most hard-core, the most rugged, the most *real*?

"Personally, I only ever travel in third class," said a jaded-looking Brit with reptilian eyelids. "It took me forty-six hours to make it here from Kunming, but it's the only way to experience anything."

"Oh, hard seat is the only way to go," a bearded New Zealander quickly agreed. "I did practically the whole eighteen-hour trip from Xian to Beijing standing up in hard seat because the car was so packed. There was no ventilation and no working toilets. Everyone was coughing and spitting. I even slept standing up. I was the only Westerner in the whole car."

"When my boyfriend and I went to India, we made sure to get a private meeting with the Dalai Lama—because otherwise, why go at all, right?" said a Danish woman, reaching behind her to tap her cigarette ash into an empty beer can by her feet.

"We traveled for eight days by local bus through the mountains. We had dysentery and there was nothing to eat but rice with maggots. But it cost only six dollars apiece, instead of the three hundred dollars the tourists pay to go in a group, and then they don't even get to meet the Dalai Lama. They just take pictures outside the temple. The way we did it was just so much more spiritual and *genuine*."

Soon we were all vying to establish our backpackers' street cred, to prove how intrepidly we'd been traveling, how much discomfort we'd incurred at how little expense. The irony of this was wholly lost on us. We were too young and myopic to recognize the perversity of a logic that equates voluntary deprivation with authentic experience. We thought that by wearing burlap pajamas, contracting intestinal parasites, and opting to ride in third class with "the people," we were somehow being less Western and more Asian. It never seemed to occur to us that only privileged Westerners travel to developing countries in the first place, then use them as playgrounds and laboratories for our own enrichment. Only privileged Westerners consider it a badge of honor to forsake modern amenities for a two-dollar-a-night roach-infested guesthouse. Only privileged Westerners sit around drinking beers at prices the natives can't afford while sentimentalizing the nation's lower standard of living and adopting it as a lifestyle.

The Asians we were seeing, of course, didn't live famished, agrarian lives due to some sort of Eastern spirituality or enlightenment. Give most of the world's population our money and opportunity, and they weren't going slumming at all. They were booking a Club Med vacation in Cancun and drinking a mai tai.

Granted, it was good, even admirable, that we young backpackers at least attempted to break through the barriers of culture and class to experience firsthand how people in Southeast Asia really lived. But we were kidding ourselves in thinking that we were somehow transcending our Western privileges by doing this.

Back in Greenwich Village, I'd once heard a self-styled preacher dressed in African kente cloth sermonizing for the Nation of Islam from atop a milk crate in Washington Square Park.

"AN-THRO-POLOGY," he'd fairly spit. "Anthro-pology. Only the white man could've invented *anthro-pology*. And for that, *we* demand an *a*-pology. Only the white man could've relegated all the other cultures of the world to a curiosity, a subject to be *subjected* to his study. Only the white man could decide that *all* the other cultures in this world are implicitly inferior. Only the white man could decide that all other cultures in this world must be *demystified.* Think about the hubris, brothers and sisters. Think about the arrogance it takes to say, 'We are going to observe cultures *less developed* than ours, *different* from ours, in order to see what we can learn about our *primeval* selves.' Think about the supreme egotism it takes to create a field of study in which your culture is the baseline—the norm against which all other cultures of the world are measured.

"Brothers and sisters," the man went on, saliva spraying from his mouth, "do *Eskimos* come down to Wall Street, pitch a tent in the stock exchange, and say, 'We're here to observe your culture'? Do *Zulu warriors* go to the Dalton School on the Upper East Side and demand to measure the height of all its children in the name of *research*? Do *Filipinos* travel to farm towns in Kansas on a *Fulbright scholarship,* then walk into someone's dining room during Thanksgiving to announce, 'We've come to record this sacred ritual of yours. Carry on as if we aren't here. After living among you, we're going back to Manila to publish articles about you and stick photographs of your family in a museum'. Does this happen, brothers and sisters? No, it does not. Only the white man shows up uninvited. Only the white man treats the rest of the world like a *specimen*. Only the white man turns his voyeurism into a so-called *social science*."

I'd thought he had a point. But sitting in the guest-house in Beijing, Claire and I got as caught up in the moment as everyone else. We glanced at each other conspiratorially, like the straight-A students we were, determined to score the highest marks in the class for derring-do and advanced voyeurism.

"I'm sorry, but I have a question," Claire interrupted, clearing her throat. "How do *you* guys deal with the military police? I mean, two weeks ago, when we went home with this Chinese friend of ours to this town that wasn't on the map, we got questioned right away because we didn't have an alien travel permit. How have you handled this sort of situation?"

The crowd grew quiet. "You got stopped by the military police?"

Claire shrugged. "Hasn't everybody?"

Watching her blink innocently and rotate her wrists in that sinuous way she had, I absolutely loved her. It was hard not to laugh.

"I mean, isn't it pretty standard," Claire said, "if you arrive someplace where Westerners haven't ever been before?"

Slowly she began unfurling our story, performing it like a striptease, letting a few odd details drop here and there. I interrupted at intervals, tossing off a few titillating asides, until people's curiosity was aroused and they pressed us to reveal more. Soon we had taken center stage, painting scenes for our riveted audience, acting out the various characters, finishing each other's sentences. As travelers were galvanized around us, we described the foreign affairs officer appearing in our Dinghai hotel room, the surreal all-fish ten-course luncheon served to us in vacuum-packed silence, and Jonnie's family's house with its refrigerator used as a storage locker. Almost as an afterthought, we recounted our harrowing encounter with the Chinese rural medical system: the poultry in the waiting room, the hole-in-the-ground latrine, the rusty syringe.

By the time we finished, the room was eerily silent.

"Wow," the New Zealander said after a spell. "You were very lucky to get out of there, is all I can say. There was a Belgian girl who got sick in Chengdu. She was hallucinating because she had an extremely high fever. The Chinese locked her in a mental institution. They wouldn't let her out for a year."

"Yeah, I heard about that girl, too," said the Brit somberly, setting down his beer can. "The Chinese don't look kindly on mental illness."

"They don't look kindly on any sick foreigners, period. You two are really, really lucky you got out of that hospital is all I can say." The New Zealander shook his head.

Beneath the white-hot spotlight of their attention,

Claire and I exchanged little smiles of carnivorous glee. In the scramble for unique adventures and experience, finally we were winning.

The next morning, however, Claire was in a snit again. She stomped around the room, flinging her dirty clothing this way and that.

"I have to get out of here. This room is disgusting," she snapped, stuffing a pile of crumpled laundry into her backpack. "I can't sleep here. I can't even think straight."

To keep the cockroaches off the mattresses, we'd moved the beds away from the walls and slept with the lights on. Despite the relentless hissing and clanking of the pipes, the room had stayed as cold as a meat locker all night, too, so we'd slept in virtually all of our clothes, one grimy layer piled on top of another. In the end, it hadn't been that dissimilar to being on the train. Neither of us had slept much, and my cough was now markedly worse.

"Go to the Great Wall today if you want, but I'm staying here," Claire announced, yanking off her gray cardigan and balling it up.

"What? You don't want to see the Great Wall?"

Our plan had been to take the CITS bus leaving from the hotel that morning after breakfast. Trevor and all his friends were going on it, too, loaded down with goodies for his birthday party. He'd instructed us to bring sleeping bags and flashlights.

"Please, I have absolutely zero desire to behave like some idiotic tourist," Claire sniffed. "I mean, going to China and seeing the Great Wall—how fucking unoriginal is that? I want to do something bold."

"What are you talking about? The Great Wall *is* bold," I cried. " 'Hey. Let's build a wall and seal off all of Mongolia'—I mean, talk about chutzpah."

But Claire refused to stop rummaging through her backpack and look at me. I couldn't tell if she was honestly opposed to the idea or simply punishing me for my romance with Trevor.

"C'mon, Claire," I pleaded. Ever since we hatched our plans back at the International House of Pancakes, we'd been talking about climbing the Great Wall together. It'd been one of our primary goals for the whole trip. Plus, though I was loath to admit this, if Trevor blew me off and ended up spending the night with Adele or Luxana instead, I didn't want to be left sleeping alone on the wall, stewing in rejection and heartache.

"C'mon, Genevieve," I prodded. "Think about how cool it's going to be to tell everyone that we camped out on the Great Wall."

Claire glanced at me disdainfully. "The only thing that's good for is getting arrested. Trevor and those guys are lunatics. If they get caught sleeping out there, they'll probably spend the next seven years in a Chinese prison."

"Okay, we don't have to sleep out, if you don't want to," I said, trying to conceal my disappointment. "We can just go there, turn around, and come back. But you can't miss out—"

Claire crossed her arms and tilted her head, as if considering me from a different angle. "Look. Go," she said peevishly, with a dismissive flutter of her hand. "Go see it for both of us, okay? I actually need to stay here and take care of some business."

"Business?"

She looked at me cryptically. "I can't...I don't...There's a contact I have to make here today."

"A contact?"

She exhaled with exasperation. "*Forget it.*"

When I continued to stare at her, she conceded, "Look, it's something to do with my father, my father and his business, okay? And Adom. And that's all I can say right now. I just...I don't want to get into it."

She snatched up her toiletry bag, strode into the bathroom, and clicked the lock behind her. I heard the shower twist on. But a moment later, she poked her blond, disheveled head back out through the door.

"Look, just go, okay?" she said over the running water. "Have fun. See Trevor. Do—whatever. But don't tell anyone what I've just told you, okay? And don't get arrested, either. I'm serious, Suze."

By bus, it took two hours to reach the Great Wall at Badaling. Trevor sat in the back with Adele, Luxana, and a contingent of shaggy, derelict travelers who appeared to have spent the majority of their time in Asia cultivating bizarre facial hair and playing Hacky Sack. When I first boarded the bus, he motioned for me to come and sit on his lap, but I declined; now that I appeared to be just another girl in his harem, the prospect of being with him wasn't nearly so appealing. Although he clamped his hand over his heart and feigned being stabbed, he made no attempt to move up to join me. I sat instead beside two quiet, affable Canadian women in sun hats and lemon-yellow cardigans who attempted to follow the route along in their guidebook. Slowly the housing projects and industrial buildings of the city gave way to desolate countryside.

Several miles before we arrived, the road descended into a ravine, and we started to catch glimpses of the Great Wall snaking over the pleated mountains. The sight was thrilling, a jolt of adrenaline. When we arrived in the little parking lot beneath the entrance, there wasn't much besides a ticket booth, a crude snack cart, and a small lean-to selling souvenir T-shirts. As soon as we poured out of the bus, it was like a starter pistol had gone off. Everyone raced up the hill at the same time. We not only wanted to be the first ones on the Great Wall, but to get away from everyone else. Mind you, there were perhaps thirty of us all told, but we had each somehow decided that we constituted a mob. We each wanted this experience to be ours alone. We all seemed to be under the impression that we were the only people ever to set foot there.

One of the Canadian women shouted, "I've heard that the right side, the steeper side, is better and less crowded." As soon as we got our tickets, the three of us dashed up the ancient stone steps scaling the wall on the right.

When we emerged from the guardhouse at the top, the view was magnificent. The Wall appeared to be draped over the mountains like bunting.

But I refused to stop and take it in. Not yet. I wanted to hike to the highest point possible first, beyond any vestige of modern civilization, and see it as it was five hundred years ago.

The two Canadians and I climbed doggedly. The tepid shower at the hotel had done nothing to improve my respiratory system. My chest hurt each time I inhaled; I couldn't seem to get enough air into my lungs. The more we climbed, the more distance we gained, the farther out we got from the entrance and the others, the more exhilarating and perilous it felt. Amazingly, the wall was entirely unsupervised. There were no emergency call boxes, public address systems, tourist information kiosks, or guards. It had simply been left to molder there as it had been moldering for centuries, slinking up and down over the mountains, crumbling and serpentine. Ostensibly we could've climbed all the way to Mongolia without anybody noticing or caring.

Finally we were beyond the last tourist. When the Canadians stopped to take pictures, I told them I'd see them on the way back down. It was just me now, panting and wheezing, struggling on alone at the crest.

The view was astounding. For 360 degrees around me, there were nothing but mountains and the single sinuous wall slithering all the way to the horizon in either direction. I was a city kid. I'd never stood on top of a ridge like this before. I'd never experienced such topography. The wall felt sacred and majestic. There was no sound but the ruffling of the wind. I felt as though I were standing on the roof of the world.

Looking out over the stones and the hills, I experienced a seizure of joy.

The wall and its landscape existed beyond all petty, quotidian fears. There was only stone, permanence, the curvature of the earth. The wind was as relentless and rhythmic as the tide. Standing there, I felt my anxiety dissolve. I suddenly no longer had bickering parents hurtling toward divorce. My student loans evaporated into the ether. I stopped glancing over my shoulder. My flat, thin hair, my glasses, my belly vanished. The college advisors demanding

"So Now What Are You Going to Do?"; my rejection letters from publishers, magazines, scholarship committees; the disapproving looks from Claire; our daunting itinerary traced on a world map in fluorescent pink Magic Marker; the chronic voices deep in my own head saying: *Who do you think you are? You'll never amount to anything. You're untalented and unlovable. You will die alone.* —all of this was banished by a slow suffusion of peace. At the Great Wall, I no longer feared my own powerlessness and insignificance. *All individuals are nothing,* the stones seemed to say, *just a speck in the continuum.* Whether we're beautiful or skeletal, whether we're sharecroppers or neurosurgeons, whether we fight in wars or give birth to children, whether we eat tofu or watch Morton Downey Jr. on television, whether we're tormented lovers or house cleaners loaded down with shopping bags on the subway train, whether we're Chinese or American—all of this is irrelevant. In the end, we're all just atomic particles destined to be reabsorbed into the cosmos. *And it's okay.* Life will come and go, over and over. Only the mountains and this wall have managed to endure.

I stood transfixed, soaking in my thoughts, listening to the wind and the scrape of my own strangulated breathing. Clouds slid by. The light shifted. The mountainsides turned from green to gold. Eventually the sun sank into my line of vision, refracting into blades of copper. I turned and started to make my way back down to the populated section of the wall. In the distance, I could see Trevor and his ragtag friends climbing together over the crumbling stones with their sleeping bags, their musical instruments, their knapsacks bulging with liquor. They were going to camp for the night in a guardhouse.

It would be so easy to call out his name and hobble after him. He would wait for me, I knew. He'd take me in his arms, slide his hand down my back, kiss my neck hungrily. For weeks, I'd been teasing myself with licentious fantasies. Now I could do it, really do it with him, right here. Watch the sun go down, then voom! How wild would that be? What kind of a story would *that* make? Think of the bragging rights. There didn't seem to be anyone patrolling the wall at all. We could truly get away with it. Trevor and I: we could fuck right here under the stars, with a view to Mongolia—then titillate ourselves with the memory of it for the rest of our waking lives.

But the Great Wall was a cathedral. I could see that now. Partying on it, strewing the place with empty liquor bottles and milky condoms, was a desecration. As much as I liked to see myself as some sort of erotic outlaw, the truth was, I couldn't bring myself to do something so obnoxious and illegal. I found myself instead slowly descending the wall one step at a time, taking care not to twist an ankle. In the distance, I could make out Trevor's muscular V-shaped back, receding over the stones.

The next evening, I would sit beside him in his Beijing hotel room as he packed for a morning train to Xian. He would tell me that I missed the most amazing night of his life—and when he kissed me tenderly and murmured, "God, you're gorgeous, girlie. The things I could've done to you up there," I would feel a huge kick of regret.

But that afternoon I simply made my way back down to the entrance, forked over fifty yuan for a crimson souvenir sweatshirt reading *I Climbed the Great Wall of China,* and obediently boarded the bus back to Beijing with the other docile, law-abiding, gum-chewing tourists.

———

Back at the hotel, Claire was gone. All our belongings were gone. Our room had been vacated, the beds stripped, though the door remained ajar and the lightbulbs still burned, casting ghoulish reflections over the wallpaper. "Claire?" I shouted.

Stupidly I checked inside the closets and the bathtub, as if she might be hiding in them. Just as I began to panic, she appeared behind me in the doorway.

"Oh, there you are," she said dully. Her newly washed hair was tucked up in her towel, and she was dressed in her pin-striped pajamas, which had started to pill and turn gray. Her eyes were puffy and pink-rimmed. "I got us moved to a better room." She turned on her heels and headed down the hallway, her flip-flops slapping against the linoleum.

Our new room was a mirror image of the first, except that the wallpaper was an angry red and the bathroom fixtures were mustard colored. "No bugs," she said, blowing her nose. "I made sure."

She'd taken the liberty, I saw, of unpacking our things and arranging our toiletries neatly on one of the shelves. Plopping down on the bed she'd claimed for herself, she picked up Lonely Planet and resumed reading, seemingly oblivious to my presence. I stood there, not knowing quite how to respond. I was beginning to feel like I needed a *TV Guide* just to keep track of her moods.

Slowly I removed my day pack and unpeeled the Velcro straps of my Reeboks. Inexplicably I felt compelled to do all of this as quietly as possible.

"Oh," she said finally, looking up, "I forgot to ask. How was the wall? You didn't sleep out?"

I shook my head and sat down on the mattress beside her. "Oh, Claire. It was the most amazing thing I've ever seen in my life. Please. I want to go back there with you. I want to spend my birthday on the Great Wall of China. Not like Trevor. No wild party. Just you and me. You really have to see it."

I expected her to fight. But she just shrugged limply. "Sure. Okay. If that's what you want."

Then her voice broke. She started to weep.

"Claire?"

Her cry gave way to a wail. She covered her face with her hands.

I grabbed her by the shoulders. "Claire, what is it?"

For a moment she heaved with emotion.

"Oh, God," she said at last, blowing her nose, "the day went so well at first. I rented a bicycle and went to the Grand Hotel Beijing and had tea, okay? Proper tea, like they might serve at the Plaza. They serve it with cream and gingerbread, and you sit in Western armchairs and listen to classical music, and it's clean and warm and quiet, and it feels so civilized. Civilized and elegant—nobody's spitting. Nobody's frying vegetables in the gutter. And the waiters speak English. And then? Then I biked over to the Main Post Office, by Tiananmen, and put in a collect call home. It took an hour and forty-five minutes for them to put me through, but my father was there, and Dominic and Alexander were home for the weekend, so I got to talk to all of them. And it was just so great to hear their voices, you know? It was evening there, and everyone had finished dinner. And then, later, after I went around and did my research, and, you know, *stuff,* and did some reconnaissance and all that, I came back here, and I just really, really wanted to talk to them some more. And the hotel can book collect calls from here, too, I found out—it just takes longer. So I waited in our room for, like, two hours, and the call finally came through — and, and I heard my father's voice again, and oh, Susie. He was really upset. It was, like, four o'clock in the morning back there, and he was crying to me and shouting and begging me to come home. And I just felt … I felt … there were all these cockroaches running all over the walls and this awful banging from the courtyard — I could barely even hear him — and I hadn't had anything to eat except for the cookies at the Grand Hotel, because when I was out on the bike, the only dumpling house I could find along Qianmen — the Chinese in it were all just staring and staring at me like I was some kind of freak — and then I heard my father's voice, and he sounded so worried — "

She keeled forward, hugging her stomach, and let out an anguished sob.

"Oh, Claire." I reached over and stroked her hair. "I get homesick, too."

Claire sat up. "No. It's not that." She blew her nose again. "It's — so I get off the phone with him, right? And I go downstairs and demand that we get another room because I just can't take another minute of the cockroaches crawling all over the place, and it's this huge hassle, Suze. The guy at the front desk doesn't understand a word of English, and it takes an eternity, and finally I check out *this* room and move all of our stuff into it, and I sit down, right? And I just try to calm myself down for a while, right, so I open the guidebook and a map I got to figure out a plan for tomorrow. And then I see—I see *this* . . ."

She unfurled a Chinese tourist map of Beijing and jabbed her index finger in the middle. There, amid little dots corresponding to names on the legend, was one for a small building labeled "PLO."

"PLO," she cried. "What the fuck is the PLO doing here?"

I studied the map. The PLO building appeared to be in an area crammed with embassies and government buildings. "Are you sure it's the *'PLO'* PLO and not, maybe, I don't know? The People's Leadership Office or something?"

It seemed unlikely to me that the People's Republic of China had much to do with Yasir Arafat. It seemed even less likely that the Palestine Liberation Organization, which in 1986 was still widely classified as a terrorist organization, would have one of its headquarters openly listed on a tourist map.

Claire glared at me. "Yes, it's the PLO!" she yelled. She grabbed the map away and threw it on the floor. She buried her face in her hands and let out another sob, her blond hair tumbling forward.

"This is not good," she cried after a moment, blowing her nose. "We could be in terrible danger."

I sat there, stunned, not sure what to say. On September 5, two weeks before we'd left for Hong Kong, a Pan Am flight had been hijacked in Pakistan. While I'd been serving Harvey Wallbangers and answering telephones in New York City, and Claire had been basting herself in Ban de Soleil in Hilton Head, terrorists had gone through the cabin of Flight 73 collecting passengers' passports and singling out Israelis and Americans. Three other hijackings had taken place the previous year, including one of a TWA flight by Hezbollah, who'd killed an American, and another by Palestinian militants, who'd taken over a cruise ship and murdered a disabled American Jew. For days, the news had reported on how the terrorists had thrown him and his wheelchair overboard.

Yet although these incidents were alarming, none of them resonated that much or transformed the American national psyche. The Cold War was at its height, and everyone in the United States was far more preoccupied with the possibility of nuclear war with the Soviet Union. The culture was full of it. "No Nukes" rallies and rock concerts. Movies like *Top Gun* and *War Games*. An apocalyptic made-for-TV movie *The Day After* that was screened nationally, with call-in psychologists on hand for viewers traumatized by scenes of atomic Armageddon. President Reagan tested a microphone once by saying, "My fellow Americans, I'm pleased to tell you today that I've signed legislation that will outlaw Russia forever. We begin bombing in five minutes" (*Ha-ha! Just kidding, folks!*), and people went batshit. Certainly, nuclear annihilation was the foremost fear in my mind. For years, every night before I went to sleep, I prayed,

Please, God, don't let everything blow up in a mush-room cloud.

Even if there really was an outpost of the PLO in Beijing, it didn't seem to me like much to worry about. The PLO, ETA, the IRA, the Brigada Rosa, Abu Nidal, the Contras, the Shining Path, skinheads: someone was always building a bomb in a basement somewhere. The PLO, to me, seemed like the least of our problems.

Granted, two years later, in 1988, a friend of mine would be blown up aboard Pan Am Flight 103 over Scotland, and I wouldn't be nearly so sanguine after that. And after September 11, 2001, I would become so hysterical and traumatized I'd require medication.

But at that precise moment in history, I was still young and unfazed. Even if there actually was a PLO office in China, why on earth would the Palestinians waste their time on two backpackers holed up in a fleabag hotel with a bunch of tampons, some paper-back novels, and an astrology book?

"Look," I said gently. "I don't really think they'd be targeting *us,* Claire. I mean, for starters, your last name is Dutch and mine is English. It's not like we're named Shlomo and Lipschitz, and we're going around waving American flags or anything—"

She stared at me with alarm. "Susie," she whis-pered, "you don't *know* what these people are cap-able of."

She wiped her eyes with the palms of her hands,

sniffled, and readjusted herself on the bed until she was facing me.

"Okay." Taking my hand, she cleared her throat. "You know how you told me you have a secret mistrust of Germans? And you know how I got on your case about it? Well, I guess I owe you an apology. Because I have the same sort of prejudice. Except that mine's toward the Arabs. They're dangerous, Susie. They're crazy and fanatical. I don't trust them, and Adom doesn't trust them, and neither does my father. He says that they're going to cause more trouble in this world than anything we've seen so far. And, Suze, he *knows* things. And so do I. I have special information, Suze. *I have information about what's coming up.*"

"What's coming up?" I said warily. Her tone was suddenly chilling. "What do you mean?"

She shook her head. "I can't say. Just promise me we'll be careful? If I say not to talk to someone or to stay away from someplace, do you promise you'll listen?"

I stared at her. It seemed to me she was being completely irrational. For a moment I was utterly dumbstruck. I felt a flood of anxiety.

But then I realized.

The small daily privations and discomforts of China were becoming cumulative, wearing Claire down like iron filings, messing with her head. She was sleep deprived and possibly malnourished. For nearly three weeks, she'd been subsisting mostly on toast, dumplings, rice, malaria pills, and beer. I'd seen her at meals: She hadn't been eating. Our socks and shirts were crunchy with grime. Bundled in layers, we were always either freezing or sweating. And then of course she'd been sick. China was exhausting her. It was like three weeks straight of pulling all-nighters. It could make anyone paranoid.

I decided to humor her. "Okay. I promise. We'll be careful," I said, giving her a reassuring squeeze. "But in return, promise me something? That you'll eat a little more? And try to get some sleep?"

————

The next morning, Claire announced that she wanted us to leave Beijing as soon as possible; we should celebrate my birthday on the Great Wall, then skedaddle. "We've got to go someplace peaceful, someplace in the country, with rivers and trees," she said. "Let's go south to Guilin. Everyone says it's beautiful there, and warm. I just know I'll feel calmer."

This sounded like a fine plan to me. Every time I inhaled now, it felt as if I'd cracked a rib, and the pollution was giving me headaches. A few more days in Beijing were about all I could handle.

As soon as we finished breakfast, we rented bicycles and headed up toward the train station to book tickets. It was so cold that pedaling felt like whiplash. By the time we reached the City Moat, we'd lost all feeling in our fingers. The clothing stalls along the canal sold vinyl jackets trimmed with fake fur and old army surplus overcoats. Claire propped her bike up against one of the booths and tried on an enormous military coat. It enveloped her in padding; she no longer looked human so much as like a big olive-colored sausage roll.

"This is perfect," she said, drawing the hood up. It was so big, it fell down over her forehead, visually scalping her. "Camouflage. No one will be able to tell who the hell I am in this, what nationality."

I didn't have the heart to tell her that putting on a Chinese army coat did nothing to hide the fact that she was five-nine and blond. Her hair peeked out of the hood in yellow-white filaments.

Meanwhile, the only outerwear I could find that fit over my breasts was an ugly bubblegum-pink acrylic sweater. I looked like a giant powder puff. The two of us now made quite a sight. If we thought we'd garnered looks from the Chinese *before,* I suspected we really were in for a shock now.

By the time we reached the train station, there was a long line just to get the little paper tickets that entitled us to wait in the CITS line. When we finally got those, we sat on the wooden benches interminably. The cavernous waiting room was smoky and dank. I couldn't stop coughing. Everyone who walked by openly stared at us, chewing, spitting. "What?" Claire snapped at them. "What are you looking at? What is so fucking interesting?"

"Easy, Genevieve," I said.

Another hour went by. The woman behind the CITS ticket window was no more than six feet away from us. Although fully aware of our presence, she slid beads around on an abacus for a little while, then thumbed through a stack of receipts wrapped in a rubber band, licking her fingertips and moving her lips as she counted. When she was finally finished, she stared off into infinity. After a good fifteen minutes, she checked her watch and rearranged herself on her stool. Just when we thought she would finally deign to help us, she reached below the counter, pulled out a small apple, and began coring it with a pocketknife.

Claire grew more and more agitated, which made me oddly Zen-like. Back in New York City, my impulse would've been to beat the ticket seller to death with her goddamn abacus, but now that we were deep in the People's Republic of China, I thought: *Well, what can we do, really?* A certain philosophical resignation set in. Or perhaps the Communist bureaucracy had simply worn me down.

Finally Claire snapped, "Okay. That's it." Grabbing her wallet out of her shoulder bag, she pulled out a fistful of FEC notes and stomped over to the CITS desk.

"Look, don't tell me you don't speak English because I know that you do," she said, pounding the ticket counter. "And don't act like you don't see us sitting over there, because I know damn well that you do, too. We have been waiting for almost two hours. And I don't know who you think you are, but you should know one thing. My father is a very important businessman back in America. And once I tell him how you people have ignored us and abused our goodwill, you will not hear the end of it."

I stepped up behind Claire, took her by the elbow, and tried to guide her back over to the bench. She flailed angrily, jerking her arm away. "No, Susie. This is bullshit." She turned to the CITS representative, who now sat so motionless, she appeared to be fossilized.

"We've filled out the forms, we've brought our passports, we have all the correct change, we've got our wait-on-the-goddamn-bench tickets, and there's nobody else here. So what's the problem? Why the hell are you ignoring us?"

A CITS manager with a gold nameplate reading "Ed" came scurrying over.

"Yes, miss?" he said uneasily. "Can I help you?" He swung open the little half door that separated the waiting area from the ticket counter and made his way around to the CITS window.

"Well, gee. Let's see. I'm at the train station. And I'm at the ticket counter. So, as radical as this may sound, I'm here because I actually want to buy some train tickets — not just sit on a bench all day with my thumb up my ass," Claire said.

"Okay, you give us forms. You give us passports, please," Ed said.

"We want two hard sleeper tickets to Guilin. Leaving the morning of October 23. Is that too much to ask?"

"Yes. You give us forms. You give us passport."

As soon as we handed over our documents, he disappeared.

"Jesus fucking Christ," Claire muttered. She leaned against the counter tapping her foot, refusing to look at me. Her hair was frizzled with static. Her cheeks were wind-burned and swollen, giving her a wild, engorged look. With her long military coat, she was quite a sight.

"What the hell do you have to do to get a goddamn train ticket in this country is what I'd like to know," she announced to no one in particular.

After ten minutes, Ed reappeared and handed us back our passports. "Okay. Yes. Here you are."

"How much are the tickets?" Claire asked.

He ignored her and said something instead to the CITS woman in Mandarin. She tore off two slips of rice paper and slid them beneath the window toward us.

"Next ticket to Guilin available in six days," Ed said.

"Six days?" Claire cried. "Are you kidding me?"

"Sir, *ching*," I said obsequiously, stepping demurely

up to the window, "are you sure that perhaps there isn't anything earlier—"

"You know, back in America, my father is a very important businessman," Claire said loudly. "We are special guests from America—"

"You pay now. You come back in three day. You bring receipts, collect tickets. Then train leave three more day after," Ed said. "You have two hard sleeper, foreigner price."

With a snort of disgust, Claire snatched the receipts up and shoved them in her purse. "When we come back in three days, do we have to wait again, or can we just walk straight up to your counter this time?"

Ed pointed back at the first ticket counter. "When you come back, you take ticket. You wait on bench. When we call ticket number, you collect tickets."

"Of course. More tickets, more waiting. That's all you have in this goddamn country. Tickets and waiting. Oh yeah, and phlegm." She shook her head and looked at me. "I don't see how the Chinese think they're ever going to amount to anything in this world. Their whole fucking system is medieval."

———

The next morning, as we got dressed in shivering silence, Claire said, "I need to spend the day alone. I've got more business to attend to."

"More business?" Claire seemed to want to spend more and more time on her own, scribbling feverishly in her notebook and bicycling into the city for hours on end. "I'm sorry, but what kind of business?"

She looked at me cryptically. "Sweetie, Libras shouldn't ask questions."

I just didn't have it in me to argue, so I rented a bicycle and pedaled despondently toward the city center alone. I arranged to meet Cynthia and her boys after lunch; until then I wasn't quite sure what to do with myself. Just outside the Temple of Heaven, I got a flat tire again, and I had to walk the bicycle half a mile beyond the park before I could find someone in the *hutong* to repair it. By the time the bike was fixed, I was nearly in tears.

My loneliness was outsized, festering. I felt as if I was starting to warp. To console myself, I imagined as I biked to Tiananmen Square that I was being filmed. *So, Ms. Gilman, here you are, the only American biking along with thousands of Chinese through the streets of Beijing. Please tell the audience back home about how you've managed to function so well in such a radically challenging environment.* I pictured vast, adoring audiences being wowed as they witnessed me purchasing a bunch of bananas on Qianmen Road. "My, isn't that impressive?" they'd marvel as I sputtered the words *hello, four,* and *thank you* in Chinese to a fruit vendor. "What a linguistic genius."

When this fantasy ran its course, I cast about for

something else to occupy my mind. Since Trevor was gone, I began imagining that my lover Jake was actually pedaling on a bicycle alongside me, urging me on. Since he'd backpacked through India, I thought he might be uniquely able to understand how you could travel to one of the most populous nations on earth, only to feel massively lonely and estranged. I began inventing conversations with him in my head. Ironically, it seemed that the best way to deal with the reality of China was to retreat into fantasy.

Cynthia, Warren, and Anthony were waiting for me with their bicycles just outside the Forbidden City. It was their last day in Beijing; the next morning, they were taking a train to Guangzhou in order to cross the border back into Hong Kong on a hydrofoil.

Cynthia shook her head incredulously. "It's only been three weeks, but I feel like we've been here a year. Can you believe it? Time is so distorted in China. It's like another dimension."

Warren zoomed ahead of us through the boulevards, pumping faster and faster on his peeling black bike. As we raced to keep up, the sun pressed wanly through the haze, warming the streets. The sky burned an unnatural cotton-candy pink. The squat tiled houses and corrugated storefronts whipped past. Part of what made Beijing appear so gray and industrial, I realized, was its total lack of commercialism—no billboards, neon signs, gaudy advertisements; no tantalizing piles of junky plastic goods in the shops. The only vibrancy was the crimson of the Chinese flag and the gate to the Forbidden City. And oh, yes. The enormous portrait of Mao.

We biked to Behai Park, then up, down, everywhere. By the time they dropped me off at the Grand Hotel Beijing to meet Claire for tea, my legs were jellied. Balancing on her bike, Cynthia pulled a tiny pad out of her day pack and scribbled down her home address.

"Please." She pressed it into my hand. "If you're ever in Southern California—"

"Likewise," I said, jotting my parents' address on the inside cover of her guidebook, "if you ever want to take the boys sightseeing in New York—"

As they pedaled back down Chang'an Boulevard, the three of them glanced back one last time and waved. Watching their blond heads bobbing, then dissolving into the sea of dark hair, I felt a stab of grief. I found myself already missing their unconditional warmth, their pioneer spirit. Any time I'd been with them, they made me feel like family. Now I would never see them again.

———

He was a gangly man, with a narrow, pleasant face and a basketball player's build: airplane shoulders, rangy arms, spatula hands. His legs were too big to fit beneath the table, so he jotted on a legal pad balanced on one knee, his tie flung carelessly over his shoulder.

Although he was Asian, something about the over-size, unapologetic sprawl of him seemed strangely familiar.

"Excuse me," I said, "but do you speak English?"

He glanced up. "Let's hope so." He smiled, adjust-ing his glasses. "I grew up in Baltimore."

His name was Lee, and of course I could join him, he said. I dropped gratefully onto the empty chair across from his. The tea room was filled to capac-ity. Tired and ill-at-ease, I began to babble. Besides Cynthia and her boys, Lee was the first American I'd encountered in weeks. *Thanks. I've just spent eight hours on a bicycle. I'm waiting for someone. God only knows where she is. I don't mean to bother you.*

"It's not a problem." Lee capped his fountain pen and set it on the table. Gold cuff links like ampersands glinted on his wrists. "What brings you to Beijing?"

When I shrugged and said, "Just backpacking around," he whistled through his teeth. "Wow. This doesn't seem like the kind of place you'd want to be on your own for any extended period of time." He sat back and studied me, frowning. "I'm impressed," he said finally, as if he'd just decided. "Want some tea?"

Lee was a Korean-American investment banker working for a small group of venture capitalists; this was his second trip to Beijing. He was staying at the Lido Holiday Inn on the outskirts of the city.

"It's almost hermetically sealed over there, but that's just fine with me," he laughed as he speared a slice of lemon and passed me the little plate. "They've got a bowling alley, a swimming pool, a 'foreigners only' supermarket. It's in the middle of nowhere, but then again"—he smiled drily—"so is the rest of China."

As we traded stories, I learned that Lee had attended Harvard Business School, was an antique car enthusiast, and used to play squash competitively. Although he'd grown up in Maryland "addicted to television and Oreos," he now lived in Mayfair and spent the bulk of his time traveling to Singapore, Japan, and Korea on business. Only recently, now that Deng Xiaoping had implemented plans for modernization, was his company considering investing in China. But Lee was skeptical. "I just don't see how this country is going to turn itself around anytime soon," he said frankly. "Industrially, it's anywhere between sixty to eighty years behind us, and that's not even counting the rural areas. And the infrastructure is terrible."

As he stirred his tea, he looked wistful. He seemed accustomed to solitude. Lee was thirty-six. If we'd met in the States, we'd have had absolutely no reason to sit together and probably nothing to say. But here? We had that special camaraderie of the displaced, of sad people with suitcases.

Claire arrived suddenly, in a flurry of apologies, carrying two enormous plastic shopping bags from the Friendship Store that knocked against the tables as she passed breathlessly through the room. I watched

Lee watch her, taking in the sylph of her, the Chablis of her hair, her glistening, attenuated neck.

He jumped to his feet and sought out another chair. "Please, allow me," he said, circling around and pulling it out for her. Before she could sit, he grabbed her hand and shook it. "Your friend's told me so much about you. Can I get you some tea?"

Summoning the waiter, he insisted that Claire and I order something to eat from the little menu as well. Then he sat back, his face newly alive, and watched Claire as she went about settling herself in, sorting out her bags and her wallet and her Windbreaker as if she were nesting. When the waiter returned with two cheese sandwiches on a silver tray, Lee paid the bill and glanced at his watch. It was obvious from the look on his face that he was late.

"Tonight, will you allow me to take you both out for Peking duck?" he asked. "There's a famous restaurant right by Qianmen Gate. It's the best in the city."

I spread our map out across the table and he circled the address for us with his fancy onyx pen.

"Take a cab there," he instructed. "I'll pay for it. Just have the driver take you to this corner and I'll be waiting on the curb."

After he left, Claire and I sat alone in the Baroque tea room, chewing our spongy cheese sandwiches. The processed yellow cheese stuck to the roofs of our mouths, making it difficult to talk, but it was a reprieve from the acrid, bone-riddled stir-fry we'd been eating all week at our hotel. The tea room had nearly emptied. From somewhere, a violinist played a concerto. A waiter in a white jacket stood woodenly beneath a dusty chandelier. It felt a little like being in a funeral parlor, though after the grimy *hutongs* and crowded boulevards, not unpleasantly so.

"Lee seems nice, doesn't he?" I wiggled my eyebrows. "I think he likes you, Genevieve."

Claire stretched her arms high over her head and closed her eyes. "Mmm," she murmured.

"I've missed you, you know," I said. "I feel like I haven't seen you for days."

Claire swallowed with difficulty and blinked at me fuzzily for an instant, as if she wasn't quite sure who I was. "Sorry?" she said.

An uneasy silence bubbled between us.

Brushing the crumbs from my mouth, I tried again. "That's so nice of Lee, isn't it, taking us out to dinner tonight?"

Claire reached across the table, plucked two sugar cubes with the silver tongs, and dropped them perfunctorily into her tea. "Well, we're being looked after now," she said. Drawing her cup to her mouth, she winked at me. "Don't ask me to explain, but I'm pretty certain Lee is a friend of Adom's. And they've been in contact. Through the bank. And Adom's network."

"Excuse me?"

But Claire refused to elaborate. She smiled faintly

to herself and began humming. It was a moment of oddness. Yet I let it pass. It seemed Claire's fantasy life had grown at least as fanciful and vivid as my own.

Quite frankly, I didn't know what else to say.

———————

For my birthday, God came to Beijing in the form of a lashing rainstorm. It began at midnight and tapered off before sunrise. When we awoke, the city was a revelation. The smog and dust had cleared, leaving in their wake a crystalline geometry of low buildings beneath a vivid turquoise sky. The fall air smelled of wet leaves and wood smoke. It was bracing and crisp. For the first time since we'd arrived in China, I felt like I could breathe.

As the CITS bus wove its way through the ravine and the first segments of the Great Wall became visible, Claire pressed her face to the window and gasped, "Oh, that *is* beyond awesome. You're right. It's almost holy."

I jiggled in my seat with excitement—and relief.

The night before, over dinner with Lee, Claire had continued to remain strangely quiet. While a white-jacketed waiter expertly carved up a duck in front of us, then bundled it into pancakes dabbed with plum sauce and scallions, it had fallen to me to keep the conversation going. While Lee and I laughed and drank bottle after bottle of Tsingtao, Claire sullenly picked at her food, unwrapping the pancakes and tweezing out slivers of scallions with her chopsticks. Several times, she excused herself to go to the bathroom, leaving most of her duck unfinished.

During dessert, Lee invited us to come out to the Lido Holiday Inn for a special birthday dinner the following evening when we returned from the Great Wall. I was surprised when Claire accepted.

"Well, why wouldn't I?" she said archly. "He's one of Adom's contacts."

Now, as the two of us began climbing the Great Wall, she seemed restored, squealing with glee, pointing, pirouetting. "Hold this a moment, okay? But don't look inside!" She thrust her big plastic Friendship Store shopping bag at me and twirled along the wall.

"Oh, my God, Zsa Zsa, you were so absolutely right," she said breathlessly. "This is un-fucking believable."

She, too, wanted to climb up high along the ridge. "But not too far. I want to make sure there are witnesses around."

"Witnesses?"

She laughed mischievously and pranced ahead. "Okay, here!" she pointed to a section. When I caught up to her, she'd already hoisted herself up between the parapets. "Come." She motioned to me to take a seat beside her on the stones. "Close your eyes."

I gripped the edge of the wall uneasily. The sun burned feverish orange cauliflowers beneath my eyelids, and I experienced a moment of vertigo. I could hear the wind over the mountains. Beside me came a rustling, a liquid plunk. Whatever Claire was doing seemed to be taking a long time. Then I heard a scrape of flint.

"Okay, open!"

Before me on the wall was a vanilla birthday cake with a lone fat red candle burning in the center and a bottle of Baileys Irish Cream liqueur.

"Happy birthday to you!" Claire sang, handing me a stack of presents wrapped in brown paper.

I gasped. "Oh my God. Claire, where on earth did you get all this stuff?" I looked at the cake, the gifts, our plastic collapsible cups thoughtfully placed beside the bottle.

"It wasn't easy." She laughed. When I blew out the candle, she handed me her Swiss Army knife. "First piece is yours."

"I can't believe this," I said. "A Western cake. How did you find this?"

She grinned and waggled her finger at me. "Uh-uh-uh. I told you not to ask too many questions before your birthday, Ms. Libra. Really," she said with a toss of her hair. "How could I possibly show up here today without something amazing planned? How could we *not* celebrate your twenty-second birthday on the Great Wall of China?"

We sat slugging Baileys directly from the bottle (the collapsible cups, we discovered, would not stop collapsing) and eating the vanilla cake, which was dense and grainy, like cornbread. A couple of Norwegian tourists hiked by. "See, witnesses," Claire pointed. "Please. Come join us." She waved them over and curved her arm around me proudly. "It's my friend's birthday!"

As we handed them a slice of cake, they sang me "Happy Birthday" in Norwegian. Some Japanese women passed by and sang "Happy Birthday" in Japanese. Claire beckoned more tourists to join us. I got serenaded in Spanish, French, and Dutch and had my picture taken by a Swiss. Someone unwrapped a chocolate bar and passed it around. Someone else handed me a wildflower they'd picked near the bus. A Chinese man in a jumpsuit suddenly appeared with a broom—apparently the wall did have a maintenance staff, after all—and Claire coaxed him over, saying, *"Ching? Ching?"* until he nervously joined us for a slice of cake. Soon it was a multinational party. There were roughly eighteen people visiting the wall that day, and all of them got a swig of Baileys out of the bottle. Everyone sang together tipsily.

"Oh, sweetie," Claire said rapturously. "This is *exactly* how I imagined it. This is exactly what I wanted for you today. People from all over. The sunlight. The cake. Tell me that the world can *possibly* get better than this?"

When the party finally broke up, it was close to sunset. Claire and I brushed the crumbs off the wall and picked up the litter. "Wait, open your presents," she urged. Somehow, she had managed to buy me a paperback book of Chinese women writers translated into English. A bright yellow silk scarf. A pair of carved wooden combs. And a red velvet hat studded with sequins that looks like a cross between a skullcap and a fez.

"I wanted to buy two of them and make them into an X-rated bra for you, but I could only find one," she teased.

I looked at her, my generous friend with her fine-boned face, her happy sense of conviction. She had bathed me in love. "Thank you," I whispered, my eyes starting to tear. "This is the most beautiful birthday ever."

———

That night we splurged on a taxi. At the Lido Holiday Inn, Lee was waiting for us in the lobby. "Happy birthday," he said, ushering us into the restaurant. "Order whatever you like." We were seated on taupe-covered velveteen banquettes beneath an ugly modern chandelier. The menu was in English, the food Western. I was amazed how comforting this felt; when we'd returned from the Great Wall, I'd tried to put in a collect call to my parents. I'd waited for over an hour, but the operator couldn't get a line out of Beijing. Now, seeing hamburgers, barbecue ribs, and spaghetti on the menu, I felt connected to home. I ordered the ribs, Claire the spaghetti; when they arrived, we saw they were barely disguised spareribs and lo mein. But I was too hungry and tired to care. This time it was Claire who did most of the talking while I sat chewing in a dreamy stupor.

When we finished our meal, Lee wished me happy birthday again and handed us each a thick bar of Swiss chocolate and a pack of Doublemint gum. We were beside ourselves. Suddenly, I understood what life must have been like for people during World War Two. Stockings! Chocolate! Then it occurred to me that this was what life was like for the Chinese every day. Everything was rationed. Everything was a luxury.

"What's your pleasure?" Lee asked. "They've got a bowling alley here, a pool, a disco."

Since I was the birthday girl, I got to choose, so of course I chose the disco. As we headed upstairs in the purring mirrored elevator, then walked down the plushly carpeted hallways, I did not see a single Chinese guest on the premises.

Juliana's Discotheque had a mirror ball and silly music videos playing overhead on an enormous screen. A clump of Westerners flailed and gyrated spastically to "One Night in Bangkok" and the theme song from *Ghost Busters*. While Claire and Lee sidled up to the bar, I walked over to the dance floor. Bananarama's "Venus" thumped on, and I started dancing by myself.

A compact, muscular African man slid over to me, took my hand, and started boogying. He was wearing an English Beat T-shirt and a black felt fedora.

"I'm Chief," he shouted over the music.

"I'm Susie," I shouted back. At the bar, Lee was leaning toward Claire and whispering in her ear intently. They were both holding wineglasses by their stems.

"Say 'Happy birthday,'" shouted Chief, pointing to himself. "Today's me birthday."

"No kidding! Today's my birthday, too!"

He stopped dancing for a minute. "You're bleedin' kidding me!"

"Nuh-Nuh. I just had a party today on the Great Wall of China," I shouted. I loved saying that, loved hearing the way it sounded.

Chief feigned offense. "You had a party. And you didn't invite me?"

"I didn't know you."

"You do now. Where're you from, Susie?"

"New York. You?"

"Grew up in London. Me mum's half Jamaican, half British, and me dad's African. I'm here visiting him. He's the ambassador from Ghana."

We danced to one song, then another. Claire and Lee meandered onto the dance floor. I noticed Lee had his hand on the small of Claire's back. I introduced them to Chief over the throb of the music.

When Chief mentioned that his father was the ambassador to Ghana, Claire flinched as if she'd been stung. She stepped back and studied him outright, like a specimen.

"Yeah." I rolled my eyes at her. "And it's Chief's birthday, too. He says he's twenty-one today. How 'bout that?"

"She and me, we're born on the exact same day," he boasted, gesturing between us. Wrapping his arm around my waist, he drew me toward him. "So how 'bout it, luv? A birthday kiss to celebrate?"

"Okay," Claire said abruptly. "Time to go. We're out of here."

Ten minutes later, in the taxi jiggling back toward our guesthouse, she was utterly silent.

"You didn't have to do that, you know," I said. "I can handle myself. The guy was totally harmless."

"Harmless?" Claire said bitterly, turning to face me in the darkened cab. "Susie, you have no idea who that guy is."

"So? We were just dancing."

Her eyes bore into me. "You don't get it, do you?" she said. "His father is the ambassador to *Ghana*? And our so-so friend 'Jonnie' was living and working in *Ghana*."

"So?"

"So? Don't you see the connection? Susie, how do you suppose this guy Chief just happened to know it was your birthday?"

"Because I told him," I said irritably. "He told me that it was his birthday, so then I said something like, 'Gee, what a coincidence.'"

"I see," said Claire sourly. "And you don't think

that that was a setup? That he didn't *pretend* it was his birthday just to engage you?"

"Sure, I do — in order to *get laid*. Guys do that all the time. 'Oh, baby, today's my birthday. Oh, baby, tomorrow I leave for the army. Oh, baby, my dog just died.' For all you know, he made up the story about his dad being an ambassador to Ghana, too. Guys talk shit all the time, Claire."

"Oh. You think so," she said viciously. "You're just lucky we have Lee on our side."

"Lee? He was totally all over *you* tonight, in case you hadn't noticed."

"He has to act that way," she snapped. "It's his *job*."

"It's his *job*? To do what? Pretend that's he's a lonely businessman hitting on you?"

"Please," Claire whispered. She held up her hand and shut her eyes, barricading herself against me. "Don't ask me to explain. Stop asking me to say things that I'm not allowed to tell you."

"That you're not *allowed* to tell me? Oh, please, Claire," I said angrily, turning to face the window. "Enough with the melodrama already. Give it a rest, will you?"

———

From then on, she boycotted me. She sat in our hotel room writing manically in her journal and speaking only when necessary, in monosyllables. After we bicycled to the train station to pick up our tickets to Guilin, she said, "I'll see you at dinner. I've got appointments." Before I could respond, she pedaled off.

I had no idea what was happening. *So we had an argument about a couple of idiot guys. So what?* Nothing was making any sense anymore. All I could hope was that it would pass. I'd lived my whole life around mercurial people. My mother was practically her own weather system. When people got into a snit, I'd found, it was best just to tiptoe around and give them a wide berth. Soon enough, they'd get over it. Plus, I reminded myself, Claire was a Gemini—Jekyll and Hyde almost by definition. *Wait it out,* I told myself. *She'll come around.*

For two days I bicycled arduously around Beijing in the cold by myself. I went to the dreary, authoritarian People's Museum. I went to the post office and spent two hours waiting in a Plexiglas booth for a collect phone call to go through to my parents, who turned out not to be home. Though I was reluctant to do it, I finally visited the Friendship Store. Entering it felt to me like crossing a picket line. I bought a three-dollar can of Coca-Cola and tried on a silk bathrobe.

I wrote dozens of postcards. Later I would find out that only those in which I praised China got through to America; the cards on which I wrote "travel here is difficult" somehow never arrived. I wrote my friend Maggie a long letter on Grand Hotel Beijing stationery. When she finally received it, it had clearly been opened, read, and resealed. There were even Chinese notations on the outside.

The more steeped in loneliness I became, the more florid my fantasy life grew. Jake was drinking tea with me, eating bean paste dumplings with me in the *hutongs*, making love to me illicitly on the banks of Qianhai Lake.

If I heard a Muzak version of "Let It Be" in the Grand Hotel elevator, I decided it was an aural postcard from home. When I saw a young Chinese man selling boiled eggs on the street, I imagined he was my friend Steve Blumenthal from high school, who sold Larry's Italian Ices from a pushcart in lower Manhattan. When I saw acupuncture needles in a window, I heard the voice of my grandmother. "Oh, Susie love, I am so proud of you." Everything became a metaphor, a talisman, a sign that I was still actually connected to people—that I wasn't so completely on my own.

On our last full day in Beijing, I begged Claire, "Whatever I did, I'm sorry. Just please be my friend again. Come out and play with me?"

She raked her hands back through her hair and blinked rapidly. "Oh, sweetie." She scratched the patch of redness beneath her ear, at the base of her neck. "It's not you. It's me. I'm just really, really tired, is all."

We took a city bus up to the Forbidden City. Outside the ticket booth, we were approached by a young Chinese man neatly dressed in a button-down shirt and a cheap, carefully knotted tie. He held a small red school notebook.

"Excuse me, but I am student at Beijing University," he said. "My name is Sam. I come here to Forbidden City to practice my English. May I kindly ask you to employ me as your guide during your visit?"

For the next two hours, Sam led us through the Forbidden City. His tour consisted mostly of escorting us through the site and reading aloud the English plaques that we could've just as easily read ourselves. Nonetheless, we were touched by his earnestness.

The Forbidden City, he informed us, was believed to have been built with 9,999.5 rooms because 10,000 was considered the number of divine perfection; apparently even the emperors acknowledged that heaven was not possible on earth. Given that Claire and I came from a culture that named every trailer park, time share, and subdivision "Paradise Grove," we found this impressive.

Like so many other Chinese, Sam questioned us relentlessly about America: *How can I learn about your political system? What books do you read? How come you say you are a democracy when so many people in America do not vote in elections?*

Oddly, his rapid-fire questions didn't bother Claire. While she was increasingly suspicious of Westerners, she seemed to have become immune to the Chinese. She happily told Sam that her three stepbrothers all had advanced degrees, that her father was an extremely important American businessman, and that she herself was preparing to become a teacher "on a global scale" — which was, frankly, news to me.

"A teacher?" Sam said, delightedly. "Do you think you could send me some books?"

———————

"That guy, Sam," I said as we walked back from the bus stop. "It's so sad, really. He's brilliant, and he knows there's this whole world outside that he can't access. It's got to be so frustrating, don't you think?"

But Claire wasn't listening. She was standing transfixed on the pathway to our hotel. A few yards away, by the entrance, a large family of dark-haired, sepia-skinned tourists was climbing out of a taxi. The women were dressed in long peasant skirts and shawls. The one man — presumably the family patriarch — wore an embroidered waistcoat. His face was hawkish and mustached; as they unloaded their satchels, they laughed and chatted away in a language I didn't recognize.

"Oh, shit," Claire murmured. "It's *them*."

Yanking me by the arm, she dashed into the lobby, barked at the hotel receptionist to give us the key to room 107, then raced up the stairs.

"Claire, what the hell—"

She ran down the hall with me at her heels. She pulled me into our room, slammed the door shut behind us, and locked it.

"Okay. Okay, that's it," she cried, panting. "That's it. From now on, neither one of us is stepping outside."

"What?" I cried. "Are you crazy? Claire, they're just tourists!"

"That's what you think. I *know* who they are. I'm not taking any chances. We're eating dinner in here tonight. We've got peanuts and almond cakes. And then tomorrow we wait for breakfast to finish. Once everybody leaves, we get the bus to the train station, then spend the day waiting there instead, until we're off—"

"Oh, for chrissake, Claire." I sat down on the bed. "You're being totally irrational. I don't even think they're Arabs."

"Guilin is off the beaten path. We'll be much safer there."

"They could be Romanian or Portuguese."

"We are not leaving until it's safe, do you understand?"

When she said this, I couldn't deny it: A little alarm went off, a trigger wire of panic. She sounded nuts. But she wasn't. She couldn't be. She was *Claire*. And we were like conjoined twins at this point. We were Zsa Zsa and Genevieve, ten thousand miles from home—from anywhere. All we had was each other.

And that's when I first wondered: Could there be some truth to what she was saying? Maybe something devious *was* going on. Perhaps Claire and her father were actually working for an outfit like the CIA. It wasn't that far-fetched, actually. The CIA routinely recruited from the Ivy League. They'd been at Brown just that past spring, in fact, trolling for new hires while my leftie friends protested outside. Claire was a Republican. This was the Cold War. Was it really inconceivable that she'd be working covertly for our government? Not at all. She really might know things that I didn't. Certainly it wouldn't be the first time.

Now *I* was sounding crazy. I stopped and tried to calm myself down. This was all just the delirium of China, I told myself. A by-product of sleep deprivation and overactive imaginations. But then again, I couldn't be sure. Whatever Claire was going through—whatever I was going through—it would pass. It simply had to.

Yet I passed the night sleeplessly, visions of the CIA and the PLO tumbling around in my brain. As soon as Claire stepped into the shower the next morning, I hurried downstairs. I tried to explain to the desk clerk that I needed to make a collect call to the United States in private; was it possible to put a call through to the hall phone instead of to our room? Significantly, the word *privacy* does not exist in Mandarin. But after much pantomiming, the clerk seemed to understand.

For the next two and a half hours, I waited. Claire went about packing her bags as if nothing were wrong, humming along loudly to Duran Duran on her Walkman. I could hear other guests tromping back from breakfast, locking and unlocking their doors, dragging their luggage downstairs. Our train didn't depart for Guilin until seven p.m. that evening, but I worried my call wouldn't go through before checkout at noon.

Finally there was a pounding on the door. "Your call ready," the clerk shouted. "You take in hallway. Quick!"

Before Claire could react, I ran out to the telephone on the landing.

Through the receiver, I could hear the crackle-static of the overseas line, then two operators speaking Chinese, then a dull, delayed ringing that seemed to be broadcast through an echo chamber. My heart thumped wildly. I crossed my fingers. *Please pick up,* I whispered. *Please be home. Oh, Mom, I need to talk to you so badly. I need some perspective. It's all getting a little crazy here. I don't know which end is up anymore.*

A moment later came a click.

"Hello?" my mother said. It sounded as if she were speaking in a wind tunnel.

"I have a collect call from Miss Susan Gilman from Beijing, China," a foreign operator announced. "Will you accept the charges?"

"Yes, I will," my mother said quickly. There was another sharp click. "Hello?"

"Mom!"

"Susie—"

"Oh, Mom. It's so good to hear your voice!"

"It's good to hear yours, too," she blurted. "But listen. Do you think you could call back in an hour? I'm sorry, but the World Series is on. The Mets are playing for the first time in seventeen years. And it's the bottom of the tenth—the tenth inning of the sixth game, can you believe it? Boston's up by one game, the score's tied, the Mets have two outs, a man on third, and Mookie Wilson just made strike two. It's unbelievable. I hate to do this, but can we talk later instead? Oh, my God. Wilson just hit a foul. Oh, my God. Look at that. I don't believe it. Okay. Gotta go."

With that, she hung up.

I stood alone in the hallway, stunned, staring at the black plastic comma in my hand. When I glanced up, Claire was behind me with our backpacks, looking like a hunted animal.

"Are you ready? What are you doing?" She foisted my bag at me. "C'mon. The coast is clear."

人

Chapter 8

Guilin

THE TRAIN TO Guilin takes thirty-four hours. The only food we've managed to bring with us is six pastries from the French bakery and two greasy bags of dumplings. When our Chinese bunkmates see this, they grow concerned. Like aunts and uncles, they begin foisting chopsticks on us and little metal lunch pails full of rice and sautéed vegetables. Even though they have scarcely more food than we do, they urge *ching, ching*—please, please—insisting we share their dinners.

A few hours later, their parental faces begin to blur. I grow woozy. My throat burns as if someone has ripped a bandage off it. By the time the train lurches to a halt in Guilin, I'm shaking. Claire bundles me in her thick Chinese army coat and eases me off the train. Rain comes down in sheets. The air smells botanical, of wet soil and leaves.

A gold room pinwheels around me. Dingy wall-paper, a roaring toilet, a sizzling radiator splinter into shards, folding into patterns as if through a kaleido-scope. My teeth are chattering so hard, they feel like they'll shatter. I'm sprawled on the stone floor of a temple — oh, the cold is so good against my burn-ing face! Hundreds of flickering votive candles have been placed around me as if I'm a human sacrifice, and Buddhist monks wrapped in saffron robes waltz in, chanting in a procession. Jake suddenly appears draped in an ivory silk toga; he kneels down beside me and kisses me hotly, then begins making love to me with increasing violence, until my head is bang-ing against the floor and throbbing in pain. His face melts, dripping between my fingers like plasma, and he turns into Trevor, standing before me in the Temple of Heaven with his arms crossed. I'm doing a striptease for him, but my clothes are endlessly layered. As soon as I remove one garment, another springs up underneath it. I'm hot! I'm suffocating! I want my clothing off! I tear and thrash, but when I finally disrobe, I'm just a smear of flesh, and Trevor is shaking me worriedly. "Are you okay?" I open my eyes. Claire's face hovers over me. "Here. Drink some of this," she whispers, pressing a dented tin cup to my lips.

The room tilts. The Mets are playing the World Series in Tiananmen Square. I'm watching first base-man Keith Hernandez pitching directly beneath the portrait of Mao Zedong, and Jonnie is sitting beside me on the bleachers eating popcorn. *Shay shay nee. This is exactly what I need,* he says, though his voice is Claire's voice, and a Chinese man I don't recognize is poking his head through a black lacquered doorway and eyeing me nervously. *I'm telling you, she's fine!* Warren and Anthony ride bicycles back and forth between first and second base, waving. Someone is hammering the roof with a bicycle chain. "I can't believe this is all they have to eat," Claire fumes, opening her palm to reveal a huge cockroach.

Then she's leaning over me, insisting, "Just one little bite, okay? You need to eat." And suddenly I'm propped up in a bed and she's proffering a sweet dumpling stuffed with gooey red bean paste. The sheets are damp. Do I imagine her telling me that her father has a business contact in Guilin? "I'm sorry, but we just can't let the Chinese know you're sick," she says. "You know what happens. We've got to steer clear of the doctors and hospitals here."

It is nighttime, it is morning. Claire is writing in her journal, Claire is gone. I crawl to the bathroom on my hands and knees. Somewhere Oingo Boingo is singing. My glands are swollen; it's nearly impossible to breathe. I am back in bed with both Trevor and Jake. They are kissing my forehead, performing cunnilingus. I come in my sleep. When I wake up, I am weeping. I am alone. I have never felt so forsaken in my life. It hurts to swallow. *Mommy!* I hear myself cry. I'm curled like a snail beneath my puffy sleeping bag. *Mommy!* Claire is saying, "This is the best I could find." She leans over and presses her hand to my cheek. "You're a little cooler, I think. Here, try this."

She gives me a pill, a bottle of soda.

I swallow with difficulty, and the room goes dark.

———

It took three days for my fever to break. While I lay immobilized in the grungy Overseas Hotel by the train station, Claire stepped out intermittently, returning with wet, tangled hair, wet clothes, wet plastic bags full of whatever provisions she could find in a grocery up the road. Often she sat in the bed across from mine keeping vigil, reading paperbacks and writing in her journal. "I'm so sorry," I groaned. "I'm keeping you from exploring."

"It's okay," she said. "It's still pouring rain, so there's not much to see. Besides, I don't mind just chilling out for a few days under the radar."

On the fourth morning, I finally felt better. Claire and I did a load of my laundry in the bathtub. It was a new day, a fresh start. But after breakfast, Claire came down with the same illness I'd had. I watched her face inflame, her forehead sequin with sweat. "No hospital, no doctor," she cried hoarsely. She writhed in her bed, kicking off the sheets, then burrowing deep beneath her sleeping bag. She called out, "Dominic,

Edward, Alexander! Feed Medium the noodles!" then wailed, "Oh, Adom, Adom." Later, when she sat up weakly and I served her orange soda, she whispered, "Don't tell anyone where we are. Whoever is working for Adom has alerted the authorities and endangered us." She started shivering again.

Thankfully her fever dissipated more quickly than mine, and the next day the rain finally stopped. It felt like we'd been sick forever, like we'd been existing in a world of time-lapse photography where we alone remained inert while everything around us had whizzed by and vanished into the ether.

We immediately spent several hours at the CITS office next door booking airplane tickets to Guangzhou. At sixty dollars apiece, domestic flights in China were considered expensive and wimpy, but neither of us were in any hurry to get back on those trains anytime soon. We were itchy to get moving again, too—we'd lost all enthusiasm for Guilin—and the next leg of our itinerary, we agreed, had to be easier. As we'd learned the hard way, the very first thing you should do upon arriving in any city in China was to start making reservations to get the hell out of it. Sure enough, the CITS agent—another grudging, bureaucratic cipher—informed us that the next available flight to Guangzhou wouldn't be for another four days.

"Fuck it. We'll take it," Claire said wearily. "I'm not spending fourteen hours trapped in another hard sleeper when flying takes fifty-five minutes." Once we forked over our money, the woman gave us a hand-written receipt.

"You come back later, collect tickets," she warned. "Tickets not refundable. Tickets cannot be changed."

———

Millions of years ago, the region of Guilin was a pre-historic sea. When the water receded, it left in its wake a valley of karsts—landscapes of huge, transmogri-fied limestone formations that look like pulled taffy, melted wax, the interior of a lava lamp. Now the city was nestled among these fantastical mountains; there was even one in the center called Solitary Beauty Peak, with a temple perched on top. The climate was subtropical, the streets dense with perfumed foliage.

Most buildings in Guilin were small and so heav-ily streaked with moss they appeared to be scorched. On the eastern edge of the town, they gave way to the languid Li River, across which was an expansive public garden known as Seven Star Park. Most every-thing in the town was either beautiful or strange. It felt humid, lush, drugged.

Along the main thoroughfare, we came upon a row of curious restaurants. They looked like pet stores. Bamboo cages stacked outside contained small live dogs, snakes, bamboo rats, pigeons, and beavers, and basins full of eels, crabs, and turtles. A Chinese man knelt down and pointed to a pair of turtles. A waiter hoisted them up and carried them inside. "Ew," Claire gasped. "I think I'm going to be sick."

As we hurried past, I kept wheeling around to see if the restaurants with their menageries were in fact still there. Since my fever, it was becoming increasingly difficult to separate hallucination from reality. In Guilin, apparently, you could sit in a tropical garden and feast on a zoo. Claire was strangely disengaged. She stared ahead, scratching the angry red patch on the side of her neck and humming faintly to herself.

On a rise above a broad lawn stood the town's one fancy modern tourist hotel, the Osmanthus. Built of white concrete and tinted glass, it looked like a 1970s spaceship plopped down in a flower bed. Claire exhaled. "Finally, civilization. Mind if we go inside?"

The lobby gleamed with polished linoleum and brass elevator banks. Overhead, a modern crystal chandelier jutted down ominously like a clutch of stalactites. Claire sank into one of the fat vinyl couches and closed her eyes. Chinese Muzak played faintly in the background. "Thank God," she murmured. "Better." In a moment she fell asleep.

I sat there for almost an hour, wondering what to do. Although I was light-headed, my limbs felt leaden. The Muzak stopped. A few Japanese tourists cut across the lobby lugging Samsonite suitcases.

When Claire finally stirred, she said, "I'm going to go back to the guesthouse and lie down. I can't be seen here any longer." With some difficulty, she hoisted herself up from the couch and hobbled across the lobby toward the hotel restaurant. "Look," she said, pointing to the menu posted on the entrance. "All English. And no dogs or cats. Only normal Chinese food."

She turned to me. "You should stay, sweetie. Have a decent dinner. You've been cooped up for days. And I could use a little time on my own to get reestablished."

Before I could object, she staggered out through the revolving glass doors. Suddenly I found myself alone again. Evening was setting in. I glanced inside the tourist restaurant. Except for one table of women, it was virtually empty. I felt torn, but Claire was right: I hadn't eaten a full meal in almost a week.

Back in Beijing, I'd ameliorated my loneliness by daydreaming about my loved ones, imagining them standing beside me in fruit stalls and alleyways. But after my fever, I couldn't even fantasize about Jake or Trevor anymore—or anyone from home, for that matter. They'd become fused with my nightmares; their faces had melted like Salvador Dalí's clocks, dripping with illness and delirium. Now I had to sever myself from them completely. America, New York, my friends, my family: They were relegated to the past now, abandoned in another dimension. The only enveloping reality was China.

In the United States, I never would have dreamed of approaching strangers and asking if I could join them for dinner, but here, what did I have to lose? The game had changed entirely. Perhaps, this was what true liberty was: nothing left to tether you, plus an absence of code and shame.

Three Swedish women were traveling together, and they were more than happy to shift their chairs around to accommodate me. *Oh, you're alone? By all means, join us. Here.* They passed me a platter. *Have some sautéed greens. Have some glazed pork. How long have you been in Guilin?*

I explained that my friend and I had been sick all week in the Overseas Hotel by the train station. We hadn't really seen much.

"Get out of your hotel," said a square-jawed woman with aviator glasses and a spiky pinecone of a haircut. "Check into the Guilin Guesthouse instead. That's where all the interesting backpackers are. It's on the top floor of a building near the park, and it has wonderful views of the karsts. Better yet, go to Yangshuo. It's only an hour away from here by bus, and it's so much more beautiful than Guilin. It's just a tiny little village in the countryside."

"You can take boat rides on the river and watch the cormorant fishing at night," said the second woman, who had tanned, leathery skin. "Go for hikes. Rent bicycles."

"All around it are nothing but rice fields and mountains," added the third. "We spent an entire week there. It's the most beautiful place in China."

"Go," said the first woman. "Trust us. It's paradise."

———

"I don't want us to be around other people," Claire shouted when I told her about the Guilin Guesthouse. "Don't you get it? And how do you know you can trust these women?"

"Why on earth would they lie?" I said. "You said you wanted to go someplace remote."

Claire slumped back against her headboard and glowered at me. "I thought you promised you'd listen to me."

I looked at her, exasperated. Then I sat down on the edge of the bed with my head in my hands. I was exhausted, I realized, and I was getting depressed. Our hotel room smelled gamy. All of our possessions were strewn about willy-nilly, a mud slide of laundry, hiking boots, underwear, books. Orange peels were rotting in a trash can in the corner. The interior pockets of our backpacks were coated with a thin, greasy film of peppermint oil from our soap bottles, which had leaked all over everything.

"Claire," I whispered. "I really can't take this anymore."

"Take what?"

"This paranoia, your refusal to engage."

"I'm not being paranoid, Suze. I *know* things."

"What's happened to you, Claire? Where are you lately?"

"What are you talking about? I'm right here."

"You used to be...we...Christ," I said despairingly. "Are you feeling okay?"

"Fine. Perfect. Couldn't be better. Why? Are *you* feeling okay?"

I glanced at her. "I am so lonely, it's not funny." I hadn't expected to say this, though I realized it was true. Claire looked as though she'd been punctured.

"How can you be lonely?" she said. "We're together practically all the time."

"No. No, we're not. Half the time you're off somewhere, and even when you're here, you're...I don't know. I feel like, when we first came here—okay, I admit, I was totally freaked out—but we were supposed to be, like, this *team*."

I threw up my hands dispiritedly. I couldn't even articulate or get my own head around exactly what I was feeling. Somehow the Claire I knew and admired so much back at Brown—the graceful, animated, self-assured Claire, the Claire who was jubilant, with her wonderful sense of the preposterous, her extravagant intellect, her Nietzsche board, her *Sweeties*, her cascading laugh, her can-do adventurism — somehow she seemed to have dissipated here. She was being transformed into a suspicious, brooding harridan. She was taking herself far too seriously. *When was the last time we truly laughed together?*

But to be fair, it felt like I was dissolving, too. In China, I was having trouble knowing who I was anymore. There was nothing familiar to reinforce my sense of self: no loved ones, teachers, report cards. While I'd once imagined I was savvy, here in Asia it had become abundantly clear that I was not. While I'd once liked to think of myself as this wild, outré nymphomaniac, here in Asia I'd learned otherwise. Certainly, the primary tool I'd always relied upon for the bulk of my personality — the English language — was no longer at my disposal much. What was really left of me?

When I looked in the mirror now, I saw a stranger. After being in Asia for a full month, Chinese faces were becoming the norm to me, while Western features appeared increasingly alien and grotesque. With my crude, exaggerated nose, my convex brow, my giblet eyelids and lips, I was literally having trouble recognizing myself. I was a fractured Picasso, a hideous distortion.

"I need to get out of this cocoon," I said softly. "I want us to hang out and laugh and — I dunno — socialize? Have fun again?"

Claire cradled her elbows in her palms and chewed

on her lip. "Okay, fine," she said bitterly, scratching
her neck. "We'll change guesthouses. But I'm warn-
ing you right now. I need to go off by myself for a little while. There's still work I need to do." She reached
for her notebook, opened it decisively, and avoided
my gaze. "I need to find out who our next connection
is, who's the guardian."

This patently made no sense, but by this point I
was too tired to argue.

The next morning we packed up our backpacks and
made our pilgrimage to the Guilin Guesthouse in
the center of town. While its dormitory had floor-
to-ceiling windows overlooking the karsts, the view
was obscured by laundry lines zigzagging across
the room, draped with various people's laundered
T-shirts and underwear, which flapped over their
beds like national flags. The Swedes were right: All
the interesting backpackers stayed here. Four Japanese tourists were sitting cross-legged on the floor
deseeding an enormous bag of marijuana. In a land
of surveillance, their audacity amazed me. The room
was freezing cold and smelled like a bong.

"Well, here you go, Zsa Zsa," Claire said causti-
cally. "We're out of our cocoon. Happy?"

She sank down on her bed and massaged her temples. "Christ, my head is killing me. I've got to eat

something halfway decent this morning. I need fried rice. You want to go get fried rice?"

I shook my head. Since my fever, all I could eat in the mornings was bread.

"Okay, well, I'll meet you back here later then."

Left in the dorm room, I encountered another traveler named Laurent, who was also in search of a Western-style breakfast. Laurent was Swiss and spoke a little Mandarin, though since each region of China had its own dialect, his skills were of limited use in Guilin. At a café on Zongshan Road, he finally managed to order eggs and Chinese sweet rolls for us. After forty-five minutes, only the scrambled eggs arrived. They were the color of tiger lilies, and we ate them with chopsticks.

Laurent left to catch a train to Kunming. Returning to the guesthouse, I found Claire hovering over two of the Japanese potheads with her broken Instamatic.

"I'm selling my camera," she said over her shoulder.

"Excuse me?" Not only was the camera inoperable, it was listed on our customs form; we had to be able to produce it on our way back out of China. "But it's broken," I said. "And we'll need it to leave."

Claire looked at me furiously. "It's not broken," she shouted with a flick of her wrist. "It's never been used." She turned back to the Japanese guy. He was sitting on the floor staring ahead vacantly, his arms between his knees.

"I just don't know how to use it," she said sweetly. "It's a really great camera."

The guy continued staring at the bed frame. "No thank you," he murmured.

"No, really. It's a terrific camera." Claire held it out to him impatiently. "Look. Top of the line."

"Claire," I said softly. "I don't think he wants it."

"Shut up," she snapped. "Don't interfere. I'm trying to *do* something here!"

She said "do something" as if she was in the middle of deciphering a code, threading a needle, or performing arthroscopic surgery. But what she was really trying to do, it seemed, was unload her junk on another traveler. I didn't know what the hell she was thinking. This from the girl who'd taken a boy with cerebral palsy to his prom? Who refused on principle to trade on the black market? So far there hadn't been a single traveler or Chinese local who'd been dishonest or ungenerous with us. There was an unspoken code of honor here. What was happening?

"Claire, please," I whispered. "Don't do this. It's really bad karma."

"Oh, fuck your karma." She turned back to the Japanese. "Only sixty dollars. It's an excellent camera."

The guy glanced laconically at his equally stoned girlfriend. "No, it is okay. No thank you."

"Okay. Fifty, then. Fifty dollars."

"We already have a camera. See?" The girlfriend held up a top-of-the-line Nikon that easily cost a thousand dollars. "But on Zongshan Road, there are several camera repair shops. I'm sure they can fix yours."

"It's not broken! I'm telling you!" Claire cried. "Fifty dollars. For a top-of-the-line camera!"

Finally, tired of enduring her, the Japanese guy grabbed the Instamatic, flipped it over, and pointed to the cracked chassis.

"Okay, so maybe it needs some repairs." Claire faltered. "But still, oh—just take it, okay?" She thrust it at him.

He glanced away coldly.

"As a gift. I mean. I meant, just take it *as a gift*. When I said fifty dollars, what I really meant was, that's how much I *paid* for it, okay?" She was clearly backpedaling now. "I want you to have it." She smiled disingenuously. "Not to buy. It's a gift, okay. A fifty-dollar gift. Do. You. Understand? You see, I just can't carry it around anymore—see? It's too heavy for my backpack."

The Japanese couple got up and walked away. Amazingly, Claire pursued them all the way to the elevator. "C'mon. Take it. I said it was a *present,* okay?"

After they left, she sank down on her bed and looked dejectedly at the broken Instamatic. "I'm sorry I snapped at you," she said after a moment. "But I was trying to *do* something important."

I crossed my arms. "It's pretty uncool to try selling off a broken camera."

"Don't tell me what's uncool!" she exploded. "It's none of your business what I do! And besides, this camera isn't broken. I just don't know how to use it!"

"You *sat* on it!" I screamed. "And it *is* my business if you go around selling other people junk, because we rely on them and then they won't trust us!"

"Shut up!" she shrieked. "You have absolutely no idea what you're talking about. Leave my business alone!"

"Fine! I'll be more than happy to." I snatched up my ugly pink sweater, then jabbed at the elevator buttons. "You want to be left alone? Fine! You're alone!"

When I got downstairs, panting and nearly in tears, I started hurrying through the streets of Guilin, down one lane, then another, without really looking where I was going. *What just happened up there? What on earth is going on?* I crossed a small bridge, then passed a post office, trying to get a handle on my emotions. I reviewed the argument like sports footage, trying to determine exactly where things started to go wrong. On Zongshan Road, I passed two tourists standing outside a restaurant pointing to a beaver in a cage. "So you cook it with ginger?" the woman said loudly to a waiter. *Oh my God,* I thought. *This is insane.* I stopped and tried to catch my breath. I was wheezing asthmatically. Out of the corner of my eye, I saw a flash of dark green. It was Claire, in her army coat, trailing me.

That evening, we sat across from each other on our dormitory beds like adversaries. When other travelers returned from their day of sightseeing, I made a big show of chatting with them, laughing and joking around. Occasionally I shot Claire a look as if to say: *See, other people aren't acting like assholes.* When a Dutch couple invited us to join them and some New Zealanders for dinner, I accepted for the both of us. Claire glared at me, but when it was time to leave, she put on some lip gloss and followed sulkily. We walked en masse to Zongshan Road, where, to my relief, the Dutch chose a restaurant that did not have live dogs, rats, turtles, snakes, beavers, or cats on display outside.

"Hey, I'm all for sampling the cuisine of different cultures," I announced as we sat down. "But I draw the line at puppies." Claire, I noticed, kept glancing back at the cages outside the restaurant next door. Although we all made a point of ordering only vegetarian fried noodles, vegetarian fried rice, and deluxe fried vegetables, when our dinners arrived, she pushed her food around on her plate without touching it. The Dutch kept ordering bottles of beer and passing them sloppily around the table. By the time we returned to the guesthouse, everyone was giggling and stumbling about with our arms draped around each other. The icy room was sweet with marijuana

smoke, and two Japanese girls sat on their beds singing pop songs. Claire sat down beside me and gently
leaned her head on my shoulder. Slowly, softly, she
began to sing along with the others, her eyes filling
with tears.

When I awoke the next morning in my clothes, it
was dawn; the rest of the dormitory was still asleep.
The horizon was vermilion, marigold orange, and
irradiant yellow, backlighting rows upon rows of
karsts shaped like enormous gumdrops, their silhou-
ettes blueing to violet in the rising sun. The colors
were so spectacular and electric, they appeared almost
spray-painted.

"Claire," I whispered, nudging her. "Wake up. You
have to see this."

She stirred, sat up, and blinked out at the unearthly,
psychedelic dawn.

"Isn't that amazing?" I said.

She nodded forlornly, looking as if she was going
to weep. "Let's go to Yangshuo," she pleaded softly,
gripping my hand. "Let's go today, okay? Please? As
soon as possible."

———

Buses left every hour, and we took the first one after
breakfast. We were the only Westerners onboard.
Claire slid into a seat by a window, then spent the
ride with her eyes transfixed on the road and her
Walkman playing at full volume. Every four min-

utes, she pushed the replay button, listening to the same song over and over again. Although I was prone to doing the exact same thing myself, after about half an hour, the incessant clicking and whirring got on my nerves.

I was coughing nonstop now: a deep, tubercular hacking; most of the other passengers on board the bus had it, too. We were a hallelujah chorus of contagion. Beyond the windows, the busy highway from Guilin quickly gave way to a rutted road. The landscape grew wild and dense; tendrils of fog coiled around the mountains. More and more of the karsts emerged until we were in a forest of limestone formations. They towered over us, unnerving in their enormity, in their haunting, Paleozoic beauty. Eventually the bus entered a valley. Sun broke through, glittering on the rice paddies and irrigation streams. Water buffalo lumbered about. There was one ramshackle roadside store made from bamboo, and then beyond it, nothing but billows of tropical vegetation along a river. We were deep in the countryside now, with tall grasses and fields as liquidly green as absinthe. At the foot of a solitary limestone karst peak the bus turned sharply and lurched onto a wide dirt road. About a hundred yards down was a row of single-story concrete buildings. The driver stopped abruptly in the dust. As soon as the automatic doors jerked open, all the Chinese clamored out. Swept along with them, Claire and I were forced to descend, unsure of where we were.

"Yangshuo?" Claire shouted, pointing at the ground. Before the driver could respond, a crowd of fresh Chinese passengers pushed past us and climbed on board with their bundles and bags, everyone talking and jostling at once. It was impossible to hear or see anything over their heads. There was a jerking sound, a belch of exhaust, and the bus took off again.

We stood on the edge of the road, blinking into the white-hot daylight.

It was summery now. Claire took off her army coat and pulled her hair back into a ponytail; I stuffed my ugly pink sweater into my backpack. Since there seemed to be no other place to go, we hoisted our bags and trudged along the dirt road toward the little outcrop of buildings. Except for a few Chinese men squatting outside and chewing, the stretch was deserted, like a tumbleweed town in a Western.

That is, until we turned the corner.

We found ourselves at the beginning of a leafy cobblestone lane. In the distance, music was playing. As we followed the road and drew closer, the tune became familiar: It was Creedence Clearwater Revival. John Fogerty was belting out, "Some folks are born, made to wave the flag, Ooh, they're red-white-and-blue." Through a clearing in the trees, we came upon a small open-air café with a sign nailed above it: "Green Lotus Peak Inn." Beneath it, someone had added a postscript on a smaller plank of wood:

"Have a Cold Beer and Enjoy the Local Talent." And beneath that, on still another plank: "Home Style Cooking Just Like Mother Used To." Backpackers in tank tops and shorts sat sunning themselves around little wooden tables dotted with half-finished pink and yellow frothy drinks. Two shirtless guys were stretched out with their hands knitted behind their heads, their bare torsos tilted and gleaming in the light like sheets of newly pressed metal. The gnashing *whuuzzz* of a blender drowned out the music.

"Jesus," Claire murmured. "Look."

Inside the café hung a menu on a chalkboard:

Pancake
Banana Pancake
Chocolate Pancake
Waffle
Banana Waffle
Chocolate Waffle
Hamburger
Beef Stew
Grill Cheese
Macaroni Cheese
Milk Shake

Next door to the café, we saw a stall full of used and bootlegged cassette tapes. BUY, TRADE MUSIC!!! Further down was a funky jewelry stand selling beaded necklaces and brass bangles, then a booth full of used Western paperback books labeled *English. German. Spanish.* At the end of the lane stood a shack of a travel office with a fluorescent yellow placard in front: *Bus tickets! Train tickets! Air tickets! Bike rentals! Cormorant night fishing tour! English spoken! Fast + Easy bookings!* Across from that, an open-air bar and restaurant had put up a sign announcing simply:

PIZZA.

At first we thought it was a mirage. We were in the middle of nowhere—ground zero of prehistory—and yet we'd stumbled into an oasis of Western hippie youth culture and English nestled among the ancient karsts. The blender stopped at the same moment the Creedence Clearwater song ended. There was nothing but the delicate clinking of glasses, a low thrum of conversation, twittering birds.

"Is this for real?" I said.

A young waitress stepped out of the café with an empty tray tucked under her arm. Blinking, she shielded her eyes from the sun. She was Chinese, though there was something strangely Western looking about her. She was tall and slim, dressed in a pink, puffed-sleeve blouse and a beige dirndl. Her shoulder-length hair was cut across her forehead in thick bangs, but the front locks were pulled back with a pink polka-dot ribbon. When she smiled, her full-moon face looked satiny and untarnished.

"Hello. Welcome to the Green Lotus Peak Inn." She stepped lightly among the tables to greet us.

"I am Lisa." When she reached us, she did something truly astonishing. She put down her tray and hugged me.

The strangest feeling overtook me: I'd met this woman before. I knew her already. She couldn't be any older than Claire and me. Buoyant, aspiring, she was a Chinese version of us: a kindred spirit, a sister from a different life, perhaps. And yet while her face was girlish and bright, her eyes were soulful, almost melancholy. There was something maternal about her. Claire sensed this too. For the first time in a while, her posture relaxed and her face lost its pinched, furrowed quality.

"Wow. Hi," Lisa exclaimed, opening her long, slender arms. Claire, the notorious non-hugger, hugged Lisa too.

Lisa held Claire in her embrace for a moment, then stepped back and tenderly brushed a lock of Claire's hair out of her face.

"Oh, your gold hair," she said. "You are both very pretty girls. Where are you from?"

When we told her America, she said, "Oh, you have come very long way. You very far from home. Must be very hard. You miss home, yes? But here in Yangshuo, no worries. I speak English, and we have food you like. You need place to stay, yes?"

Claire and I nodded dumbly. In China, the simplest tasks—peeing, eating, buying a ticket—had become so difficult and degrading, they'd worn us down, made us buckle and contort. Only now that we were suddenly relieved of the effort of having to fend for ourselves did we fully appreciate what a strain it had been. We found ourselves tearing up.

"Ooh," said Lisa sympathetically, touching her hand to Claire's cheek. "Don't cry. You in good hands now. Go down road, make left, then right. You see sign. Garden Guesthouse. You get nice room there. Then, you come back here and I cook for you. Good food. Just like Mom make."

With his broken English, the proprietor of the Garden Guesthouse communicated that he had accommodations for us provided we didn't mind sharing our room with another traveler. He led us into a thatched hut with three beds situated on crude platforms high above the dirt floor; they weren't so much beds as tables shrouded in mosquito netting. Shared showers and squat toilets were located in a small concrete barracks across the courtyard.

Back in Shanghai or Beijing, accommodations like this set us on edge. But here in the countryside of Yangshuo, they seemed charmingly rustic.

"Very Gilligan's Island," Claire remarked, setting down her backpack and surveying the room. "Almost like camping. All we need now are kerosene lamps and pith helmets and maybe some sort of pet monkey?"

Her good spirits were a relief. At Lisa's, we dug blissfully into enormous stacks of banana pancakes, moaning with pleasure each time we swallowed. Van Morrison sang "Brown Eyed Girl" from the tape deck behind the counter. And the guys! There seemed to be more varieties of beautiful young men than pancakes at that café; virile chess players simmering with concentration; bed-headed Apollos in sandals and hemp tunics; tanned backpackers gripping pineapple milk shakes in muscular hands and threading fresh rolls of film into their cameras as if preparing for battle. The air seemed to shimmer with pheromones. Behind the café, the Green Lotus Peak rose up like a patron saint. The breeze was scented with frangipani. The Swedes had been right: This was paradise.

Claire beckoned to me across the table. "See? I told you we should come here." She flung her hair back.

I laughed.

"I'm serious," she whispered, leaning in close. "We were *meant* to meet Lisa. Don't you see? She's our protector. *She's* the connection."

"Excuse me, ladies." One of the chess players stood over us. He had dark, leonine hair and a gaze alone that could pin me to the wall like a butterfly. I instantly felt myself on high alert.

"I'm Than. My friends and I"—he pointed back at his table—"we'd like to buy you two a beer, if that's all right."

I ran my hand through my hair so that it fell over

one eye in what I hoped was a seductive manner. "As long as you come over and drink it with us."

Claire gave me a swift kick underneath the table. But Than was already signaling to his friends and, in seconds, we were thoroughly invaded. An Englishman named Simon and a German named Gustav drew up chairs beside us, set their empty glasses down, and opened up their portable chessboard. Gustav offered around a package of Marlboros, then tucked it into his breast pocket and called out to Lisa to bring over five more Tsingtaos. Simon and Than hoisted their glasses. "To peace, love, and understanding in Yangshuo!" Snaking their arms over the back of our chairs, they reclined with satisfaction.

"Ah. Sunshine, cold beer, two beautiful girls, and a chess set," Than said. "What more can you ask for?"

"A third girl?" suggested Simon. "So tell me." He scooted his chair closer to Claire. "Where you're from, where you've been, where you're going. What you think of the geopolitical situation in Micronesia—"

"What you prefer," Than interrupted. "Totalitarian dictatorships or free-market cannibalism?"

"Women with facial hair or men with breasts," said Gustav.

I scowled with mock annoyance. "I have to choose?"

They laughed, and in the concentrated beam of their attention, I felt myself bloom. It was an enor-

mous relief to flirt, to banter and joke and be friv-
olous; the frisson of laughter and hormones made
me feel alive again, more like my old self. Had we
been back at college, surrounded by attentive men,
engaged in some playfully preposterous philosophical
debate, I know that Claire would've happily dug in,
issuing witty comments with a sly look on her face.
This intellectual ping-ponging was exactly her thing.
*Whose life would make a better musical: Socrates' or
Dolly Parton's?* But she just sat there stiffly. Whenever the men tried to engage her, she pulled her collar
tightly around her throat and answered curtly: *No.
Whatever. I really couldn't tell you.*

Their beers finished, the men folded up their chessboard; they'd rented bikes to take into the mountains
for the day. "Do you want to join us?" Than asked.
"I'm sure we can find two more bicycles."

"No, thank you," Claire responded frostily. "We
don't go off into the wilderness with strange men
we've just met."

I shot her a furious look. The three men exchanged
glances, shrugged, and left with their backpacks.

"Excuse me," I said. "But what exactly is your
problem? Those guys were totally into us."

Claire narrowed her eyes at me. "What's *my* problem? Susie, you have absolutely no idea who those
men are."

"So what? You think they're a bunch of chess-
playing, bike-riding ax murderers? Can't we just take

a chance and have some fun together with some cute guys for once? Can't we just be spontaneous?"

Claire sucked in her cheeks and crossed her arms. "You don't know what they want from us. My father is very important, you know."

"Christ." I leaned across the table. "Who cares about your father, Claire? Those guys have been back-packing around Asia for the past eighteen months. They're Europeans. You think they give a shit?"

"They have ulterior motives."

"Yeah? Well, so do I. They're hot, they're straight, they're single—"

She didn't smile. "Susie," she said in a low, vicious tone, "do you understand that people here in China are watching us?"

I looked at her with exasperation. "No shit. We're in a Communist country."

"No. I'm not talking about that. *Other* people, Suze. You're not even aware of it. But I am. I see them. Eyeing us. Sizing us up. You really do have no idea what's going on here, do you?"

Then she shook her head and waved her hands as if to erase what she'd just said. "Forget it," she sighed, her tone suddenly turning conciliatory. "Look, I'm still not a hundred percent. I'm still a little off kilter from the fever. I'm feeling claustrophobic. Let's just walk, okay? Get some fresh air."

Lisa recommended a path following the Li River out of the village, making a long, lazy loop through the countryside. We walked single file in silence, listening to the rustle of the water. Along the riverbank, the earth was loamy. The air had a sweet, mineral scent. A formation of geese flapped overhead. The sun was hot on our backs, but the steady breeze was like a balm. Slowly the path deviated away from the river and descended inland into a glittering expanse of rice paddies. They glowed green, like phosphorus.

"Lisa," Claire mused. "Lisa is so nice. Lisa is a truly wise and caring person. She reminds me of my mother." She stopped. "Do you ever miss someone so much you physically ache?"

"Yeah," I said vaguely. "Mostly guys, I guess."

Claire crossed her arms and walked off. With her brisk, determined gait and her long legs, she put a good twelve feet between us instantly. It was impossible to keep up. I hurried behind as best I could. She strode ahead, humming loudly "I've Been Working on the Railroad." As I began to gain on her, she broke into a run. She bolted down into the fields, cutting through the rice paddy.

"Claire!" I raced after her.

But Claire was an athlete. Her lithe body zigzagged farther and farther away as she sprinted through the fields toward a point in the distance where two women in coolie hats were working.

Pursuing her, I found I could barely breathe. I had to stop every ten feet or so with my hands on my knees. I was spitting up thick gobs of yellow mucus now. I couldn't seem to get enough of it out of my lungs. When, coughing and gasping, I finally reached the point where Claire had stopped, I saw that she, too, was now bent over in the grass. But she wasn't struggling to catch her breath. She was working. She'd grabbed a small sickle away from the older woman and was bent over beside the woman's daughter, harvesting rice. In unison, Claire and the younger Chinese woman each grabbed a hank of rice the way you might grab a hank of someone's hair, sliced it off near the roots with the sickle, and dropped it into a metal bucket. They were doing this in complete silence.

The older woman stood over Claire, perplexed. Strangely, neither Claire nor the younger woman acknowledged my presence. They continued working together in sync, as if they'd been working alongside each other for years, as if what they were doing was totally natural and practiced.

"Claire?"

She continued thwacking away wordlessly.

The older woman looked at me with resignation. Hurrying over to a small bamboo shed at the edge of the paddy, she returned with two more sickles and held one out as if to say: *I suppose that you, too, have come to help us harvest?*

"*Shay shay nee,*" I murmured. The old woman squatted in the paddy beside me and demonstrated how to use it.

For a while, the four of us harvested rice together

in complete silence. It was hard work, but the rhythm of it quickly became hypnotic. Soon I was aware only of the curve of my back; the cool, damp feel of the rice in my fist; the hefty, weighted swing of my right arm; then the satisfying, fibrous tear of the rice coming free from the earth. *Bend, grab, swing, rip. Bend, grab, swing, rip.* All of us performed it together: *Bend, grab, swing, rip.*

I felt as if I'd liquefied, transcended all boundaries of myself and seeped into the countryside around me: the geese overhead, the delicate thrash of trees in the wind, the simmering sunshine. *Bend, grab, swing, rip.* I was no longer an individual, but a bundle of sensation: my spine burning, the earthy musk of the soil, the plants sticking to my hands, the colors of the two Chinese women — red thread wrapped around the tips of their black braids, dusty navy blue uniforms, straw-colored hats — contrasting sharply against the incandescent green of the paddy.

Bend, grab, swing, rip. The ground was rutted and wet. The air was clean and cool as water. The pile of rice mounted in the bucket.

When Claire disappeared, I didn't realize it right away. One minute she was bent over a few yards away from me, fervently hacking the plants; the next minute she was gone. I stood up, glanced around. There was nothing but a sea of green. I called out her name.

The elderly Chinese women nudged me and

pointed to a spot about ten yards away. There on the ground amid the tallest rice plants, Claire was lying on her back with her arms crossed over her chest like a sarcophagus.

"Claire?"

She opened her eyes sleepily. "You ready?" she said dreamily. "Boy, is that sun hot." She stood up slowly and brushed herself off. Tromping over to the Chinese women, she relinquished her farm implement, then strode purposefully back across the field toward the path.

I hurried after her up onto the hiking trail. "Excuse me," I grabbed her by the arm, "but what the hell are you doing?"

She jerked away, her nose crinkling with disgust. "You said you wanted us to be more spontaneous. So? I was being spontaneous. I was literally going off the beaten path. Trying something new. What the fuck is your *problem*?"

"My problem? What the fuck is *your* fucking problem? That's what my problem is."

Did Lewis and Clark ever get on each other's nerves? In the depths of East Africa, did Richard Burton and John Speke ever irritate each other so much that they just wanted to reach over and whack each other upside the head? Did Sir Francis Drake ever sulkily give his crew the silent treatment? What about Sir Edmund Hillary and Tenzing Norgay? Did they bicker all the way up and down Everest? All I'd ever read about in school were glorious discoveries and epic adventures, undertaken with a seemingly blithe braveness and steadfast camaraderie. But now I'd nearly had it with Claire, and she'd clearly had it with me. This was the one dilemma I'd never anticipated during our trip. How on earth did people do it? Never mind finding the source of the Nile or circumnavigating the globe: Just traveling without killing each other was accomplishment enough.

Claire and I trudged on, seething in silence. We were in the middle of a Chinese wonderland of geology, botany, and agriculture, but all I could focus on was a catalogue of personal grievances. *Claire's such a fucking narcissist, inventing all these little melodramas in which the entire world is allied against her all the time—as if people don't have bigger and better things to do.* And oh, is she spoiled! Who brings a Gucci wallet to the People's Republic of China? And that way she flicks back her hair and elongates her neck like she's so superior—and says *please* not like a question but as a definitive! And what's with the picky eating? Who *diets* in a Third World country? And the prudishness! All that frigidity and judgmentalness and "Ew, a cockroach!" Can't she just loosen up for a minute? Look at her with those guys at the café: She's got a stick so far up her ass, it's a wonder she doesn't spit wood chips.

To be fair, at this very same moment, Claire was undoubtedly assembling an equally damning assessment of me. *Look at her, slutting around. She's supposed to be this big feminist, but really she's just boy-crazy. Why the hell didn't she just stay home and hang out in that bar she worked at? Does she have any idea how pathetic she looks?* She is sick, too, of my sloppiness—the pile of balled-up Kleenex on the floor by my bed is enough to make anyone psychotic. And that idiotic astrology. Oh, and my verbosity! Can't I ever just talk in sentences instead of anecdotes? Does everything have to be a fucking story? What I need are editors, not friends. As for my in-your-face New York attitude? Maybe I think I'm being urban and sophisticated, but really, I just come across as vulgar and Jewish half the time. Honestly, I should see myself. I should get it through my head once and for all that the whole world does not in fact revolve around Manhattan.

We were so busy stewing in our righteousness and indictments that we almost didn't see the man standing directly before us in a clearing, holding a camera. A shaft of sunlight beamed down on him. His presence there in the woods was so incongruous, he appeared to have been conjured on the spot by a magician, brought to life by a handful of pixie dust. He was Western and quietly handsome: square-jawed and thoughtful-looking, with thick sandy hair and melancholy deep-set eyes. He raised his camera and aimed it directly at us.

"Whoa," Claire cried.

The man lowered it, startled. "Oh. I'm so sorry,"

he said. "I did not see you." His accent was musical and difficult to place; I suspected he was Swedish. He appeared to be in his mid-twenties. He was dressed neatly in jeans and a polo shirt with a Windbreaker knotted around his waist. Although he was not much taller than Claire, he had a lean, well-proportioned body: solid shoulders and legs, arms faintly striated with muscle. "It is very beautiful here, yah?" he said.

Claire shifted her weight from one foot to the other.

"What are you?" she demanded, sizing him up baldly, evaluating the space between them. "Where do you come from?"

"Me?" the man said almost sheepishly. "Oh, I am German."

Claire glared as if he'd confessed to a crime. Yet I found him instantly adorable: so masculine but sweet-faced.

"Are you lost?" I said "Do you want to walk with us?"

"Oh, no. I am not lost," he said with a modest laugh. "But I'm happy to walk with you. I have been trying to capture this landscape on film, but it is very hard. The postcards and photographs, they do not do it justice, I think." He screwed his lens cap back on and slung his camera across his chest like a bandolier. When he raised his arms, I could see the smooth plane of his abdomen below his polo shirt.

Claire sulked.

"So, how long have you been in China?" he asked politely.

She gazed off across the fields without responding.

"One month," I offered. "Just backpacking."

"Really?" said the man, turning to me. "I am impressed. I think that is a very long time in a place like this. It is very difficult."

Claire walked off, yanking leaves off the low-lying shrubs as she went.

"Ignore her." I rolled my eyes. "She's been moody all day."

The man stared after her, frowning.

"She's recovering from a fever," I said.

The man smiled. His brown eyes crinkled; his face was like curtains parting.

"We're actually circling the globe," I told him, trying to sound nonchalant. "India. France. Thailand. Egypt. You know. That sort of thing."

The man laughed. "Not in that order, I hope."

Nervously I giggled. Then I started coughing. Embarrassingly, I couldn't stop. I doubled over, hacking and gasping, until I stumbled backward over a tree root. The man grabbed me around the waist to steady me.

"Whoa." I clung to him. He smelled wonderful, of linen and pine. Aware that he was embracing me, he drew back.

"Uh-oh." He laughed bashfully.

"Well. This is weird," I proclaimed. "Cute guy out of nowhere."

"Yah. It is really funny. I just run into you in the woods."

For a moment, we stared at the ground shyly.

"Well, I guess I should say now, 'Hello. My name's Eckehardt.'"

"Eckehardt?" I struggled to pronounce it.

"Yah. Eckehardt Grimm."

"Grimm? You're kidding me. Like the fairy-tale author?"

"I guess so," he said.

———

As we strolled along behind Claire, Eckehardt and I poured out our stories to one another. In his neat clothes (vaguely strange German versions of American sportswear: the proportions slightly off, the stitching thicker and too bright, the fabric stiffer, the brand names unheard of), Eckehardt didn't resemble the other backpackers in China, who all had a scruffy, degenerate look to them. He was more adult somehow. He was in China as the very first German postgraduate student to attend a polytechnic institute in Nanjing as part of a new exchange program. The program had just ended and now he was finally on vacation. For three months he'd been the only Westerner on a Chinese campus—the only Westerner at all, in fact, wherever he went.

"Oh, in certain ways, it was very nice," he said. "I was treated like a king. The Chinese, they did everything for me. They made all my reservations. I was their special guest. They cooked for me, cleaned for me. Of course they also knew my every move, everything about me. The woman who cleaned my room, she went through all my things. Every day. Even my underwear. They read all my letters. It was quite funny. I go to the bathroom, and suddenly everybody else has to go, too."

Delightedly, I also learned that Eckehardt wasn't married and didn't have a girlfriend back home either, though there seemed to be a whiff of recent heart-break around him.

On a certain level, the whole conversation between us was just elevator music to me—an insipid, superficial rendition of a growing attraction transpiring beneath the surface.

By the time we completed the circuit through the countryside and arrived back in Yangshuo, all two streets of it, I was fairly drunk with desire for this man—this man whom I'd known exactly fifty-five minutes. Claire was waiting for us at the entrance to the path, however.

"So, mystery man," she teased, sauntering over coquettishly, motioning to him with a serpentine flick of her hand. "You finally made it out of the wilderness."

"Yah." Eckehardt laughed. "Though it's not much of a wilderness when there's a path right through it."

"Listen, I was just wondering"—she fingered the

gold chain around her throat—"where are you staying tonight?"

"Where am I staying?"

Claire ran her fingers slowly through her hair so
that it caught in the sun and glittered, then gave
him a big doe-eyed gaze and a pout. Her attempts at
seduction were so exaggerated, they were almost bur-
lesque, a parody of someone genuinely flirting. Still, I
felt like punching her. *What was she doing?*

"You are staying in Yangshuo, aren't you?" she said
in a breathy little-girl voice, touching him lightly on
the wrist. "Certainly you're not sleeping out there in
those woods."

Eckehardt looked flustered. He seemed to have as
much trouble recognizing this strange character as I
did. "Oh, I am staying here at a place called the Garden Guesthouse. They have put me in this room with
two other people. I am hoping they are not too crazy."
He laughed nervously.

"The Garden Guesthouse?" I exclaimed. "That's
where we're staying. What's your room number?"

"Five."

"That's our room." For a moment I was ecstatic: I'd
be sharing a room with Eckehardt! But then, I realized, so would Claire, and I felt a flood of resentment.

"Oh, you are joking?" said Eckehardt. "I am sharing your room with you?"

He looked from me to Claire. It was hard to tell
whether he was smiling or grimacing.

"Well then, sir," Claire said extravagantly, with a small pirouette. "What do you propose we do for the evening?"

Eckehardt said he'd hoped to take a boat excursion at night on the Li River to see the cormorant fishing. When he asked us if we'd like to join him, I noted with satisfaction that he looked directly at me, not Claire.

"Of course I'd love to go," Claire announced.

"Well, me, too," I said.

"Good. Well. Fine," Claire said. "Susie, why don't you run ahead then, and buy us tickets?"

"Oh, no," Eckehardt said with a start. "Please, I will buy them. I have to go to the travel agent here. Tomorrow I am going first to Guilin by bus, then to Kunming on the train. Although I made the reservation days ago, you know China. Just picking up the tickets could take hours. So I will arrange the boat trip too, while I am there. I will meet you later at the restaurant?"

He shot me a quick, private smile, which Claire, to my great delight, didn't fail to register.

As he headed off down the lane, I felt a tug of longing. Claire watched him too. She kicked at the dirt path with the toe of her Timberlands.

"Oh, please. Don't tell me you have a crush on a *German* now," she said.

"Why not? He's totally cute. You were the one who said a person's nationality shouldn't matter."

"Jesus, Suze. He's a homunculus. Look at him. He's barely an inch taller than me." She kicked a pebble across the footpath. "The Hun. Like Churchill said, 'They're either at your feet or at your throat.'"

She spun around on her heels and blinked rapidly into the sunlight. "I'm going to Lisa's café," she said acidly. "Come or don't come. Do as you like."

———

By early evening, the Green Lotus Peak Inn had become an open-air nightclub. Hurricane candles flickered on the tables, K.C. and the Sunshine Band blasted from the tape player, and overturned wooden crates doubled as chairs for an overflowing crowd. Simon and Gustav were clustered around a table with another German, a Bulgarian, and a Swiss guy, who were all taking turns tossing back shots of rice vodka. Each time one of them swallowed, everyone in the café cheered and began singing, "Aw, that's the way, *uh-huh uh-huh*, I like it . . ." With the assortment of accents, it was quite a sound. The Bulgarian was wearing a Mao cap hanging over one eye that he intermittently pulled off and tossed in the air. When Gustav saw us, he started to wave me over, but Simon tugged on his sleeve and whispered something to him, and he stopped.

The blender growled and the *tttzzzztttt!* of pancake batter splattering against the hot grill was constant. Other travelers slonked beer glasses together, shouted across the café, and tossed postcards to one another like Frisbees. Occasionally a local Chinese man trudged past, barefoot, carrying buckets of water suspended from a yoke around his neck, though no one seemed to notice him.

No sooner were Claire and I seated than a group of British teenagers in matching polo shirts barreled into the café. "Tsingtao beer!" they shouted.

They were high school students from Hong Kong on a class trip to China.

"This country sucks," a boy announced.

"We've been here four days and all we've eaten is bloody cabbage. The food is disgusting!" said a girl beside him.

"We hate China. We can't wait to go home."

"Tsingtao!" they chorused. "We need beer!"

Lisa maneuvered through this brouhaha with aplomb, gracefully setting down heavy platters of pancakes and beef stew in front of the travelers, then whisking away empty glasses and hugging everyone who entered. Watching her, I knew exactly what she was experiencing: The Green Lotus Peak Inn was not that different from the West End Bar where I'd worked that summer. Yet she never appeared to lose her cool or enthusiasm. The café was bathed in her goodwill. "Lee-sah! Lee-sah!" the crowd started chanting. "We love Lee-sah!"

Finally she arrived at our table.

"Please," Claire said, gesturing to the empty chair

beside her. "Sit for a minute? Talk to us? Lisa, you're the only worthwhile person in this whole place."

Lisa smiled bashfully in the candlelight and adjusted the polka-dot ribbon in her hair. "Oh, you are so nice. Very kind girls," she said, touching Claire lightly on the shoulder.

"So are you, Lisa," said Claire. "I'm serious. You're the nicest person we've met in all of China. I mean it. You are our friend."

"You know, back home in America," I confessed, "I'm a waitress, too. Just like you."

Lisa frowned. "You are waitress in America?"

I nodded proudly.

It was hard to tell whether she was impressed by this or disappointed.

"Lisa, please," Claire said, redirecting her attention. "Tell me. What are you doing here? How did you know to communicate with us? How do you speak English so well?"

Lisa gathered us in closely in a conspiracy of girls. "Do you know who Yao are?"

We shook our heads.

"Yao are Chinese minority. We come from west. But I marry foreigner. I come here to work for him. My family not like this. So I know what it is like for travelers. I know what it is like to feel alone, no family, no friends.

"My husband, he know a little English. He teach me. When we open café, I learn more English from travelers. I say, 'I know you very far from home. What you miss most?' And they all say, 'Cooking like Mom makes.' So I say, 'You teach me, and then I can cook like Mom.' And so the Germans teach me pancakes. Pancakes with bananas. Pancakes with apples. A boy from England teach me beef stew. Lady from Belgium teach me waffles. The first Americans I meet, Americans like you, they teach me hamburgers and milk shakes. The more I cook like Mom, the more people come here to Lisa's café, and the more cooking they teach me, the more I learn English."

When she finished, she sat back with a mournful look in her eyes.

Slowly Claire and I each reached across the table and grasped one of her hands in ours. The three of us sat there, blinking into the candlelight amid the din. For a moment we really did feel like sisters.

————

Eckehardt buys tickets for a ten p.m. fishing excursion. When he joins us at Lisa's, he slides in beside me and clasps my hand in full view of Claire. It's official now, and I feel a jolt of anticipation. Claire is speaking intently to Lisa, and I find myself secretly hoping that she'll decline to come along with us. But when the time to depart rolls around, she stands up and says, "So are we ready to go?"

At night, the area surrounding the two streets of Yangshuo is completely unlit. If a sliver of moon hadn't been out, there would have been no light at all except for the stars. The blackness is disorienting. Eckehardt thoughtfully retrieves all of our flashlights from the guesthouse, and we make our way single file through the dark toward the river, poking our beams out ahead of us. Claire takes the lead. Eckehardt comes up beside me and puts his arm around my waist and we walk together, nuzzling. I want him so badly I feel drunk. The stars overhead are massive; the sky is a stadium. When Eckehardt and I stop and try to spot the constellations, everything's skewed. We're further south than I've ever been in my life, just above the Tropic of Cancer. Nothing is located where I've been taught it is.

The fishing boat is little more than a canoe with a thatched roof cresting over it. Lurching against the dock, it seems eminently capable of capsizing. The fisherman holds up a single small lantern and ushers us on board with a grunt. The bulb sputters; it casts weak greenish-gold beams across the water for a few feet before dissipating into the blackness. There are only three other tourists on board, and all of them look worried. Certainly there are no life jackets or life preservers. The fisherman shouts harshly at his assistant, who balances precariously on the bow and casts the boat away from the shore using a long bamboo pole. The hull rocks violently. Instantly, the shore vanishes.

Moments later, we hear a furious flapping. As the boat sways, half a dozen cormorants are led out from cages into the water. Until this very moment, I haven't really been clear about what, exactly, cormorant fishing is. Now I see that cormorants are long-necked birds that look like hybrids between storks and pelicans. When cormorants spy a fish, they swoop down into the water and scoop it up in their gullets. The fishermen, however, have screwed brass rings around their throats to cut off their esophagus; when the birds catch fish, they're prevented from swallowing, and the fishermen yank open their mouths to retrieve the catch. The birds, in effect, have become living nets and harpoons.

The cormorants dive-bombing into the lake, the fishermen wrestling them back onto the boat, then prying the fish out their gullets as the birds thrash and bleat in strangled protest—it's a brutal, otherworldly spectacle. Each time a fish is caught, I have to look away; I grip Eckehardt tightly and bury my face in his chest. Rationally I know this fishing method is not a matter of sadism but survival, a necessity born of poverty and hunger in the world's most populous country. Only recently has it even begun to double as a small, lucrative tourist attraction. The people in the hillsides around Yangshuo, Lisa has told us, often go hungry. But watching their night fishing is unbearable. I glance over at Claire. She is standing a little bit away from us, hunched over the hull of the boat with her head in her fists. Each time she hears the sounds of the birds, she flinches. Wordlessly Eckehardt extends his arm, touches her lightly on the back, and draws her toward us.

"Get away from me," she hisses.

When the boat docks, she scrambles off before we do. We come upon her five minutes later, sitting on the ground in the middle of the footpath. Her legs are splayed out in front of her like a doll's and she's emptied her purse out in the dirt, her passport, traveler's checks, lip gloss, and Kleenex all heaped in the dust.

"How could you possibly show me those birds?" she sobs. "Why on earth did you have me watch that? What's wrong with you people?"

She leaps up, gathers up the contents of her purse, stuffs it all back into her bag, then tears off through the darkness in the direction of Lisa's.

Eckehardt looks after her. "Uh-oh," he says with dismay. "I think the fishing was not very much fun for her."

"Augh," I say with exasperation. "Nothing is very much fun for her anymore. And frankly, I've just about had it with her soap operas."

I turn in to him and wrap my arms around his waist. My heart is beating wildly, and I can feel the rise and fall of his breathing through his rib cage.

"She is your friend," Eckehardt says, running his hand gently over the nape of my neck. "She seems pretty upset. Are you sure you don't want to go after her?"

I shake my head. It seems like ages since I've been held. Traveling lately has felt like solitary confinement; having been sick and feverish among the crowds, I've felt almost invisible, dissociated from myself and even my body. When Eckehardt runs his hands down along my spine, it's like fire to parchment, a whole philharmonic orchestra tuning up and coming to life, a flag being raised. I refuse to give this up. I can't bear to walk away for yet another one of Claire's little melodramas. *Please,* I think, *just let me keep feeling this a few minutes longer.*

"She's being manipulative," I say. "She's jealous. She's staged this tantrum precisely so that I'll go after her instead of being here with you."

"Are you sure?"

I nod. "I'm going to be traveling with her an entire year. She's going to have to get used to the fact that if, say, I ever meet this totally hot guy, say, just standing there in the woods in the middle of Southwest China—"

Before I can finish, he kisses me.

He kisses me, and I go up in flames.

There are no trees nearby, no thick grasses, no bench. So we just stand there on the pebbled path by the embankment kissing as the stars shift position in the sky overhead.

Finally Eckehardt says, "What should we do?"

I sigh. "We're sharing a room with her. I just don't feel right about that. That would be totally uncool."

He nods. "Okay. Then. I guess this is it. We should probably head back to the guesthouse."

Reluctantly we make our way through the empty streets of Yangshuo, our flashlights jiggling over the muddy cobblestones. By now the Green Lotus Peak Inn is shut for the night and the lone street lamp has been switched off. When we aim the beam at Eckehardt's digital watch, we're shocked to see it's almost two o'clock in the morning. Outside in the courtyard of the Garden Guesthouse, only Simon and Gustav are still awake, sitting in a stupor around a barrel top crowded with empty bottles and a half-finished chess game. They can barely raise their heads to acknowledge us as we slink past; Gustav grunts incoherently.

When we reach our hut, Room 5, Eckehardt tries the door and finds it's already unlocked. Before he opens it, though, he steps back into the courtyard and kisses me one long, last time. "Good night," he whispers. "Sleep well. And thank you for the very beautiful evening."

We've agreed that I'll return to the room a few minutes ahead of him to diffuse some of the awkwardness. As I slip inside, I feel a click of panic.

Claire's body is silhouetted peacefully beneath her tent of mosquito netting. When I lean in close, I see, to my great relief, that her eyes are shut and fluttering rapidly beneath their luminous lids. Her breathing is deep and regular; it sounds like the tide scraping back and forth over the sand.

"Eckehardt," I whisper when he pads in a few minutes later, his shoes in his hands for good measure.
"She's totally asleep."

Even though it is nearly pitch-dark, I can see him
smiling faintly. I can see him beckoning me toward
him. I can see him gently lift up the mosquito net
draped over his bed like an expectant groom lifting
the veil from the face of his bride.

Chapter 9

Yangshuo

CLAIRE IS ALREADY awake and showered and pulling on her hiking boots when I stir. I roll over into a mosaic of sunlight and watch her through the mosquito net. In the bed adjacent to mine, Eckehardt is still asleep, his chest heaving, his forearm flung over his eyes. Claire moves perfunctorily about the room, tossing her possessions haphazardly into her backpack. Her wet hair drips on the floor. Her face has a raw, beaten look, as though she's been crying.

When she notices I'm awake, she says coldly, "I'm going to Lisa's café for breakfast. I want to see Lisa."

"I'll come with you," I groan, rolling over again. "Just give me a minute to shower."

She grabs her purse and loops it over her head. "I'm going *now.*"

Then, agitated, she removes it. "Christ," she swears,

"I'm so fucking sick of lugging all of this shit around with me all the time."

She empties the contents out into her backpack, snatches up a few items she deems useful, stuffs them back into her purse, and storms out.

I sit up slowly, stretching. I feel a nagging sense of obligation to patch things up with her and behave contritely, though all I really feel is resentment. *So what if for one single night of our trip, I made out with a guy instead of indulging her?*

Climbing down from my bed is difficult. My back and shoulders are sore from harvesting rice the day before. My lips feel deliciously bruised. I tiptoe back to Eckehardt's bed. The sun casts a shadow of lace over his blankets. Though he's shifted position, he's still asleep. I watch him for a moment, his solemn lips, his long eyelashes, the square of his chin with its gentle cleft, his torso shuddering slightly as he breathes. I reach through the mosquito net to touch him. He groans, looks up at me sleepily, and smiles.

"*Nee how*," he says softly.

"*Nee how*."

"Claire's gone to Lisa's for breakfast," I tell him. "I think I should probably join her."

"Yah. I think that is a good idea," he yawns.

While he lies watching me, I undress, wrap myself in a towel, and gather up my toiletry bag.

"Of course you are entitled to join me in the shower

if you want," I tease. "Otherwise, wait for me later, so that we can say a proper goodbye?"

He rolls onto his side and looks at me with bemusement, his sandy hair flopping into his eyes. "Yah. Okay." He rubs his forehead groggily. "I think I can do that."

Across the courtyard, the showers are little stalls with saloon doors and the usual pipe jutting out of the wall. I stand in the muddy corridor in my towel and flip-flops, listening to the sparrows as I wait for the water to turn from glacial to simply freezing. Finally I relinquish my towel, give a yelp, and begin soaping myself up as quickly as possible.

A moment later, as I'm covered head-to-toe in peppermint lather, I hear a door swing open and footsteps slapping across the concrete.

"Susie?" a man calls.

"Ecke?" I shout. "I'm in the last stall. The one on the end."

But it isn't Eckehardt at all. It's Gustav, the chess player from the day before. He arrives in front of my stall breathlessly, as if he's just run a great distance.

"I am sorry, but you better come quickly," he pants. "Your friend, she is really going crazy. She is in Lisa's café, screaming. She is yelling at people and knocking over furniture."

"What?"

"Lisa says you should come right away."

"Oh, Jesus, okay, I'm coming. Tell her I'll be there as fast as I can."

Fuck fuck fuck fuck fuck, I say aloud, rinsing myself in the ice water. *Claire, what the hell are you pulling?* Yanking my towel around me, I dash across the courtyard, my flip-flops in my hands and soap suds trailing behind me. In the hut, Eckehardt is already dressed and rapidly lacing his sneakers.

"Claire's making a scene," I say.

"Yah, I know. That guy told me." He snatches up his Windbreaker as I wriggle into my clothing as quickly as possible: Traveling with a limited wardrobe has its benefits. We hurry outside and down the lane while I'm still stuffing my feet into my Reeboks, past the pizza bar, the travel agent, the funky jewelry booth. When we arrive at the Green Lotus Peak Inn, I notice a few travelers clustered outside whispering.

Inside, the café is chillingly empty. Several chairs have been knocked over and there is an abandoned half-eaten breakfast on one of the tables. As soon as Lisa sees us, she hurries over.

"Lisa, what happened?"

"I so sorry," she says. "Something very bad happen."

"Where's Claire?"

"I don't know. She was here. She very, very upset. She crying to me. She telling me she in very big trouble. When other travelers come in, she yell at them. I try to make her calm. I tell that man to go find you. But then someone come in for breakfast and she get very upset." With her chin, Lisa gestures toward a skinny backpacker with a Vandyke beard who's hunkered down at the corner table.

"Hey, man. I'm sorry," he says, holding up his fork defensively. "I just wanted some waffles."

"Your friend, she see this man, she start screaming all over again," Lisa says. "Then she stand up, knock over chairs, and run outside."

"Oh, Christ," I say, dropping my head in my hands. "She's gone too far this time."

"Do you know which direction she went?" Eckehardt asks.

Lisa points.

"I am so, so sorry," I say, righting the overturned chairs. "Please, Lisa, if Claire comes back, tell her to wait here, okay?"

Eckehardt and I hurry down the lane—he scans the left side of the street while I scan the right, in case Claire's ducked inside somewhere. We don't see her. We turn onto the other main thoroughfare. Yangshuo consists of just two streets, a single axis with a few small lanes deviating off of it.

The second street is wider, longer, and dustier. It's lined with bulky concrete buildings and no tourist spots. This is where the locals do business. There's a post office, a machinist's, a squalid grocery selling a few canned goods. The street dips down, then curves around a bend. Moving through it, I feel my heart banging away in my rib cage. I've had it with Claire and her tantrums, her desperate bids for attention.

Midway down the block, Chinese pedestrians appear to be fleeing in our direction. They hurry past us, glancing back nervously and clutching their possessions to their chests. "Uh-oh," says Eckehardt. "There she is."

In the middle of the road stands Claire. She is flailing her arms and thrashing at the air as if she's caught in the middle of a giant cobweb, as if she's fending off an attack. "GET AWAY FROM ME!" she screams.

Her face is wild-eyed, ablaze. "WHAT ARE YOU LOOKING AT, HUH?" she shouts belligerently at two backpackers. They sidestep her quickly, averting their eyes. She glowers at a Chinese woman and recoils. "I TOLD YOU TO STAY AWAY FROM ME." Sweat is soaking visibly through the armpits of her white alligator shirt. "I KNOW WHAT YOU'RE UP TO. YOU THINK THIS IS FUNNY?"

"Oh, my God," I whisper. This is so above and beyond anything I've ever seen her do. Her face is hot pink, her lips shiny with spittle. Her hair is so disheveled, it looks electrified. She is like a bomb about to detonate. An old Chinese man shuffles by with a basket of lettuce lashed to his back. "DON'T YOU DARE TOUCH ME," she shrieks.

Eckehardt and I run up to her, and she jerks around. "Claire, it's me," I say. I wrap my arms around her tightly, trying to contain her. "Please, Claire, calm down."

"Oh, Susie," she cries, collapsing into me. "They're watching me. They're after us."

She wipes her eyes with her wrists. "I don't know what it is," she says emphatically, "but it's *big*. And it's *international*. And it's out to get us. It includes the CIA and the Mossad and probably the FBI. They're trying to kill us, Susie. You and me both. We're in terrible, terrible danger."

"Ssh, ssh, it's okay," I whisper—even though as I embrace her, I exchange horrified glances with Eckehardt. *Is she kidding?* I'm surprised by how bony she feels. Her ribs and her spine jut through her shirt. Since arriving in China, she's lost an unnerving amount of weight.

"Oh, Susie," she sobs. "We're in way over our heads!"

"Okay, listen. We're going to get you out of here, Claire," I say softly. "We're going to pack up and go back to Guilin today on the bus, okay? And then tomorrow we're going to fly to Guangzhou. We've got those plane tickets, remember? And then from Guangzhou we're going straight to Hong Kong. And from there we're going to take you back home to Connecticut, where it's safe. Everything's okay, you understand?"

So this is it, I realize. *The ignominious end of our glorious trip.*

"EVERYTHING'S NOT OKAY," Claire shouts. She grips me by the forearms. "DON'T YOU SEE? THE CIA AND THE MOSSAD AND THE FBI ARE AFTER US."

"Claire," I say, but her voice is growing increasingly shrill, snowballing toward delirium.

"Listen to me." I grip her cheeks between my hands. "WE ARE NOT IN ANY DANGER. DO YOU UNDERSTAND?"

She wrenches my hands away and starts punching and clawing at me, hollering, "GET AWAY FROM ME!"

Eckehardt moves to pull her off me, but before he can, my hand swings back almost reflexively and I smack her hard across the face.

The crack is sharp as a whip.

Claire staggers back a moment, and we both look at my palm, stunned.

"Claire. You've got to cool it now," I whisper, my voice shaking. "You can't be screaming like that here. You're hysterical."

She stands there, panting, her hand on her jaw.

"I'm sorry, but I had to do that," I say tearfully. "Now, I want you to take a deep breath. Do you hear me? Breathe."

She inhales spasmodically, her low lip trembling.

"That's it," I say. "Good. Now another."

She stands there for another minute, slowly breathing in.

Then she bolts. She tears off down the street and runs around the bend.

"Oh, fuck," I say. Eckehardt and I run after her, but I can no longer keep up. My lungs just won't absorb enough air. They feel cauterized and sore. Wheezing, I half run, half stagger. Eckehardt turns back to assist me. By the time we round the corner, Claire has made it up the dirt road. It's the same road where the hourly bus from Guilin let us off just the day before. At that very moment, in fact, a bus is sitting there, chugging exhaust and discharging its passengers.

Claire barrels headlong into the waiting crowd and elbows her way to the front of the line. A second later, I see her force her way onto the bus, her shoulder bag flouncing, her blond hair haywire.

By the time Eckehardt and I catch up to her, the rest of the passengers have already crammed on board. It is so full, the driver is having trouble getting the automatic doors to clomp shut. It's a tangle of bodies, bundles, poultry, plastic bags; everyone's mashed together shouting and spitting. There's no possible way of getting on, and there's no possible way of getting anyone off, either. Claire has somehow managed to squeeze herself into a tiny space between the driver and the rest of the passengers, her back wedged against a Fiberglas partition. It's only because she's so tall and blond that I'm able to spot her in the crush.

"Claire!" I shout as Eckehardt bangs on the half-folded door, calling out, *"Ching! Ching!"* and gesturing for the bus driver to stop.

Claire turns in the direction of my voice. Her eyes look glassy and unfocused. But when she spots me, her face suddenly relaxes with recognition.

"Sweetie," she says softly, waving. Her voice is singsong. "Do you have any change for the bus? All I have is this."

She holds open her purse. It's empty except for a tube of lip gloss and her traveler's checks held together with a hair scrunchie.

"Get off the bus!" I shout.

"I can't." She reaches over her head and sweeps all of her hair languidly over one shoulder. She glances down at Eckehardt and me almost pityingly.

"Listen, I just need a little space," she sighs. "I'm feeling a little claustrophobic, is all. I just need some room to breathe. Take the next bus back to Guilin, okay? Bring all my stuff and meet me at the Osmanthus Hotel. I'll have a bath, use a Western toilet, and I promise I'll be better. I just need a little money, okay?"

I don't know what the hell to do. The driver is jamming the bus into gear. I try reaching past the passengers barricading the door, but no one can budge. I feel in my pockets. All of my Chinese money is back at the Garden Guesthouse; Eckehardt pulls some twenty-yuan notes from his wallet, balls them up, and tosses them to Claire over the crush of heads.

"Thanks, guys. A steak dinner later, I promise," she calls out, catching the money and slipping it into her bag. "Sorry. I'm just freaking out a little. I need to feel the road under me for a while and I'll be fine."

The doors jerk shut. The engine growls, and Eckehardt and I are suddenly left standing in a puff of diesel fumes, watching the dented metal loaf of it lurch forward, then turn the corner and disappear.

"Excuse me, but what the hell just happened here?" I grip the sides of my head incredulously. "Did you see that? Who was that?"

"I think," says Eckehardt worriedly, "that your friend has some real problems."

Back at the Garden Guesthouse, I discover that Claire really has left everything behind: her passport, her Gucci wallet full of Chinese money, $600 in American cash, her phalanx of credit cards, her international driver's license — even her around-the-world plane ticket. Gathering it up, I find myself hating her.

"Fucking little princess," I mutter. "Acting out like that. Leaving me with all her shit so that she can go off and have a bubble bath. Who does she think I am? Her housekeeper? Her personal Sherpa?"

Eckehardt watches me with consternation.

"She grew up with a maid, you know," I say. "She's used to other people cleaning up her messes."

"Oh, Susie," he says, shaking his head. "I do not think she was acting out."

"Oh, of course she was," I declare bitterly, reaching for a pile of her dirty socks and stuffing them angrily into her pack. "Did you see how rational she was in the end, once she got on that bus? It was like, poof! All of a sudden, she's not in any danger anymore. She just wants to hang out at a fancy hotel.

"You know what?" I say suddenly, looking him straight in the eye, "she's jealous because you and I hooked up. Every time on this trip, whenever a guy pays me more attention than he pays her, she gets all moody and bent out of shape and suddenly has these little *crises*."

Eckehardt stares at the ground.

"I think I should tell you," he says, "last night, after you'd gone back to your bed, she tried to sleep with me."

"What?"

"Oh, no, no," he says quickly, waving his hands. "It was not like that. But it was very strange. She woke me up and climbed into my bed."

I hurl down her canteen. "See, that's exactly what I mean. It's not enough that she's rich and beautiful and probably going to law school next year, and that she's Phi Beta Kappa and has this steady boyfriend back home. She just can't stand it when *I* get the cute guys. She can't stand not being the best at absolutely everything."

"She was crying," Eckehardt says. "She was telling me about her mother being dead, and about how much she is missing her. And she is saying that she is trying to telephone her family, but that the phones here do not work. Maybe, yah, she is also jealous. But she was very troubled."

"When did this happen? You and I were up until at least three a.m."

"Four? Four-thirty?" He shrugs. "I told her to try and go to sleep. I said that I was thinking she would feel better in the morning. But when I wouldn't let her stay in my bed, oh, she got very angry. She slapped me. She took her Walkman and stormed out."

I pause and stare at Claire's blue rubber flip-flops in my hand. "Oh, Christ, Ecke," I say.

That's when it hits me, when I allow myself to think the thought I've been refusing to entertain: Maybe my friend is not merely playacting. Maybe she truly is losing her mind.

The paranoia, the secretiveness, the mood swings: I've been chalking all of it up, of course, to the stresses of travel, plus Claire's own penchant for fabulism. You have to remember too that both of us at this moment are fresh out of college. We've spent the last ten years steeped in the histrionics of growing up. Back at Brown, our classmates staged hunger strikes to protest apartheid. A fraternity bricked up its front patio to create a swimming pool, then filled it with beer; when they got expelled, they hired a skywriter

to fly overhead during graduation in protest. After a
guy in our freshman dorm got a C in engineering,
he went to Japan to visit his brother for a week and
ended up staying a year. My roommate got into the
habit of picking coffee with the Sandinistas in Nica-
ragua each semester in order to sort out her "issues."
Another friend would regularly pound on my door
at four o'clock in the morning yelling that it was an
emergency, then rush in holding an album by Echo
and the Bunnymen. "You have totally *got* to hear this
song," he'd shout, charging over to my turntable.
"It's going to blow the top of your fucking head off."
Another, after a breakup, slept on my floor for a week
and ate nothing but Twizzlers. And then, of course,
there was me—the queen of hyperbole—who'd
checked into health services for a week after a dis-
tressing telephone call from my father.

At this stage in our lives, Claire and I have a conception of "appropriate behavior" that is beyond operatic.
And in China, certainly, nothing seems normal anyway; even the constellations are skewed. Is Claire mentally ill or merely freaked out? I honestly cannot tell.

What *is* indisputable, though, is that it's over.
Claire's psychological health is at least questionable,
and dealing with her has propelled me to the edge of
a nervous breakdown myself. Both of us are disintegrating. It's time to go home. I've got to make arrangements as quickly as possible. I look at my watch. The
next bus for Guilin leaves in forty-eight minutes.

Lisa puts her arm around me as I explain. Although I deliberately omit the part about the CIA, the FBI, and the Mossad, once I describe Claire's behavior out loud, it really does sound crazy.

"Your friend, she very sick." Lisa frowns. "This no good. This very, very bad."

"I'm going to have to take her home," I say miserably. "Ecke went to get my bus ticket, but I really need to contact our parents. Is there any place here where I can make a collect call to America?"

This is a long shot, I realize, but Lisa thinks for a minute, then leads me back behind the café, down a narrow wooded lane. At the end of it, beneath a willow tree, stands a wooden shack with a corrugated roof. It looks like a refreshment stand. Lisa knocks on the door. Inside, a man is sitting at a crude wooden table cluttered with packages of biscuits. She says something to him. For a moment he and Lisa seem to negotiate. Then he pulls out a rice paper notebook and hands me a pen.

"Write down your name, address, and phone number you want to call," Lisa instructs. When I finish, the man leads us around the back of the shed to what looks like an outhouse and motions for me to wait there.

"Phone call maybe take long time," Lisa says. "I must go back to café. You wait, yes?"

I stand there by myself, staring out at the meadow and the jagged emerald karst. Even though it is early November, it feels like a lazy summer day; the air is humid and trilling with crickets. It is hard to reconcile this tranquility with the turmoil I've just experienced. It's hard to believe we arrived here only a day ago. The gooey banana pancakes. Lisa with her polka-dot hair ribbon. Eckehardt revealed in the clearing. The stars, the brass rings glittering around the throats of the cormorants. Claire sobbing on the pebbled ground. Eckehardt kissing me, his fingertips tracing my clavicle. The entire sojourn in Yangshuo feels unreal. And yet it's impossible to fathom that in just a few days, Claire and I will be back in the U.S.A. Strangely, it's hard to fathom us being anywhere else but here.

Claire. At that very moment, her bus should be more than halfway to Guilin, weaving its way through the karsts. I imagine her shifting uncomfortably in her seat, hugging her purse like a shield, the bus jostling over the pitted road.

Suddenly I get the terrible feeling that I should never have let her go off alone. How did I allow that? Did I have any choice? I try to imagine some way in which I might've convinced the driver to halt the bus, or barring that, gotten myself onto it. But nothing seems plausible, and besides, what would've happened then? We'd have left everything behind in Yangshuo—backpacks, passports, money—and it would only have compounded the problem, because then we'd have to turn around and find some way to come back. And what if she became irrational again? She's taller, stronger, faster than I am. How on earth would I manage her?

Pacing in front of the phone booth, I begin to grasp the enormity of what I may be up against.

The man reemerges from the outhouse, gesturing. Miraculously, the call has gone through to America in only twelve minutes — record time.

I pick up the heavy Bakelite receiver. There is a roar of static, then the distant ocean sound of my parents' phone ringing. Back in New York, it is ten o'clock at night. "C'mon, damn it," I murmur. But nobody answers.

I scribble down my grandmother's phone number and thrust it at the man, pleading, "*Ching?*" There's now only twenty-one minutes until the bus leaves.

Luckily, this time the connection overseas goes through almost immediately, and my grandmother picks up her phone on the second ring.

"Oh, Susie darling. What a lovely surprise," she cries over the hissing and sizzle. "How is China?"

"Fine. Great. We have to come home immediately," I say. "I can't talk long, and I can't go into detail. But I need you to call Mom and Dad, and tell them to contact the Van Houtens."

"But why?" says my grandmother. "You've only just left. And you worked so hard for —"

"Claire is sick. We need to come home."

"*Bubeleh,* can't you just get her to a doctor? Or put her on a plane—"

"It's complicated. She's not sick *physically.*" I enunciate carefully. "Do you understand?"

If at all possible, I want to avoid saying words like *mental illness* or *nervous breakdown* over the phone. The line keeps clicking whenever I speak; I suspect it's being tapped.

My grandmother thankfully grasps the situation instantly. "I see. Is she *rational*? Is she *depressed*?"

"I don't know," I say. "But we need to come home."

"I see. Susie, is she a danger to herself?"

"Again, I don't know," I say. "I don't think so. But I really can't talk anymore, okay? I'm in this small village. There's a bus leaving for the city soon. Can you please call everyone and explain? We're going to check into this big Western-style hotel, and I'll try to contact them from there."

"Absolutely, *bubeleh.* You take good care of yourself," my grandmother says.

Then, just as we're about to hang up, she adds as an afterthought: "Oh, whatever you do, don't let her out of your sight, you understand?"

———

When Eckehardt returns from the travel agent, he has some bad news: The next bus to Guilin will not be leaving for another two hours. The Chinese apparently enjoy leisurely lunch breaks as much as the rest of the world.

I tell myself that perhaps a two-hour delay won't be that big a deal; perhaps the situation with Claire isn't nearly as dire as I've made it out to be. Perhaps once she's installed herself into the Osmanthus Hotel, ordered a grilled cheese sandwich, and reclined in a bathtub, she'll feel clearheaded again. She might not even notice I'm late.

But when I proceed to check out of the Garden Guesthouse, the proprietor starts yelling at me.

"You friend, you friend," he shouts, pointing angrily to the grimy metal clock on his desk and tapping on the number 4. He pantomimes sleeping, then someone pounding on the door.

"Why she wake us up?" cries his wife, who pushes through the curtain dividing the office from their kitchen. She is carrying a huge tureen full of soup that slops onto the floor. "She wake us up two o'clock. She wake us up four o'clock. She wake us up five o'clock. She ask to make telephone. Who make telephone at five o'clock morning?" she demands. "Why she no sleep?"

By the time I finish paying the bill, I'm nearly in tears.

"Oh, God, Eckehardt," I cry. "What am I supposed to do now? She's going to be alone out there for hours."

I lean into him. He puts one hand on my hip, the

other on the back of my head. For a moment, I stand there clutching him in the courtyard.

"I'm from New York City. I'm supposed to be tough." I sniffle. "I'm supposed to be able to handle stuff like this." I gesture at Claire's backpack. "But I can barely even carry her goddamned bag."

"Oh, I am afraid this is not a very good situation for you," he says mournfully, touching my shoulder. "I think maybe I will come with you to Guilin, yah?"

I glance up at him, blinking with disbelief, unable to believe my good luck, afraid that if I reveal the depth of my desperation and gratitude, he'll change his mind. "But you wanted to see the karsts before you left. You were supposed to spend the whole day here."

He shrugs. "I don't think that will be very much fun for me. I have to go to Guilin anyway for my train tonight. So I will just go a little earlier."

Eckehardt has known me exactly nineteen hours, Lisa twenty-four. But in the course of a single day, the two of them have become my family. They are all that stand between me and an utter free fall into helplessness.

At the Green Lotus Peak Inn, I am so choked with emotion, I can barely eat lunch. Lisa stands before me in her apron and her cheap, lace-trimmed gingham blouse, gimlet-eyed and smiling. "Here, Susie," she says, touching my shoulder, stroking my hair. "Special pancake for your trip. Chocolate and banana."

Her face has such innocence and yearning, it breaks my heart. I cannot bear to leave her behind. Sitting there, I can see the life she will be condemned to live: endlessly washing dishes for her husband, serving beer to foreigners. Most likely, she will have one child, followed by a series of forced abortions. She will do as she's told by the local authorities, who control if and when Chinese citizens can ever leave their own province. If she does not keep her ambitions in check, she may very well be punished. Slowly her intelligence will curdle, her face will grow prematurely lined and weary, and in ten years' time, she will look twenty years older and feel contorted and embittered. This moment—when she is young and radiant and still buoyed by the adventure of meeting people from around the world and learning to cook their favorite meals—this, I suspect, will be the sweet spot in her life. The high point. From here on in, her future is a treadmill, a foregone conclusion.

And meanwhile, Claire Van Houten will likely slip out of her delirium once she orders a medium-rare steak, drinks several bottles of spring water, and sleeps beneath freshly laundered bed linens. Once back in the United States, my friend will go on to some magna cum laude greatness—a partnership in a white-glove law firm, a Princetonian husband, a gabled house in Connecticut (Graycliff, Briarwood Falls), which she will fill with ruddy, tennis-playing children and heavy coffee-table art books. She will have her hair cut by Vidal Sassoon, a cordovan leather briefcase, a trusteeship on the board of a museum. She will sail, recalibrate. Our time here in China will be remembered only as some misguided youthful impetuousness akin to a lost weekend or a smashed-up convertible. Her stepmother will be the only one ever to mention it, referring to it under her breath as "that little nastiness back in Asia."

And me? An astrologer, a novelist, the next Gloria Steinem? Whatever my future holds, I have to be sure it'll be cushier and a lot more expansive than Lisa's.

It is not enough to hug her goodbye and say "*Shay shay nee*" profusely. I believe a grand gesture is required, something that will emboss us in each other's lives and link us across the ocean. Impulsively I run next door to the jewelry stall and find two souvenir bracelets made of heavy, tarnished brass engraved with the Chinese characters for good luck and long life.

I present one of them to Lisa. "You wear one, and I'll wear the other, and every time we look at it, we'll remember each other," I say gravely, twisting mine over my wrist. It feels heavy, almost like a shackle. "See? This will be our bond, no matter where we are in the world."

Lisa slides hers on, adjusts it, and smiles at me sadly. "You very good friend," she whispers, touching my cheek. We place our wrists side by side, so that the bracelets touch and we can admire them. Then we burst out crying like the two twenty-two-year-olds we are, pulsating with sentiment.

"I'll come back here one day, I promise," I weep. In my heart, I suspect I'm lying; I can't imagine ever setting foot in this supremely difficult country again. But I really do want to believe that I'll return to Yangshuo one day if only for Lisa: that I will rescue her the way that she has helped me.

"I'll come back again under better circumstances. Maybe I'll be married. Maybe we'll both have children, and we'll show them these bracelets, and we'll tell them how we met, and we'll laugh."

Sniffling, I write down my parents' address for her, and Lisa writes down hers for me. We hug as if I'm a soldier marching off into battle.

"Goodbye, Susie." She waves forlornly. Then she picks up her tray and heads slowly back inside the Green Lotus Peak Inn, where rows of pancakes and hamburgers are growing cold on the countertop waiting to be served, and a group of drunken backpackers have begun pounding on the table with their forks, chanting, "Lee-sah! Lee-sah!"

"Goodbye, Lisa," I call after her hoarsely. Then I hoist my overstuffed backpack onto my bruised shoulders with a grunt, and Eckehardt and I make our way down the lane toward the bus depot, dragging Claire's backpack on the dusty ground between us like a corpse.

Of course the bus breaks down.

Halfway to Guilin, there is a gnashing and shudder, and it wheezes to a halt. We are all forced to disembark and wait on the shoulder of the road while the hood of the bus is raised, and all the Chinese take turns peering into the guts of it and proffering opinions. Cigarettes are offered around. Mechanics are fetched and parts slowly accumulated. Most of the passengers walk down to a small roadside teahouse and install themselves there. They drink from chipped cups, smoke more cigarettes, and play a game using ivory tiles like dominoes. Even the driver does not appear to be in any sort of hurry.

Eckehardt and I stand off a little ways under a tree, my back pressed against his chest, his arms entwined around my waist. We watch the occasional bicycle or truck rumble past, leaving tread marks imprinted on the road. We squint up at the formations of geese flapping across the pale blue sky. Neither of us says much. We just breathe in unison.

When the bus is finally repaired, it sputters into Guilin two hours behind schedule. Eckehardt and I arrive in the lobby of the Osmanthus Hotel sweaty and drained.

The tiled lobby is shiny; it smells sharply of ammonia. A strange, xylophonic Chinese Muzak plays softly in the background. Claire is not there.

Eckehardt sinks down on one of the sofas and guards our backpacks while I hastily search the restaurant, the gift shop, the travel office, the fancy Western steak house upstairs on the mezzanine. For some reason, I'm not surprised when she does not appear, though each time I search a room and find it empty, I find myself feeling increasingly unsettled. Finally I head back to the reception desk and ring the bell. After several minutes, a clerk appears, a prim girl with a starched white blouse and a slightly woebegone look. I show her Claire's passport.

"Have you seen this girl here?" I point. "Has she checked in yet or left a message for me? Her name is Claire Van Houten."

The clerk looks at the passport and nods. "You like room, yes?"

"No. I want to know if she's checked in. *This* girl." I point again to Claire's photograph. It must have been taken when Claire was a freshman. Her face still has that childish, unfinished roundness to it. She's smiling goofily. Her hair, which falls past her shoulders, is feathery and white-blond. How the receptionist can think this is my passport is beyond me; I suppose all Westerners look alike to her.

"Did Claire Van Houten — *her,* not me — did she check in already?"

The receptionist looks at me blankly. "You like number one room, yes?"

Exasperated, I tuck the passport away and rummage through Claire's things for the phrase book. Watching me, the receptionist announces, "No passport, no room."

Of course, there's no way Claire could've checked in, I realize, without the items I'm carrying with me. So where is she, then? My uneasiness thickens.

"Excuse me, but is there anyone here who speaks English?"

"English?" she repeats unsurely. "Yes, okay. One minute." She disappears behind the wall. The Muzak continues playing; it sounds strangely like an Asian rendition of Engelbert Humperdinck's "After the Lovin'." After ten minutes, no one returns. I walk back over to the sofas.

"Ecke, she's not here," I say worriedly. "Maybe she went for a walk or she's at the park? Can you wait here with the bags, in case she shows up, while I go look for her?"

Eckehardt checks his watch and frowns. I sense that I'm finally exhausting his chivalry. "Yah, okay." He motions to the inside pocket of his Windbreaker. "But I am sorry I do not have so much time left. The train to Kunming is leaving at eight o'clock, and so I have to be there at seven."

"It's only four p.m. now. I promise, I won't be gone more than thirty, forty minutes tops. Guilin's not so big. It won't take me long to find her. Please?"

Now, as I push through the glass doors and step out onto the humid sidewalk, I positively hate Claire.

I still can't help but suspect it's her jealousy that's at the root of all this — that she orchestrated this fiasco just to punish me for having a fling. This is perhaps naive and selfish, but my logic is similar to that of female jurors who blame rape victims for wearing short skirts: As long as you insist that people have control over their actions, you're buffered against having to confront the true anarchy and craziness of the world. If Claire has done this deliberately, it means she's still rational. Nasty and vindictive, yes, but not mentally ill.

On impulse, I return to the Guilin Guesthouse. But she isn't there, and no one has seen her. I hurry down Zhongshan Road, past its restaurants like pet stores. An entire Chinese town slides by me: rudimentary shops; a fretwork of parked bicycles; men sitting out on the sidewalk on folding chairs smoking cigarettes; women squatting by the gutter, rinsing laundry in plastic buckets full of soapy water. Old electric fans rotating lazily in dirty windows.

At the turnstile to Solitary Beauty Peak, I hastily buy a ticket at the foreigner's price and race through, looking under trees and scanning the lawn areas. But Claire isn't there, either. Now I'm really starting to panic; I was certain she'd be at the park sitting on a bench by the pond. The only other place she could conceivably still be is the large public garden on the other side of the river. Seven Star Park is at least half a mile away, but I don't have time to wait for a bus.

I half walk, half jog as fast as my lungs will let me; I arrive twenty minutes later panting and gasping.

Seven Star Park is vast and circuitous, with sculptural rock formations and thickets of tropical foliage. It's impossible for me to search it thoroughly. The only people I come across are a New Zealand couple with terry-cloth sun visors and cameras. The woman keeps squinting up at the karst formations and saying, "Which one is that?" unaware that her husband has already wandered toward the next point of interest, his nose in the guidebook. When I show them Claire's picture and ask if they've seen her, they shake their heads. "Sorry." They've been in the park since noon, picnicking.

It is now five-fifteen in the evening; I've been gone from the Osmanthus much longer than promised. I've scoured the entire town, and there's no sign of my friend. A sickening feeling begins to take hold of me.

I climb on a bus heading back to Zhongshan Road, praying that by the time I return to the hotel, Claire will have somehow magically materialized. I try to visualize her sitting beside Eckehardt on the plastic sofa, flinging her hair over her shoulder, twirling her wrists in that sinuous way she has, talking animatedly. I try convincing myself that she probably just got tired, lay down someplace secluded in the park—the way she did in the rice paddy—and fell asleep. Or that she simply parked herself in a teahouse somewhere and forgot about the time.

But somehow I know that this is not the case, and my panic and dread escalate. Sure enough, when I return to the hotel, Eckehardt is sitting alone on the edge of the couch with his hands on his knees glancing around anxiously. The lobby is as empty as it was when I left it.

Claire is officially missing.

"I am so sorry, but she has not shown up," Eckehardt says. "Did you find her?"

I shake my head.

From the moment her bus had left Yangshuo, I'd imagined a whole range of possible outcomes. I half expected that once I reached the Osmanthus, I'd find Claire at a table by the window, finishing off a whipped cream dessert and a cup of Nescafé, fully restored and chatting away amiably to some waitress. I also half expected that once she saw me, she'd have the gall to behave sullenly, as if I'd somehow ruined her party. I pictured her frowning at me contemptuously and giving me the silent treatment. Alternately, I also pictured her screaming at me in the lobby, or curled up in a stall in the ladies' room, ostensibly hiding from the CIA. Whatever state I found her in, I was certain that we would have another fight, and I'd braced myself for this.

But the possibility that Claire would just not show up at all simply hadn't occurred to me.

Her bus went directly to Guilin. It made no stops along the way. Had it broken down, we would've seen it. I have all of her identification and money with me. She knows that we're scheduled to fly to Guangzhou the next day. Even if she was being dramatic or trying to punish me, she wouldn't have stayed away this long deliberately.

Where the hell is she?

I get a terrible feeling in the pit of my stomach.

The afternoon light is in its death throes, filling the lobby with a fiery gloss. Soon it will be dark outside. Eckehardt will have to leave for his 28-hour train journey to Kunming, and I will be left alone with Claire's abandoned backpack and not a friend in the world to help me.

I'm seized with panic. A tour bus pulls up the circular driveway and dispatches a group of Japanese tourists; I race outside shouting, "Does anyone here speak English?" to no avail.

As a handful of Western travelers slowly begin straggling back after their day's sightseeing, I waylay them by the elevators, desperately pointing to Claire's photograph. When that doesn't pan out, I berserkly ring the bell at the reception desk. A different young woman appears, but her English is equally limited.

"Is there a *doctor* here?" I beg. Perhaps *doctor* is a word she knows; perhaps a doctor will know some English. But the receptionist stares at me with irritation. Finally she disappears and returns with a tall middle-aged man in tow. He is wearing a polyester tie, a polyester suit, and a brass name tag: MANAGER: GEORGE.

When I say, "George, please, I need some help. Do you speak English?" he nods agreeably. "Yes, we have number one room. You need exchange money?"

I sink down beside Eckehardt in tears. "Ecke, she's gone. I don't know what I'm going to do. I can't communicate, I can't—nothing!"

Just then another tour bus pulls up into the circular driveway and starts unloading passengers. These are Westerners—retirees in plaid Bermuda shorts and golf pants, with spun-sugar hair and pomaded, overly optimistic comb-overs. Most of them wear matching knitwear shirts embroidered with the logo of a travel company.

"Excuse me," I cry, "do you have a Chinese guide? Do you have an interpreter?"

A chubby British woman in a tracksuit points to a Chinese woman with close-cropped hair holding a clipboard. She appears to be arguing with the driver about luggage he's piling on the sidewalk.

"Excuse me, *ching. Shay shay nee*," I interrupt breathlessly. "But do you speak any English? I need some help. It's an emergency."

She cocks her head, squints at me, and adjusts the frames of her wire-rim glasses. "Yes," she says slowly, guardedly. "I speak some English. Why? Is there a problem?"

Within ten minutes, the lobby of the Osmanthus Hotel is flooded with interpreters and military police. Suddenly it looks like Command Central. It seems that as soon as the tour guide, Jane, said the words *missing* and *American* to the hotel manager, everyone stopped regarding me as just another annoying big nose and began to realize that they might actually have an emergency on their hands.

A private car stops short in front of the hotel and a woman in a pin-striped dress suit swings her legs down onto the sidewalk and marches into the lobby carrying a notebook. Jane introduces her to me as Jane, also. This second Jane has a level gaze and pleasant face. Her hair is pulled back in a ponytail. She escorts me back over to the couch where Eckehardt is sitting and asks me to please repeat my story.

I explain very carefully that my friend and I had a big fight in Yangshuo, and that my friend got so angry, she stormed off and jumped on the bus to Guilin without thinking. I tell Jane that when I ran after my friend, she said that she just needed to let her temper cool off a bit. She instructed me to get her backpack and meet her back here at the Osmanthus Hotel at noon. I told Jane that I followed my friend to Guilin as quickly as possible, but that the bus broke down, and when I finally arrived here four hours later, my friend was nowhere to be found. I tell her that I've searched all over town.

Of course I studiously avoid any mention of Claire's screaming in the streets, her questionable mental state, and her paranoid convictions that the CIA, FBI, and Mossad are trying to assassinate her.

When Jane asks me, "How well do you know this girl?" I reply, "Not that well, really." In the event that the Chinese somehow do get wind of Claire's rants about the CIA, I realize I need to distance myself as much as possible. It's not going to help either of us if the Chinese decide that both of us are spies or threats to national security.

"Could your friend have checked into another hotel here?" Jane asks.

I shake my head. "She has nothing with her. I have all of her documents and valuables," I say. "Her passport. All her money and credit cards."

Jane asks to see them. Reluctantly I hand over Claire's passport and wallet. Jane glances briefly at the wallet and hands it back to me. But she holds fast to Claire's passport and studies the picture intently.

"She has no money with her at all?" she asks after a moment.

"Only about eighty yuan in remninbi," I say. "She also has her American traveler's checks."

"I see," says Jane, still frowning at the photograph. Finally she closes the passport and returns it.

A moment later, though, she brings George, the

hotel manager, over to me, and has me repeat the whole story to him again. His English proves to be far better than he initially let on. He, too, studies Claire's passport for a disconcertingly long time, then asks me abruptly: Could she be somewhere else in the vicinity? How much money does she have with her? How well do I know her?

Then Jane brings over two men in military uniforms and has me repeat the whole story yet again. The men are unsmiling and not nearly as amicable as either she or George. They question me in far greater detail, too:

How tall is your friend? (Five-nine.)

What was she wearing? (Khaki slacks, a white alligator shirt, Timberland hiking boots, a brown leather purse with a brass buckle, a silver Windbreaker, gold S-chain bracelets, a matching fourteen-karat gold necklace with a horseshoe charm.)

How can you be certain of this? (Trust me. We're backpacking. We really only have one outfit apiece with us. Her other shirt, the peach-colored one, is dirty.)

What did you argue about? ("A boy, of course," I say, rolling my eyes for effect. "It was stupid.")

They ask me what Claire's profession is, what her parents do, how long we've been in China, and where we've traveled so far. Their tone sets me on edge.

When they finally finish questioning me, one of the officers tucks Claire's passport into his pocket and says, "We will be needing to keep this for now." He disappears behind the reception area with the manager. A whole platoon of military officers seems to be swarming around the lobby, along with several well-dressed Chinese men and women who look like stockbrokers or beaucrats. The Muzak has stopped playing, but the lobby is now completely abuzz. Aware that some sort of drama is unfolding, the Western hotel guests try to appear inconspicuous as they gravitate toward the couch, attempting to eavesdrop.

It is now 6:05 p.m. For all intents and purposes, Claire has been missing for over seven hours. In fifty-five minutes, Eckehardt will have to leave me in order to make his train to Kunming. George, the hotel manager, reappears, accompanied by the two military policemen who questioned me.

"We have contacted Guilin police, Yangshuo police, and Bureau of Foreign Affairs. So far, very sorry. No one has seen your friend," he says solemnly. "Now we will contact hospitals."

I look despairingly at Eckehardt, then drop my head in my hands. "Oh, God."

He picks up his day pack. "I am going to the train station now," he announces. "I am not sure that I can, but I will see if maybe I can change my ticket for tomorrow instead, yah?"

"Oh, thank you," I sob. "Ecke, I am so sorry."

"No, it is okay." He sighs. "I cannot leave you here like this. But I cannot promise I will get another ticket. It is twenty-eight hours to Kunming. I do not think I will be able to travel unless I can get another ticket in hard sleeper."

Either way, he promises, he will return, if only to say goodbye. Leaving his own bag at my feet, he hurries out of the hotel and down the circular driveway.

I sit alone on the couch, blowing my nose and watching him disappear. I suddenly feel as if someone's clubbed me over the head. *This is really happening,* I keep telling myself. *You are not dreaming. Claire has actually vanished in the middle of Southwest China.* All the officials and police remain stationed at strategic points around the lobby. It is clear from the way they keep glancing at me that I'm being kept under surveillance. George has assured me that as soon as he has any more news, he will let me know immediately. Until then, all I can do is pray.

Suddenly a pretty, fresh-faced Western woman climbs over the side of the couch and slides down beside me with a little flounce. "Wow, what is all of this?" she says cheerily, as if she's settling in to watch a movie. "You think it's a convention?"

She has short auburn hair and a sly feline smile. Her gray-blue eyes are flecked with hazel. One is wider than the other, giving her face a slight asymmetry. She's dressed in hiking shorts and a nubby white pullover the texture of a baby's blanket. Reaching into a purple fanny pack clipped around her waist, she pulls out a roll of toffees, pops one into her mouth, and begins chomping away.

"You want some?" she says, more to the lobby than to me. "Jeez Louise. This sightseeing. It's sometimes more exhausting than work, enh?" Her voice has the earnest, perky twang of someone from Minnesota.

George the manager comes hurrying over. "Miss Gilman. Yes. We just speak to Guilin hospital. So sorry. Your friend not there."

"Thanks," I say miserably, relieved but also not relieved. "Christ," I murmur as he scurries back to the reception counter. "Where the hell is she?"

The woman slows down her chewing and stares at me dubiously. "Wow," she says. "What *is* going on here? You're crying. Are you okay?"

I look at her helplessly. "My friend is missing."

"Jeez Louise. For how long?"

I sniffle. "Seven, maybe eight hours. Or not. I'm not sure where I lost her exactly. She was leaving Yangshuo. We were supposed to meet here after noon. I'm not sure now if she ever made it."

The woman resumes chewing. "Wow," she says again, processing this. "How exactly do you lose someone?"

"We had a fight." I wipe my cheeks briskly. "She got angry. Jumped on a bus. You know."

"Well. That's a little extreme," the women declares frankly.

"Oh, you don't know the half of it," I say.

A blond, bearded man approaches us hesitantly. He's dressed in hiking shorts too and what looks like the top half of green hospital scrubs. "Uh, Sandy?" he says nervously, scratching the back of his head. "Uh, do you have the door key? I, uh, I can't find mine."

A look of intense irritation flickers across the woman's face, and she digs down into her fanny pack. "This woman just lost her friend," she informs him, snapping her fingers. "Just like that. That's why all these police are here." She looks at me knowingly and rolls her eyes. "Kyle here thought it was because some Chinese party bigwig was arriving. He thinks that just because we're in China, he's going to be rubbing shoulders with Deng Xiaoping."

Kyle looks at me, his eyes shining. "Well, they actually have hot water here, so I assumed maybe someone important was coming. You lost your friend?"

Slowly I explain my predicament to him and Sandy much the same way I explained it to the Chinese, in a sanitized, protracted fashion, careful not to mention anything about madness, paranoia, or covert intelligence agencies. When I finish, I say, "I really hope she shows up soon. We're supposed to fly to Guangzhou tomorrow. If we miss that flight, I have no idea how I'll manage to get her home."

"Get her home? To the United States?" Sandy scowls, tucking in her chin. "Jeez Louise, lady. Why would you do a thing like that? Because you've had a fight and she's acting like a baby?"

"Well, it's complicated—"

"Lordy. Look, if you don't want to travel with her after this, well, I can certainly see why. But there's no reason you should forfeit all *your* adventures. Just put her on a plane. But don't you go with her. Heck," Sandy says, gesturing with her chin over at Kyle. "Kyle and I can barely stand each other half the time—can we, Kyle?—but you don't see us throwing in the towel."

I look at them helplessly. With all of these Chinese officials milling around, there is no way I can risk telling them the truth.

"The thing is," I shrug, "who would I travel with? Claire and I, we planned this whole trip together."

"So travel with us," Sandy declares, throwing open her arms, as if the conclusion is obvious. "We're great to travel with. Backpackers hook up with us all the time. Kyle and I, we're loads of fun. We're Canadians, so we're intelligent and easygoing, but not show-offy or demanding like you Americans. Kyle here's worked in a hospital, and I'm sort of a nurse, so we're very practical and levelheaded. Not like some of these drug-heads roaming around here. And I've been teaching English in Shanghai all year, so you won't have to spend another minute in China if you don't want. In a couple of weeks, we're going to Bali, then Thailand, and just lie on a beach drinking piña coladas, eh? By all means, don't go home!"

"Absolutely," Kyle nods. "How many times again

in your life will you ever have this chance? We may even go see the Dalai Lama in India later."

They look at me coaxingly. "Well," I say vaguely, "we'll see, okay?"

I don't have the heart to admit to them that at this moment, I actually *want* to go home. I'm frightened, I'm physically sick, I'm exhausted; getting the hell out of Asia will only be an enormous relief to me. And the truth is, this trip was really Claire's idea. I simply can't muster up any enthusiasm for doing it without her. Alone—or with anyone else—I have neither the nerve nor the appetite. It's Genevieve and Zsa Zsa, or nothing.

Seven o'clock comes and goes.

Sandy checks her watch. "The restaurant's open. Kyle, what do you say we go get some dinner?"

Slowly she stands up. I notice that one of her knees is crosshatched and scarred. "Don't forget what I told you, enh?" She points at me admonishingly. "As soon as they find that friend of yours, you put her on a plane and come travel with us. We'll be at the steak house upstairs if you want to join us for dinner. Kyle here takes forever to eat, so no rush. We'll probably be there through breakfast."

As I watch her walk off, a voice calls, "Susie!" Eckehardt hurries across the lobby, waving a slip of paper. His temples are shiny with sweat. "They changed my ticket. A hard sleeper, leaving tomorrow," he says breathlessly. "It was the last one. But the CITS woman, she was very nice. Oh, I am very, very lucky, yah?"

I throw my arms around him. This man is a savior, my Teutonic knight. "Thank you," I whisper over and over again, burying my face in the crook of his neck.

He smiles wearily. "You think maybe later, though, we can have that steak dinner?"

As night descends, the number of Chinese officials slowly thins out and the lobby grows chilly. The chandelier overhead comes on dimly. In the reduced light, the tiled walls and the marble floor glisten darkly, their surfaces suddenly appearing harder and more impenetrable. Eckehardt slumps next to me with his head propped against my shoulder. I continue to stare watchfully out into the darkness. Now that it is black outside, it is clear that Claire cannot be anyplace good. Is she unconscious in the thicket somewhere? Half dead in a cave? What if she never reappears? What if she becomes one of those ghoulish mysteries I used to read about as a kid, like the one about the boy in Kansas who simply vanished from the cornfield behind his parents' farmhouse one evening? The Chinese are now checking all of the hospitals throughout Guangxi province. If she's sick or, or, or...I don't even want to think it. Nobody knows yet for sure. Until they do, I'm not placing any calls to our parents.

Claire. I remember her in the student lounge our

freshman year, throwing back her head with laughter and proclaiming, "*You* are brilliant." Claire loping across the green with her elegant catwalk stride, her hips thrust slightly forward, her hands tucked into the pockets of her long white coat. Claire leaning across the table at IHOP, her fork poised in midair, declaring, "Okay, sweetie. Now we absolutely have to travel." My friend, with her cornflower-blue eyes, her irritating habits, her imagination and humor, her love of complicated books, her silly faces, her flamboyant enthusiasm, her athletic vigor, her inborn physical grace. *Oh, God, where is she? Please, please. Don't let this happen. Deliver her safely somehow.*

―――――

At eight-thirty that evening, George and one of the military officers suddenly reappear.

"Miss Gilman," George announces. "I have very good news. We have found your friend. She is with the Yangshuo police. She is safe, and they are taking care of her. They will bring her here to you in the morning."

That is all he says, but my relief is so volcanic, I am instantly transported, incoherent with gratitude.

"Oh, *shay shay nee, shay shay nee*," I cry. It takes all my restraint not to throw my arms around him.

"You and your friend here," he continues, gesturing to Eckehardt, "you will please stay here at the

Osmanthus Hotel tonight as our special guests. We give you number one room at special student rate."

"Yes, of course, thank you." I nod vigorously. He leads me over to the counter, hands me the registration to fill out, and tucks my passport into one of the room cubbies in exchange for its key. Eckehardt and I haul the three backpacks triumphantly into the elevator.

"Oh, Ecke, they found her, they found her!" I clap.

"Yah, I know. That is very good," he says. "I was very worried."

"Oh, me too," I say. "Thank God she's all right. I was worried sick."

I press the elevator button and announce, "Good. Now that I know she's fine, I can kill her."

We drop the backpacks in the room and head immediately downstairs to the mezzanine restaurant. Now that all is well, we feel positively inebriated.

"Okay," I say, pulling Claire's Gucci wallet out of my day pack and waving it around in the air, "dinner's on Claire tonight! Order the whole menu if you want."

We order two glasses of white wine at fifty yuan apiece. "To Claire," we toast. "To the Yangshuo police!" Neither of us can stop laughing. We can barely concentrate on the menu. We order shrimp cocktail, pâté, sirloin steaks, French fries. Before the waiter has even finished writing down our order, I race ahead to the dessert section and cry, "Look, hot fudge sundaes."

"Yah, and apple strudel," says Eckehardt. "That is so funny here."

"Well, order whatever," I proclaim. "Like I said, Claire's treating."

We sit with our fingers laced together across the heavy white tablecloth, watching the votive candles flicker. Now that we know that all has ended well, we replay the day's events with gusto: "And then, when she ran down the street?" "Oh, yah, and when she jumped on the bus?" What was a living nightmare twenty minutes earlier is now a wild adventure, a delirious believe-it-or-not.

When our food arrives, we fall upon it. We are ravenous. The "Western" dishes turn out to be caricatures of themselves, peculiar Chinese approximations using local ingredients. The shrimps are served with their shells and heads still on in a gelatinous sweet-and-sour dip. The steaks have been marinated in soy sauce, the French fries prepared in a wok. Eckehardt and I devour all of it, tearing the shrimp from their casings with our fingers, dunking the French fries in the cocktail sauce, spearing multiple chunks of steak with our forks, laughing as we chew. We then order two more glasses of wine. "To Claire," we cheer again, clinking our glasses.

By the time the waiter has cleared away our dessert plates, we both look a little stunned.

Eckehardt stares at me. "I cannot believe I just met you yesterday in the forest." He shakes his head. "I was just standing there. And there you were. And then it turns out we are staying in the same guest room?"

"I know." I smile. "It's crazy. No one would believe it. And now look at where we are." I reach across the table and squeeze his hand. The idea that Eckehardt and I will now actually get to spend a night alone together in this fancy hotel sends a thrill shooting through me. It almost makes everything worth it.

He gazes at me. We both sense what is coming. "Well?" He smiles.

Leaving the restaurant, we run into Sandy and Kyle, sitting at a table in the corner. Sandy is leaning back in her chair, coolly watching Kyle as he painstakingly finishes a slice of cream cake. He is scraping the excess frosting up off his plate with the side of his fork as if it were cocaine.

"Hey, lady, did they ever find your friend?" she calls out.

"Yeah, they did. She's in Yangshuo. She's fine. The police are bringing her by in the morning." I introduce her and Kyle to Eckehardt. "This is my knight in shining armor. He fairly saved my life today."

"Oh, no," Eckehardt laughs, waving his hand embarrassedly.

"Well, then, knight in shining armor. Don't you think Susie here should just put this friend of hers on a plane and keep traveling with us?"

"Oh, I do not know about that." Eckehardt shakes his head. "Her friend, she was really going—"

"Why don't we see in the morning," I interrupt. "After I've had a chance to sleep on it. I really don't want to make any decisions before Claire comes back, if that's okay."

Sandy nods. "Good thinking. Boy, are you smart, lady," she teases, crinkling her nose. "Are sure you're not Canadian?"

———

Our hotel room is not much more glamorous than a Motel 6. It has two twin beds with plastic coverlets, modular, built-in furniture, and a single lopsided floor lamp leaning between two polyurethane chairs. But by Chinese standards, it's luxurious. It's also the first time in my life I've shared a hotel room with a man.

I sit on the edge of one of the beds while Eckehardt rummages through his backpack. I watch the muscles in his arm flex slightly as he pulls out his various belongings: his shampoo, his shaving cream, his bottle of aspirin, all these mundane products labeled peculiarly in German. His hair falls into his eyes whenever he leans over. When he realizes I'm watching him, he smiles shyly. He is a mixture of both sensuality and kindness. This is such a rare combination in anyone.

I am swooning with gratitude. I feel as though I

am in love with him. "Hey," I say, lightly touching his shoulder. "I'm sorry about all of this. You got a lot more than you bargained for with me."

He shrugs. "For three months, I have been without anyone to talk to. Now I am spending the night with a beautiful woman. It is not too terrible."

An image forms in my head. Slipping into the bathroom, I turn on the shower and strip.

"Hey, Eckehardt," I sing out, tossing first my bra, then my panties back out into the bedroom. "Would you come here, please?"

I have big erotic plans for us. Yet the reality is that after all of the running around and emotional turmoil of the day, the two of us are caked in perspiration and dust. And I, at least, do not smell very good.

Once we are facing each other beneath the merciless bluish glare of the bathroom light, we become bashful. We step gingerly, almost shyly into the steep, narrow orange tub. For a moment, we just stand there propped against each other with our eyes closed. Eckehardt turns the knob higher. The spray pulsates down on us. I have not had a hot shower in almost five weeks. The sensation is all-consuming. Slowly we begin to scrub our scalps with earnest dedication. We get very intent on shampooing, then with methodically getting the dirt out from underneath our fingernails and the clefts between our toes. When we have effectively sanded ourselves clean, we take turns standing under the spray and sighing with relief.

Wrapped cozily in the hotel's terry-cloth towels, we emerge from the fogged-up bathroom and drop down onto the bed in a stupor. Gently Eckehardt turns my face toward his and kisses me, and I fumble for the damp towel around his waist. But it's no match for our exhaustion. As we ease down onto the bed, we can't help it; his head drops heavily onto my shoulder, and I collapse beside him limply with my head flung back. With the lights still blazing and the wet towels stuck to us, we fall instantly, doggedly, asleep.

†

Chapter 10

Guilin

THE RING IS jarring and shrill as a baby's cry. Jolted awake, I fumble for the receiver. The earpiece is cold against my cheek.

"Is this Miss Susan Gilman?" a man's voice asks, unmistakably Chinese. "My name is Jonnie. I am a friend."

"Huh?" It takes me a moment to remember where I am. A damp bath towel is stuck to my knees. The light on the nightstand casts a lurid apricot glow over the room like a heat lamp. "Excuse me?"

"Miss Gilman. I need to talk to you. I have just been to the Yangshuo police station. I have just seen your friend."

I sit up. "You've seen Claire?"

"I would like to talk to you about her. It is important."

"Is she okay?"

"I am here in the lobby. I need you to come downstairs immediately."

With that, he hangs up.

I throw back the covers, my heart pounding.

"What is it?" Eckehardt says groggily.

"Some guy downstairs says he's just seen Claire." I feel around for my glasses in a panic. "Christ. What time is it?" The room is in complete disarray. I have no idea where anything is. I can't locate my bra, my panties, my Reeboks. Finding my pants and T-shirt on the floor of the bathroom, I pull them on without any underwear.

"It is three o'clock in the morning," Eckehardt says, squinting at his watch.

I jam my feet into my flip-flops. "He told me to meet him immediately."

Reluctantly Eckehardt sits up. "Do you think I should come with you?"

I hunt around for the room key. "You've done enough. Wait here. Go back to sleep if you can."

Hurrying down the corridor, I feel waterlogged with exhaustion but also strangely adrenalized. "C'mon, you piece-of-shit elevator." I watch the illuminated strip overhead slowly tick off the floors. When I finally reach the lobby, there's no one behind the reception counter and no one seated in the cluster of shiny chocolate-brown sofas. The restaurant has been shuttered for the night, its floor sign reading "Welcome" turned to face the wall. It's eerie. The lights are still burning, but the place is completely deserted.

"Jonnie?" I call out. My voice echoes off the tiles.

I push through the glass doors. Outside, the warm night air is pungent with fermentation. The pavement glistens with humidity. I walk a few yards down the circular driveway, but the asphalt quickly gives way to darkness, a vacuum of silence.

"Jonnie?" There is a rustling in the bushes behind me. But when I turn around, no one is there.

"What happened?" Eckehardt groans from the bed. In my absence, he's pulled on a pair of white cotton briefs and an inside-out undershirt with the label on the front. His hair is a tumult.

"No one was there. You think it's someone's sick idea of a joke?"

That moment, the telephone rings again.

"Where are you, Miss Gilman?" the man barks. "I told you to come downstairs immediately."

"I did. Where are *you*? I searched all over. You weren't there."

"You searched the front lobby," says the voice. "I am in the back. The *back* lobby. You come down here to the back lobby. Immediately. Please."

What back lobby? I'm fully awake now. Something is not adding up.

"Look, it's three a.m.," I say. "I'm not running around downstairs looking for some stranger in some back lobby somewhere. You wanna talk to me? Then come upstairs to my room."

I slam down the phone and roll my eyes. "Christ," I snort. "How much you wanna bet this guy isn't even at the right hotel? Sometimes it seems like this whole country is run by the New York City Department of Motor Vehicles."

Three minutes later, there is a loud, insistent knock on my door. Opening it, I find a young Chinese man squinting at me through small wire-rim glasses. He is dressed like a middle-aged college professor in a cable-knit sweater and blue polka-dot tie. He appears uncomfortable in these clothes, as if they've been rented for the occasion. He holds before him an oxblood leather briefcase. Flanking him are two military police officers in full uniform.

The officers have faces like carvings on Easter Island. They stare at me stonily from beneath their green and gold caps. The sharp seams of their uniforms are delineated with red piping. Gold epaulets hang from their shoulders like stiff vegetable brushes.

"Hello, Miss Gilman," the young man announces brightly. "I am your friend, Jonnie. I have come to help you." His affability is a direct contrast to the two officers looming behind him like a pair of executioners. Strangely, this Jonnie does look similar to the "real" Jonnie from Dinghai. He's got the same bowl haircut, the same eager-to-please beagle eyes. He nods at the officers. In unison, they all take a step forward.

When a stranger arrives unannounced on your doorstep in the middle of the night accompanied by the military police, many people, I suspect, would get nervous and demand to contact their embassy. I am smack in the middle of a Communist country known for its human rights abuses and political torture. Amazingly, in my fatigue and disorientation, I simply wave them inside like the hostess of a Tupperware party.

I accept that Jonnie is exactly who he tells me he is — a university student whom the Yangshuo police have recruited to help out in this situation as a translator. I assume, too, that the only reason he has a pair of military escorts with him is to help him find the correct hotel and perhaps for dramatic effect; doesn't everyone love an entourage? The fact that he has arrived on my doorstep at three a.m. — when it takes only fifty-five minutes to drive between Yangshuo and Guilin — in no way strikes me as odd, either: I figure that's how long it's taken the Chinese to get their act together. Infrastructure, after all, isn't exactly the strong suit here.

I feel genuinely sorry for the officers, in fact. They've no doubt had to climb out of bed in the middle of the night and get all dressed up in the dark to trek over here while their wives and kids continue sleeping.

"Please. Come in. Sorry there's no minibar," I say. "You guys want some tea? There's an electric kettle in the bathroom. And there are cookies, too. Cookies, guys? Anything?"

The officers fix me with an icy gaze. Jonnie smiles with embarrassment. "Please. That will not be necessary."

"You sure? Because I think there's a pack of cookies in my backpack."

Instead, Jonnie moves one of the hotel's cushioned chairs so that it is directly facing the other. "Why do you not have a seat and we will talk?" He sits down in the chair closest to the door. The two officers remain standing, positioning themselves on either side of him.

Lowering myself into the chair opposite him, I finally realize where my bra is. When I tossed it out of the bathroom earlier that evening, it landed on top of the floor lamp. Jonnie is now seated directly beneath it. The lacy underwire cups are unfurled sequentially above his head like an obscene banner for a peep show. There's no way to remove it discreetly from the lampshade, though leaving it dangling there is preposterous. I can't look at him and *not* see it. I wonder if the two officers have noticed.

"So you've seen Claire?" I say. My bra, I can't help

but observe, is long overdue for a wash. "Is she all right?"

Jonnie's back stiffens and he frowns. "Yes. She is fine."

Before I can ask anything further, he reaches into a shirt pocket beneath his sweater. To my surprise, he pulls out her passport.

"This young woman, is she a good friend of yours?" Jonnie asks.

I shrug, trying to appear as nonchalant as possible. "Not a *good* friend," I say cagily. I feel guilty saying this; it's as if I'm abandoning her. But I can't help sensing that it's still to our advantage to have me establish some distance between us.

"I went to university with her. But I didn't really know her until just before graduation, when she said she wanted to travel to China, and I was, like, 'Hey. So do I.'"

"Why?" I ask. "What did she say?"

Staring down at her passport, Jonnie runs his fingers over the number punched into the leathery blue cover like Braille. His hands, I notice, are small and smooth, the nails buffed like the pinkish insides of shells.

"Would you please describe your friend's family please?" he says.

Again, I shrug. "I'm not really sure I can. She has three stepbrothers who've all gone to university. They're all very smart. Very upstanding citizens. Her

mom—I mean, her stepmom—seems nice enough.
Big dog lover, very into homemaking and stuff. And
her father, he is a *very* important businessman, you
know."

Saying this, I'm appalled to hear my voice inflected
with the same preening tone as Claire's. Yet suddenly
Mr. Van Houten's wealth and prominence don't seem
like such bad things to trumpet.

"Is Claire still at the police station," I ask, "or have
they put her up at a hotel?"

Jonnie glances at his watch. "Would you tell me,
please, exactly what happened yesterday?"

I sigh. In a nation lacking photocopiers, computers, faxes, and typewriters, most Chinese, I assume,
can only verify information by asking the same questions over and over.

Yet again I recount my sanitized version of events.
That Claire and I had a fight. That she impulsively
jumped on a bus in order to put some distance
between us. That she instructed me to meet her here
at the Osmanthus Hotel, but never showed up. And
that's it. End of story.

I've been repeating this so much that I'm actually
starting to believe it myself—that we simply had a
fight over a boy after traveling together for weeks on
end, stockpiling all sorts of resentments between us.

"It was a silly argument." I shrug. "I really don't
know what happened."

For the first time Jonnie glances at me in a way

that suggests he does not quite believe me. He leans back in his chair and crosses his arms.

"You say you have all of her belongings with you. All of her valuables and identification?"

"Yeah. She was really annoyed. I guess she just forgot them. Or, you know, she wanted to leave me with all her stuff to carry, as, like, punishment." I smile at him broadly, in what I hope is an expression brimming with cooperation and goodwill. For some reason, the air-conditioning has clicked off, and the room is growing uncomfortably warm. It smells of varnish, mildew, cabbagey body odor.

"Obviously, I had Claire's passport," I tell him, "which I gave the authorities as soon as they asked for it. I also have her wallet, which has her driver's license in it, and her credit cards, and both her Chinese and American money—"

"So she had no money with her when she got on the bus to Guilin?" Jonnie interrupts.

"Well, we gave her some at the last minute. About eighty yuan."

And that's when all the pieces suddenly come together, and it clicks.

The money that Eckehardt tossed Claire as the bus doors were slamming shut: It was Chinese money, renminbi. Even though shopkeepers gave us change in renminbi all the time, possessing it as a foreigner was technically illegal. When Claire tried to buy a bus ticket using local money, the driver must have felt obliged to refuse it and handed her over to the local authorities. This is why she never made it to Guilin; this is how she's disappeared. I feel a flood of relief. Of course! China is practically built on bureaucrats and tickets.

At the police station, no doubt Claire had tried to cash her traveler's checks for FEC money. But without her identification, there was no way she could've done this, and without her phrase books, there was no way she could've communicated anything to the officers either. I imagine her standing inside some dank concrete outpost in the countryside, pantomiming furiously before an indifferent police chief. She points at the chunky telephone on his desk, then to her bundle of American Express traveler's checks. With her finger, she outlines the shape of a rectangle in the air, then mimes driving toward Guilin. When he does not respond, perhaps she looks around in vain for a pen and a pad of paper in order to draw an American flag. Finally, distraught and tear-streaked with frustration, she begs, *"Ni shou ying wen ma?"*

Yet the policemen in Guangxi province speak only a dialect, so her Mandarin is useless. Having absolutely no idea who she is, where she's from, or what she wants, the officers regard her first with contempt, then with a growing combination of pity and perplexity. They have no idea what to do with her. They cannot simply release her onto the side of the road. She is a mysterious foreigner without any FEC money, ID, or a ticket.

In my mind's eye, Claire is then shown to a metal folding chair in the corner and instructed to take a seat. A kindly older officer arrives with a tin bowl full of noodle soup, a pair of chopsticks, a lone, dented spoon. She sits there holding it despondently while the police stand around the desk gesticulating and arguing about what to do next. Locals, who've heard that a strange blond big nose is at the precinct, start dropping by to sneak peeks at her through the open doorway. They set down their bundles, their enormous baskets stuffed full of bok choy and scallions, and motion and call to their neighbors to come and see. People point and light cigarettes and even attempt to offer her one through the window. Finally Claire has had enough. Setting down her bowl, she stands up defiantly, shoos them away, and is about to make a scene when the police chief's telephone rings. An alert has been issued across the province from the manager of the Osmanthus Hotel. *An American woman in Guilin says her friend is missing. She says she was on a bus from Yangshuo without money or ID.* Quickly the Chinese put two and two together.

So now here at last is the final piece of the puzzle. Jonnie, I conclude, has been dispatched to confirm Claire's identity and get the money needed to release her. Perhaps she will be required not only to pay for her bus ticket but also to sign some sort of bogus confession admitting to having traded on the black market. Perhaps the Chinese have incurred expenses for her meals and a hotel room that they want me to reimburse. Whatever: In a moment this fiasco will finally be over. I have plenty of FEC money. Better yet, I have all of Claire's ID, so she can cash her traveler's checks directly.

"Listen. It's okay. Claire has traveler's checks with her," I reassure Jonnie. "Over a thousand dollars' worth. They're inside her purse."

Jonnie frowns. He glances fleetingly at the officers on either side of him, then leans forward. "There is no purse," he says flatly.

"Yes there is," I say. "She had it with her when she left. It's dark brown leather, with a big brass buckle. It looks like a saddlebag, but it's a purse."

"There is no purse," he repeats. "Your friend's purse is gone."

The way he says this sends a chill through me. A terrible feeling takes hold.

"What? What happened? Was she robbed?" I suddenly imagine someone yanking the bag from Claire's shoulder, smacking her across the face with the buckle.

Jonnie looks me dead in the eye. "Her purse is in the river," he says, as if this explains everything.

"The river? What river? How did it get in a river?"

"Your friend took it with her," he says plainly, "when she jumped in."

————

The room constricts and distorts around me as if viewed through a fish-eye lens. I blink rapidly in the dim orange light. I don't think I've heard him correctly. I'm suddenly aware only of the bedside clock ticking ominously, the exhaust fan whirring in the bathroom, my own congested breathing.

"Claire jumped in a river?" I say after a moment.

"Yes. But do not worry," Jonnie adds hurriedly. "The peasants fished her out."

"Peasants?"

"Yes. And they gave her clothes."

"Clothes?" I say faintly. "What happened to her clothes?"

"It seems she took them off," he replies, "when she jumped in the river."

Claire, who didn't even want me to see her in the communal shower at the Pujiang? She tore off her Izod shirt and her khaki wrinkle-free pants and flung herself off a bridge in the middle of Southwest China? No matter how erratic and paranoid her behavior was, she never once struck me as suicidal. And until this very minute, I've still somehow kept telling myself that the scene she made on the streets of Yangshuo was just that, a *scene*—that she was *acting*.

"No," I say emphatically. "Claire didn't do that."

"I am so sorry," Jonnie says, nodding. "But I am afraid that she did."

He regards me with genuine sadness.

"Christ," I cry, clamping my hands over my mouth. "Jumped in a river? What the hell was she trying to do? Is she crazy?"

Not realizing that I am being rhetorical, Jonnie nods. "Yes," he declares. "We do think she is crazy. We think that she has tried to die."

Despite the vast cultural and linguistic differences that exist around the world, certain acts, it seems, are interpreted universally: Voluntarily throw yourself off a bridge for no apparent reason, and it's generally assumed that you're trying to kill yourself.

Eyeing me steadily, Jonnie leans forward with his fingers spread across his knees. "We need to know if you do, too, Miss Gilman," he says.

"If I do what?"

He enunciates each word slowly, as if he is loading a pistol: "We...need...to...know...if...you...thi nk...your...friend...is...crazy."

We, he has said. *We* is plural.

That's when it dawns on me that Jonnie is not a student.

My friend, an American, has just attempted suicide on Chinese soil. She has stripped herself of all belongings and identification. And for all I know, she was overheard screaming about the CIA, the FBI, and the Mossad beforehand. This is not some trifling matter of an unpaid bus ticket or a public temper tantrum. This is a big fucking deal. And the Chinese know it. They have her in custody. None of these three men in my hotel room are temporary hires, fumbling bureaucrats, or local Keystone Cops at all. They are skilled, high-level Communist and military officials. They have woken me up at three a.m. deliberately. They want to catch me off guard in order to get information — confirmation, perhaps, of something they already know or suspect. I am not being briefed casually about Claire's condition whatsoever. I am being interrogated.

I reel from my own foolishness. How could I have been so naive? How could I have been so oblivious? Claire's unraveling, her hurtling toward suicide, the machinations of the Chinese authorities — have I absorbed absolutely nothing? For seven weeks I've been tromping around Asia, candy-coated in deflective stupidity. Now Claire is being held in a local jail somewhere, and I am in way over my head. *In every way imaginable, I am so far from home.* I set off to conquer the world, and here's what it's resulted in: three Chinese police officials grilling me in a cramped hotel room while my friend is detained somewhere in a Guanxi cell.

Jonnie stares at me. "Please, answer us. Do you think your friend is crazy?" he repeats.

I glance fleetingly toward Eckehardt, lying motionless beneath the acrylic bedspread; the officers haven't acknowledged his presence. I don't want them to, either. Still, I instinctively look to him for answers he cannot possibly have. How on earth am I supposed to answer this?

Of course I think Claire is crazy. She's delusional, she's gone missing, she's jumped in a river. But I'll be damned if I tell the Chinese this. I haven't forgotten what the British traveler back at our hotel in Beijing had told us: *This Belgian girl was hallucinating because she had a fever, and so the Chinese put her in a mental institution, and they wouldn't let her out for over a year.* I haven't forgotten Tom in Shanghai, either, sent to a prison camp for owning a *Playboy*.

I have to get Claire out of police custody as quickly as possible—before she says or does anything that might further indict her—and get her back to the United States pronto. But how can I explain her actions to them in any way that makes sense—in a way that will convince them to release her to me?

Oh, Claire, I think wretchedly. *I wish you were here.* Claire, who sweet-talked the officer in Dinghai and routinely chatted her way out of speeding tickets in Rhode Island: She'd be far better equipped to deal with this than I am. Me, I'm just some clueless, fumphering asshole from New York.

In this situation, I wonder in my panic, what would she do?

Straightening my back and crossing my legs, I

affect her posture, attempting to channel her. "Is my friend crazy? Oh, no. She's just *homesick*," I tell Jonnie breezily with a flick of my wrist. "She's homesick for her family, homesick for her boyfriend. We American girls, when we get homesick—wow—we just get really emotional.

"Of course," I add gently, "I can see how her behavior might seem bizarre to you, since you're Chinese. But trust me, Jonnie, what Claire did is pretty typical for an American girl."

As I say this out loud, it sounds saccharine and disingenuous to me. And yet it doesn't strike me as wholly unreasonable, either. Since Jonnie and the officers are men, I hope and pray they'll readily believe that Claire and I are prone to hysterics simply because we are women. For a moment, I decide, I've got to sell out the sisterhood; sexism has got to be manipulated to full advantage here. Instinct tells me, too, to play up our Americanness; this, after all, is our real X factor, our wild card, the quality that renders us truly enigmatic to the Chinese.

"She is just homesick?" Jonnie repeats dubiously.

"A homesick *American*," I correct. "Please let me try to explain my friend's behavior in a way that makes sense." I re-cross my legs, take a deep breath, and smile at him winningly.

I actually have no idea where to go with this. My mind races through its database of trivia and information, calculating algorithms of what might formulate the best, most convincing excuse. I'm a writer; fabrication should be my strong suit. To lie decently, I know I'll have to be audacious. And I'll need what's known in fiction writing as a significant detail—some unusual, highly specific invention delivered with such authority as to make it seem plausible. Ideally this detail should be something that Jonnie himself might be able to relate to, that hooks him in. But what? The situation here is so dramatic and extreme, it's practically an opera.

And that's when it hits me.

"Jonnie, you're a highly educated man," I say silkily. "I mean, you're in a position of authority. You speak impeccable English. So I trust you've heard of William Shakespeare, yes?"

I don't wait for a reply. "Shakespeare, as you know, is the preeminent playwright in Western culture. His plays in America are very much like your operas here in China. Everybody sees them, everyone grows up with them. And one of Shakespeare's most famous plays is *Romeo and Juliet*. It's a little like one of your famous operas here, actually—that one with the emperor and the concubine? Anyway, in *Romeo and Juliet*, these two young lovers, oh, they want so desperately to be together. But their families forbid it. And so when Juliet can no longer stand to live without her Romeo, she *fakes suicide* in order to be with him."

Jonnie looks confused; clearly he's not following me. But he is Chinese: If he doubts me or has absolutely no idea what I'm talking about, it's my hope he'll want to save face and refrain from embarrassing either of us by admitting it.

"So you see," I continue, "when we girls in America *really* miss our boyfriends, we sometimes act just like Juliet in the play. We fake killing ourselves to prove how in love we are. We make these big grand dramatic gestures in public—screaming, flinging ourselves about, declaring that we can't live without them, and so forth. We become *incredibly* operatic. We Americans even have a phrase for it. We call it 'Pulling a Juliet.' Of course not everyone does this," I add quickly. "But Claire has been *so* homesick and missing her boyfriend *so* much, she probably just couldn't help herself."

Jonnie presses his palms together and brings his fingertips to his lips ponderously. "I see," he says slowly in a way that suggests he doesn't see at all. "You're saying she jumped in the river because she misses her boyfriend?"

"Now, I understand that it was foolish of her to pull a stunt like this here in China, where your people cannot possibly be familiar with our quirky American ways," I say. "And frankly I can't blame you for being alarmed. To an outsider, I can only imagine how crazy she seemed. But please, believe me when I tell you,

Jonnie, that my friend is simply a typical American girl in love. And we American girls in love—well, frankly, we're all just a bunch of lunatics."

I sit back, utterly spent. I've spoken with absolute conviction and certitude, yet I sense that Jonnie isn't buying it. He is not a dumb man. He likely recognizes a boatload of bullshit when he hears it.

"Please. Remember," I add beseechingly, sitting forward in my chair. "America is a very young country. And so we Americans often act like very young people. We are not as wise or as mature as your nation. We have not yet learned to control our emotions. We're independent and materialistic, and we're rarely satisfied with what we have. As a nationality, we're like teenagers. Often we're just in thrall to our own desires. And now, through my friend's actions, well, you've just seen this firsthand. It's embarrassing, but there you have it."

Jonnie cocks his head and studies me. This last bit I've said seems to resonate with him—perhaps, I realize suddenly, because it is actually true. We Americans *are* the teenagers of the world, brimming with enthusiasm and arrogance, innocence and narcissism, creativity and emotion, thinking we know everything, that we're invincible, that the world revolves around us. I have proffered him a genuine insight. And in this cultural context, my explanation of Claire's behavior does make a perverse kind of sense—perhaps at least just enough to get us off the hook.

Jonnie shifts in his chair. He pulls a handkerchief from his pocket, removes his eyeglasses, and polishes each lens with deliberate, unhurried motions. My pulse quickens.

"So you do not think that your friend has gone crazy and tried to kill herself?" he says finally, replacing his glasses.

"Oh, no. Not at all," I say brightly, laughingly. "But I do think she needs to go home, *immediately*. She needs to be reunited with her boyfriend. The worst thing for an American family is to have a daughter make a huge, emotional display like this without any resolution. It's a huge embarrassment. The best thing you can do, Jonnie, is to bring her to me in the morning, and let me take her straight back to America. As soon as she sees her family and her boyfriend, she'll calm right down. I promise. It's the only way to help her."

Jonnie tilts his head and crosses one small hand over the other, clearly weighing his options. He does not strike me as an unreasonable man, and I suspect that neither he nor the rest of the Chinese relish the prospect of incarcerating Claire, creating an international incident, and having to serve as her custodians for any lengthy period of time. They have their own problems, after all, their own population to feed and police. Perhaps Jonnie has merely been looking for a way to save face all along — for some semi-credible explanation to present to his superiors as a pretext for releasing Claire. Perhaps, like the hotel staff in Dinghai, the authorities are actually anxious to dispense with her — to make sure that if she is going to go crazy and kill herself, she won't do it on their soil.

Yet what if she has been telling them that she's being hunted by American and Israeli intelligence agencies? What if they think they have a valid reason to detain her?

I decide not to wait for a verdict. "So good, you'll bring her to me in the morning," I say heartily, proffering my hand. "What time works for you? Eight o'clock? Nine? You wanna split the difference and say eight-thirty?"

Before he can respond, I say, "Beautiful. Oh, Jonnie. Thank you so much." I grasp his hand bathetically.

"Really, I cannot thank you enough," I gush — and at this moment, I genuinely can't. "You have been such a help to us, coming here the way you have. I understand how strange this must all seem to you, and I'm so sorry you had to get caught up in this. Please let me apologize again for my friend's behavior. But you and everyone here have acted *so* admirably. You've been such good hosts to us. You've done not only a great service to Claire and her family, but to the entire United States of America by keeping her safe and being so understanding. Really. And please tell these two fine gentlemen who've accompanied you here, and everyone at the Osmanthus Hotel, and all the police back in Yangshuo '*shay shay nee*' for me, too, will you?"

Jonnie can't help it: He smiles sheepishly. When I refuse to stop shaking his hand, he actually blushes.

"So you'll bring her to me at eight-thirty then?" I say, rising.

Slowly he stands up, awkwardly gripping his briefcase. "Okay, yes," he stammers. The tops of his ears are flushed and glistening.

"Great." I usher him and the two officers quickly toward the door. "Then I'll see you again in a few hours. My heroes! Really, you guys—you're the best! And again, *shay shay nee!*"

After they leave, I lock the door and lean against it, listening for the sound of their footsteps receding and the elevator doors dinging open. When I'm certain they're gone, I whirl around and look at Eckehardt, wild-eyed.

"Claire took off all her clothes and jumped into a river?" I yell. "Is she fucking crazy?"

I jerk open the zipper to her backpack and begin tearing through her belongings.

"How did I miss this, Ecke?" I rummage through her laundry, her towels, her Ziploc bags full of medications. "How did I not see this coming?"

Eckehardt sits up in bed and shakes his head. "Wow, this is very bad news. This is not a very good situation at all. I did not think she would do something like this."

"Okay, yeah, but you've known her what? A day? I've known her for almost four years. What kind of a fucking moron am I?" I dump the remainder of Claire's things onto the floor and paw through them. "Where is it?"

Her precious journal: It must hold some clue, some evidence of her undoing and everything I've so clearly missed.

I shake out her one remaining dirty polo shirt, her sleeping bag, her soft gray cardigan that now's an accordion of wrinkles. She doesn't have many clothes left. "It has to be here."

Finally I unearth her notebook, wrapped in her yellow towel, pushed into the inner Velcro pocket of her backpack behind the internal frame. But when I open it, I find that, except for the first five pages, the journal is virtually blank. After a few entries written in Hong Kong and one aboard the *Jin Jiang*, they peter out. "What?" I flip through hundreds of empty pages, one virginal white sheet after another, the blue-threaded lines unmarked. "How can this be?"

On one random page, I do find she's copied down a quote: *No victor believes in chance.* It's unattributed, though I can guess whose it is. On another is a half-finished list of expenses accrued in Hong Kong. Further on, in the center section, I spy a single entry for early October, hastily written in Claire's sloping, flowery script. I tell myself I'm not going to pry—I just want to skim for any words like *suicide* or *depressed*—but when I see my own name embedded in the paragraph, I can't help reading it twice. Claire gives a brief description of the Friendship Store and Remnin Square in Shanghai, details our tedious boat tour on the Huangpu River, then notes:

Last night, Susie fooled around w. creepy sailor guy, then got all freaked out that he might have given her AIDS because he has tattoos and she thought maybe the ink and needles could carry HIV. Spent afternoon assuring her that she does not have AIDS, especially since they did not even have sex! She is such a hypochondriac, it is not to be believed. Three days ago she had headache & became convinced it was brain tumor. She is really driving me crazy w. all her imaginary illnesses.

"Excuse me," I say aloud, glancing up from the notebook. "*I* drove *her* crazy?"

Then, in the very back of the journal, I come upon a dense collection of markings. Aimless doodles, chains of loop-de-loops, discordant trapezoids, mushroom clouds, Greek letters, lightning bolts, arrangements that look vaguely like fish bones, chicken scratches dotted with stars, fantastical, incoherent equations. For a moment I wonder if it's some sort of secret code, but there's no rhyme or reason to any of them. Her scribbles grow increasingly more cramped and ingrown, and some sections of them have been circled repeatedly with arrows pointing to them diagonally across the page. It's almost a private language, a secret geometry. A few notes are written hastily on the sides: "Make contact." "Must tell Alex if poss." "Noodles, tea, soup for din." "Collect call 4:17, 43Y, bike rental 15Y." They go on for several pages without any regard for the margins, then stop abruptly.

There is no trace at all of any world curriculum.

"There's nothing here," I whisper. "It's like a phantom diary."

"Maybe she did not plan to do what she did," Eckehardt suggests.

"Oh, my God, Ecke." I set down the journal and bring my fist to my mouth. "What did I let her do?"

Suddenly I see Claire in a state of madness and terror. It is earlier that afternoon. She has run onto a crude suspension bridge swaying high above a river. Her eyes dart about like a trapped animal's.

Seizing her purse, she pulls it from her shoulder and hurls it into the water as if it's about to explode. Trembling, she hoists one long, slender leg over the cable, then the other. With her toes curled tightly against the splintery edge of the bridge, she inhales, opening her arms and leaning into the air like a sail into the wind. With a yelp, she pitches forward and plunges.

I could've stopped her. I could've paid attention, been more generous. But instead, I neglected her. I let her run off. With my hypochondria and horniness, I literally helped push her over the edge.

"Oh, Susie, I do not think you did anything wrong," Eckehardt says as I sob. "You have saved her. You have convinced the Chinese to release her."

"Nuh-uh," I wail, my voice scorched with grief. "Oh, Claire," I gasp. "I'm so sorry. Oh, Claire. Forgive me."

———

It is four a.m., it is five a.m., and then it is almost sunrise. Maybe Eckehardt finally sleeps; maybe he just lies there with his eyes shut, leaden with exhaustion. But I'm awake, sniffling and blowing my nose as I pace about the room trying to wrap my mind around everything that's transpired. As soon as it seems like it might be a reasonable hour, I put my bra on under my sweatshirt and lace up my Reeboks (located, finally, under the bed) and hurry downstairs to the reception desk. If the young woman working there has any idea what has recently transpired in my room, she betrays no knowledge of it.

"Hello. Yes. May I help?" she says, her small, heart-shaped face a blank screen, her ponytail bobbing obediently.

"I need to place a collect phone call to the United States," I say in a low voice. "Can I do that here?"

"Yes. Collect phone call. Yes," she nods.

Reaching under the counter, she pulls out a form and turns it around so it's facing me. Painstakingly I write out my parents' phone number, then fill in my passport details. The young woman is diligent. To make sure she's got it right, she reads the phone number back to me when I'm done.

"Okay, yes," she says again. "Collect phone call to U.S.A. You wait in room, yes?"

"Do you have any idea how long it'll take to go through?" It is 5:30 a.m. here in China. This means it's either 4:30 or 5:30 p.m. back in New York; I'm too dazed by this point to recall the exact time difference.

The young woman shrugs. "Maybe one hour, maybe two. You wait in room, yes?"

"Okay," I say. Then, as I'm turning to leave, something important occurs to me. "Hey," I say, trying to sound as casual as possible, "I need to change some money today. So I'm just going to hold on to my passport, all right?"

———

Back in the room, I fill my money belt with all of Claire's and my valuables and secure it tightly around my waist beneath my sweatshirt. I hurriedly repack all of Claire's belongings, discarding anything that isn't absolutely necessary. I have no idea what kind of state she'll be in when the authorities return her to me—agitated, suicidal, weepy? I have to assume she'll be in no shape to carry her own backpack. Anything of hers that I own also, such as peppermint soap, Tylenol, or a flashlight, I discard. Her paperbacks of

Nietzsche and Ayn Rand I leave on the desk for the next traveler to read. Her ungainly Chinese army coat I hang in the small closet. The unused, cumbersome water purifier I tuck in a drawer. I consider discarding the broken camera as well, but I figure we already have enough problems without getting questioned by customs. I also hold on to her canteen, since it was a gift from her stepbrother Dominic. When I'm finally done culling her stuff, her pack, while not light-weight, is manageable.

Our plane tickets to Guangzhou are for 1:30 p.m., and we're supposed to be at the airport at least thirty minutes beforehand. I try to figure out how I'll get Claire and her bag—plus mine—to the airport single-handedly, then navigate a sprawling city of three million. I've already dispensed with the idea of budget traveling. From here on in, it's taxis and four-star hotels only. If we have to burn through all our money, so be it. I simply can't risk the possibility of Claire flipping out at the first sight of a squat toilet or making another scene on a bus. The challenge will be finding four-star accommodations without the help of CITS. Lonely Planet lists only hostels and pensions, yet I refuse to interact with a single Chinese "tourist" official.

Remarkably, I never attempt to contact the American embassy. It's located over a thousand miles away in Beijing, while the one U.S. consulate in Guangzhou is just a satellite office for passports and visas only.

Trying to contact the embassy—either by phone or in person—would not only delay our departure, I fear, but reignite the suspicions of the Chinese. I have an acute sense that time is of the essence. At any moment Claire could fire off like a synapse or the military police could change their minds; I worry that a telegram will arrive from somewhere informing them that in America there is no such thing as "pulling a Juliet." All I can think is that I need to hustle my friend out of the People's Republic as quickly and inconspicuously as possible.

When I was little, my father taught me to ride waves in the Atlantic. Standing beside him waist deep in the ocean, I was thrilled but terrified. If I didn't dive directly into the wall of water barreling toward me, it would pull me under. Holding my breath, I'd plunge headlong into the breaking wave, then immediately struggle to regain my footing and prepare for the next. Facing down the ocean, I was no longer aware of the blazing blue sky overhead, the glittering silt between my toes, or my mother unwrapping sandwiches on a beach towel on the sand nearby. I was aware only of the wave directly in front of me, the thunderous, impending trauma of it.

This is how I become in Guilin now: nothing but parasympathetic nervous system, tunnel vision, and pure, animal reflex. All I'm cognizant of is the obstacles directly in front of me. Everything else has fallen away.

I reorganize my bags, repack my toiletries, brush my teeth. *Will I need money for bribes?* I wonder. I take out a few small bills, tuck them in my pocket.

Finally, when there's nothing left to do, I drop down on the bed beside Eckehardt and sit, catatonically listening to my own labored breathing. The first shafts of sunlight glint through the curtains and creep across the baseboards. Eckehardt stirs.

"Hello," I say softly, stroking his hair.

"Hello," he murmurs, feeling for my hand.

It feels like we are married. It's hard to believe I've known this man less than forty-eight hours. Reaching down, I press the back of my palm to his cheek. His skin is moist, and he's beginning to grow beard stubble the color of ale—a shade lighter than the hair on his head.

"Oh, Ecke," I say. "Thank you so much for staying with me. I can't imagine having to go through this alone."

He blinks up at me blearily. "Yah." He rubs his forehead. "I was worried. Those policemen, they might have taken you away with them, yah?"

At first I assume he's joking. But it makes perfect sense. Military police arriving on a doorstep in the middle of the night? Of course.

"Jesus," I say. "What if you hadn't been here?"

Bitterly I flash upon Gunter with his rucksack full of tea twigs, departing for the train station in the middle of Claire's health crisis in Dinghai. Then, shamefully, I recall how Claire and I ourselves dashed selfishly down the platform at the Shanghai Terminus, pretending not to notice that we were abandoning Jonnie—humiliating him after all of his generosity. Eckehardt Grimm, with his fairy-tale name: This German stranger has gone to extraordinary lengths for us. He is a far better person than I am, than I possibly ever will be. He has forfeited his vacation to help two insolent American girls, one of whom, no less, is... *Does he know?* Suddenly it seems imperative I tell him.

"Hey, Ecke," I whisper, squeezing his hand. "There's something I think you should know."

"Mm?" His eyes are halfway closed again.

"Eckehardt," I say haltingly, "I'm Jewish."

My confession, I believe, is monumental. We're the next generation, after all: Here in China, in our own small, poignant way, we are writing a new, inspiring chapter, redeeming the hideous history of our peoples. Then I panic. What if hearing this makes him hate me?

Eckehardt stretches sleepily. "Yah?" He yawns into the crook of his elbow. "I was raised Catholic myself. Though obviously"—he laughs, motioning to the disheveled bed we've just shared—"not a very good one."

Sitting up groggily, he rakes his fingers through

his hair. "Oh. I need some coffee. Do you think the restaurant is open for breakfast yet?"

I stare at him. Whatever I expected his reaction would be, nonchalance was not it. But this, I realize, is the best possible response. It's the best possible response in the entire world.

"I've got a collect phone call to wait for," I say. "Please, go on ahead. Order anything you want and sign it to the room."

I suddenly recall that the night before, I'd promised the two Canadians, Sandy and Kyle, that I'd have breakfast with them to discuss traveling together. Now the idea seems so absurd, it's practically science fiction.

"If you see that Canadian couple in the restaurant, would you please send them my apologies?"

"Yah. Okay." As Eckehardt tucks in his shirt and threads his belt through the loops in his jeans, I wonder how on earth I'm going to make it through the rest of my ordeal without him.

Then something occurs to me. The night before, on the couch in the lobby, Sandy had said: *Kyle here's worked in a hospital, and I'm a sort of nurse.*

I freeze. "Wait a second, Ecke. Can you make sure to find them? And tell Sandy exactly what's happened? And then can you please ask if her if she'd come up here immediately?"

After he's gone, I sit down heavily on the edge of

the bed and stare at our backpacks lined up neatly by the doorway, each one zipped and labeled, ready for the long trip back home. I smooth my hands aimlessly over the bedspread. The hotel walls are thin, and through them, I can hear faucets squeaking and water glugging through pipes overhead. A closet door rattles open and shut. Footsteps approach, then fade down the hallway. Outside, a woman shouts something in Chinese; then a ventilator kicks on, throbbing and humming. A bicycle bell *cha-ching*s. A dog barks. Around me, Guilin is waking up.

In just a few days' time, I will be halfway around the world again. I try to fast-forward ahead past the treacherousness that await to the time when I am finally home in our New York apartment on the twelfth floor, and my family and I are all sitting down to dinner around a table set specially with linen napkins and wineglasses, and my mother is passing around a platter of crisp roast chicken and bowls full of glazed carrots and egg noodles shiny with butter. I try to imagine hurrying down the steps into the subway on 96th Street, into the roar and the velocity of the IRT, then emerging at Sheridan Square to stride triumphantly through the streets of Greenwich Village in my gold ankle boots. I try to picture being reunited with my friends, and giggling over giant frozen margaritas at Caramba! and dancing ecstatically beneath the roving magenta spotlights at the Palladium — all of this drama and scariness over and done with and relegated to the past as a bad hiccup in time.

But it's impossible. All I can do is sit here in the People's Republic of China and hope that the police will make good on their word. All I can do is listen anxiously to my own labored breathing. All I can do is wait.

十一

Chapter 11

Guangzhou

THERE IS A half hour of silence. Dread accumulates like clouds in a turbulent sky. The bedside clock ticks ominously. Then everything seems to detonate at once.

Eckehardt hurries back with two slices of bread wrapped in a napkin. "Sandy, she is coming," he says breathlessly. A moment later, Sandy strides into our room in her fuzzy white sweatshirt and Bermuda shorts.

"Lordy, I've seen people get into a pickle before, but yours takes the cake. Your friend's lucky, you know. The Chinese aren't big on letting crazy foreigners run loose in their country."

Summoned to the rescue, she is efficiency personified. She plants herself in the middle of the room with her hands on her hips as if she plans to either clean or invade it. "Mind if I take a look through her stuff, see if she's on anything?"

I dig out Claire's quilted toiletry bag, and Sandy rifles through it. "Malaria pills. Laxatives. Midol. Nope. Nothing unusual."

"Hello," a police officer announces, poking his head through our door. Three officers march in and silently take up position by the window. It seems we are now hosting an open house. Military police officers appear in the hallway outside, along with George, the hotel manager, who stands on the threshold with an imperious-looking Chinese woman in a frilly white blouse buttoned to the neck. All of them are talking at once in the language I can't understand and pacing around.

"Your friend," George announces. "Yes. They are bringing her."

At the end of the corridor, there is a sudden commotion. More police pile out of the elevator; Jonnie, my so-called student interpreter, is among them, still dressed in his V-neck sweater vest and blue polka-dot tie. Amid the cluster of olive-green army hats moving toward me, I catch a glimmer of blond hair. The men grow nearer and nearer until they are directly in front of me, and then they step aside to reveal Claire standing slumped and dazed between two military escorts.

Her face is pale and swollen. Hanging lankly like seaweed, her hair is sprinkled with tiny bits of twigs, her bangs matted against her forehead. Her left cheek has been raked with scratches like bloody perforations.

"Hey," she says, almost inaudibly. She rubs her left elbow as if she is polishing it and stares at the carpet.

Absurdly, the peasants who found her have dressed her in a bright orange souvenir T-shirt reading "I Climbed the Great Wall of China" and navy blue pants from a Mao uniform that are so small, they fall only to her calves. Her red, puffy feet are swimming in an enormous pair of the cheap plastic sandals that guesthouses provide for use in public showers: thick soles with molded rubber crosses over the toes. She has to shuffle in order to walk in them.

This hodgepodge of clothing is a testament to the peasants' poverty and generosity, yet it only makes her look more deranged.

Her gold bracelets, I notice, are gone. So is her gold horseshoe on its slender gold chain. There is something of a broken puppet about her, a marionette with its strings snipped; her movements are twitchy, then listless. A vital nerve has been extracted from her, an electrical wire yanked out. Behind her eyes is deadness. Her mouth is dumbly agape.

"Wow. Talk about making an entrance," I say, attempting a joke.

With great difficulty, Claire smiles. "Yeah, I really showed them, huh?"

"Are you all right?"

Jerking her head to one side, she stares at the wall and starts humming.

"Okay. We're going to get you home." I motion to Sandy. "Claire, this is a friend and a professional nurse."

"Well, look at you, so tall and gorgeous," Sandy says, stepping forward. Her voice is the aural equivalent of a plush toy: velvety, comforting, preposterously cheerful. "I've been here in China a long time. Believe you me, I know how rough it can be. But don't you worry. You're in good hands now. I'll bet more than anything you'd like a nice hot bath, wouldn't you?"

For a moment, Claire appraises her. Then she swallows and nods. She looks as if she's about to cry.

"Well, guess what? We have plenty of hot water here. What do you say I take you inside, and we get you all cleaned up? Won't that feel better?"

Sandy guides Claire carefully by the elbow over the threshold. "Okay, everybody out," she barks at the officers milling around the beds. "*Gai wah qwen.* Vamoose."

The officers, I see, have been busy rummaging through our drawers and closets. "What is this?" one of them demands, pointing to Claire's Chinese army coat. "Who does this belong to?"

"What do you care?" Sandy snaps. "They sell those all over. You know that. Now, go wait outside."

"And this?" The man holds up the blue plastic

water purifier I discarded in the desk. With its white plastic tubing, it looks incendiary.

"It's a water purifier," I say.

"Why you put it in desk?" the officer asks.

"Look. Save your questions for later, okay?" Sandy points to the doorway. Her audacity impresses me. "This girl needs a bath and a rest. You're not going to accomplish anything by badgering her."

One of the officers begins arguing with Sandy in English; another chimes in in Chinese. Claire stands beside Sandy with her eyes closed, humming faintly to herself, her head lolling against her clavicle.

"If you want someone in here, then send a woman." Sandy plants her hands on her hips. "I'm not having a bunch of men hovering over her while she's taking a bath."

As another officer begins shouting at Sandy in Chinese, the telephone rings. My collect call has finally gone through to America. It is, of course, the worst possible timing. Lunging across the bed, I grab the receiver. "Hello?" I cry. There is a crackling sound like fat roasting. "Mom?"

"Susie, where are you? Your grandmother called with the news. Are you with Claire? Are you two all right?"

Pushing past me, one of the officers pulls the drawers out of the nightstand and overturns them. I crouch between the two beds with my hand cupped around the receiver. There's absolutely no way to speak without either the Chinese or Claire hearing every word.

"Mom, what a pleasant surprise. We are absolutely, super-duper fine," I say saccharinely. "Everything here is just peachy swell."

I pray that she will detect the falsity in my voice and realize that I am talking to her under duress.

For a moment, there is a hissing silence.

"Mom, do you understand what I'm saying?"

"Yes," she says finally. "I think I do. You can't talk freely. People are listening?"

"Exactly." Glancing over at the military police, I present them with a pacifying smile, then reach for Eckehardt's hand and squeeze it so hard I practically crush it.

"Okay." My mother exhales into the receiver. "Just answer yes or no. Is Claire okay?"

"Um. Not sure."

"Is she there with you?"

"Yeah. Along with a lot of other folks here at the hotel, who are all being super-duper friendly, Mom. Especially the Chinese police."

"Okay. Got it," she says worriedly. "Are you in danger?"

"Again, not sure."

"Okay. Should I just keep asking you questions, then?"

"Why don't you do that? That's a very good idea."

Never before in our lives have my mother and I

been in such perfect sync. We are almost telepathically fused, the phone line between us a shared central nervous system.

"How serious is it? Your grandmother said you have to come home immediately. Can you give me any idea why?"

"Well," I say cryptically, "Claire's out of money."

"Out of money? What happened to her money?"

"Oh. It's in the river," I say lightly, aware of the irony and absurdity of my response as I say it.

"In the river?"

"You know," I say casually. "The river Claire decided to go into."

The military officers begin to clamber out. Sandy steers Claire into the bathroom, locking the door behind them with a click. Two Chinese women have been left to guard us instead—the one in the white frilly blouse, parked in the chair beneath the floor lamp, another in full uniform standing rigidly by the window. I have no idea how much English they understand.

"Uh-oh, I think I'm getting the picture," my mother says anxiously. "Suze, did Claire jump in the river?"

"Mmm-hmm. Exactly."

"Susie, can she swim?"

At this moment, I love my mother more than anything; she knows the Van Houtens are avid sailors with a bright turquoise pool in their backyard. But she has figured out a way to get me to confirm Claire's mind-set and intentions, the full-blown awfulness of exactly what has happened.

"No."

My mother can no longer help herself. "Suze, has Claire completely flipped?"

"Majorly, Mom."

———

Through a conversation conducted in ellipses, improvised code, and verbal charades, my mother grasps that although Claire has disassembled, neither of us can simply stay put and wait for help to arrive. I have to get us out of China as quickly as possible. She promises to contact the Van Houtens, who are currently in Hilton Head, and get everyone on standby, ready at a moment's notice to receive overseas phone calls, wire money, book airplane tickets.

As soon as I hang up, Sandy sticks her head out of the bathroom. "Hey, can you please come here for a moment and bring in some clothes?" Her voice, I notice, has the same artificial cheeriness that I have just used with my mother. It is the tone of people aware that they're under surveillance.

In the bathroom, I see that Claire's pallor is returning and her eyes are less vacant, though her expression is now increasingly that of someone being persecuted. She refuses to look at me or acknowledge me in any way. Shame shoots through me. *This is all my fault*, I think.

Since she no longer owns any pants or shoes, I give her my violet tank dress to wear, along with her own blue rubber flip-flops and her wrinkled gray cardigan. Sartorially, it's only one cut above the souvenir T-shirt and the Mao uniform. After Sandy dresses Claire, she leads her like a child over to the chairs in the corner and asks Eckehardt to watch her for a few minutes. She steers me out into the hallway to a deserted alcove by the elevator thrumming with white noise from the air shaft.

"Okay, here's the deal," she whispers. "When I gave Claire a bath, I took the opportunity to give her a medical exam. She's got scratches on her hands, arms, and chest from a tree branch. But otherwise, physically, she's fine. No sign of anything broken or sprained. No sign of any sort of abuse. Nobody's mistreated her at all."

"Did she tell you what happened?"

Sandy exhales. "I've got some good news and some bad news. The good news is that your friend did not try to commit suicide. She did not jump off a bridge. She told me that she walked into the river very calmly."

"I knew she wasn't suicidal!" I exclaim with a little clap, feeling vindicated. "So what's the bad news, then?"

"She walked into the river," says Sandy, "because she believed it would help her escape the assassins sent by the CIA. And she insists that the water was calling to her."

———

Back in the room, Eckehardt sits beside Claire, holding her hand and whispering to her. While he talks, she stares straight ahead, seemingly captivated by molecules dancing in the air before her.

Sandy kneels before her with a cup of tea and a pill. "Here, take this."

Mechanically, Claire obeys.

Eckehardt pulls me aside. "I think you should know, when I went to sit with her, she told me that she is hearing voices. She asked me to just keep talking to her so that she does not have to listen to them. I did not know what to say, so I just talked about the weather."

I lean back against the wall for a moment. "Christ." I blink up at the ceiling tiles. *How did it come to all this?*

"I think the Chinese, they are nervous," Eckehardt continues. "They do not want a foreigner to kill herself in their country. That would be very embarrassing for them, yah?"

I pull Sandy into the bathroom, turn on the faucet to drown out the sound, and relay this latest bit of information.

"Your friend may be schizophrenic, psychotic, or

just having your basic garden-variety breakdown," Sandy says. "I don't know. I've just given her some Valium that I picked up in South Korea." She waggles an amber-colored vial of pills. "But she's not the only one I'm worried about. Can this guy Eckehardt go with you to Guangzhou and Hong Kong?"

I shake my head. "I've only just met him, really."

Sandy looks worried. "Then I think you need a Valium, too, lady. No offense, but this is way too much for anyone to handle by themselves, and you're not looking so good. I don't like the sound of your cough, either."

"I don't need Valium," I say. "If Claire's like this, I need to remain as clearheaded as possible. I'm from New York. I'm tough. I'll deal with it."

Sandy sighs. "Yeah, but, honey, we're not in New York City now," she says delicately. "We're in China. Trust me. I've lived here a year. You have no idea what you're up against."

Of course she is right. "Well, if that's the case, then what I really need is for you to come with me," I say. My own brazenness surprises me. "Come with me to the airport or to Guangzhou, even to Hong Kong if you can. Help me, and I promise I'll put you up in four-star hotels and pay all of your expenses, both there and back." Opening my money belt, I pull out a fistful of cash. "See? I'm good for it. I earned this as a waitress. I'm not going to stick you with the tab."

Sandy crosses her arms and frowns.

"Let me get this straight. You're asking me, a total stranger, to accompany you and your nutcase friend to another city, possibly all the way to Hong Kong, on a moment's notice?"

Before I can plead my case further, she hoots, "Jeez Louise. How wild would that be? I love it. The look on Kyle's face alone might be worth it."

"So you'll actually consider it?" I cannot believe my great fortune. Sandy might as well be a superhero landing before me with a bright red maple leaf emblazoned on her chest, a gold lasso at her hip.

"On three conditions." She holds up her hand. "One"—she ticks off on a finger, "absolutely no whining. We're going to have our hands full with baby Claire here, and I can only care for one infant at a time. You whine, I leave, got it?"

I nod.

"Two. I am Canadian. This is not only a separate nationality from America, but a superior one. If I ever hear you pulling that American crap—you know, saying that Canadians are really just Americans except more boring, or making wisecracks about county mounties and ice hockey—so help you God, lady, you and your friend will be out on your Yankee doodle bums in a heartbeat, understand?"

"Okay," I say with mock disgruntlement. "No Canada jokes."

She smiles mischievously. It feels both good and

strange to joke with someone again, to feel that easy camaraderie.

"Lastly, three, I want us to make this as fun as possible. Treat it as an adventure, not a tragedy, okay? Because believe you me, I need a vacation so badly, I'm even willing to sign up with you two, that's how desperate I am. Between living here in China and traveling with Kyle, I'm just about ready to jump in a river myself."

"Really?" I say, genuinely surprised. "But I thought you said you were having such a great time."

Sandy drops her pill vial into her toiletry bag. "Sure I am. That's why I just happen to be traveling with a bottle full of South Korean tranquilizers."

Within fifteen minutes, Sandy's overnight bag is packed, Eckehardt has hailed a taxi to the airport for us, and the three of us have coaxed Claire down to the lobby with her backpack. Yet at checkout, George, the manager, refuses to relinquish Claire's passport.

"Yes, I am so sorry," he says, "but that will not be possible."

First he insists that he does not have permission to release the passport. Then he claims he no longer has the passport. Finally he implies that the authorities have confiscated the passport. Whatever, it has vanished, and without her passport, Claire is unable to check into another hotel, purchase train or bus tickets, or board an airplane even domestically. Technically she is no longer in police custody, yet the Chinese have managed to incarcerate her by fiat.

I start panicking, but Sandy remains unfazed.

"What did I say about whining?" she says, slinging her small purple knapsack cavalierly over her shoulder. "Trust me, if I've learned one thing after a year in this country, it's how to get around the system."

"I'm putting these girls on the next plane to Guangzhou," she announces breezily to Kyle, who has arrived to see us off. "I'm not sure when I'll be back. If I can't get on the flight with them, I'll be back in two hours. If I can get on, I'll see you in two days. If I wind up going as far as Hong Kong, I'll see you at the end of the week."

Kyle stands there in his hospital scrubs and his jute sandals. "You want me to continue sightseeing here without you?"

Sandy rolls her eyes. "No, Kyle. I expect you to do nothing but sit around the Osmanthus waiting for me indefinitely."

My farewell to Eckehardt is distinctly more heartfelt: I kiss him desperately; he touches my face tenderly and tells me to please be careful and to write to him in Germany as soon as I get home. The two of us hug, and I bury my head in his shoulder weeping, "Thank you. *Danke. Shay shay nee*," until Sandy says, "Jeez Louise, you two. Enough with the mushy stuff."

Then, Eckehardt and Kyle are hoisting up our backpacks with those purposeful, heroic motions men use whenever they're required to lift anything, and they parade the bags out to the waiting taxi and deposit them in the trunk while Sandy and I slowly escort Claire across the lobby. We've put her Walkman on her with the volume turned up to the max to drown out the voices in her head, and the Valium is kicking in. She is in such a daze now that Sandy and I each have to take an arm and lead her like an invalid through the glass doors. Once we have lowered her gingerly into the backseat of the cab, Sandy slides in beside her. "See. That wasn't so bad at all, was it? We'll have you home in no time."

Claire snuggles against her with her eyes closed. "Sandy. Mm. Like Mother," she murmurs.

I give Eckehardt one last kiss goodbye and begin crying all over again.

"You've saved my life," I whisper.

"It was not so terrible," he laughs.

He shuts the door with a sad little smile, and the taxi pulls away from the curb with a jerk. The two of us watch each other wistfully through the mud-splattered back windshield until the cab lurches over the speed bump in the driveway and turns into the street, and we are abruptly cut off from one another's view and that is it. Auf Wiedersehen. It is likely that we will never see each other again.

The Guilin airport is little more than a drafty airplane hangar with a couple of counters and offices set up along one wall. In 1986, China's only airline is CAAC, which Westerners joke is an abbreviation for "China Air Always Crashes." Rumor has it that if you manage to survive a CAAC flight intact, you get candies and a present from the crew upon landing.

No matter how much wangling Sandy does, the CAAC representative insists that there are no more seats available on the afternoon flight to Guangzhou. I sit with Claire in the dismal, empty waiting area nervously eyeing the clock as Sandy demands to speak to one agent, then another. Finally she stalks back over to where we're sitting, hoists Claire's pack onto her own shoulders, and commands, "Come on, we're boarding."

"You got a ticket?"

Sandy's ability to navigate China continues to wow me; she is thoroughly undaunted by the culture or her own limited linguistic abilities. "Nope. We're just getting on."

"Without checking in or anything?"

"Look, I've had enough of this bureaucracy. I'm sorry, but I'm Canadian. There's only so much incivility I can take. We're just going to board the plane. What are they going to do to us?"

I look at her incredulously. "Put us in jail? Arrest us?"

"Please. We're foreigners. No one will dare. Besides, your friend here doesn't have a passport, so what else can we do?"

For a moment I wonder if perhaps Claire is not the only delusional person among us. But Sandy charges toward the security area and motions for us to follow, and so we do.

The security area consists of a lone Formica table and a turnstile with a couple of young Chinese officers lingering behind it. They smile at us agreeably.

"*Nee how.*"

"*Nee how*," we parrot back—even Claire, who's now bobbing her head spasmodically in time to the music blasting on her Walkman. "Everybody Wants to Rule the World" emanates tinnily from the headphones.

"Ticket, please," says the head officer. He examines mine and Claire's, then looks expectantly at Sandy.

"I am their official government escort," she announces coolly, holding out her Chinese ID card from the university where she teaches English. The officer studies the card uncertainly but, to my great relief, does not challenge her. He asks instead to see our passports. When Claire does not produce hers, the officer frowns and says something in Chinese. His colleague leans over and demands, "Where is other passport?"

"She lost it," I say.

"No get on plane without passport."

"But that's exactly why we're going to Guangzhou. To go to the American consulate to replace her lost passport."

The officer looks confused.

"We can't show you a passport if you don't let us through," Sandy seconds, louder and more slowly, as if this might in any way clarify the situation. "She needs a new one. And she can only get one in Guangzhou."

"Get new passport? Where is old one?" says the officer.

"It's in the river," I tell him.

Sandy looks at Claire and me. "Oh, fuck it," she says. "Run."

The three of us bolt through the turnstile and dash out onto the tarmac into the hot wind, our backpacks jiggling on our shoulders. The plane is already revving its engines with an ear-piercing whistle; the propellers are beginning to rotate lazily, and a lone worker in a Mao uniform is just about to disengage the mobile stairway away from the fuselage.

"No! Wait!" Sandy yells. For some reason, all three of us are laughing wildly, running as fast as we can across the asphalt.

If this were fiction, of course, I could embellish this scene. Chinese military officers would begin chasing after us across the tarmac with their guns drawn, calling hurriedly for reinforcements while the three of us dramatically scramble up the stairs to the airplane, tumbling breathlessly into the cockpit at the very last minute amid a hail of bullets.

But the fact is that when we run, I glance back to see that only one of the officers has walked out onto the tarmac after us. After a moment he shrugs and wanders back to his post behind the security table, where he and his colleagues proceed to light cigarettes and watch us through the plate glass window with only mild interest. Perhaps they assume we won't make it onto the plane; perhaps they just don't feel like running; perhaps they have decided that it's easier to let three crazy Westerners become somebody else's problem in Guangzhou.

Whatever the reason, they let Claire, Sandy, and me race up the staircase at the last possible second and stumble into the airplane just as the hatch is closing. Already strapped into their jump seats, the startled flight attendants leap up, grab our tickets, then look at us, bewildered.

Glancing around the cabin, we see that the CAAC representatives were not lying. There are exactly two seats left on the entire flight—1A and 1B—which have been reserved for Claire and me. Otherwise the plane is full. There is absolutely no place for Sandy to sit. Yet the doors have been shut and the plane is already pivoting slowly around on the tarmac.

"Oh, that's okay," Sandy says, smiling prettily at

the panicked flight attendants. "I'll just share a seat here with my friend Claire."

Somehow she manages to raise the armrest, wedge into the space between Claire and me, and stretch the seatbelt across both of them. "See?" she laughs, scrunching her nose and clipping in the buckle. "All snug as a bug."

With our backpacks piled on the floor by our feet, we are breaking every standard passenger safety rule in commercial aviation. And yet nobody halts the plane. *China Air Always Crashes!* As the cabin shudders and vibrates, we feel it accumulating velocity until the engine shrieks and the entire body seems to release, catapulting forward. We are suddenly aloft, airborne, lifting higher and higher up over the jagged karsts, over the metallic rivers and soft green rice paddies, over the misty pearl-gray city of Guilin, until the view from the tiny window is nothing but blurred patchwork, and we have left Guangxi province, with all of its terror and beauty and heartbreak, behind.

———

As soon as we land, we have other problems. We have to go through passport control in Guangzhou, which, unlike Guilin, appears to be highly functional, with a Plexiglas booth staffed by military police who are actually paying attention.

Mercifully, the checkpoint official seems to be used to frantic Westerners appearing before him empty-handed and teary-eyed, explaining that they've come to Guangzhou for replacement passports. The moment we launch into our tale of woe, he pulls out a mimeographed map of the city with various foreign consulates circled on it in red. But as he issues Claire a special transit waiver that allows her to leave the airport, he warns us that she has to obtain a Chinese emergency visa as well. It doesn't matter that we're planning on leaving for Hong Kong the next morning. Without an emergency visa in her replacement passport, he explains, the Chinese will prohibit her from exiting and detain her. The government has a distinct sense of irony: If you don't have official proof that you've been admitted into the country in the first place, they'll refuse to let you out of it.

What's more, the official explains, if Claire does not obtain an emergency visa on the very same day as her new passport, she will be considered illegal and risk being arrested or detained that evening. We have to proceed to both offices *immediately*.

As luck would have it, the American consulate and the Chinese foreign visa office are on opposite ends of the city. And, like good bureaucracies everywhere, their doors come down like guillotines at precisely five o'clock. It is currently 2:54 p.m.

"Why you arrive so late?" the official scolds. "Most people, they need new passport, they arrive Guangzhou first thing in morning."

"Gee, thanks. Okay then. Telling us this is really

helpful," Sandy snorts as she pulls Claire through the turnstile. "We'll just go jump in our time machine now."

We have no option but to split up. Logically, as a fellow American, I should be the one to escort Claire to the American consulate. But Claire's relationship to Sandy has become positively umbilical. She clings to Sandy and becomes agitated whenever Sandy disengages herself to do so much as tie her shoe or use the ladies' room. "Sandy, where are you going?" she cries, groping like a blind person.

"Oh, Sandy," she coos, "don't leave, okay?" Me, on the other hand, she snubs outright. When she overhears us discussing the logistics, she yanks off her headphones and says anxiously, "I only want to go with Sandy."

And so Sandy, the great Canadian, ends up taking Claire to the American consulate while I get dropped off at the Chinese foreign visa office to get a jump on the paperwork.

The visa office is housed in an ornate beaux arts town house with flaking wrought-iron gates left over from French colonial times. A line of grungy backpackers extends from the emergency visa counter through the musty reception hall to the entrance foyer. Standing there, I worry that I won't even reach the front of the line before closing time. People inch up glacially. Only one bureaucrat is manning the entire operation—an elderly Chinese man in a gray muslin uniform who moves so slowly, he might as well be practicing tai chi. Each time someone finally arrives at the counter, he hands them a series of forms, which they fill out at a side table or while sitting cross-legged on the parquet floor. He then reviews their paperwork as if attempting to memorize it. Eventually he stamps it with a satisfying *thwomp!* that echoes throughout the hall. The backpackers flee clutching their passports like prizes that might at any moment be revoked, their faces shiny with relief.

It is 3:24 when I arrive. Then it is 3:27, 3:34, 3:41, 3:52. Checking the time becomes an insatiable itch. I tap my foot, bite my nails, pull my split ends apart, and glance miserably around the high-ceilinged waiting area, which smells of wet clay. I find myself despising Claire, then feeling guilty for resenting somebody who is helpless and mentally ill and so clearly suffering; I am a heinous person. I think longingly of Eckehardt. Just imagining the journey ahead gives me vertigo. How on earth am I going to get Claire all the way back to New York by myself in the state that she's in?

As closing time nears, the man behind the counter gets eager to finish. *Thwomp, thwomp, thwomp!* There are only six people ahead of me, then five. When it is finally my turn, there is still no sign of Sandy and Claire. I take the forms and fill them out in the corner, leaving blank the sections that require her new passport number. I am the only one left in the office.

The administrator waves me over impatiently. It is 5:02 p.m. Claire and Sandy are still not back from the American consulate. Shafts of dusty sunlight are receding across the parquet floor.

"Ni shou ying wen ma?" I ask. This is Mandarin, not Cantonese, I realize but the man seems to understand. He shakes his head. His benign, plump face is tea-colored, grandfatherly. Holding out his small crepe-skinned palm, he motions for me to turn in my application.

When I refuse, he points again to the clock overhead. *It's closing time. Now or never.*

I fumble through my day pack for the Cantonese phrase book, locate the characters for *friend* and *ten minutes,* and point to them.

The administrator sighs. Pulling a metal box from beneath the counter, he puts his rubber stamp away and locks it with resignation.

"No, please!" I cry.

He walks over to the bank of large windows and systematically begins closing the blinds with a tug and a *thwip!* As he proceeds from one window to the next, I hurry after him, pleading in some sort of demented hybrid of English and Mandarin and tapping at my watch. After regarding me pitifully for a moment, he disappears into a little doorway beside the counter. For a moment I think that perhaps he has opted to help me after all. But he reemerges with a broom and begins sliding it across the floor. He glances at me once sympathetically as if to say, *I am so sorry I cannot help you, but I do not understand what you want.*

In a few more minutes, he will begin switching off the lights. He will insist that I leave and lock the door behind me. Then what? I survey the office frantically for something to seize upon, for some instrument to help me. There is nothing. In my frustration, my eyes fill up with tears.

I step in front of his broom. "Please." I clasp my hands together. "You don't speak any English?" For the life of me, I don't know how else to communicate. "*Parlez-vous français?*" I say stupidly.

The man stops. Reaching up beneath his cap, he runs his hand over his pate in amazement. "*Mais oui, mademoiselle. Je parle français,*" he says. "*Et vous aussi?*"

———

Twenty minutes later, when Claire and Sandy finally arrive at the foreign visa office, Mr. Chiang and I are hunkered over my 913-page volume of *Linda Goodman's Love Signs* and I am explaining to him in French that as a Sagittarius in Western astrology ("*le sagittaire, un cheval*") he is most naturally compatible with Leo and Aries ("*le lion et le bélier*") while Chiang is explaining to me in turn—also in French—that since I was born in the Year of the Dragon ("*le dragon*"), I should have absolutely no problem getting along with my brother, who was born in the Year of the Monkey ("*le singe*"), but that I should always watch out for the pig and the rat. The fact that he's a Sagittarius tickles him immensely, he says, because in Chinese astrology, he was born in the Year of the Horse. "*C'est parfait, non?*" we cheer in unison. "*Cheval et cheval! En deux cultures différents, la même signe!*"

Sandy stands there looking at me as if I, too, have now lost my mind.

"Claire, Sandy!" I cry, leaping up. "*Monsieur Chiang*," I say magnanimously, "*je vous present mes deux amies, Claire et Sandy.*"

Beaming, Mr. Chiang escorts them over to the counter. He has already heard my truncated version of our saga. Pulling out his metal box, he removes his rubber stamp and embosses Claire's passport with a flourish. An emergency visa is only good for twenty-four hours, he says apologetically, but at least Claire will no longer be illegal. We now have exactly one full day to get her out of China.

There is a maritime travel office by the wharf, Mr. Chiang says, where we can purchase hydrofoil tickets to Hong Kong. He's not certain, but he thinks it's open until six o'clock.

"*Bon voyage!*" He waves as he locks the wrought-iron gates. "*Et bon courage!*"

"I can't fucking believe it," I say as our taxi jounces toward the waterfront. "The guy spoke fluent French.

Said he learned it during colonial times before World War Two, working on the docks. What're the chances of *that*?"

"Sounds like you had an easier time than I did," Sandy grumbles. Reaching over, she checks to make sure that Claire's Walkman is still on high, then tells me that the staffers at the U.S. consulate behaved like a couple of frat boys.

"They were calling each other Scooter and Biff and punching each other on the arm and tossing this Nerf football back and forth as if we weren't even there. When I finally got their attention and told them what had happened, that Claire had a breakdown and needed a new passport and so forth, they just looked at me like, *So. What do you expect us to do?*

"And I said, 'Look, I'm Canadian. I found her in a lot of trouble, so I brought her here. I'm just trying to help.' So then they asked to see *my* passport. And when they saw I was Canadian, they said, 'Well, how do we know that your friend here isn't Canadian too, and that you're not just scheming to get her an American passport so you can live in the U.S.?'

"Well, Lordy, Suze, I just about lost it then. 'Look,' I said. 'This girl is an American. If you don't want to help *me* help her, fine. I'm out of here. She's your problem now.' And Claire is sitting there on a bench humming to herself, her eyes practically rolling back into her head, and your purple dress hiked up over her knees, and she's swatting at the air and starting to yell at people, getting all paranoid because the Valium's wearing off. 'There she is.' I pointed. 'Have fun.' And I walked out.

"And they took one look at Claire, and suddenly the consulate guy comes running out after me, shouting, 'Ma'am, I'm sorry. Please. Come back, ma'am. We'll get your friend a new passport. Please. I'll even make you coffee.' And back inside they're leafing through the consulate handbook trying to figure out what to do, and calling their boss, and finally, *tah-dah*. They give her a passport. And the coffee they made me was really good, too. But Lordy, Lordy, Lordy. I am telling you, lady. You Americans, you're worse than the Communists."

That evening, with three hydrofoil tickets finally in hand, we check into one of the fanciest hotels in Guangzhou, a modern high-rise with its name spelled across the top in cherry-red neon characters. We're required to hand over all three of our passports, which makes Sandy and me very leery. We can't imagine that the authorities in Guangxi aren't out looking for Claire, methodically connecting the dots.

Ironically, Claire herself seems unfazed. Our deluxe double room costs seventy-five dollars a night and smells of pineapple air freshener. Although it is scarcely more luxurious than the Osmanthus, it has two queen-size beds with brocaded coverlets and an immaculate Western bathroom. An air conditioner purrs reliably in the corner. Claire sighs contentedly and sinks into a club chair by the window. She is like a candle melting. Then she turns to me, scratches her neck compulsively, and says the only thing that she will say directly to me that entire day. Pointing at the foil-wrapped chocolates glinting on each pillow, she murmurs, "Mints."

Since it is the only place where Sandy and I can talk out of earshot of Claire, the bathroom becomes our command center. Both of us are nervous that the authorities will track us down and detain us before we can cross the border the next morning. We are also worried that Claire will have another delusional episode. Perching on the edge of the tub, Sandy sorts through her medications. "I have exactly seven Valium left. If you give her one every twelve hours, you can keep her sedated through Friday." Then she steps outside, helps Claire into her pajamas, and tucks her into bed. Although it is barely seven p.m., it feels as though it's midnight. Even in bed, Claire is still wearing her Walkman.

"Go. Get yourself some dinner downstairs," Sandy instructs as she strokes Claire's hair. "Once she's asleep, I'll join you if I can."

I sit alone at a banquette in the hotel's peculiar faux-Polynesian-themed restaurant, keeping my eye out for military police. Every waitress, every busboy makes me flinch. Between forkfuls of sweet-and-sour chicken, I glance around uneasily and cough. *I* have now become the fearful, suspicious paranoiac. The irony of this is not lost on me. My nerves make it difficult to eat, but I force myself. It's been twenty-four hours since my last meal. That celebratory wine-soaked dinner with Eckehardt seems surreal and very faraway now, the back end of a telescope.

Halfway through my meal, Sandy slides into the padded seat across from me. "Jeez Louise," she groans, spreading her arms across the tabletop and dropping her head between them. "I need a drink." Summoning the waiter, she orders two mai tais and another plate of sweet-and-sour chicken. "You Americans are exhausting."

I wait until she has had something to eat and we're chewing on the orange rinds from our second round of cocktails. Then I move my decimated plate aside and lean toward her. "Okay, please tell me."

Sandy sighs and runs her index finger around the sticky red rim of her glass. "Well, she believed people were after her. Assassins," she begins.

"CIA, Mossad, FBI. Special agents. She said she'd been picking up signals. But once she got on board the bus to Guilin, she said, and you and Eckehardt were there outside, she suddenly felt calm and safe again, like maybe she'd thrown them off her track and that she'd be okay if she could just get to Guilin.

"But then, after about fifteen minutes riding the

bus, she said her panic started to return. She felt increasingly endangered, constricted, like she couldn't breathe, and this pressure was building up behind her eyes. She claims voices were telling her they could pinpoint her using their special satellite, and there was all this noise from the Chinese on the bus, too, and the engine roaring, and people were staring and pointing at her and laughing at her and spitting, and it was building to a crescendo. She thought her head was going to explode from all the chatter, and that the CIA agents were monitoring the bus until it reached a predesignated point where they could climb on board and abduct her. She said she had to get off immediately. And so she started screaming and grabbing at the driver's arm, ordering him to open the doors. And he did. He stopped short on the side of the road and let her off. All she remembers is that it was in a wooded area with a stream below."

As Sandy recounts Claire's story, I try to imagine it. The bus pulls away, disappearing beneath a veil of trees, and Claire is suddenly alone in the whispery stillness. From overhead comes the mournful caw of a bird. The trees rustle in the wind. But Claire knows this tranquility is an illusion. Above her, the karsts appear to be melting. It's disintegrating—the landscape is poisoned, she decides. It's all part of the plot. She knows. She knows too much, in fact—which is partly why the CIA is trying to kill her.

The way an animal can sense a predator stalking

it, she feels her assassins closing in. She has got to keep moving. If she descends the embankment, she can reach the stream. Water. It can throw hunters off your scent.

On either side are dense tropical forests. The slope is steeper than she anticipated. Losing her footing, she slips and skids down a ways on her backside, ripping her left pants leg on a knob of roots protruding from the earth. As she picks herself up and brushes herself off, she feels an increasing sense of urgency. There's no time left. They're coming! Hurrying down to the stream, she begins following it. At one point she pulls a fistful of what she thinks are spearmint leaves off a bush and rubs them all over her palms and her neck, hoping this will help to throw the assassins off her trail. But then she hears a voice behind her saying *We've got a lock on you* and she breaks into a run, half stumbling through the bushes, leaping over rocky outcroppings alongside the stream. She dashes through the woods until it is just a blur of green and brown and all she's aware of is the bass beat of her own frenzied heart and her blood pounding relentlessly in her ears, and the slap of wet leaves underfoot, and the voices somewhere intoning, *All systems on red alert. We're closing in.*

Suddenly she runs through a clearing and finds herself at the edge of a river. The water is fast-moving. It sounds like rain, and this sound obliterates anything sinister. When the sunlight hits the current, it turns to quicksilver, dancing and sparkling—like jewels on her mother's throat. She is momentarily overcome by a memory: her mother dressed to go out to a Christmas party, leaning over to kiss her good night. As she bends over Claire's bed, her breasts swell in their emerald-green bodice, and her necklace dangles above Claire like a pendulum. Claire remembers the glossy crescents of her mother's neckline, the waxy scent of her cranberry-colored lipstick, her perfume, Ma Griffe—and she remembers reaching up to grasp the tantalizing necklace—she couldn't have been more than three years old—and her mother laughing and wrapping her hand tenderly over Claire's tiny fist, saying, "Uh-uh, darling. Don't touch."

Her mother. *Oh, Mom,* she cries aloud. *Please, where are you?* Suddenly she misses her mother so furiously, she aches. Then, staring into the river, she sees her. Not her mother exactly, but the distilled essence of her. The "oversoul," Emerson called it, and here it is, infused with her mother's spirit, diaphanous in the water. And she can hear it now, too, calling to her, beckoning, urging: *Come to me. I will protect you. Here the assassins will not be able to get you.* She sees the water opening its arms.

The rocks at the edge are slippery, but Claire squats down on them and manages to lower herself in one leg at a time. She hadn't imagined the river to be so cold. Nor had she expected it to be quite so deep. Straightening up and fumbling for her footing, she finds she is already submerged up to her waist, and the current is strong. *That's it. You brave and beautiful girl. Come to me.* She manages to take a few steps away from the shore, but it is a struggle. Her Timberlands have filled with water; they might as well be cement, and her goddamn bag is weighing her down, too. She's got to get rid of it. Lifting it over her head, she swings the bag by its strap and releases it toward the shore. But it falls short of its mark and lands in the water with a *thwuck!* where because of the weight of the leather, it quickly fills and begins to sink. Yet Claire feels only relief. The bag was just an albatross, something the CIA could use to identify her. Quickly, she rips off her thin gold necklace and bracelets and flings them across the water, too. They're chains, after all. She has to be free of them! No ID! She craves weightlessness. Perhaps if she relieves herself of enough belongings, she will finally be able to alleviate this terrible pressure in her head.

With difficulty, she bends over in the rushing water and undoes one of her shoes, then the other. At one point she loses her balance and falls face forward into the river. Water goes up her nose, and with the current tearing at her limbs, it is hard to regain her balance, but she does, coughing and sputtering. Her hair and all her clothes are now soaked, though without her shoes, it's so much better! She can almost swim! But her clothes are waterlogged, weighing her down. *Take them off,* the river whispers. *Liberate yourself. Come to me.* She can't get them off quickly enough. She wriggles out of her shirt and lets the river carry it off, and for a moment she feels a wash of joy, but then she is suddenly aware of her sopping wet bra binding her ribs, and so she yanks that off too. As soon as she dispenses with that—watching the Lycra twist and unfurl dervishly in the water as it's carried away downstream—she realizes that it's her canvas pants that are really holding her hostage. They're an encasement, an iron cast. *Get rid of them,* the river commands. *And I will wrap you in my protection.*

And so Claire performs a sort of trancelike strip-tease until she is naked in the center of the river, with the water rising up to her armpits, churning furiously around her, cleansing her, rebirthing her, until for one shining moment she really does believe that she is at one with the river, that the river is her mother's arms, that she is cradled in a liquid, perfect love. And she both feels herself unleashed and electrically alive inside her own glistening skin, and sees herself too, from above, as if she is hovering in the air over the river looking down at her gleaming white body, an axis in the center of a swirling of water that radiates out from her in shards of dazzling light, like a galaxy of mirrors.

But you can't stand naked and ecstatic in a river for long. As the first vestiges of hypothermia began to numb and needle her skin, Claire's anxiety begins to return. What if the CIA has radar? The FBI and the Mossad could be hiding in the foliage lining the shore, targeting her in the crosshairs of their assault weapons. She can hear their voices again, intermittently fading in and out as if filtered through the static of a shortwave radio. *We've got you now. We know the coordinates.* They're back! The sun slides behind a cloud, casting the river into shadow, turning the surface of the water slate-colored and impenetrable. Her teeth are chattering so hard she accidently bites her lower lip. Viscous, salty liquid begins filling her mouth. The rocks on the riverbed scrape the soles of her feet and batter her toes. She is in terrible danger. She realizes she has done nothing at all to escape. She has got to get out of here immediately!

Yet her muscles have atrophied from the cold, and she's losing the feeling in her feet. Moving through the water now is like slogging through quicksand. She struggles, windmilling her arms through the current. It's exhausting, and the river is tugging her steadily downstream. As it accumulates speed, she finds herself fighting to remain standing and in control. Her shoulders feel as if they'll be yanked from their sockets. It would be so easy, she thinks suddenly, just to let go. Surrender. *I feel like I have been carrying so much for so long. Why. Not. Just. Let. Go?*

And the river whispers to her sinuously: *Yes. That's right. Come to me, and I will carry you.*

She spreads her arms wide and leans back, lifting her legs off the riverbed with a flutter, and the water seems to rise up to meet her, buoyantly, and then it whisks her off, pinwheeling her in the current, churning, washing over her, flooding her ears and her nose, faster and faster, more and more relentlessly, until she can't breathe and she can't lift up her head, and for a terrifying moment she thinks, *This is it. I'm going to drown.* But then she hears a hideous crunching and the sound of wood splintering, and a burning slap hits her violently across the side of her face and all the way down along the left side of her torso, and she stops. It is a tree felled by a storm, extending halfway across the river. She has slammed right into it; its branches have caught her like a giant outstretched hand. As she grips it, and slowly struggles to stand up, she suddenly sees two figures watching her from the riverbank. But they are not CIA agents or Mossad sharpshooters at all. They are two small, astonished Chinese children in ragged pants and straw hats, clutching a dented pail.

This time the collect call goes through to my parents immediately. In the privacy of the bathroom, I explain to them exactly what has happened. Sandy sits beside me on the edge of the tub listening.

If the phone is tapped, so be it. I find myself speaking with reckless abandon. I'm simply too exhausted to keep my words in check anymore. This must be how totalitarian governments wear people down;

the citizens acquiesce simply because they run out of steam to resist.

My mother jots down the number of our hotel. Ten minutes later, the Van Houtens call from Hilton Head. Claire's father is on one extension, her stepmom on the other. Prior to our departure, I met them only twice. Their disembodied voices sound strange to me; they don't correlate with how I remember them. Mrs. Van Houten's voice is girlish and tentative; Claire's father's is trembling with emotion. Over and over they tell me how grateful they are. I have saved their daughter's life. Nobody hurt her, did they? And am I okay? Of course they'll cover any expenses I incur whatsoever. "Don't you worry about the money," Mr. Van Houten says. "Just bring my little girl home. Your mother says you're with a Canadian nurse. Do you have an exit strategy?"

I tell them that I've arranged for Sandy to accompany us to Hong Kong on a hydrofoil leaving the next morning. From there, I suppose, we'll check into a fancy hotel until I can book a direct flight for Claire and me back to New York.

"Well, what about this nurse?" Mr. Van Houten says. "Can't she come with you?"

"Oh, I don't think she can come with us all the way to New York City." I tug at Sandy's arm and point at the phone incredulously. "She didn't even plan to come this far. She left her boyfriend and all her stuff back in Guilin."

"Tell her I'll pay her whatever she wants. Better yet, put her on the phone."

I hand the receiver to Sandy.

"Hey there," she says cheerily, "are you Claire's dad?" I listen as she gives the Van Houtens a complete medical report and answers questions about Claire's fever, appetite, and weight. I watch her nod and say, "Uh-huh...Uh-huh. I see. Jeez Louise. Well, that's certainly generous of you. Well, I have to think about it, if you don't mind...Yes, I certainly understand..."

When she hangs up, she giggles. "Wow. He's begging me to come with you all the way back to New York. Can you imagine?"

I have to struggle to rein in my enthusiasm, my galloping, voluptuous hope. Having Sandy escort us all the way home would be a godsend; it is simply too fabulous to contemplate. "Well, you did say you needed a vacation." I try to sound nonchalant. "Have you ever seen the Statue of Liberty? Walked across the Brooklyn Bridge? If you come to New York, you know, I can show you around. Give you a real insider's tour."

She sighs. "Yeah. But it's what? A twenty-four-hour plane ride?"

"True. But how many times in your life will you get to be a savior *and* get an all-expenses-paid trip to New York?"

She laughs. "Lordy, I tell Kyle I'm going to the airport for a couple of hours, then next thing you know, I'm halfway around the world? Wow, it is tempting," she admits. "But I have to think about it. I mean, all I have with me is a toothbrush and three pairs of underwear."

"Of course." Suddenly I feel foolish. "Look, I'm sorry. Already, you've done more than enough. You've really saved us. I mean, if you hadn't come with me today—" My eyes start to tear up.

"Oh, shush. It's what I do," Sandy says. "If someone's in trouble, I help them. But as far as New York's concerned, let's just see how things are tomorrow morning, okay?"

A moment later, Claire wakes up, wailing like a baby. "Where is everybody?" she cries hoarsely.

"We're in the bathroom."

"I have to use it. Is it a real bathroom? Are there bugs?" She sobs. "I have to go. Please help me."

When we arrive at her bedside, she pushes me away violently. "Only Sandy!" she screams.

From across the bed Sandy shoots me a look of concession.

And that's how we decide.

十二

Chapter 12

Hong Kong

AFTER SIX WEEKS in the People's Republic of China, Hong Kong is the New Jerusalem. It is Nirvana, Mecca, and Xanadu all rolled into one. Look, we squeal, pointing out the window of our air-conditioned taxi. A Hilton Hotel! McDonald's! A doughnut shop! Everything once anathema is now thrilling. The malls, the gargantuan neon billboards, the jewelry stores, the touristy dim sum restaurants with English menus displayed on the sidewalk. The hawkers ambushing pedestrians with armloads of fake Rolexes. All those jubilant colors! Those name brands! The skyline!

"Oh, a Ponderosa steak house," Sandy sighs. "What do you say we all get a big, juicy sirloin steak and a baked potato for lunch?"

"Mm," Claire murmurs as she sits huddled between us with her Walkman still playing. "Potato."

Even Hong Kong's stultifying humidity now seems charmingly atmospheric. Ditto for the oily bay bobbing with fishing junks and tankers, its waterfront hemmed by advertisements. It's like a tropical New York City, I think, exuberant with commercialism. The air smells of crab and overripe fruit. I am amazed what a relief it is to return, to alight from the hydrofoil and hear the declarative *fwok!* of a rubber stamp hitting my passport. *Visitor permitted to remain for ninety days from date of entry as shown below.*

As soon as the cab drops us off in front of the Kowloon Holiday Inn, I hurry ahead to the reception desk.

"Please," I say breathlessly to the young Chinese clerk dressed in a silk Nehru jacket. On the counter is a gold vase full of orchids and a bowl of peppermints wrapped in cellophane. A bellhop stands by with a luggage trolley that looks like an oversize birdcage.

"Do you speak English? And if so, can you tell me, your deluxe rooms, do they have hot water and Western toilets? And is there toilet paper, or do we have to supply our own?"

The clerk smiles at me bemusedly. Leaning over the polished countertop, he grips my hands in his white-gloved palms. "Yes, we have everything. Welcome to Hong Kong, Miss. You're not in China anymore."

Indiana Jones and the Temple of Doom is playing in endless loops on the pay-per-view channel. Sandy and I park Claire in front of the TV, locate the yellow pages, and get to work. I'm coughing so much at this point, I can barely complete a sentence; I sound like a truck engine idling. It's Sandy who telephones the airlines. My job is to walk over to the marvel that is the Ponderosa Steak House.

By the time I return with three lunches, Sandy has some news. Seats are in fact available on the next flight from Hong Kong to New York via Japan. The problem is that they're $7,000 apiece. "They expect you to book in advance," she frowns. "Anything last minute and one way is a fortune."

Even though the Van Houtens have insisted that money is no object, neither of us can fathom spending so much. In 1986, $21,000 is roughly the average American's annual salary. For all I know too, it's the entire GNP of Dinghai. Plus, none of us have that high a limit on our credit cards.

"Our only other option is to wait," Sandy sighs. "The student discounters say that Korean Air has a flight to New York via Seoul that's only $2,500 one way. But it's not available till Saturday."

It is currently Wednesday. Sandy and I look at each other.

"How much Valium do we have left?" I ask.

Claire is now mostly restive. Every so often, a look of agitation darts across her face. But she begins going to the bathroom unassisted and eating — voraciously, in fact. She eats her steak with her hands, dunks chunks of baked potato directly into the sour cream, and licks her fingers before polishing off three white dinner rolls, a small Caesar side salad, and a large, gelatinous slice of apple pie. At the end of the meal, she sits back on the bed and says contentedly to no one in particular, "Thanks. That was good."

Then she dozes off, the bluish glare from the television flickering over her profile.

While I watch over Claire, Sandy heads over to the student discount travel agency. An hour later, she has three tickets in hand, the itinerary painstakingly written out on each one in shaky block letters:

SATURDAY, NOV. 7
dep. HK 7:10 a.m., arr. Seoul 11:25 a.m.
dep. Seoul 12:45 p.m., arr. JFK 12:55 a.m. Nov. 8

There it is. Seats 14A, B, and C in the no smoking section. We are finally going home.

We sprawl across the two queen-size beds in a torpor. Even though it is daytime, we keep the curtains drawn like a convalescence ward. We watch television for hours, thumb listlessly through the tourist magazines on the nightstand, and when we're really feeling energetic, play card games of cribbage. Whenever Claire dozes off, Sandy urges me to go out.

"Explore Hong Kong, lady. Have some fun. You've earned it."

But the truth is, I have no interest in sightseeing. My lungs ache terribly. Every time I inhale, it feels like a truss tightening. For a few minutes one afternoon, I do wander down Nathan Road in a daze. I stare at the store windows crammed with skeins of pink and bauxite-colored pearls. I glance at the roast ducks and racks of spareribs hanging like mobiles in the windows of the restaurants. But after a few minutes, I head back to the hotel coughing.

Sandy doesn't feel much like playing tourist, either. Although she insists she's saving her energy for New York, she's clearly far happier just to sit inside the air-conditioned splendor of the Holiday Inn, ordering French fries and club sandwiches slathered in mayonnaise from room service and watching television, which she hasn't seen in almost a year. Outside it is the first week of November, but all three of us are oblivious to the world. We all seem to be in a state of shock.

While Claire naps, Sandy and I engage in the classically female ritual of pouring our hearts out to one another over bags of M&M's from the vending machine.

Kyle, I learn quickly, is not Sandy's boyfriend, but simply a staffer at the hospital where she worked back in Calgary.

"He worked the night shift," she laughs. "I barely knew him. But one day in Shanghai I sent a postcard back to my unit at the hospital, saying, 'Hey, everyone, China is neat. Wish you were here.' That sort of thing. The next thing I know, I get this letter from Kyle saying he's coming to visit.

"And by the time I get it, of course, it's like the day before he's supposed to arrive. He's never been outside of Canada before. When he gets off the train in Shanghai, the guy doesn't even know how to fold a map. So right away I read him the riot act. I tell him that we're no longer in the hospital, so I am off duty. If we're going to travel together, he's got to learn how to stand on his own two feet.

"So every day when I go to teach, I kick him out of my flat. 'Kyle, you're not coming back here until you learn five words in Mandarin,' or 'Today, you're going by yourself to book us train tickets to Suzhou.' And that's how it's been now for almost two months. Leaving him alone in Guilin will be the best thing that's ever happened to him. He's a sweet guy, but Lordy, does he ever need to grow a backbone. And boy, do I need a break from Asia."

Yet her journey, I discover, is not without its romantic underpinnings. Hovering over her is the specter of a man. She pulls out a snapshot. Xavier.

He is a dashing Mexican doctor with cheekbones like scalpels. In 1984, Xavier did a year's residency in Calgary. During that time, he wooed Sandy away from a pharmacist she'd been dating. The week before he left, he proposed. "Come with me to Mexico," he said, holding out his hand like a quivering flower. "We'll open a clinic on the beach and make babies and grow old together in the sun."

Love-struck, Sandy spent the next six months hammering out their wedding plans. "I had the white dress. I had the white sandals encrusted with crystals," she says. "I was ready."

Three days before she was supposed to leave, Xavier broke it off. "No explanation, nothing," Sandy says. "I cried for a month."

And then just as she was moving on, a year to the date from when she was supposed to have gotten married, Xavier reappeared on her doorstep.

"He told me, 'My love, I have made a terrible mistake. I've been a fool to let you go.' Then he got down on one knee and proposed to me all over again."

Sandy crumples up the empty M&M bag and lobs it triumphantly into the garbage can. "Believe you me, it was like something out of a movie. I'd been dreaming of a scene like that from the moment he'd called off our wedding.

"But once Xavier was actually right there in front of me, a really funny thing happened." She raises an eyebrow. "Instead of feeling angry or relieved, I just felt this strange wave of calm. For the first time in my life, I felt like my destiny was my own.

"I realized that before I pledged my life to anyone, I needed to live some of it myself first. I'd always wanted to do something wild and daring. I suddenly wasn't sure if I'd actually wanted to marry Xavier because I loved him, or because I just loved the idea of being whisked off to Mexico.

"And so, when I saw an ad in a newspaper for English teachers in China, I knew I had to go. I sent in my application, bought myself a backpack, and told Xavier *Hasta luego.* See you in a year."

"Wow." I sit back against the bed and look at her. I am enormously impressed. I have always been smitten with the idea of women walking away from a man on a bended knee, forsaking marriage for adventure. Yet I have never met anyone who has actually done this.

"So?" I can't help asking, "Do you know if you want to marry him yet?"

"The problem is, there's just so much more to see." Sandy stretches dreamily. "Thailand. India. Nepal. I feel like I'm only just getting started." She tilts her head. "What do you say we go to Bali first once we get back? Christmas on Kuta Beach?"

I stare at her blankly. For a moment I have no idea what she's talking about. Then it dawns on me: Sandy is still under the impression that I'll be returning to Asia with her once we deposit Claire back home. I never did get around to telling her at the Osmanthus that I wouldn't be continuing on with her and Kyle. Now she assumes it's a done deal.

Looking at her, I'm loath to tell her that I'm secretly ticking off the hours until we land at JFK, that I can't imagine ever wanting to come back here again. That I am perhaps far more like Claire at this moment than she knows: sick, exhausted, freaked out—a liability who just wants to be helped home.

So instead I simply nod and say, "Bali? Sure. Great. Cool." Then I look away, feeling fraudulent and craven.

When Claire is awake, she continues to monopolize Sandy, whispering and fawning, "Oh, Sandy. I don't know what I'd have done without you." Whenever I speak, however, she looks at me as if I'm an irritant she can barely tolerate. I begin to feel as though I'm back in elementary school, being frozen out of the popular clique by girls in the schoolyard.

After two days, my nerves are frayed.

"Claire isn't sick," I whisper venomously to Sandy in the bathroom. "She's just being a bitch, is all."

Sandy sighs. "Well, I think it's more complicated than that. But you are right. She's treating you horribly."

"I don't fucking get it," I say miserably—though in my heart of hearts, I actually do. My guilt, in fact, is starting to feel like a vise, crushing my stomach and thorax, squeezing my shoulders. I sit on the faux marble toilet seat and stare at the floor tiles. "It's because it's all my fault," I say softly.

"Excuse me?"

"When Claire began having her fantasies about Adom and the CIA, I just thought she was horny and homesick. When she started making all these cryptic comments and going off by herself in Beijing, I just thought she was being melodramatic. And when she threw that fit in Yangshuo, I just thought she was being a spoiled brat. That she was pissed because I was hooking up with Eckehardt. So I ignored her."

I start to cry. "I wasn't there when she needed me. If I had been, none of this would've happened. But I just had to fool around with some guy, didn't I? I just had to let her get on that bus. I could've lain down in front of it to keep it from driving off. But did I do that? No."

Sandy looks at me, aghast.

"I know." I yank the toilet paper from its roll and blow my nose in it. "And the thing is, my friends are usually the most important thing to me. But I was such a fucking idiot. I was lonely. I had my head up my ass. I didn't even see—"

"Stop it," Sandy hisses. Standing up, she reaches over, grabs the wadded toilet paper out of my hand, and hurls it into the trash can underneath the sink. "Since when are you so special?"

"Huh?"

"Who do you think you are, lady, the second coming of Jesus? 'Oh,'" she says mockingly, "'If only I had been there.' I'm sorry, but you need to get a clue, honey. Your friend is mentally ill. Nothing you did or didn't do made her go crazy. You think that if you just hadn't kissed some guy, Claire would be perfectly fine? You think if you'd somehow been magically able to pull her off that bus, she wouldn't be hearing voices? Please. That's like saying, 'If I'd been a better friend, she wouldn't have gotten cancer.' Jeez Louise. You really think you have that much power?"

"But, Sandy, *she* thinks it's my fault, too." I blink tearfully up at the ceiling. "She keeps looking at me like I've violated her. Why does she hate me so much?"

Sandy's face softens. She kneels down before me and brushes a strand of hair out of my face. "Because," she says gently, "you saved her life. She's embarrassed. Trust me. I've worked in a hospital. Nothing can make people feel more resentful and humiliated than needing to be rescued."

———

Finally, after three days in our own little biosphere of the Kowloon Holiday Inn, it is time to depart. Early Saturday morning, we arrive at Kai Tak Airport in excellent spirits. Our backpacks feel as light as balloons. It is barely daybreak. Light is beginning to seep up from the horizon and silhouette the mountains. The airport is more deserted than when Claire and I arrived there seven weeks ago. In the ghostly terminal, it doesn't seem possible that we are actually going home.

And then we discover we're not.

"I'm sorry," says the airline representative at the check-in, handing us back our tickets. "But these were for yesterday."

"What?" Sandy and I say in unison.

The clerk leans over and points with his ballpoint pen to the line on our tickets where the travel agent has written in Saturday, November 7.

"While it is Saturday," he concedes, "today is November 8. The seventh was yesterday, Friday. Whoever filled these out made a mistake. They booked you on the flight that left yesterday. You're no longer on the manifest."

At that moment, I experience what feels like a coronary fibrillation. "Well, isn't there any room left on the flight leaving today?"

The clerk scans the manifest and frowns. "There's still space on the flight as far as Seoul. But after that, the connection to New York is completely booked. In fact, that flight appears to be sold out for the rest of the week."

I look desperately at Sandy, who looks desperately at Claire, who slowly removes her headphones and looks desperately at both of us. We all stand there for a moment in a triangle of horrified disbelief. "Oh, my

God," I say. Then simultaneously all three of us burst into tears.

"Please, you've got to help us," Sandy pleads desperately across the counter. "We have got to get home. It's a matter of life or death."

———————

Airline representatives, it seems, will sometimes go to extraordinary lengths to keep customers from making a scene at their check-in counter.

No sooner do all three of us start weeping, begging, and arguing than a manager rushes over. Then another. In a few minutes, the counter is almost a reenactment of the lobby at the Osmanthus Hotel the day that Claire disappeared, except now the people who keep materializing in uniforms are Korean Air representatives. They take turns staring at our tickets and frowning, then barking things into walkie-talkies and making telephone calls and throwing up their hands in frustration. It is not our fault, Sandy and I keep insisting, thumping the desk. The tickets say *Saturday* first, so why would we think to show up on Friday? We purchased these in good faith. Korean Air should honor that.

Proposals are put forth, none of them acceptable. One of them is that we simply re-book the flight for the following week. "Spend a few days here in Hong Kong and go sightseeing," one of the representatives suggests chirpily. "Why, you can even get a tourist visa and spend a few days in the People's Republic of China if you want."

Another informs us that she can refund our money and get us on a United flight leaving Monday. "It's business class," she says. "One way will run you ten thousand dollars a ticket."

Finally the check-in clerk comes up with a solution. We can in fact leave for New York City today, provided we're not terribly picky about arriving anytime soon.

"I can get you on a flight to Seoul immediately," he says. "There's a stop in Taipei, but you don't have to deplane." From Seoul, however, we'll have to reclaim our luggage and check in all over again at a different terminal, then endure a nine-hour layover in South Korea for a flight to Hawaii. Once we land in Honolulu, he might be able to get us on a flight to Los Angeles on stand-by, in which case, we'll have only a four-hour layover on Oahu. But there are no guarantees, so we might spend a night in Hawaii.

Provided we do make the flight to L.A., we'll have a four-hour layover for the last leg of the trip to New York. But we'll be arriving at LaGuardia, not JFK, he says.

I tell him that at this point, I don't really think it matters.

"Oh, but one other thing," he adds. "That flight to New York? It isn't direct, either. There's a forty-

minute stopover in Philadelphia where you may have
to switch planes."

———————

Is there any reason to fill you in on every interminable detail of this journey? All anyone really needs
to know is this: By the time the Korean Air representatives finish rerouting us and handing us the revised
paperwork, we nearly miss our flight.

Since we have no time for Claire and I to contact
our parents before departing, I have the perverse thrill
of calling them collect at two o'clock in the morning
from a pay phone in South Korea.

Nine hours later, just before boarding the flight
to Hawaii, an announcement comes over the loudspeaker: *Passenger Miss Claire Van Houten, please
report immediately to security.*

Of course as soon as Claire hears her name boom-
ing over the PA system, she seizes up in a panic. Her
paranoia reignites. And by this point, of course, the
last Valium is gone.

Armed with her passport, I go in her place.

It turns out that the U.S. Army canteen that her
stepbrother Dominic gave her has set off the metal
detectors in the baggage handling area and made the
South Koreans extremely nervous. After disembow-
eling her entire backpack for inspection, the security
officers finally release both it and me, though they
insist on confiscating the canteen.

By the time we land in Honolulu, we have already been traveling twenty hours, and the gate attendant there says to us, "Oh, we've heard so much about you." Word, it seems, has traveled. The three of us are starting to be treated like marathon runners following a grueling, nearly insurmountable course through the sky. Every airport we land at, Korean Air personnel come out to greet us, cheer us on, urge us forward.

"Let's see if there's something else we can do to help you girls out," says the clerk in Honolulu, typing our names into her computer. By the time we board the plane to L.A. four hours later, we're so groggy and disoriented, we don't understand right away what has happened. Why are we being segregated from the rest of the passengers? How did our seats get so big and puffy? Since when do they serve crab cakes for lunch? It's not until the flight attendant hands us a wine list that we realize we've been upgraded to business class.

The nearer we get to Mainland U.S.A., the more animated and lucid Claire becomes. She begins flinging her blond hair over her shoulders again, laughing in her old, melodic voice, and even deigns to address me directly. "Hey, Zsa Zsa," she calls airily from her seat across the aisle, "mind lending me your Chapstick?"

By the time we've landed in L.A. and have taken our meal vouchers to the glass sky restaurant, she is actively flirting with the waiters, quoting Schopenhauer, and demonstrating to Sandy her facility with different accents.

"New York's is a cinch," she says, swirling a French fry around in an enormous dollop of ketchup. "I want a piece of *chawklit.*"

She giggles, and I feel like punching her. I'm growing increasingly worried that by the time we finally arrive at LaGuardia, Claire will be fully restored. She'll stride blithely off the plane, air-kissing everyone and behaving like a returning diva while I'll stand there looking like some lunatic who ran around Chicken Little–style, claiming the sky was falling when it so obviously wasn't. *Honestly,* I imagine Claire saying, *I really have no idea what all this fuss was about. Frankly, I think Susie cooked up a little melodrama just because she wanted to come home.*

As I watch Claire unwrap a drinking straw and jab it into a strawberry milk shake, I have to resist pulling her into the bathroom and slapping her around. *Listen,* I want to growl, *after everything everyone's gone through for you, you'd better crawl off that plane in New York foaming at the mouth.*

But by the time we finally arrive at LaGuardia Airport at 6:45 a.m. Monday morning, we have been traveling for almost forty straight hours. All three of us are shattered and incoherent, none more so than Claire.

So many times in Asia, I'd imagined our triumphant return. It would be late summer of 1987, and since my brother would be home from college, he'd smartly rally my friends to surprise me at the airport. I'd disembark to see a big hand-lettered "Welcome Home" banner and loved ones throwing fistfuls of confetti and uncorking bottles of champagne.

If I was feeling particularly grandiose, I liked to imagine that paparazzi would be waiting. On the relentless train rides through China, I kept myself entertained by inventing interviews between Barbara Walters and me. "Well, Barbara," I'd say diffidently, "sure, China was a challenge. But really, it was nothing that a seasoned traveler couldn't handle."

Instead, exactly seven weeks to the day of our departure, I am staggering off a plane back in New York coughing violently and spitting up fluid, while Claire shuffles behind me looking stunned and demented in my now filthy, ill-fitting purple tank dress and a pair of plastic flip-flops. She is helped along by Sandy, a Canadian nurse with two-toned eyes whom nobody else knows and who, in her pilling white sweatshirt and plaid Bermuda shorts, looks almost as disheveled as we do.

In 1986, families are still permitted to meet their loved ones right at the gate, and Claire's stepbrothers are out in force: Dominic, Edward, and Alexander are waiting with their shirtsleeves rolled up like a team of emergency rescue workers. Parker is also there, Claire's milquetoast boyfriend whom all of us seem to have forgotten. He hovers right by the gate in his Bass Weejuns holding a paper cone of yellow roses. As soon as he spies Claire, he races past the cordons and embraces her desperately. "You're home, it's all going to be okay," he murmurs into her hair. She stands there woodenly, letting herself be hugged. The scratches on her face, I can see now, are starkly visible in the bleached light of the arrivals gate. She looks papery and frail.

A moment later, our parents are upon us, weeping and hugging. As I embrace my father, then my mother, I hear everyone in the Van Houten clan taking turns introducing themselves to Sandy and thanking her profusely. "Oh, it's Susie who's the real hero," she insists generously. "No, it's Sandy," I say.

Everybody treats Claire very gingerly. As she stands bewildered among them, her father barrels over, crying, "You saved my little girl," and hugging me so tightly my ribs almost crack. I am crying now, Sandy is crying, even my father is crying. The only one who isn't crying is Claire. She glances around in a daze, as if she is not quite sure where she is.

Somehow Dominic and Alexander appear with our backpacks, thoughtfully collected from the baggage claim. Claire's father and mascara-streaked stepmother begin shaking our hands strenuously. "Let's all talk later, shall we? Once the girls have settled in?" And then, putting their arms around Claire, they whisk her away toward a limousine waiting just beyond the arrival doors.

Her stepbrothers and Parker hurry after her, crowding around her protectively like a phalanx of bodyguards. Watching them, I am suddenly reminded of the Chinese military police clustered around her just days before in the hallway of the Osmanthus Hotel. As the Van Houtens recede, I see in their midst a glimmer of Claire's blond hair. But then her stepbrothers close rank around her, and whatever remains visible of her is eclipsed, and all I am left with is a wall of their broad masculine backs and the bulk of her father's tweed overcoat, moving toward the exit. The glass doors slide open, a chauffeur comes around to the back of the limousine, a trunk slams, and in a flash they are gone.

Less then fourteen minutes after our arrival, Sandy and I find ourselves standing alone with my parents by the empty luggage carousel at LaGuardia. Beyond the doors, the November sun is rising brilliantly. An entire city is stirring and coming to life like a sleeping dragon bathed in gold, oblivious to all that has just happened to us.

My bedroom back in Manhattan is exactly the same. A Rolling Stones poster, stacks of old *Glamour* magazines, a twin bed with flowery sheets, dust gathering on my record albums. The only proof that I've been away is a single postcard from Shanghai tucked into the frame of the mirror over my dresser. I'd sent it to my parents the day after we'd arrived. Reading it now is eerie. *China is beautiful. Streets all lit up. Big celebrations. Food delicious. Already made two friends—Jonnie and Gunter. Claire great company. Next stop Beijing? Tibet? Having a blast.*

My brother's abandoned bedroom has been set up for Sandy, his collection of rubber gorilla masks, art supplies, and piles of *Mad* magazine tucked discreetly into his closet.

Before either of us shower or unpack, however, my father insists that Sandy and I make up a list of all our expenses.

"Compile everything while it's still fresh in your mind," he says. "I want to take a bill over to the Van Houtens as quickly as possible."

For the moment, the Van Houtens are staying in a corporate apartment on Sutton Place. It's unclear how long they'll remain there.

Although neither of my parents says it outright, they are concerned. They do not understand why the Van Houtens did not fly to Asia themselves to rescue their daughter. Certainly they have the resources. Couldn't they at least have met us in Hong Kong? Their decision to leave it to me and a strange nurse to get Claire back home smacks of expediency. Now that Sandy and I have effectively cleaned up the Van Houtens' mess for them, my parents fear that they will simply disappear and stick us with the bill.

Neither Sandy nor I imagine this will happen. And yet I know my parents have a point. When I was waitressing, the most well-to-do customers were inevitably the ones who'd stiff me on the tip. No one ever got rich, it seemed, being generous with the help.

Sandy and I empty our backpacks and pockets. Receipts are everywhere.

My round-the-world airplane ticket is now invalid since I've backtracked; I suppose I can negotiate a refund with the airline. "No," my father instructs. "Have the Van Houtens reimburse you for the remainder, then give them the ticket to deal with. It's not your fault you had to come home. Also, they should pay for your airfare back to Asia as well."

When I look startled, he says, "I want you to have that option. You worked hard for that money. It's not fair to expect you to shell it out again."

I worry that my father is being a hardnose, that it's wrong and unseemly to get busy with money at a time like this. Claire is still my friend, and I feel guilty asking the Van Houtens to pay me back when they so clearly have more pressing problems to deal with at the moment.

But Sandy shakes her head, "Nuh-uh, lady. Your dad here is right. People always think that taking care of others should be its own reward, that being a hero shouldn't come with a price tag. But work in a cardiac care unit for a couple weeks, then tell me if you still think that. The Van Houtens made sure their daughter was taken care of. Your dad is just making sure his is too."

By the time Sandy and I finish compiling our expenses, including the cost of three flights back from Hong Kong, the Van Houtens owe us over eleven thousand dollars. Neither of us can quite believe it. "Good," my father says. "Now give me the bill and go take a shower."

By the time we finish primping and napping, he is already back from Sutton Place. Mr. Van Houten, he reports, had been just as eager to take care of business. "Tell the girls thanks again," he'd told my father. "We'll talk more once they've rested." Without blinking, he then cut my dad a banker's check for almost twelve thousand dollars. My father insisted on including a fee for Sandy's nursing services, too. Mr. Van Houten had been happy to pay it.

By noon, Mr. Van Houten's check has already cleared. My father arrives home with a thick envelope. He tosses it on the dining table, and a landslide of hundred-dollar bills spills out. The jade-green money is everywhere, fluttering to the floor like leaves.

———

What worries *me* however, is the inevitable phone call. All day long I turn it over in my mind, formulating how exactly to phrase things.

None of our parents, you see, know the details yet.

All they learned from my distressed phone calls from China was that Claire had become mentally ill, experienced a breakdown, and become a danger to herself. But beyond that, they do not know the specifics. The only question the Van Houtens have ever asked about Claire's mental state during the crisis is: "Is she rational?"

Now they are going to require a list of her symptoms in detail: her increasingly paranoid delusions, the fact that she was hearing voices, the fact that she disrobed publicly and went into a river and nearly killed herself, albeit inadvertently. And I am the one who is going to have to give it to them.

Finally, around four p.m., the telephone rings. Mr. Van Houten is on one line, Claire's stepmother on another, and their family doctor in New Canaan, Connecticut, connected via conference call.

"We are truly sorry to have to bother you," Mr. Van Houten begins, his voice shaking. "But as you can imagine, we have so many questions."

Their doctor starts by asking me about Claire's physical state: her diet, what medications she'd been taking, if she'd ever run a fever. For about half an hour, I answer these as carefully as I can. We all know what he is really leading up to, and as he works his way through his list, the line grows tense and I feel my heart pounding harder and harder as I try to devise the least painful way to explain things.

Finally the doctor takes a deep breath. "Okay," he says, "I need to know, too. Was she at all sexually active during the trip?"

No, I tell him. Not at all. "But she was having some romantic fantasies that—"

Before I can finish, I can hear all three parties on the other end of the phone exhale.

"Okay then," the doctor says with relief. "Thank you so much for all your time. I think that's all we need to know, don't you, Drummond?"

"Yes, I think so," says Claire's father. "Thank you so much again, Susan."

With that, they hang up.

————

Later that evening, however, there is one more phone call. It is from Parker. He is at a pay phone on First Avenue, several blocks from the Van Houtens' corporate apartment.

"No one wants to hear the truth," he says soberly. "I realize it can't be pretty. But if anyone's ever going to really help her, someone needs to know."

Forty-five minutes later, he is at my parents' doorstep. He is dressed in the same down vest and Bass Weejuns he was wearing that morning at the airport. His hair is still immaculately glued across his forehead like a hairpiece, though he is no longer wearing a webbed belt with little whales on it. He is smaller than I remember him being at school. He is barely

Claire's height and compactly built, a sort of miniature man with sad, watery green eyes. He holds out a small tin of expensive Danish butter cookies as a house gift for my mother. "I am so, so sorry to disturb you," he says.

My mother ushers him over to our dining room, sets down a bottle of bubbly water, then leaves. It is just Parker, Sandy, and me now. He takes a sip from his glass and looks at me bleakly.

"Okay," he says, bracing himself. "Start from the beginning."

And so, meticulously, I begin. I tell him everything in all its terrible unfurling: Claire's cryptic comments; her mounting belief that the CIA, the FBI, and the Mossad were keeping tabs on us; her secret forays to do business in Beijing; how she became convinced that the PLO had gotten involved. I tell him about her fear of other tourists, her bizarre attempt to give away her broken camera, her lying down like a corpse in the middle of the rice paddy. And then I get to Yangshuo with Lisa, the tantrums, the nocturnal phone calls, and then to the final, horrible, prolonged denouement. I do not embellish, nor do I flinch. I present to him not only Claire but myself as well, as accurately and dispassionately as I can, the two of us in all our nakedness, fallibility, and confusion — with the police, with each other. Per Parker's instructions, I do not spare him any of the details.

That is, except for one. When I mention Adom, I

present him only as someone Claire developed a crush on from afar, then cultivated into a romance entirely in her own head. For all I know, this might have actually been what happened after all. And if it wasn't, well. When I look at Parker's sad green eyes—unflinching in their loyal, brave love—it seems to me there's been enough heartache already.

————

In the days that follow, I take Sandy on a whirlwind tour of New York City—the Statue of Liberty, the World Trade Center, the Brooklyn Bridge—"to see what all the fuss is about." To my great satisfaction, she is impressed. We also take me to a pulmonary specialist, who immediately orders a series of blood tests and X-rays, then informs me that I have severe bronchitis and a bacterial infection similar to mononucleosis.

"How long have you had this?" he asks. When I tell him about six weeks—that I contracted it in Shanghai—he asks me what the hospitals are like in China.

"Terrible," I say. "Why?"

"Because if you hadn't come back here when you did, you would've ended up in one."

He puts me on a high-level dose of antibiotics for a month and orders me to come back in seventy-two hours. When Sandy asks if I can possibly fly back to

Asia next week, the doctor says, "Only if she wants to do it in an oxygen tent."

Sandy looks crestfallen. But I secretly feel like I've been given a "Get Out of Jail Free" card. I will have at least a month now to wriggle out of returning to Asia altogether.

At the Liberty Travel Agency, Sandy alone books a return flight to Hong Kong for the end of that week. Then I take her to the galleries in SoHo. My favorite coffeehouses in Greenwich Village. The Metropolitan Museum of Art.

Yet here's what we do not do: see the Van Houtens. Although I'd expected we'd speak to them regularly — and perhaps visit Claire — oddly, they do not call us, and anytime I telephone the corporate apartment of Sutton Place, no one answers.

———

A week later, my parents drive Sandy to the international terminal at JFK Airport, where I myself had departed back in September.

"So listen, lady," Sandy says at the final call for boarding. She adjusts her small purple backpack with a shrug, then plants one of her hands firmly on each of my shoulders like a sergeant conferring an order on a corporal. "You'll meet me in Hong Kong in three weeks. I'll call you as soon as I get settled back there, and we'll confirm exactly where and when. You got that? In the meantime, just book yourself a ticket and don't worry. Kyle and I will be waiting for you."

I nod vigorously. "Thanks," I say. "You're amazing." As she turns and heads down the gangway toward the plane, I wave insanely, brimming with admiration for her. I shout, "Travel safely. See you soon!" And yet I know that I am lying. I will never see her again. I will never head back to Asia. I just do not have it in me to get on another damn plane and begin traveling with a backpack all over again. The departure lounge is the proverbial fork in the road; Sandy has taken one direction, I the other. I tell myself I'm really okay with this.

———

When I was little, I used to have indulgent little daydreams in which I was declared dead purely by accident. Before I could set the record straight, however, my funeral would be held, and I'd get the thrill of witnessing it from behind a potted plant in the chapel. After listening to all the glowing eulogies given about me, I'd nonchalantly reappear to revel in my friends' and family's adoration, their euphoric disbelief.

After I see Sandy off to Asia, this is not too dissimilar from what happens in New York. My friends in Manhattan who said goodbye to me just two months earlier have essentially given me up for dead (which is what New Yorkers tend do if somebody ventures beyond the Hudson). Now suddenly they find me

waiting in their lobbies, sitting at tables at the restaurants where they're bartending, leaving surprise
messages for them on their answering machines. My
friend Maggie works at Tiffany's. When I appear like
a ghost in the china department and say "Yo, babes"
she nearly drops a $420 gravy boat. Every time some-
one squeals and throws their arms around me, I experience a thrill of love.

I even manage to hook up with Jake again. "Whoa,
look at you," he says, gallantly flinging open the door
of his parents' East Side apartment. "The adventurer
has returned. What happened? Tell me everything."
Sitting across from him on the sofa, however, I find
myself struggling to reconcile the flesh-and-blood
guy before me in a rumpled pin-striped shirt with
the lover I fantasized about during my loneliest hours
in Beijing, who accompanied me through the grimy,
chaotic *hutongs,* then decomposed in my arms as I
hallucinated with fever in Guilin. When he hands
me a glass of wine and marvels, "I can't believe you're
back already," he has no idea of the surreality he's participated in over the past seven weeks.

Oh, but it's great to be home! To be waking up in
the same bed that I've slept in since I was eight, to
be walking down all the familiar streets, reveling in
the craziness and familiarity that is New York, New
York! Even my parents seem to be just the way they
used to be, but better. They're easy with each other,
walking to Zabar's hand in hand on Saturday after-

noons, contentedly reading the Sunday *Times* in the morning sunlight. Our family life is surprisingly cozy and tranquil.

And yet after about two weeks of reuniting with all my dearest friends, I find myself feeling slightly like a war veteran—agitated, displaced, out of sync with the culture. While my friends around me are consumed with their entry-level magazine jobs, nightclubbing, grad school applications, learning computer languages, their new roommates in their new shared walk-up apartments—while they rehash jokes from movies and episodes of *Cheers* I haven't seen and obsess about their unpublished poetry, their acting auditions, their thighs, their workouts, their student loans—I find my mind straying back to China, to Jonnie seated among his family in Dinghai and the old man in Beijing who helped us fix our bicycles, to Lisa waiting tables amidst the karsts of Guilin. I think of all the women washing clothing and vegetables in plastic buckets in the gutters. Of Tom meeting us clandestinely in the azalea bushes. I see the throngs of people clogging the overpass on Nanjing Road, their Mao uniforms inky blue, the gray street below slick with rain. The phosphorescent rice paddies. The little girl with pigtails stepping forward shyly to welcome us before a crowd of beaming onlookers in Hangpu Park. I see the tangles of bicycles. The dumplings sizzling in hot sesame oil in a filthy wok. The profound kindness in the eyes of the people, again and again and again.

Whenever I think of these things, I feel an exquisite pang of longing.

I find myself starting to feel oddly depressed; it's almost like I know too much simply to be in the moment anymore, to enjoy what I used to relish so uncritically. I'm aware that there is a bigger, far more complicated world out there than I'd ever realized, and just like the students at Beijing University, I've glimpsed it only fleetingly, peripherally. I've sensed the vast expanse of my own ignorance now. I feel antsy and constricted and a deep, almost sexual yearning for velocity, for some sort of raw, transcendent experience that I cannot even begin to articulate.

I am terrified to go back to China, to reactivate all that anxiety. Being unleashed into an incomprehensible culture felt paradoxically like climbing a mountain and plunging over a precipice. If I learned one thing by going abroad, it is that I am not by nature an adventurer. For all my bravado, I am hesitant, nervous, neurotic. I am a parochial New Yorker.

And yet.

Three weeks later, to my great shock and surprise, my parents see me off at JFK again with the same backpack, the same eight-item wardrobe, the same Lonely Planet guidebook, and this time a small deck of Aquarian Tarot cards instead of heavy Linda Goodman. In my hand is a one-way ticket back to Hong Kong, courtesy of the Van Houtens, and Sandy is meeting me at Kai Tak Airport, just as we'd planned, although this time, we've agreed, I'll check into the Holiday Inn for a few nights until I can get acclimated. From Hong Kong, maybe we'll go to Bali. Or Thailand. We'll decide once I get there. We don't have any concrete plans. We'll just go where the world takes us, until we see all that we can see and absorb all that we can learn. I find myself craving this, even though I am still terrified. As I walk toward the gangway, waving goodbye again to my teary-eyed parents, my heart is beating violently, like a bird breaking free of its cage, and my hands are clammy and sparkling with fear. But I smile and I turn and I go.

It seems I'm that sort of girl after all.

Afterwards

I NEVER SAW Claire Van Houten again.

That morning in November in 1986 when I deposited her into the arms of her father, she ducked down into a limousine outside LaGuardia Airport and vanished from my life.

When I boarded the plane back to Hong Kong four weeks later to resume traveling, I had no idea that I would, in fact, end up circumnavigating the globe just as she and I had planned that spring night back at the IHOP. I trekked through Bali, Jakarta, Singapore, Malaysia, Thailand, and Sri Lanka, then soldiered on to Western Europe and the Middle East. All told, I ended up traveling ten months.

Since then I've acquired more stamps in my passport than I'd ever dreamed. As a journalist, I've covered assignments overseas in Poland and Austria. As a teacher, I've led students on an educational tour of Britain. As a tourist, I've been lucky enough to tromp through Red Square in a miniskirt and dance salsa on the beaches of Venezuela.

On our first wedding anniversary, my husband, the Amazing Bob, and I move to Switzerland. His international employer sends him around the world. We go on safari in Tanzania, kiss at the Taj Mahal.

In October 2005, Bob is invited to a conference in Beijing. As luck would have it, I have a writing assignment: Hong Kong Disneyland is opening. As far as irony goes, this is the jackpot. Walt Disney was a rabid anti-Communist. Now his Magic Kingdom will be singing "Be Our Guest" to the biggest Communist regime on the planet. The working title of my article is "Mickey Mao."

While we're there, Bob and I decide to retrace my steps from 1986. We're able to do this because China now has a network of domestic airlines that makes it easy to hop from Beijing to Shanghai to Guilin in a matter of days. In another sign of just how much has changed, I now think that paying $110 for a plane ticket is a bargain.

There have not yet been the epic earthquakes, floods, or 2008 Olympic Games. Widespread visuals of twenty-first-century China have not yet been broadcast around the world. Only a few stock tourist images have repeatedly appeared. So everywhere we go is a revelation, a shock.

On the highway from the airport, the air is so thick with particles, our taxi seems to be hurtling into a void. Beijing is now permanently engulfed in a blizzard of pollution, a chemical snow. Ghoulish clusters of fifty-story buildings rise out of the smog. Outlines of modern office buildings — miles upon miles of them — slowly take shape. We pass a stadium, a riot of overpasses. Boulevards converge, huge tributaries of honking cars.

At the hotel, white-gloved porters take our bags and usher us past an Armani boutique into a soaring glass atrium. A cool, cathedral hush fills the lobby. "Hello, Ms. Gilman," says a blond receptionist. "We're overbooked, so we've upgraded you to a suite."

The suite is bigger than our apartment back home. A plasma-screen TV is embedded in the wall above the marble Jacuzzi.

The Temple of Heaven is closed for renovations. Most of the *hutongs* where Claire and I ate dumplings have been bulldozed. Tour groups are led through the few remaining alleyways in bicycle rickshaws.

At the Wangfujing pedestrian mall, a bank of televisions throb with music videos of an Asian rapper named Will performing a hip-hop song, "Will Is MVP."

"I'm back, yo, you like it," he shouts, aping Eminem. "*Shay shay nee.* MVP."

A private air-conditioned taxi with a guide whisks us to the Great Wall. A cable car has now been constructed at Badaling to transport visitors directly to the top, and a miniature roller coaster careens down the side to a snack bar. As Bob and I climb the stones with thousands of other tourists, we see power lines and cell towers.

Our guide, Tina, a giddy young woman in her twenties, wears rhinestone cat-eye glasses and tangerine-colored lipstick, her hair in a dozen loony barrettes.

"I take you for traditional Chinese refreshment, yes?" she says, playing with the ring tones on her cell phone.

Before we can protest, the car pulls into a Chinese Friendship Store, where we are subjected to a twenty-minute hard sell for what looks like drinkable potpourri, silk pajamas, and decorative jade snuffboxes. It doesn't take a genius to figure out that Tina is getting a kickback.

"They should rename it," Bob says afterward as we flop down on our bed at the hotel with a bag full of cloisonné chopsticks and a canister of lichee tea. "The Great Mall of China."

"Are you spelling that M-A-L-L or M-A-U-L?" I snort.

"Both," he laughs.

———

Competing smells of urine, lacquer, and roast duck still permeate the streets. Avenues still have patchy sycamore trees and paving stones like pressed tin. The same ramshackle assortment of wheelbarrows and rusty pushcarts clutter the sidewalks. But in less than twenty years, the country has progressed a century.

I feel like an archaeologist, looking desperately for some small fragment from the past. On a corner of Chang'an Avenue, flapping in the wind above a darkened restaurant is the tattered red awning of Maxim's. But the restaurant seems to have disappeared; a gargantuan apartment building rises above it.

At the edge of Tiananmen Square, there's a new Metro station and a 7-Eleven convenience store. A young Chinese man approaches. "Excuse me. But do you speak English?"

"*Nee how.* Yes," I exclaim. Finally something familiar: a Beijing University student still eager to make contact.

The young man hands us a card. Lucky Dragon Silk Paintings, Ltd. "You like special silk paintings? Come, I show you, yes? For you, special price."

Bob and I wend our way through the crowds to the entrance of the Forbidden City. There, exactly two decades earlier, I was supposed to meet an Australian sailor named Trevor on his birthday. Now I stand there and kiss my husband instead. The enormous portrait of Mao Zedong continues to stare down at us benevolently. It alone has not changed.

———

My sweet, troubled friend with that incredible laugh. In China, I find myself homesick for her. She is one of the few people on this planet who can truly appreciate the enormity of what I am witnessing, who can share in my shock and disbelief. I try imagining her reaction to Shanghai, which is now a futuristic city straight out of science fiction, with strobe lights orbiting the tripod of the Oriental Pearl TV Tower each night. I long to take digital photos with my cell phone of the Pujiang—which still exists, refurbished as a hip, historic boutique hotel—and text, "You won't believe where I am." I want to send her postcards of the two giant pagodas, one silver and one gold, that now rise like Excalibur swords out of a newly created lake in the center of Guilin. *This entire country has undergone an extreme makeover*, I'd write. *As Nietzsche said ...*

But of course this is impossible.

To be fair, Claire is with me always. Every time I board a plane, I still feel as if I'm about to undergo a triple bypass. My own internal hardwiring for cowardice, my emotional, personal GPS still whispers to me insidiously, *Go home. You can't handle this.* But then I hear her voice like a mantra, urging me on: *I have faith in you. You can do this.*

I would not be living my life the way I am today if it wasn't for her. Claire Van Houten unleashed something in me; she set me off on a path far beyond anything I ever imagined for myself or believed I was capable of doing. In this way, back in China in 1986, she saved my life, too.

But as far as she — or Jonnie, for that matter — is concerned, I cannot offer you the happy ending I wished for, the redemption and reunion this story demands. Truth may be stranger and wilder than fiction, but it's also more frustrating in its refusal to conform to a neat little narrative. Of course I've done the requisite Googling. I've scanned our alumni directories and newsletters. I've looked up phone numbers. But to no avail. And I can't say I've pushed it either. Because I suspect that clearly, Claire would rather not be found.

For closure, I can only offer you this.

On our last day in Guilin, before heading home, Bob and I take a cruise down the Li River.

Such cruises are now a huge tourist business. They're showboats with full kitchens on board, some with lounges decorated like eighteenth-century French parlors. During the three-hour trip downriver to Yangshuo, passengers are served cocktails and multicourse Chinese lunches. So many boats make this trip each day that they parade down the river in an absurd beribboned flotilla.

The day we make the trip it is broiling. There is scarcely any breeze. The boat is packed. Nonetheless, the karsts are more magnificent than I remember. Two decades ago, such trips weren't possible, so I never got to see the full topography from the river, with all its phantasmagoric beauty. Guangxi province. It really is something to see. For three hours, Bob and I stand mesmerized on the deck, watching the landscape grow increasingly spectacular. The vanished prehistoric sea is a lush, shimmering Eden.

As the boat turns in to Yangshuo, this ends abruptly. Chinese kids wave to us from the docks, where dozens of hulking tour boats are now moored. Brand-new condominiums and modern hotels are terraced against the hills; a wall has been constructed along the embankment draped with a garish banner in English: "Chinese Famous Tourist County—Welcome to Yangshuo."

Scores of tour groups are shepherded by guides with bullhorns up the hill to cafés with rainbow-colored umbrellas and rows of plastic deck chairs. The woodsy hamlet of twenty years ago is now a city of 300,000.

By now, however, I'm used to this. I've grown up, and so has China. It's time to accept it. "Ah, well," I say to Bob, waving dismissively at the yellow construction cranes looming in front of the limestone karsts, "let's go get an ice cream."

Pushing through the crowds, I come across a few lanes similar to those back in 1986. One small section of Yangshuo, it seems, has not lost its funkiness. Tiny open storefronts still sell glass beads, used paperbacks, milk shakes, T-shirts. Backpackers still sit in sidewalk cafés writing postcards. The guesthouse trade survives; quirky little three-story inns sport hand-printed signs: "Western toilets! Hot water! Bike rentals! Bus tickets sold here!"

Squeezed in among the little bars and shops, I almost miss it. But there it is. A restaurant with a sign over it in gilded script: "Lisa's Hotel."

"Whoa. Is that possible?"

Bob shrugs. He's heard my stories before. "How many Lisas are there in Yangshuo?"

I honestly don't know. Back in 1986, it seemed that everyone Chinese was either a Lisa or a Jonnie. It could be her or one of a billion other people with that moniker. But what are the chances?

My heart bangs as I step inside. The restaurant is dark, cool, rustic. I look around for clues. There is a display case full of glittering Mao memorabilia. A white guy with dreadlocks sits eating a plate of stir-fried beef. Music plays faintly from somewhere: a tinny, syncopated tune. There are no blackboards listing banana pancakes.

The only other people are three young Westerner backpackers at a table with a Lonely Planet China guidebook. The two young women and a man cannot be much older than twenty. The girls wear bracelets from Thailand and leather thong anklets. One is dressed in an Indian skirt. The guy is wearing Tevas and burlap drawstring shorts. They look almost identical to backpackers twenty years ago.

"So what do *you* think?" one of the women says

to the guy, fidgeting with a digital camera. "Bali or Tibet?" Her English is harshly accented.

The guy shrugs. "I dunno. When exactly is our flight home to Tel Aviv?"

Israelis. I mull this over for a moment. It seems chillingly significant. Had I made this up, it would've seemed incredible. But here they really are.

"Excuse me," I ask, "Do any of you know if there's actually a proprietor here named Lisa?"

A voice behind me says crisply, "Yes? Can I help you?"

I turn around to find an unfamiliar middle-aged Chinese woman in a filmy black T-shirt standing in the doorway.

"I'm looking for Lisa," I say.

"I am Lisa," the woman says plainly.

I step back and study her. The Lisa I remember from the Green Lotus Peak Inn was willowy and taller than I was; this woman is barely my height. Her long disheveled hair hangs like wool down her back; her face is sweet but sad-eyed, sallow, and puffy. The Lisa I'd known had had a distinctive mantle of cheekbones; her hair was cut in bangs. She'd had that dewiness, too, that satiny sheen of exuberance and youth. But then again, that was almost twenty years ago. How old is this woman? I continue to stare at her. It's impossible to tell.

For her part, she seems to never have seen me before either. She regards me quizzically.

"I'm sorry. I think I have the wrong Lisa." I clear my throat. "Almost twenty years ago," I feel compelled to explain, "I was here in Yangshuo, traveling with a friend. And my friend, she became very sick, you see?" I point to my head and rotate my index finger in what I hope is now a universal sign for insanity. "And this woman Lisa, she worked in the one restaurant here, and when my friend and I were in trouble, she came to my rescue. She really saved me, and I promised her I'd come back here one day, and I gave—"

Lisa cuts me off short, her eyes filling with tears. "And you gave me a bracelet," she says.

———

Years ago, when Claire Van Houten and I set off for China, our futures seemed so horizonless and shining, whereas Lisa's seemed so preordained and meager. And while Claire and I believed we'd be friends forever, Lisa seemed destined to be no more than a footnote. Now, in her restaurant, Lisa and I throw our arms around each other and weep, shaking our heads in disbelief as the Israelis look on.

"I was so young then," she cries. "I did not know anything!"

"Neither did I. But you saved my life!"

After we hug and weep some more, after we have Bob take our photograph, after Lisa tells me that she wrote me and I tell her that I never got her letters, after we confess to thinking of each other during Tiananmen Square and September 11, after this great eruption of joyousness and incredulity, Lisa steers us over to a table, dispenses a girl in an apron to look after the customers, and tells us her story in earnest.

In the past two decades, she has gone from being a young waitress with a pink hair ribbon to one of Yangshuo's preeminent entrepreneurs. Today she owns and runs two guesthouses and a restaurant, and she and some American business partners are finalizing a development deal for a four-star hotel. When President Bill Clinton came to Yangshuo in the late nineties, Lisa was not only part of the delegation who welcomed him, but the proprietor who served him what he declared to be "the best coffee in Yangshuo."

"You had coffee with President Clinton?" I laugh. "Dang! I never got to do that! And I lived in Washington, D.C., for five years."

The Lonely Planet China guide now describes Lisa herself as "an institution." Often, she's called upon to address both Chinese and foreign business groups. While she and I play catch-up, she gives Bob a draft of a speech that she recently delivered to a visiting American chamber of commerce. In it, she recounts her early days in Yangshuo and explains how she first got the idea to have homesick backpackers teach her to cook Western food.

"Now everybody here makes banana pancakes,"

she says, rolling her eyes. "Now, there is a lot more competition. But back when I started, you know that I was the only one."

Today Lisa is also a mother of five. Although I have trouble following this part of her story, it seems that she divorced her first, foreign husband, then married a man chosen for her by her family. She had some biological children and adopted other daughters from nearby villages. "Otherwise, they have no future," she explains. As if on cue, one of her daughters comes into the restaurant. She looks about fourteen. On her wrist is a brass bangle identical to the one I gave Lisa twenty years ago. We both stare at it. To this day, we confess, we each still have our bracelets locked away in our jewelry boxes.

Unsurprisingly, Lisa appears wearier than she did two decades ago. The years of serving hot pancakes and cold beer to rowdy, insolent backpackers. Of doggedly making beds, scraping caked grease off the grill, scrubbing toilets, renovating guest rooms, sweeping dust from the floorboards in a country livid with dust. The years of raising children, placating authorities, courting investors. The bookkeeping, the worry: It's all visible in her eyes.

I yearn to invite her to Switzerland. *Come visit,* I want to say. *I'll take you to a spa in the Alps. You can sit in a hot tub outdoors and watch the rising steam swirl and dissolve in the mountain air like condensed milk. You can eat chocolate croissants for breakfast, drink pink wine with lunch. I'll do the hosting and the cooking for a change.*

But in 2005, the Chinese government still prohibits its citizens from traveling independently. Only tour groups are allowed to journey to approved countries with guides.

Looking at Lisa this time, I am acutely aware of my privileges and freedoms. The inequality, the gaping expanse of it between us, feels shameful and wretched.

For a moment, there is an awkward silence. We reach across the table and squeeze each other's hands.

"I told you I'd come back," I say softly. It's all I can think to say.

Lisa smiles, her face still radiant with kindness.

"This time let's stay in touch, okay?" I add.

She nods and hands me a business card. "It is so much easier now," she says. "Here. I have e-mail."

———

Just before sundown, Bob and I board a bus back to Guilin. The bus station, of course, is now bigger than it was two decades ago and even more chaotic. But the route through the karsts is the same. There are only so many ways, it seems, to navigate your way around the mountains.

The bus lurches forward. I stare out at the shifting light, at the ghostly peaks turning cobalt in the evening, and think of Claire nineteen years ago, so beautiful and full of promise, screaming at the bus driver to stop, then disembarking somewhere along this very road. Now, she is even farther away than this—lost to the world—and I have no idea where.

What really happened to her during those seven weeks in China? The only thing I know now that I didn't know then is this: Some of those malaria pills we were taking in 1986 were later proven to cause hallucinations.

Sometimes, of course, it all seems like a fever dream—the fireworks exploding over Shanghai, our furious pedaling through the violet smog of Beijing, the public toilets, the sizzling chicken bones, the stench, the duplicitous bureaucrats. Trevor conversing with his tattoos out of loneliness and feeling me up on the balcony. Cynthia trading on the black market with her precious seven- and eleven-year-old boys. Jonnie insisting that we could arrange citizenship for him at the American embassy. The drunken singing tourists eating snakes in Guilin. Eckehardt appearing like a phantom in the middle of the rice fields, having not spoken to a soul in days, weeks, months? The Communist operatives in their stiff Western clothes, speaking stilted English—weren't we all a little deranged, really? And look at this country and mine, the psychoses that have seized them—both then *and* now. Look at this world today.

As the sky grows darker, I am no longer riding a bus beside my husband through the karsts of Guangxi. I am leaning over a railing on a turbulent ship in the East China Sea. Claire is in the cabin behind me, smoothing out her sleeping bag, and so is Jonnie, smiling desperately in the pale gold light as he plays the same song of love over and over, and Gunter is there, too, meeting his opera singer near the bow. Me, I am letting the salted wind tear through my hair beneath a vortex of infinite stars. I am listening as a young Chinese man sings "Country roads, take me home," his voice wistful, the notes rising plaintively over the thrash of the waves, and I stand there with him, forever hopeful and young, yearning for a place far away that we can never go to, where we can never, ever, return.

Acknowledgments

SEVERAL PEOPLE WERE invaluable to me while writing this book. I owe them my eternal gratitude and, in some cases, a bottle of South Korean tranquilizers.

I bow before Eckehardt Grimm for not only coming to my rescue two decades ago, but for reading this twenty years later when I showed up on his doorstep in Germany. Ecke, thank you for your excellent memory, your enduring friendship, your profound kindness, and your permission to use your real, incredible name. *Danke*.

Sandy Fenton deserves a medal of honor—not only for her unbelievable altruism, but also for making sure I'd gotten this right years after our last contact, and for letting me use her name as well. Thank you, O Great Canadian, for remaining as funny, spirited, and indomitable as ever.

To Cynthia, Warren, and Anthony Lukens for their inspiration decades ago and their approval moments before press time.

To Lisa Li in Yangshuo: *Xie xie ni.*

I raise a glass to my first editor, Amy Einhorn, for her continued faith in me and for launching this project in all its messiness.

A whole case of champagne, meanwhile, goes to my current editor, Les Pockell, who from day one brought inexhaustible vision, intelligence, and enthusiasm to this book. Ditto for Grand Central Publishing's Celia Johnson, who read this repeatedly with unflagging interest. Both deserve a Nobel Prize in the yet-to-be-established field of "Humoring and Reassuring High-Maintenance Authors."

To my agent, Irene Skolnick, for taking my late-night phone calls and for years of emotional as well as professional support, and to Vida Engstrand, who went beyond all proofreading duties, giving me tons of feedback and talking me through hitting the Send button.

To my cohort and twin, Marc Acito, for his wise counsel, wit, and structural expertise, and to Floyd Sklaver for indulging us both.

To my beautiful cousin Joan Stern for brainstorming and cheering me on. To Stefanie Weiss for her reading, encouragement, and humor. To Susie and Gray Walker for their enduring interest and help in reconstructing Hong Kong in the 1980s. To Eric Messinger and Rebecca Tayne for the cookies. To Maureen McSherry and Desa Sealy Ruffin for their sympathy and support. To Lisa and Doug Grandstaff for their sushi, sympathy, and photography. To my brother, John Seeger Gilman, for artistic advice.

To the staff at Grand Central Publishing, who continue to promote and believe in my work.

To "Claire Van Houten" and "Jonnie" — wherever they are. To Jonnie, thank you for all your immense kindness and hospitality that I did not deserve twenty years ago. To Claire, thank you for insisting I not give in to fear, for opening up the world for me, for giving me my life. I wish things had turned out differently; I'll always be grateful to you.

Yet the person to whom I am most indebted is Bob Stefanski, my humble but truly brilliant husband, who has lived, breathed, and traveled through China and this book with me for three years. He has been my rock, late-night reader, and constant sounding board. I simply could not have written this without his love, patience, and insight. Bob, I thank you for everything. I give you my full heart.